Long Past Slavery

CATHERINE A. STEWART

Long Past Slavery

Representing Race in the Federal Writers' Project

The University of North Carolina Press *Chapel Hill*

*This book was published with the assistance of the Fred W. Morrison Fund
of the University of North Carolina Press and the Richard and Norma Small
Distinguished Professorship Award of Cornell College.*

© 2016 The University of North Carolina Press
Set in Arno by Westchester Publishing Services
Manufactured in the United States of America

The paper in this book meets the guidelines for permanence
and durability of the Committee on Production Guidelines for
Book Longevity of the Council on Library Resources.

The University of North Carolina Press has been a member of the
Green Press Initiative since 2003.

Cover illustration: Hands of Mr. Henry Brooks, ex-slave, Parks Ferry Road,
Greene County, Georgia. Photo by Jack Delano, 1941. Farm Security
Administration—Office of War Information Photograph Collection,
Courtesy of the Library of Congress, Prints and Photographs Division,
LC-USF34-044273-D.

Library of Congress Cataloging-in-Publication Data
Stewart, Catherine A., author.
Long past slavery : representing race in the Federal Writers' Project /
Catherine A. Stewart.
pages cm
Includes bibliographical references and index.
ISBN 978-1-4696-2626-0 (pbk : alk. paper)—ISBN 978-1-4696-2627-7 (ebook)
1. African Americans—Race identity—History—20th century. 2. African
Americans—Psychology—History—20th century. 3. Collective memory—
United States—History—20th century. 4. Federal Writers' Project.
5. Cultural pluralism—United States—History—20th century.
6. United States—Race relations—History—20th century. I. Title.
E185.625.S763 2016
305.896'0730904—dc23
2015017267

For my three favorite storytellers:
My father, Thomas Allan Stewart (1933–2001)
My mother, Marion Conger Stewart
My aunt, Joyce Winnifred Robertson.
Their voices are in mine.

Contents

Illustrations

Acknowledgments

"I want to say something warm and gracious. Goodness gracious
it's warm in here."
—Victor Borge

A book incurs many debts of gratitude and for a project that has had a lengthy
evolution, the number multiplies exponentially. Two professors at Lawrence
University, Paul Cohen and Anne Schutte, saw the makings of a historian in
me and started me on the path with a good foundation in theory and historical method. It was the Associated Colleges of the Midwest's semester program
at the Newberry Library in Chicago that sealed the deal. John Aubrey took
me into the closed stacks to show me the many treasures of the Newberry
and introduced me firsthand to the innumerable joys of archival research.

As a graduate student at the State University of New York at Stony Brook, I
had the great fortune of working with exceptionally creative scholars: Nancy
Tomes, Gene Lebovics, Bill Miller, Fred Weinstein, Kathleen Wilson, and
Gary Marker contributed significantly to my intellectual development. In
particular, my advisors, William R. Taylor and Matthew Frye Jacobson, were
unflagging in their generosity with their intellectual gifts. My debt of gratitude to both of them will remain of untold measure. Larry Levine served as
my outside reader; even posthumously, his probing and insistent questions
continue to inform my approach to historical evidence.

My deep appreciation goes to Mark Simpson-Vos, editorial director of
the University of North Carolina Press, and his dedicated assistant, Lucas
Church, who made sure my manuscript got into the right hands at the right
time, including theirs. Mark encapsulates all of the qualities an author would
most like to have in an editor—insight, enthusiasm, patience, and transpar-
ency; he thoughtfully and promptly responded to all my queries. Mikala
Guyton at Westchester Publishing Services was enormously helpful in the
final stages. Two anonymous readers provided excellent suggestions and
guidance for revision, along with their votes of confidence. Thanks, too, to
Amron Gravett.

Cornell College provided financial support for two full-year sabbatical
leaves, thanks in part to Deans Dennis Moore and Joe Dieker. A McConnell
fellowship and two McConnell travel grants helped fund essential research

trips to archives in Washington, D.C., New York City, and Florida and provided time for writing. Nancy Rawson good-naturedly and unfailingly assisted me with the administrative details, helping to ensure my receipts were in order. My colleagues in the history department, Phil Lucas, Robert Givens, and Michelle Herder, generously supported my time away from departmental responsibilities. Michelle also told me about the web series *Ask a Slave* for my public history course. Brooke Bergantzel, Cornell's instructional technology librarian, kindly stepped in at the eleventh hour to work her magic with computer formatting.

Special thanks are owed to the numerous archivists and librarians I encountered during my forays into the collections of the Library of Congress, the National Archives and Records Administration, the Schomburg Center for Research in Black Culture of the New York Public Library, and the Beinecke Rare Book and Manuscript Library at Yale University. I am especially grateful to Peggy Bulger, former director of the Archives of the American Folklife Center at the Library of Congress, who was extremely welcoming to a young researcher. On a more recent trip to the Library of Congress in 2015, Bruce Kirby of the Manuscript Division helped me dive into the NAACP records, where I made some critical discoveries. On my first trip to the National Archives and Records Administration, to look at the records of the Federal Writers' Project, an archivist in College Park took me into the stacks to show me how many linear feet of boxes I would be delving into; on a return trip, Eugene Morris took the time to explain the new classification system and helped me track down a number of materials. At the University of Iowa Libraries, Janalyn Moss generously helped me unearth some important information on members of Florida's Negro Writers' Unit using the library's extensive online databases.

Paul Camp in Special Collections at the University of South Florida Libraries was enormously helpful. On a subsequent trip, the aptly named Matt Knight was generous with the collection and his assistance, going so far as to provide long-distance research help a year later. At the P. K. Yonge Library of Florida History at the University of Florida, James Cusick and Florence M. Turcotte were exceedingly obliging hosts. Flo made sure I didn't miss any relevant treasures and was a hoot to boot. After I got home and realized I had overlooked an important document at the Carl S. Swisher Library at Jacksonville University, reference librarian Anna Large and library director David Jones kindly came to my aid. Other long-distance research assistance was generously provided by Sherry Cortes at the Georgia Historical Society, Norwood A. Kerr at the Alabama Department of Archives and History,

Ben DiBiase at the Florida Historical Society, Frances Pollard at the Virginia Historical Society, and Chris Kolbe at the Library of Virginia. Robert F. Hancock, senior curator and director of collections at the American Civil War Center, recommended that I contact the United Daughters of the Confederacy (UDC) headquarters. That tip led to one of my most memorable and enjoyable research trips. UDC archivist Teresa Roane and research librarian Betty Luck could not have been more gracious and accommodating; Ms. Roane opened up the library for an out-of-town researcher during a terrible ice storm and expedited my research by knowledgeably guiding me to the most relevant sources. She and Ms. Luck generously spent additional hours working on my research questions long distance.

A number of librarians helped to expedite my requests for image reproductions and permissions, including Florence Turcotte, Kathryn Hodson at the University of Iowa Libraries, Mary Linnemann and Mazie Bowen at the Hargrett Rare Book and Manuscript Library at the University of Georgia Libraries, Adam Watson at the State Archives of Florida, Kay Peterson at the Archives Center of the National Museum of American History, Smithsonian Institute, and Martha Kennedy, in the Prints and Photographs Division of the Library of Congress.

Mike Denham, director of the Lawton M. Chiles Jr. Center for Florida History, deserves special thanks and gratitude for encouraging me to contact Stetson Kennedy and for inviting me to Florida Southern College to talk about my work. I met Mike at Columbia University during a rewarding Gilder Lehrman Seminar on Slavery and Public Memory taught by David Blight and James Horton. Mike's invitation opened up a whole new world of material as well as adventures. In particular, the incomparable Sandra Parks took me under her wing and into her home and opened up doors, including the door to Beluthahatchee. She also shared her considerable contacts in the St. Augustine community. Author David Nolan graciously showed me around St. Augustine and shared his extensive knowledge of the area's history. Jill Poppel took me on a memorable trip to the Kingsley Plantation. Mr. Kennedy welcomed me into his home and gave me access to his voluminous personal papers and archives (now housed at the Smathers Libraries' P. K. Yonge Library of Florida History at the University of Florida). Mr. Kennedy also took me to Jacksonville to see the former headquarters of the Florida Project and visit the former location of the Negro Writers' Unit of Florida at the Clara White Mission and Museum.

I have been extremely fortunate in the friends who have provided humor, encouragement, and support, including Jill Jack, Leslie Kathleen Hankins,

Cliff Rappaport, Carol and Hernan Lacy-Salazar, Martha Boysen, Marg Strass, Shelby Vespa, and Carol Enns. Geoffrey Tomasello and Douglas Boberg provided housing and laughs for a weeklong research trip to the University of South Florida. My lifelong friend, Jennie Kay Claver, stepped in at the close of this book project to cheer me on. A number of good friends who are also talented wordsmiths read chapters and provided invaluable suggestions along the way. Special thanks goes to Rebecca Entel and Martha Boysen, as well as Doug Baynton, who read several chapters at a crucial stage and provided very helpful edits as well as encouragement. Katy Stavreva provided sage and timely advice about the many steps of the publishing process and also served as an exemplary model of how to be a dedicated teacher and generous colleague as well as a scholar. Leslie Schwalm helped me believe this book would find a publisher and a readership. My long-term writing group at Cornell, Lynne Ikach and Michelle Mouton, read many sections and provided excellent feedback on points both small and large. Ellen Hoobler also made valuable suggestions and brought a renewed sense of enthusiasm to our group and this project. Lynne Ikach provided, time and again, essential readings as well as encouragement and significantly improved this work. This book is much finer for all of these writers' generous feedback.

And then there are the people without whom this book might never have seen the light of day. My parents gave me the biggest gift of all, an understanding of the pleasures of a life of the mind. Any "mayhem" I may have "perpetrated upon the body grammatic" has been innumerably lessened by the influence my mother, the poet Marion Conger Stewart, has had on my respect for the art and craft of writing. Her partner, A. Paul Douglas, is also deserving of my thanks. The influence of my siblings, David Gene Stewart and Shepherd Verity Goodenow, is evident in these pages owing to the many conversations we have had about power and inequality in America. Two people who are closest to me gave me a room of their own to call my own at critical moments: Joyce Robertson, my aunt, provided the ideal place as well as companionship to help me start this project. My best friend, Cheryl* Ringel, using her impressive networking skills, helped with housing and every other need in D.C. for all of my research trips. Bev Klug at the University of Iowa provided essential tools for life and for the writing life. Matthew Jacobson, professor of American studies at Yale, has remained a loyal and generous mentor over the intervening decades since our time together at SUNY–Stony Brook. I also owe a large debt of gratitude to Phil Lucas, who read both rough and revised versions of chapters and generously devoted part of his sabbatical to this work. He provided excellent suggestions right up to the final submission. My husband and soul mate, David Strass, has been unfailing in his devotion to me and this project. He has cheerfully spent countless hours, days, months, and years listening and talking about all aspects of this project. He read every sentence, tracked down sources, and selflessly and generously attended to all of my citations to ensure accuracy and consistency. Therefore, any mistakes that remain are his.

Long Past Slavery

Ex-slave and wife on steps of plantation house now in decay, Greene County, Georgia. Photo by Dorothea Lange, 1937. Farm Security Administration—Office of War Information Photograph Collection, courtesy of the Library of Congress, Prints and Photographs Division, LC-USF34-017943-C.

Introduction

The railway juncture is marked by transience. . . . Polymorphous and multidirectional, scene of arrivals and departures, place betwixt and between (ever *entre les deux*), the juncture is the way-station of the blues.

—Houston A. Baker Jr., *Blues, Ideology, and Afro-American Literature: A Vernacular Theory,* 1984

In Tampa, Florida, in the fall of 1937, former slave Josephine Anderson told Jules Frost a ghost story. Anderson's tale was representative of the rich African American folk tradition of hant (a colloquial version of "haunt") stories, many of which were collected by employees, like Frost, of the Federal Writers' Project (FWP), one of the New Deal's work-relief programs.[1] As Anderson recounted, early one morning before dawn she was walking along the railroad tracks on her daily route to work when "fore I knowed it, dere was a white man walkin long side o' me. I jes thought it were somebody, but I wadn't sho, so I turn off at de fust street to get way from dere."[2] The next morning was foggy as well as dark, and Anderson found herself almost upon the white man before she realized he was there again, "bout half a step ahead o' me, his two hands restin on his be-hind. I was so close up to him I could see him as plain as I see you. He had fingernails dat long, all cleaned and polished. He was tall, an had on a derby hat, an stylish black clothes. When I walk slow he slow down, an when I stop, he stop, never oncet lookin roun. My feets make a noise on de cinders tween de rails, but he doan make a mite o' noise." Now thoroughly spooked, Anderson sought to discover whether the figure was human or spirit, saying "goo[d] and loud: 'Lookee here, Mister, I jes an old colored woman, an I knows my place, an I wisht you wouldn't walk wid me counta what folks might say.' " As soon as Anderson made this declaration, the man vanished: "he was gone; gone, like dat, without makin a sound. Den I knowed he be a hant."[3]

Anderson was one of over 2,300 African Americans interviewed as part of the FWP, one of the numerous cultural projects established under the auspices of the Works Progress Administration (WPA) of Franklin Delano Roosevelt's New Deal. Gathering oral histories from the last living generation of former slaves, the Federal Writers' Ex-Slave Project intended to record the history of slavery as well as African American folk culture from those who had experienced it firsthand. This short-lived project created the largest collection of ex-slave narratives about the institution of slavery in the United States and is still considered one of "the most enduring and noteworthy achievements of the WPA."[4] It was also an endeavor that from start to finish was riven with conflict and complexity. Competing visions of the past and conflicting views on black identity and black citizenship offered different prisms for interpreting the remembrances of former slaves.[5]

Almost all of the scholarly discussion of the WPA ex-slave narratives has focused on their use as an important corrective source for histories of slavery in the United States.[6] This book attends specifically to what they reveal about the racial politics of the New Deal's cultural projects and 1930s debates on pluralism. Although ultimately not about ghost stories, this study explores the ways the past of slavery continued to haunt New Deal attempts to lay the ghosts of slavery to rest.[7] While project administrators viewed the past, in the form of tradition, as a means of unifying a dispirited nation in the midst of crisis, New Deal cultural projects were intensely political in their appropriation of the past, particularly the legacy of slavery. Far from being "a kind of neutral ground," as Michael Kammen referred to the decade's obsession with the nation's historical past, the Ex-Slave Project became the site where competing visions of African American identity, past and present, vied for ascendance in the struggle to map the contours of black citizenship in the nation's future.[8]

There was much at stake for African Americans in the politics of this cultural project. Black intellectuals were becoming increasingly committed to (re)constructing a historical record that would foster a sense of collective pride and national identity, while educating white Americans about black achievement and entitlement to the rights of citizenship. Writing African American history into the nation's master narrative, many hoped, could serve as the foundation for achieving racial equality. The imprimatur of the federal government on this interracial collaboration to document black history accorded it a national and symbolic prominence seldom seen in public representations of the nation's past. The FWP promised a step forward in African American campaigns for equal access to popular media and the public sphere.[9]

The FWP's Ex-Slave Project marks a historic moment in which the federal government both invited and enabled African Americans (as informants, interviewers, and, in one case, as a federal director of the Project) to talk about black identity, but it also created a space in which they could address Jim

Crow.[10] The Ex-Slave Project set in motion a series of profoundly earthshaking and revelatory encounters as black and white Americans from different regions, educational backgrounds, and economic classes spoke to each other across the racial divide. Together, FWP interviewers like Jules Frost and ex-slaves like Josephine Anderson walked the boundary between the past of slavery and the present of racial segregation, between the oral traditions of southern black folk and the literary print culture of the FWP, between white and black social intercourse during Jim Crow.

The compromising circumstances of the color line in 1930s America made it almost impossible for blacks and whites to speak to one another freely about slavery. Many of the elderly African Americans interviewed for the FWP's Ex-Slave Project endured daily the interrelated injustices of sharecropping, poverty, the convict lease system, and a system of legal statutes designed to control all aspects of African Americans' lives.[11] Most African Americans viewed white questioners with suspicion often laced with fear.[12] As the writer bell hooks recalled about her Kentucky childhood, "White people were regarded as terrorists, especially those who dared to enter that segregated space of blackness. . . . What did I see in the gazes of those white men who crossed our thresholds that made me afraid, that made black children unable to speak?"[13]

African American folktales that featured otherworldly characters, such as ghosts and witches, frequently served as metaphors for the dangers posed to African Americans by whites.[14] Former slaves, drawing upon the black oral tradition, often told ghost stories as a way of commenting on the injustices of white behavior and white racial codes in the segregated South. Yet FWP interviewers unfamiliar with African American oral traditions often diminished their import, representing the ex-slaves' figurative language and metaphorical tales of the supernatural as a positivistic and literal embodiment of the naiveté and superstitious tendencies of black folk. Viewing these traditions as evidence of ex-slave informants' provincialism, they rendered them in written form in a manner to provide entertainment for potential readers.[15] Thus, while FWP interviewers like Jules Frost were engaged in writing down African American ghost stories, former slaves such as Josephine Anderson were conjuring up tales about power and racial identities. Throughout the Ex-Slave Project, vernacular expressions intersected uneasily with the literary aims and publishing ambitions of the FWP. These competing interpretations of black culture and identity exemplify the larger struggle that took place over African American identity within the FWP during the second half of the New Deal.

Anderson's haunting takes place, not incidentally, on the railroad tracks—
often a southern town's dividing line between white and black communities
and a powerful metaphor for highly charged racial geographies resulting from
Jim Crow.[16] Anderson's ghost story becomes a means of making visible the
implicit social codes still governing the interactions between white men
and black women, between Anderson and her white male questioner from
the FWP. Her ghost story provides a coded and oblique commentary on the
boundaries of the color line, both visible and invisible, but always a felt and
marked presence, much like the ghost in Anderson's tale. The railroad ties
represent a liminal site or threshold where interracial contact may take place,
but such close proximity raises questions about transgression and the unequal
risk such contact posed for African Americans; the possibility that his whiteness is corporeal may be even more frightening than if it is ethereal.[17]

In her admonition to the white man's ghost not to walk with her "counta
what folks might say," Anderson was likely signifying to her white interviewer
about her unease regarding the potentially dangerous consequences of their
conversation. A common characteristic of the black oral tradition of signifying is the use of indirect speech, whereby "the remark is, on the surface, directed toward no one in particular."[18] What makes this form of signifying
successful, however, is the choice of a subject that is pointedly relevant to the
intended listener. In a neat reversal of the traditional ghostly visitation where
it is the ghost who has a message to impart to the living, it is Anderson who
speaks and the ghost who remains silent. The specter of the white man immediately disappears when Anderson calls attention to the dangers posed by
the impropriety of their walking together.[19] Anderson effectively banishes
the ghost with the power of utterance historically denied to black women
in their interactions with white men during slavery.[20]

Numerous scholars have noted that the circumstances of the interviews
that produced the WPA slave narrative collection certainly shaped the story
that got told.[21] For example, the presence of white interviewers could con-
strain elderly African Americans who, in attempting to placate or please their
questioners, told happier tales of life under slavery and glossed over the more
gruesome and harrowing aspects of enslavement. Complicating this situation
further was the extreme poverty endured by many of these informants during
the Great Depression despite the federal relief aid promised by Roosevelt's
New Deal. Ex-slaves were asked to respond to an interviewer's list of queries,
frequently without explanation or comprehending why they were being asked
to do so.[22] A number of ex-slaves apparently mistook FWP interviewers, who
were identified as government employees, for relief workers who had come

to assess their situation for the purpose of allocating welfare monies and may have shaped their stories accordingly.[23] Yet scholars have been surprisingly slow to examine how ex-slave informants found ways to narratively "move without moving," to speak truths that may have been unwelcome or unsolicited by their interviewers.[24]

As a document of an unprecedented interracial collaboration during Jim Crow to collect ex-slave testimony, Anderson's tale epitomizes the complex and often contradictory approaches the FWP took in transforming the oral art of former slaves into written mode. The prominence of hants in Anderson's full narrative, five in total, is representative of the Ex-Slave Project's increasing emphasis on black folk culture and superstition, as federal directors' concerns over publishing led them to consider the literary possibilities of ex-slave testimony. Anderson's narrative was selected for use in Florida's public school system, as were several others written up by Jules Frost.[25] Tales like the ones Anderson related were presented by FWP employees in various ways: as examples of the inventiveness of the African American folk tradition, as evidence of black superstition as a sign of racial inferiority, or as proof of southern whites' success in inculcating fear of the supernatural within the slave population as a method of psychological control.[26] Anderson's narrative was transcribed by her white interviewer in a manner intended to be a written representation of the black vernacular, following guidelines issued by federal directors of the Ex-Slave Project. "Negro dialect" became a key trope of authenticity for the ex-slave narratives, but in this example, as in many others, FWP decisions about how to depict it on the page reveal more about how the black vernacular was used to represent black identity than about the actual speech patterns of ex-slave informants.

At all levels of the project, white employees' varied assumptions about black identity and the historical legacy of slavery came into contact, and often conflict, with African American perspectives. Although the project did employ a number of African Americans as interviewers, most notably in the states of Virginia, Louisiana, and Florida, each of which established a segregated Negro Writers' Unit (NWU), the majority of FWP interviewers involved in collecting these oral histories were southern whites. Some were members of the United Daughters of the Confederacy, an organization dedicated to rewriting the national narrative of slavery in ways that would vindicate the Confederate cause. Scholars have yet to examine carefully how white FWP interviewers chose to hear black speech and black testimony and how, as the transcribers of these stories, they interpreted and represented the black vernacular and the tales themselves, often shaping them in accordance with a nostalgic "remembrance" for the antebellum past of southern tradition, defined in large part by the existence of slavery. The long histories that shaped the stories ex-slaves told about their individual and collective pasts reveal competing voices within this radical project and show how they sought to define a black future.

Age, class, and educational differences between African American FWP employees and ex-slave informants also affected both the style and content of the ex-slave narratives. There is evidence that ex-slaves also exercised caution when speaking with black interviewers and shaped their narratives in particular ways for those listeners as well. African Americans employed by the FWP were equally invested, if not more than white employees, in shaping these narratives to represent black identity, past and present. Many, such as the members of Florida's NWU, wished to present a portrait of African American identity that emphasized not just black survival but black assimilation and racial progress. These narratives reflected the black bourgeoisie's investment in black respectability and racial uplift.[27]

This study also provides a new way of reading the ex-slave narratives of the FWP, in part by using the tools provided by black literary criticism (what some have called "vernacular criticism") in order to identify the oral and literary traditions located within these texts. This method reveals ex-slaves as strategic storytellers.[28] I view the narratives as written versions of oral performances, following John Blassingame's suggestion that scholars who wish to uncover the secrets of the slave narratives should "systematically examine the internal structures of the interviews, the recurrence of symbols and stereotypes, the sequence of episodes, and the functions they serve."[29] This makes it possible to discover within the narratives veiled commentaries articulated by ex-slave informants about segregation in the 1930s, as well as alternative histories of slavery and emancipation. A close examination at the end of the book of the tropes and rhetorical strategies contained in the ex-slave narratives illuminates, among other things, how former slaves drew upon African American oral and literary traditions to enact some measure of authorial control and create counternarratives of black history and identity.

But we cannot understand these tales, in all of their rhetorical complexities, without understanding the history of how the Ex-Slave Project came about and how 1930s debates over folk culture and black identity—past and present—affected the contests that ensued over African Americans' authority to represent the past. This study reveals how the ex-slave narratives served different functions for various authors involved in their production: as an elegiac look back at the Old South; as a means to debate federal government involvement in issues pertaining to race and economics; and, through memories of slavery, the Civil War, and emancipation, as arguments for and against African Americans' fitness for the responsibilities of citizenship.

My study takes its cue from the rich corpus of scholarship on the construction of historical memory, much of which has taken the Civil War as its primary subject.[30] As David W. Blight, James Horton, and others have amply documented, the use of the past in constructing public memories is always selective, improvisational, and highly contested.[31] Furthermore, because publics and nation-states rely heavily on narratives about the past in order to create a sense of identity and, even more important, in order to define and enforce selective rights and privileges of citizenship, the stakes over whose remembrance becomes authorized as the "collective" memory are extremely high. The creation of historical memory can become an instrument of power, undermining versions of the past that might support or contest the status quo.[32]

The start of the Ex-Slave Project in 1936 coincided with the nation's seventy-fifth anniversary of the Civil War. As a result, the Ex-Slave Project was fraught with conflict over which version of the past should be valorized as part of the nation's official public memory. By focusing on the promise and limitations of black cultural authority in the Ex-Slave Project, this study offers a close look at the troubling vicissitudes of racial politics during the New Deal and provides a more nuanced picture of African Americans' experience with state and federal authorities. It also exposes the contradictory currents of the 1930s that informed the FWP's approach to black history and culture, including the rise of social scientific authority, the commercialization of folk culture, and the ghosts of the Old South, which came together in surprising and complex ways.

The Ex-Slave Project promised a unique opportunity for African Americans to participate in this endeavor, from the highest administrative level of the FWP, where the African American poet and scholar Sterling Brown worked as the national editor of Negro Affairs; to the state and local levels, where black employees (customarily working in segregated NWUs) submitted their work to white editors and state directors; to the personal interactions that took place between FWP interviewers and former slaves. At all levels of the project, however, African Americans' authority was sharply circumscribed by the racial divide of the 1930s. Assumptions about race engendered significant controversy over what constituted "authentic" portraits of black-ness and who was best qualified to represent African American history, cul-ture, and identity. Because African American history was being recovered but also shaped in response to debates about the South's economic situation and the "Negro problem," the extensive records of the Ex-Slave Project yield op-posing perspectives on the meaning of black identity and black citizenship. The project exposed uneasy attempts to reconcile the rhetoric of democracy with the reality of racial injustice and inequality.

My study examines how FWP employees, at all levels of the project—local, state, and federal—influenced and shaped the structure and content of the ex-slave narratives, with varying degrees of success and authority. Chapters 1–4 explore how prevailing discourses about race and the "Negro problem" shaped the Ex-Slave Project's goals and methods. It also charts the impact of federal directors, such as Henry Alsberg, Brown, and the folk song collector John Lomax, on the project's representations of black culture and identity. Through a close examination of federal and state directors' admin-istrative correspondence and the guidelines federal directors issued to state directors and FWP interviewers, I explore the editorial conflicts that ensued over the meaning and significance of African cultural survivals, "Negro folk-lore," and how to transcribe "Negro dialect."[33] Central to this process was Lomax, who served as the FWP's first national advisor on folklore and folk-ways. Chapter 4 demonstrates how Lomax's approach to black informants and his definition of what constituted "authentic" folk culture shaped his direction of the Ex-Slave Project, affecting the ways the ex-slaves and their narratives would be represented.

Chapters 5–8 shift to a closer examination of African Americans' involve-ment with the WPA and the Ex-Slave Project as FWP employees at the state and federal level and also as ex-slave informants, placing particular emphasis on the ways they worked to challenge widespread assumptions about black history and culture and the methods they used to authorize their own por-trayals of black identity.[34] Using Zora Neale Hurston as a case study, chapter 6 serves as an essential counterpart to the discussion of Lomax in chapter 4, providing a comparative look at Hurston's brief career as a professionally trained ethnographer and her experiences as an employee of Florida's NWU. The contrast between Hurston's and Lomax's careers and employment with the FWP epitomizes the radical racial inequality of this era and is indicative of African Americans' lack of institutional authority to represent black culture and identity. Chapter 7 examines the strategies and methods other members of Florida's NWU (besides Hurston) adopted in order to reinscribe their authority over prevailing discourses on black culture and identity, using the ex-slaves' life histories.

Chapter 8 turns to a close examination of FWP informants to demonstrate how ex-slaves used their oral performances as a form of currency and self-commodification in their negotiations with FWP interviewers. My approach is an important departure from much of the existing scholarship on the Ex-Slave Project that gives short shrift to ex-slaves' agency within the context of the interview dynamic and provides a new way of reading the ex-slave narratives. Drawing on narratives from the Georgia Project and Florida's NWU as a comparative case study, I demonstrate the vital ways informants drew on African American vernacular traditions, such as signifying, to exert some control over the interview and also articulate their own experiences of slavery and emancipation.

The Epilogue looks at some of the immediate outcomes of the Ex-Slave Project with the official end of the FWP in 1939 and the shift to a state-supervised Writers' Project. I examine the process of appraisal the folklorist Benjamin A. Botkin instituted after 1939 to determine the value of each narrative: for publication or for deposit into the Library of Congress. The Ex-Slave Project also intersects with the larger story of African Americans and the New Deal, and the long history of the Civil Rights Movement and the continuing struggle for equality. The FWP's revolutionary decision to include black Americans in the federally sanctioned production of historical knowledge helped to permanently destabilize a white monopoly on representations of black history, culture, and identity. Working within the new framework of New Deal rhetoric and promises, African American activists and organizations like the National Association for the Advancement of Colored People (NAACP) and the Joint Committee on National Recovery were able to push successfully for black representation in the arts projects (known as Federal Project No. 1). The FWP, however, stands out among the arts projects for its appointment of an African American federal director to oversee all copy and projects related to black Americans and for pushing to employ a greater number of African American white-collar workers.[35] By including African American history, folk culture, and communities in its American Guide Series and creating special projects devoted to the black experience, the FWP staked a claim for the African American story as a central part of the American story and therefore worthy of study and federal attention. In this regard, it challenged conventional understandings about race and, through the Ex-Slave

Project, created a body of historical evidence that forever altered the terrain on which histories of slavery would be written. African Americans involved with this unique project found ways to "write back" and create their own narratives about the legacy of slavery and African Americans' past, present, and future as citizens of the nation—narratives that have had a long-term impact on how historians write the history of slavery.[36]

CHAPTER ONE

The Passing Away of the Old-Time Negro

Folk Culture, Civil War Memory, and Black Authority in the 1930s

Many southerners look back wistfully to the faithful, simple, ignorant, obedient, cheerful, old plantation Negro and deplore his disappearance. They want the New South, but the Old Negro. That Negro is disappearing forever along with the old feudalism and the old-time exclusively agricultural life.

—Ray Stannard Baker, *Following the Color Line*, 1908

The post Civil War household word among Negroes—"He's an Uncle Tom!"—which denoted reluctant toleration for the cringing type who knew his place before white folk, has been supplanted by a new word from another generation which says:—"Uncle Tom is dead!"

—Richard Wright, *Uncle Tom's Children*, 1938

"The Negroes of old times are rapidly passing away in the South and soon will be known only in history," a Federal Writers' Project (FWP) employee from Tennessee observed in an ex-slave narrative entitled "Passing of Old Time Negroes."[1] The flood of African Americans migrating to northern as well as southern cities during the first thirty years of the twentieth century led to an increased awareness of the vanishing folk traditions of a population that was rapidly acculturating to urban life. Some two million African Americans participated in this mass exodus.[2] Folklorists and historians bemoaned the imminent disappearance of the last surviving members of a generation of African Americans that had forged unique oral traditions out of African survivals and the crucible of slavery. This awareness inspired many folk collection and oral history projects in the 1920s and 1930s, including the FWP's Ex-Slave Project.[3] FWP federal and state directors frequently referred to the passing away of the oldest generation of African Americans and the waning of black rural folk traditions in an increasingly modern and industrialized society. For those engaged in the collection of black folk culture, this language of loss resonated particularly strongly, as many felt that emancipation had led the freedmen to "despise [black folk culture] as a vestige of slavery," thereby contributing to its demise.[4] Black folk culture became inextricably tied to a vision of an older generation of former slaves. There were obvious contradictions here, particularly for collectors in the 1930s, as their ex-slave informants, a generation now "rapidly passing away," had been children when emancipation came and had spent most of their lives as freedmen and freedwomen. Thus, the phrase "the old-time Negro" referred to more than just the elderly status of the last generation of African Americans to possess firsthand knowledge of slavery and folk traditions; it also evoked a sensibility that, collectors hoped, would provide a direct link to the past.

The phrase "the passing away of the old-time Negro" carried another connotation as well: for southern whites nostalgic for the antebellum era, it was code for the disappearance of a generation who accepted their place at the bottom of the racial hierarchy. In his 1904 political treatise, *The Negro: The Southerner's Problem*, the famous plantation school writer Thomas Nelson Page bemoaned the passing of the faithful Negro personas of slavery days: "That the 'old-time Negro' is passing away is one of the common sayings all over the South . . . he will soon be as extinct as the dodo. . . . No servants or retainers of any race ever identified themselves more fully with their masters." Nevertheless, white southerners quickly found ways to ensure he would not be forgotten. Beginning in the Reconstruction era, portrayals of black servitude and the mythical halcyon days of slavery were increasingly popularized through plantation school literature, the burgeoning sheet music industry, public monuments and museums dedicated to the Lost Cause, and Hollywood films. "In the Jeff Davis Museum in Richmond," sociologist Herbert Miller recalled, "there used to be an exhibit dedicated to the 'old-time Negro who is rapidly passing away.' It was a scene on a plantation, where the old-time Negroes are going about their business in an acquiescent manner, like domesticated animals."[5] These civic forms of commemoration for the antebellum South were driven by white southerners' desire to publicize a narrative of the historical past of slavery that rewrote the script of race relations (quite literally, as "faithful slaves" were renamed "former servants") and to delimit black agency as African Americans agitated for the rights of full citizenship.[6] The Old-Time Negro took on even greater saliency in the 1930s. The stereotypes of cheerful and uncomplaining black servitude that continued to abound in mass culture through the longevity of icons like Uncle Tom and Aunt Jemima were at once a response to the straitened financial circumstances of many whites and the increasingly successful attempts of black labor to organize.[7] Such minstrel tropes took on a new importance as a result of the economic crisis of the Great Depression and New Deal efforts on behalf of labor and significantly shaped the FWP to collect ex-slave narratives.

The utopian dream among some white Americans for a permanent labor force consisting of an unpaid and unresisting black underclass would reach its apogee during the Great Depression and found its ultimate embodiment in a labor-saving prototype of one of the earliest humanoid robots. Far from passing away, the Old-Time Negro would be reanimated, literally, as "Rastus, The Mechanical Negro," also referred to as "The Mechanical Slave." Built in 1930 by Westinghouse Research Laboratories, shortly after the economic collapse of Wall Street, the mechanical robot made his debut appearance at the annual convention of the American Institute of Electrical Engineers.[8] The robot's name was surely an intentional reference to another personification of black servitude created by the ready-made food industry, Rastus, the Cream of Wheat Chef. Like the smiling black images of advertising icons Aunt Jemima and Uncle Ben, Rastus evoked the down-home authenticity of southern folk culture and cuisine and blacks who were loyal, dependable, and eager to serve whites.[9] Fittingly, Rastus the Robot's movements included standing up, sitting down, and bowing. Rastus's performance involved a short "conversation" with his interlocutor (using a prerecorded soundtrack on 16-millimeter film) and a reenactment of the William Tell legend, whereby his designer "shot" an electronic arrow (actually a beam of light) at the apple on top of Rastus's head, triggering a gunpowder explosion that discharged the apple and bringing the robot "to his feet with an exclamation of dismay."[10]

Many African Americans were eager to bury these stereotypes of black servitude, and they worked on multiple fronts to correct popular misconceptions about the past and also black identity by publishing histories and postbellum slave narratives, circulating counterimages and writings through the black press and the black arts movement, creating their own forms of commemoration through Emancipation Day celebrations and public parades.[11] The political stakes were high in determining whose representations of African American identity would be valorized as authentic. As the acclaimed poet and critic Sterling Brown contended, along with other leading figures in black letters such as Langston Hughes, Richard Wright, and Zora Neale Hurston, a dialogic relationship existed between the evolution of racist stereotypes of black identity and the despotically unequal social policies they were meant to justify.[12] During the 1930s, working as part of the Roosevelt administration's New Deal programs, Brown, along with other prominent black intellectuals, writers, and artists who had come of age during the Harlem Renaissance, would challenge the monopoly white writers, social scientists, and publishing houses exercised over representations of black history, culture, and identity.

The cultural projects of the New Deal, and particularly the FWP, seemed to promise an unprecedented opportunity for African Americans to correct dangerous misrepresentations of black identity, and to help rewrite popular national narratives about slavery and post-emancipation racial inequalities. By hiring African American writers to work on projects specifically related to black history, culture, and identity, the FWP held out a radical promise for black authority by situating it within the framework of a federally sanctioned project.[13] The appointment of Brown as the editor of Negro Affairs for the FWP in 1936 seemed to herald a new era in African Americans' ongoing struggles for equal access to public discourse about racial identity, racial equality, and black citizenship. As Brown would observe about *The Negro in Virginia*, one of the few FWP studies on African Americans to achieve publication, it was a rare and significant "instance of a governmental cultural agency's sponsorship of a serious history of a minority group."[14]

Brown's responsibilities in the FWP's Office on Negro Affairs in Washington included overseeing the compilation and publication of manuscripts pertaining to African American history, culture, and contributions, while also reviewing all copy submitted by the states' project editors that pertained to African Americans.[15] For the short duration of the FWP, from 1936 to 1939, Brown seemed to be placed in a position of unprecedented authority for an African American intellectual, working to ensure that representations of black history, culture, and identity were based on fact and not on the racial phantasms that permeated American culture. Brown hoped to use his clout to create portraits of African Americans that would emphasize their contributions to the nation and help serve as a corrective to decades of racial stereotypes of black identity. For Brown, the idea of the New Negro was intimately connected to the discourse of "racial uplift" that enjoined African Americans to advance the race through self-help, moral regeneration, and educational as well as economic progress. The new image of black Americans, as educated, upwardly striving, and filled with moral rectitude, was essential for proving their entitlement to full citizenship. "Racial uplift" ideology informed and influenced FWP portraits of black history and identity produced by African American employees working in segregated Negro Writers' Units, such as Florida's.

What led the FWP to employ African Americans to work on projects related to black history and identity during an era in which white writers and folklorists still maintained their hold over the authority to represent blackness? How did the federal government become interested and involved in the collection of folk culture and, in particular, the collection of black folk traditions and oral testimony? The Ex-Slave Project and the FWP's mission to collect and document American folkways cannot be understood without the larger historical context of the 1930s: a decade in which the "Negro Question," in its multiple and often conflicting meanings, took on renewed salience as federal projects, civil rights activists, social scientists, and social documentarians focused much of their attention on the South.[16] This, along with the seventy-fifth anniversary of the Civil War, helped fuel debates over black folk culture and African American citizenship.

The Folk Movement

The FWP's decision to collect folk culture and to employ African Americans in this endeavor evolved out of a complex convergence of trends in the 1930s that included an expanding scholarly interest as well as a commercial market for folk culture, particularly African American folk culture. Folklorists were in pursuit of folk cultures that were conceived of as originating among and therefore belonging to the people, to a public domain. The Roosevelt administration sought both to recover the people's history and folkways through its patronage of public arts projects and to create its own forms that could help people accept many of the New Deal programs. The FWP was part of an administrative endeavor to revitalize American national identity through a celebration of cultural pluralism as the organic roots of democracy.[17] There was also a growing commercial market among publishers, record companies, and radio networks, and an emerging national audience for "authentic" folk culture.[18] These often conflicting pursuits were driven in part by the decade's fascination with documentary genres and a search for the "real" and the "authentic." They were also a response to growing concerns about modernization, the impact of mass culture in the form of radio, film, and the phonograph, and the mass migration of African Americans out of the rural South and into urban areas of the South and North, making the "Negro problem" or "race question" an issue of national concern and discussion.

In the early 1930s, the folklorist Benjamin Botkin, who would later be appointed as the FWP's folklore editor, proclaimed, "the folk movement must come from below upward rather than above downward."[19] Many who became involved with the folk movement of the 1930s saw it as an unprecedented opportunity to explore the culturally and regionally diverse groups that made up the fabric of American identity, such as migrant laborers, industrial workers, ethnic minorities, and African Americans. To document a previously underrepresented side of American life became a dominant theme among artists and writers of this decade. It characterized many of the cultural projects of the New Deal administration, from the photography project of the Farm Security Administration to the FWP's national guidebook series and oral history projects, and it was animated, in part, by a desire to provide a space in which representatives of these groups could speak for the record themselves. If the project of documenting the folk cultures of the United States was to be taken seriously, Botkin explained, the folk—the people themselves—must have a hand in the collection of the nation's cultural patrimony. "Otherwise," Botkin warned, "[the folk movement] may be dismissed as a patronizing gesture, a nostalgic wish, an elegiac complaint, a sporadic and abortive revival—on the part of paternalistic aristocrats going slumming, dilettantish provincials going native, defeated sectionalists going back to the soil, and anybody and everybody who cares to go collecting."[20]

Botkin's concern over who should be involved in the project to collect, salvage, and preserve the cultures of the American folk demonstrates a fine sensitivity to the politics and inherent power relationships involved in representing minority groups' cultures and identities. And yet his warning turned out to be eerily prophetic when it came to the actual implementation of the FWP. While the unifying aim behind New Deal cultural projects was to record the diversity of the American experience and to "let . . . the people speak,"[21] putting this ideal into practice raised vital questions about agency and authorship, required delicate arbitration among opposing constituencies, and created vexed debates over "authenticity" in folk culture and portrayals of the folk.[22] The FWP's enterprise to collect folk culture and local public histories would involve nothing less than the reshaping of national identity through the social production of historical memory.

In his impressive history of Popular Front cultural activity during the 1930s, Michael Denning identifies the New Deal arts projects of Federal One (in theater, music, art, and writing) as "a crucial site" for building alliances between radical artists on the relief rolls and established intellectuals who served as project administrators.[23] As Denning notes, a number of individuals working in key positions both in New Deal arts projects and the Works Progress Administration (WPA), such as Botkin, were part of a broad left-wing movement that sought to address issues of injustice arising from racial discrimination as well as labor struggles. The concept of an undifferentiated "Cultural Front," however, ignores the oppositional and necessarily confrontational relationship that was a central part of the African American left's experiences with Roosevelt's New Deal. Furthermore, it overlooks the critical role played by African American political organizations and leaders in applying consistent and necessary pressure on WPA officials, including those in the arts projects of Federal One, to address ongoing and prevalent issues of discrimination.

African American disillusionment with New Deal promises led to the tenuous coalition of civil rights organizations and leadership through the creation of the Negro Industrial League (later renamed the Joint Committee on National Recovery) and the National Negro Congress.[24] Organizations like the NAACP and the Joint Committee on National Recovery played a central role in exposing a wide range of racially discriminatory policies and actions in the WPA and the cultural projects of Federal One and demanded appropriate actions by WPA administrators to redress the greatest offenses. Their success, in many cases, demonstrates that the pluralistic aims and ambitions of New Deal programs, along with liberals in key positions (such as Henry Alsberg of the FWP and U.S. Secretary of Labor Frances Perkins), provided a political space in which such claims were heard, if not always addressed.

The white-collar relief program for writers that would later become the FWP started as part of the Federal Emergency Relief Administration in 1934. Early projects and proposals focused on local and state histories, the study of racial groups, the collection of folk culture, and interviewing ex-slaves: these became the models for FWP endeavors. Because of the emphasis on preserving America's folk heritage, one employee proposed that the federal project should be called the American Folklore Project.[25] American audiences' growing appetite for folk cultures was inextricably tied to the ascendance of social scientific forms of knowledge for the study of culture and identity. In the 1920s, amateur folk collectors such as Lydia Parrish, along with professional folklorists like John Lomax (who would later become the FWP's folklore editor), traveled into rural communities and scoured the hills to collect and preserve folk cultures that were dying out as the result of modernization.[26]

While these projects often began with the aim to create a record of these cultures for posterity, this preservationist ethos did not prevent their commercial potential from being quickly realized and capitalized upon. As Brown would later observe, "Folk arts are no longer by the folk for the folk; smart businessmen now put them up for sale."[27] The widespread interest in folk culture that characterized this decade was fraught with internal contradictions. Certainly a dynamic behind part of this folk culture phenomenon was a nostalgic longing for a pre-Depression, preindustrial past, one that seemed in retrospect to exist apart from commercialism and the acquisitiveness that characterized the volatile economy of the 1920s. New Deal cultural projects, which sought to establish noncommercial art (theater, literature, social-ethnic studies, music, and visual arts) for the public by drawing directly upon the arts of the people and the people's artists, were linked not only to the economics of the Great Depression, as the federal government sought to create jobs in the arts for the unemployed, but also to an explicit critique of the market values associated with the collapse of the stock market. Selfish individualism and materialism were blamed by many, including President Roosevelt, for directly contributing to the nation's economic woes. Roosevelt called for a renewed commitment to traditional community values as a bulwark against commercialism, avarice, and unregulated market values. The New Deal emphasized culture as the firmest foundation upon which to erect economic transformation.[28] This led to a celebration of folk cultures as the panacea to these ills; folk culture embodied the ideals of public ownership by the people and the community, as opposed to the individual or celebrity artist. Folk culture, by definition, existed outside the economic realm. Yet, as the mass media discovered a commercial market for it, folk culture became a commodity whose value was determined by its ability to transcend or remain distinctly separate from the marketplace, while adapting itself to the aesthetic conventions with which mainstream audiences were already familiar. Folk culture in the 1930s was simultaneously being pursued as an anthropological artifact, as part of the search for the pure, unspoiled folk community, and as a commercial property. Folklorists found themselves decrying the effects of commercialization upon the remnants of "authentic" folk culture, while their careers benefited from offering up that very "folk" to a mainstream American audience.

A new consumer market for all things "folk" emerged and, along with it, the exploitation of folk cultures and members of folk communities. Ironically, the fascination that drove the market relied implicitly on the authenticity of the folk cultures purveyed. The concept of authenticity became extremely important for both collectors and consumers of folk cultures, as it was inextricably intertwined with the value—both symbolic and economic—of the folk material itself. In particular, this decade marks a seminal moment in which "authentic blackness" came to be associated with the folk.[29] This discourse of authentic blackness was fostered in large part by folklorists who, fearing the complete eradication of folk cultures faced with encroaching aspects of modernization, sought out rapidly vanishing members of an older, agrarian, and largely illiterate class located in the remote regions of the South.[30] During the 1920s and 1930s, members of the black intelligentsia would also capitalize upon this fascination with the folk by turning the definition of black authenticity to their advantage as they strove to destabilize white writers' representations of black culture, history, and identity.

The Commodification of Black Culture

The newly developing industries of mass culture—radio, film, and on-site recording machines—along with the phonograph and print media all attempted to cash in on this growing fascination with the "folk." Its diverse incarnations ranged from the obsession with the West and the cowboy culture popularized through Gene Autry and Will Rogers, to the commercial marketing of African American music in the form of "race records," to the *Amos 'n' Andy* radio serial starring white actors Freeman Gosden and Charles Correll.[31] Many of the new forms of mass media sought to capitalize on a national audience for African American culture that had emerged during the 1920s, partly as an outcome of the Harlem Renaissance, and would continue into the 1930s. Hollywood's employment of African American performers reflected the growing popularity of a whole cadre of black musicians, singers, dancers, and stand-up comedians.

With the advent of sound, Hollywood studios began producing musicals that featured predominantly African American casts. Films such as King Vidor's *Hallelujah!* from MGM in 1929 starring Nina Mae McKinney, Fox Studio's *Hearts in Dixie* starring Stepin Fetchit, and RKO Radio's 1935 *Hooray for Love*, featuring Fats Waller and Bill "Bojangles" Robinson, served to showcase black entertainers' talents, who formerly could be seen and heard only in cabarets, jazz clubs, and vaudeville theaters. The commercial interest in aspects of black folk culture was also evident in Hollywood film depictions of black speech, black music in the form of spirituals, and religious revivals as portrayed in *The Green Pastures* (1936), an all-black version of the Old Testament.[32] These films located an authentic black identity in the agricultural South, contrasting rural folk with the corruption and decadence of an urban "New Negro" who had exchanged his traditional values of religion, humility, and racial deference for the immoral vices of city life, gambling, sexual licentiousness, and style in the form of the fashionable dandy.[33] Plantation imagery was a direct critique of black urban migration and reflected both northern and southern white desires for black labor to remain in the South.[34] They also drew upon the idea of black primitivism. The well-known film director King Vidor explained that his goal for *Hallelujah!* was to explore the rich culture of the "pristine Southern Negro," as opposed to "the Negro who apes the white man." Buried beneath the layers of white civilization, "the polished [urban] Negro . . . possesses, under the surface, the rhythm and abandon, the love song and laughter of those in a primitive state."[35] Although these roles were an opportunity for black performers to reach a national audience, they were structured in conformity with white audiences' expectations for black characters to embody stereotypes of African Americans as comical, childlike Uncle Toms, as critics such as Alain Locke, W. E. B. Du Bois, and Sterling Brown were quick to note.

Another key development in early twentieth-century mass media, whose roots were embedded in the commercialization of black music, was the phonograph. The nascent record industry was instrumental in finding black blues musicians and packaging them along with phonographic equipment.[36] Initially, these so-called race records were advertised and sold primarily to African American listeners.[37] But with the astounding commercial success of female blues singers in the 1920s such as Bessie Smith and Ethel Waters, companies like Paramount, Columbia Records, and Victor began mass marketing up-and-coming blues musicians nationwide.[38] By 1926, the three largest recording companies for blues musicians were selling five to six million records a year.[39] The phonograph and radio brought African American musical traditions to the metropole, but they also began to exert a centripetal force; as rural musicians became commercial performers whose sounds were broadcast for a national audience, their style made its way into rural homes, influencing and shaping the next generation of blues musicians.[40] Many at the time saw this as a corruption of authentic African American music and bemoaned the inevitable disappearance of authentic folk music as a result.

In fact, the race records industry illustrates one of the fundamental paradoxes that would emerge in the marketing of black folk culture. In order to compete successfully with the larger white-owned companies, African American–owned businesses, like the Black Swan recording company (under a board of directors that included W. E. B. Du Bois), began emphasizing the purity of their product in terms of its racial authenticity: their company motto proudly proclaimed that theirs was "The Only Genuine Colored Record— Others Are Only Passing."[41] This motto playfully invoked the very serious public debates over light-skinned blacks' ability to "pass" for whites, a practice that enabled individuals with black ancestry to partake of the rights and privileges enjoyed by whites but routinely denied to blacks under segregation. By applying the concept to cultural production, Black Swan Records and African American intellectuals drew attention to the much more widespread practice of whites masquerading as black in cultural representation. This enabled whites to animate seemingly lifelike but soulless stereotypes of the minstrel tradition; the many examples in popular culture of slaves "yearning for the good old days 'befo' de War,' " Sterling Brown pointed out, were merely speaking as "ventriloquists' dummies."[42]

Folklorists themselves, who were bringing black folk culture to the attention of the general public, also found themselves walking an uneasy line between the authenticity of their discoveries and the commodification of their protégés' "authenticity." A key example of this was folklorist John Lomax's discovery and successful marketing of the folk musician Huddie Ledbetter. Lomax, who would help direct the Ex-Slave Project as the FWP's first folklore editor, was one of the most prolific gatherers and publicizers of folk culture during this era. Lomax is still best known for the contribution he made to ethnomusicology through his incomparable collection of American folk songs and ballads. The rapid disappearance of folk cultures lent an air of urgency and importance to Lomax's work and made him increasingly interested in locating members of the black folk community who were cut off from the homogenizing forces of industrialization, the radio and the phonograph. In order to locate black folk music that still survived, Lomax traveled through the remote areas of Mississippi, Alabama, Louisiana, and Texas. Lomax's theories about what constituted "authentic" black folk culture made him particularly interested in gathering material in places where people were culturally isolated either by geography or imposed societal codes, like racial segregation. Folklorists such as Lomax would fashion themselves as the saviors of a vanishing African American folk culture; however, their arguments for the crucial role they played in the collection and preservation of black folk traditions, along with their representations and interpretations of black identity, would not go unchallenged.

The Struggle for Black Cultural Authority

The authority of folklorists such as Lomax was hotly contested by African American scholars, who were quick to observe that much of this commercial exploitation of black folk culture was based on whites' appropriation of it. As the writer and ethnographer Zora Neale Hurston lamented to her friend the poet Langston Hughes: "It makes me sick to see how these cheap white folks are grabbing our stuff and ruining it. I am almost sick—my one consolation being that they never do it right and so there is still a chance for us."[43] A younger generation of writers, coming of age in the 1920s and 1930s, such as Wright, Hughes, and Hurston, felt there was an artistic value in "authentic" folk culture that should be presented in as close to its original, earthy, and unstudied form as possible.[44] They saw in folk culture a distinct form of vernacular expression that intrinsically articulated a nascent form of black nationalism born out of a savvy awareness of power and race relations and imbued with a "racial wisdom" that had an eternal capacity for regenerating the spirit and consciousness of black Americans.[45]

Despite a growing market for representations of blackness, white authors along with white audiences, wealthy patrons, and commercial publishers continued to exercise a great deal of control over which images of blackness would be circulated in the public sphere. Much of black cultural expressiveness continued to be mediated by white audiences' and patrons' fascination with a particular trope of blackness—primitivism. This would lead some African American writers prominently associated with the Harlem Renaissance to renounce it in later years for catering to white expectations of black exoticism. Langston Hughes, in his 1940 autobiography, would describe the decade as a "period when white writers wrote about Negroes more successfully (commercially speaking) than Negroes did about themselves."[46]

Black intellectuals in the 1920s, such as W. E. B. Du Bois, Alain Locke, and Hurston, saw an intrinsic connection between the circulation of commercial images of black identity—which reinforced racist stereotypes—and political and economic systems of oppression. As the black satirist George Schuyler would observe, white writers of this period were fond of representations of African American identity that emphasized the race's innate primitivism. In these depictions, "even when [the Negro] appears to be civilized, it is only necessary to beat a tom tom or wave a rabbit's foot and he is ready to strip off his Hart Schaffner & Marx suit, grab a spear, and ride off wild-eyed on the back of a crocodile."[47] Members of the black intelligentsia such as the historian Carter G. Woodson, editor and founder of the *Journal of Negro History*, and sociologists Charles S. Johnson and E. Franklin Frazier recognized the variety of ways in which the perpetuation of harmful stereotypes of black identity had continued to justify the subjugation of African Americans.[48] To counter this, black Americans needed to reclaim the role of representing African American culture and identity as an essential political step toward equality. All viewed the collection and interpretation of African American folk heritage by black writers as a means of rescuing black history and identity from white distortion. The emerging national interest in "the real" culture of black folk made it possible for African Americans to begin the process. Spurred on in part by the endeavors of scholars like Du Bois, Woodson, and others, a movement took shape to make white America more aware of the value and legitimacy of authentic forms of African American culture as a means of challenging popular tropes of the contented slave, incompetent freedman, and exotic primitive that undermined black citizenship.[49]As Henry Louis Gates Jr. points out, "to manipulate the image of the black was, in a sense, to manipulate reality. The Public Negro Self, therefore, was an entity to be crafted."[50]

This was not the first time that African Americans had struggled to claim their authority for self-representation. As Barbara Savage notes, every historical development in the public media has been met with a campaign by African Americans for "equal access" to the demonstrable power of the cultural media in shaping public opinion.[51] During the 1920s, African Americans did make some inroads upon this white monopoly, creating their own images of blackness that began to circulate to a wider audience as part of the decade's growing interest in black culture and identity. In 1923, African American women mobilized to launch a countercampaign against the United Daughters of the Confederacy's (UDC) drive to erect a memorial statue of "mammy" in the nation's capital. Working with the black press, members of the National Association of Colored Women, including the organization's first president, Mary Church Terrell, undertook a massive letter-writing campaign to publicize an opposing image of the plight of the female slave.[52] The cultural explosion of black writers, artists, and musicians, which seemed to emerge in Harlem, helped put the spotlight on a modern black identity, the "New Negro," who was being created and defined by blacks themselves. "Uncle Tom is dead!" "A New Negro arises!" proclaimed the black press.[53]

The spirit of the New Negro had different manifestations, from overt calls for full political, social, and economic equality and black self-defense, such as those found in the socialist journal the *Messenger* and the union ranks of the Brotherhood of Sleeping Car Porters,[54] to the use of the term by literary figures such as Alain Locke to signal the progress of the race through a new self-consciousness achieved and expressed through cultural production.[55] Black political activists "waged a tug of war over the term 'New Negro,'" with black socialists like A. Philip Randolph using it to invoke a new militancy arising among the masses, while others, who sought "civil rights by copyright," made it the figurehead for a primarily bourgeois cultural movement.[56] All of its iterations, however, signified black Americans' refusal to accommodate white violence and racism, including racist stereotypes that circulated as part and parcel of a commodity culture.[57] The race consciousness that the trope of the New Negro embodied was meant to rebuild black Americans' conception of themselves as much as to challenge white Americans' assumptions about black character and potential for citizenship. Much of this discourse, however, focused on the restoration of black manhood. "Racial uplift" and the masculinist enterprise embodied in the New Negro relied in part on traditionally gendered conceptions of the roles men and women should play.[58]

As numerous reviewers of Richard Wright's *Uncle Tom's Children* observed in 1938, "the title comes from the expression of the Negroes indicating that they are no longer 'Uncle Toms,' that is, cringing servants." The *New York Herald* review warned, "The sentimentalized 'good nigger' of proprietary Southerners and tutelary Northerners is not to be found here." The poet and Harlem Renaissance alumnus Countee Cullen used the opportunity to compare the New Negro directly to the old Uncle Tom: "Uncle Tom's Children . . . are after what belongs to men; they want happiness, better homes, better economic conditions. They still find the getting hard, but (here the blood is different) they are willing to fight."[59] In this alternate and contrapuntal use of the trope of the Old-Time Negro, African American writers fervently hoped he was indeed passing away.

In the introduction to the groundbreaking 1941 literary anthology *The Negro Caravan*, editor Sterling Brown argued that stereotypes of the "self-effacing black mammy, the obsequious major-domo, the naïve folk, and the exotic primitive" had supported the racial oppression of African Americans from slavery to the racial segregation and political disenfranchisement that characterized the seventy-five years since emancipation.[60] Creative literature, Brown asserted, had too often "been a handmaiden to social policy," with white authors often interpreting "the American Negro . . . in a way to justify his exploitation."[61] A number of white writers, he noted sardonically, "offer[ed] such unimpeachable qualifications for understanding Negroes as playing with Negro children, attending Negro picnics and churches, and bossing Negro gangs," with one writer going so far as to claim that her slaveholding ancestry made her a better interpreter of "Negro character than any Negro author."[62] But clearly those most knowledgeable about African Americans belonged to that group by birthright, and must claim the authority to represent black identity previously held by whites. "Negro authors, as they mature, must be allowed the privilege and must assume the responsibility of being the ultimate portrayers of their own."[63] In order for African Americans to achieve full equality in American society, it was critical that they obtain greater control over cultural representations of black identity in the public sphere.

The Social Sciences and the "Negro Problem"

For a number of black intellectuals in the 1920s and 1930s, the social sciences became a disciplinary means or framework for educating white audiences about the slippage between "authentic" black cultural expressiveness and Hollywood's minstrel acts. It also offered a way of competing commercially with white cultural brokers, as Black Swan Records did. African American intellectuals, like Du Bois and Brown, sought to capitalize on the public's appetite for black folk culture by emphasizing the value of ethnographic portrayals over fictional caricatures. The concept of authenticity could be effectively deployed to critique whites' depiction of black culture and character. In particular, the rise of social scientific authority would help to generate a greater realism and ethnographic approach to folk culture in the 1930s. African American sociologists like Charles S. Johnson, E. Franklin Frazier, and Ralph Bunche were developing their own school of sociology that could be used as a tool of liberation for African Americans by scientifically debunking long-held racist assumptions about the nature of black behavior and identity. Robert Park trained a number of black sociologists at the University of Chicago, including Horace Cayton, Allison Davis, St. Clair Drake, Frazier, and Johnson.[64] Although Park believed that slavery had obliterated any African vestiges of an authentic and independent black cultural tradition, a view that would put him at odds with scholars such as Carter Woodson and Hurston, he also became famous for training his students in the anthropological method of "participant observation." To obtain the inside view of different social subsets in the urban environment, he had them pose as members of these communities in order to infiltrate their inner workings.[65] This approach made black researchers an absolute necessity for studies of African American communities and attitudes.[66]

Debates in the 1920s and 1930s over the relationship between racial identity and culture benefited greatly from the scholarly influence of the German American anthropologist Franz Boas. In the early decades of the twentieth century, Boas had managed to discredit much of the dominant anthropological model from the nineteenth century, an evolutionary perspective that held that biological determinants, such as racial identity, were responsible for observable differences in social structure and culture among human groups. Instead, Boasian anthropology emphasized the importance of environmental factors on cultural configurations and stressed the internal logic of group behavior. The Boasian precept that came to be known as "cultural relativism" helped to undermine hierarchical models of human development that rated cultures on a spectrum based on notions of "primitive" and "civilized." But the question of the degree of influence of factors like biology and environment remained and continued to inform debates over black equality and the "Negro problem."

In a period in which prevailing scientific belief, state laws, and Supreme Court decisions classified African Americans along with immigrants from southern and eastern Europe and Asia as racially distinct from and inferior to "whites," Boas and his followers argued in favor of assimilation and acculturation.[67] Although, like Park, Boas believed that most elements of African culture had not survived slavery, a theory that would later attract criticism from the anthropologist Melville Herskovits, he also thought that black Americans should recover their cultural heritage through education and the anthropological retrieval of folk traditions.[68] In his role as editor for the *Journal of American Folklore* and as a founder of the American Folklore Society and the Association for the Study of Negro Life and History, which he cofounded in 1915 with Woodson and Park, Boas helped to publish a large amount of African American folklore, contributing greatly, in the words of historian George Hutchinson, "to the general movement toward a reevaluation of black folk culture, a movement of critical importance for the Harlem Renaissance and that continued with historic results through the 1930s by way of the Federal Writers' Project."[69]

Arguments surrounding black folk culture were infused with assumptions about the nature of African American identity and character: Could black Americans ever fully assimilate? Or did African Americans, at some level, constitute a fundamental and irreconcilable racial other who neither could nor should integrate into the national culture? Many scholars who worked to prove the connections between African cultural traditions and those throughout the black diaspora did so to show the strength and independent value of black culture, such as the white anthropologist Herskovits, the historian Carter Woodson, and writers like Alain Locke, Hurston, and Hughes. The Harlem Renaissance of the 1920s had promoted the idea of African Americans as civilized based on the talents and abilities of black writers and artists, many of whom were embracing the idea of African cultural retention and finding ways to incorporate an African-based aesthetic into their work.

Evidence of African survivals, however, could also be marshaled to demonstrate the continuing primitivism of black Americans. As Walter Jackson has pointed out in his analysis of Herskovits's scholarship on the race question, "Most white American scholars of the early twentieth century portrayed

Africa as a land of primitive savagery. . . . If they discussed African survivals among Afro-Americans at all, it was generally in the course of arguing that these characteristics unfitted blacks for citizenship."[70] Economist Abram Harris and columnist George Schuyler, both formerly of the *Messenger*, ridiculed those associated with the Harlem Renaissance for emphasizing the connection between an African past and a contemporary black art and culture. Schuyler, known for his acerbic wit, castigated them for accepting "the old myth palmed off by Negrophobists for all these many years . . . that there are 'fundamental, eternal, and inescapable differences' between white and black Americans."[71]

During the 1930s, the so-called Negro Question, or "race problem," long considered to be of southern provenance, would now be articulated as a problem of national scope. In 1936, the regionalist Howard Odum, founder of the sociology department and Institute for Research in Social Science at the University of North Carolina, summarized the factors that had contributed to this shift: first, "the Negro population was being diffused through the nation so that the problem was national rather than southern"; second, the "racial" intermixing had created a nascent "Brown America"; third, the "social character of the Negro [was changing] as he expanded his activities and increased his cultural stature." These changing conditions, Odum maintained, made the "future of the Negro . . . essentially an American problem of development and assimilation."[72] Although the Chapel Hill sociologists would lead the way, social anthropologists from Harvard, Yale, and the University of Chicago would also descend on the South to study race relations and class structure.[73] The study of southern blacks thus became a central feature of these social scientific inquiries.

As the "Negro Question" came to the fore in 1930s popular discourse, the federal government, along with privately endowed research institutions, began to seek ways of obtaining information about African Americans. In 1927, the National Research Council created a special committee under the jurisdiction of the joint division of anthropology and psychology on the "Study of the American Negro." At the second meeting of the committee, the following mission was established: "Whereas, the negro constitutes a large fraction of our population, and Whereas, this element of our population is perhaps the least known of any part, Therefore: be it resolved that the object of this committee is the scientific study of the negro and its hybrids."[74] African Americans seemed to constitute a large unknown to white America and therefore a worthy object of study. Prestigious research institutions, such as the Carnegie Corporation and the Rockefeller Foundation, expressed interest in bringing former colonial officials of the British empire, experienced with controlling indigenous populations of people of color in a colonial context, to the United States to assess the "Negro problem" in the American South.[75] Carnegie president Frederick Keppel originally wanted a candidate with colonial experience to direct the most extensive study of the race problem in the United States, but ultimately commissioned the Swedish economist Gunnar Myrdal in 1938 to undertake the project, which was published in 1944.[76] These same institutions also considered funding the folklorist John Lomax's work to collect Negro folk songs, which, as Lomax made clear, would yield far more than just folk music. Folk songs, declared Lomax, were essentially "epic summaries of the attitudes, mores, institutions, and situations of the great proletarian population who have helped to make the South great culturally and economically," and thus offered a window on black identity.[77]

Civil War Remembrance and the "Passing Away of the Old-Time Negro"

The use of history became one of the crucial tools employed in the debates over the "Negro problem." The seventy-fifth anniversary of the Civil War rekindled long-simmering disputes over how it should be commemorated and reawakened unresolved debates over black citizenship and the role of African Americans in the national polity. Americans' fixation with Abraham Lincoln during the 1930s was part of the era's flood of Civil War remembrance. Writer and literary critic Alfred Kazin called "the passionate addiction to Lincoln" one of the "most moving aspects" of the era, and the historian Bernard De Voto viewed it as part of Americans' response to the crisis of the Great Depression: "The American people have invoked the man who, by general consent, represents the highest reach of the American character and who, in that earlier crisis, best embodied the strength of our democracy."[78] Histories, biographies, plays, and films celebrated Lincoln as the leader who had saved the Union and emancipated the slaves.[79]

President Franklin D. Roosevelt invoked Lincoln to support New Deal policies, and others drew direct parallels between them.[80] The New Deal, through its extensive government programs to address the economic crisis of the Great Depression, marked the birth of the modern social welfare state and the greatest intervention of the federal government on matters of racial inequality since Reconstruction. To many "Dixiecrats," the New Deal was all too reminiscent of the abuse of federal authority and the encroachment on states' rights that had led to the Civil War and black enfranchisement.

For African Americans still striving for the rights of citizenship, the New Deal promised a second reconstruction, and cultural projects like the FWP seemed to offer nothing less than the opportunity to finally set the historical record straight, by including African Americans as equal participants in the national narrative, and by including African American voices and perspectives on slavery, emancipation, and post-emancipation struggles for full equality.

But even in the frenzy of Lincoln mania, African American perspectives on the past would be significantly challenged. For example, the memoir of former slave Elizabeth Keckley, the dressmaker and confidante to Mary Todd Lincoln, was reissued in 1931 after decades of being out of print. *Behind the Scenes*, when it was first published in 1868, created public condemnation for its author for daring, as a black woman, to write about the first family. This time, Keckley's authorship and even her existence was questioned in a *Washington Star* article in 1935 by the historian David Barbee, who claimed that Keckley was a fictitious invention of the white abolitionist Jane Swisshelm. This set off a storm of controversy in newspapers and academic journals nationwide as prominent African American scholars, such as the noted historian Carter G. Woodson and the Reverend Dr. Francis Grimké, sought to defend the authenticity of Keckley's autobiography in the *Journal of Negro History*.[81] Significantly, an excerpt from *Behind the Scenes* was included in Brown's anthology *The Negro Caravan*, one that placed Keckley firmly within the center of the scene of private and national loss: her reminiscence of the death of President Lincoln, when she became his grieving widow's sole companion during the period of mourning. Additional selections from *The Negro Caravan* directly contested southern white writers' views of slavery and the propaganda regarding black racial difference and African Americans' unsuitability for the rights of citizenship. Woodson confronted representations of slavery as a benevolent institution, assertions that the Civil War was not about slavery, and stereotypes of miserable freedmen who found life in the North so unbearable that they eagerly returned "to the land of slavery."[82]

Conflicting representations of the Civil War era surfaced most clearly, and certainly most visibly, in the plethora of Hollywood films released during the 1930s, several of which focused on the life and legacy of Abraham Lincoln and an even greater number that were steeped in nostalgia for the antebellum South.[83] Nostalgia for white racial supremacy appeared in *Gone with the Wind*, with its iconic imagery and narrative of a pastoral, prosperous, and peaceful South and its accepted racial hierarchy, tragically brought down by tyrannical and rapacious northerners.[84] But there were many others in a similar vein, such as *Jezebel* (1938), starring Bette Davis as a plantation mistress of contented singing slaves on the aptly named "Halcyon Plantation."[85] The best-selling novel by Stark Young, *So Red the Rose* (1934), described as "'a memorial wreath' to the Old South and Confederacy," was released as a film the following year.[86] As Brown pointed out in *The Negro Caravan*, these films' images, owing to the power and popularity of this visual mass medium, had likely "done more than historians and social scientists to implant in the American mind certain inflexible concepts of Reconstruction."[87]

Ex-slaves themselves became the locus of memory making through competing forms of remembrance about slavery. There were two different types of ex-slave gatherings as a form of commemoration in the 1930s, both of which epitomize the larger struggle taking place over black identity (past and present) and both of which were documented by the FWP. During the 1930s, southern whites revived a tradition popular in the late nineteenth and early twentieth centuries by organizing "Old Slave Days" as part of local public festivities.[88] Event organizers, often town councilmen, used the promise of a meal to bring in ex-slaves—who were then put on display for attendees, both locals and tourists, singing Negro spirituals, reminiscing about slavery days, and leading the crowd in prayer. Such events emphasized the authenticity of the encounter with real former slaves but also fed visitors' nostalgia for a mythologized southern past. These events bear a disturbing resemblance to the ethnographic traveling exhibits of southern plantation life (complete with old "darkeys") popularized in the late nineteenth century.[89] The white community of Southern Pines in North Carolina instituted Old Slave Day as part of their annual spring festival in 1933. As the local paper, the *Pilot*, reported in 1935: "Last year on Old Slave Day we had more than 100 ex-slaves to whom we furnished a luncheon and gave each one a small amount of money to carry home.... These old negroes enjoyed that day better perhaps than any day in their lives."[90]

Some criticized the event as a crass commercial ploy and an insult to historical memory. One of the premier black newspapers in Virginia to consistently tackle issues of social justice, the *Norfolk Journal and Guide*, ran an editorial that was picked up by smaller papers, such as the *Norfolk Blade*. Titled "Southern Hokum for Negroes," it described the annual observance of "Slave Day" as "consisting of a round-up of 'illiterate members of the Negro race of an advanced age' who are encouraged to put on a performance for the delectation of the townsfolk and the northern tourists.... They engage in a crapshooting tournament and 'other degrading performances designed to rekindle the embers of a noble tradition—that of the departed institution of human slavery. Since this institution was abolished seventy-one years ago,

Attendants at Old Slave Day, Southern Pines, North Carolina, 1937. Portraits of African American ex-slaves from the U.S. Works Progress Administration, Federal Writers' Project slave narratives collections, courtesy of the Library of Congress, Prints and Photographs Division, LC-USZ62-125155.

the "ex-slaves" who are mobilized to entertain northerners are probably 99 per cent phony.' " The editorial suggested that such "entertainment" was unlikely to paint a just portrait of slavery: "instead of parading these memories for the entertainment of our monied visitors, we might with better grace allow them to sleep in the history books where those tourists who are hardy enough to crack them open may familiarize themselves with the departed institution in its proper perspective."[91]

The *Pilot* was quick to defend this local event as a dignified tradition, one steeped in real history as all who were invited were genuine ex-slaves: "the authenticity of these venerable negroes . . . is vouched for by the men who knew them and these are honest men," meaning white "southerners of long descent."[92] Southern Pines' Old Slave Day lasted until 1942 but lived on in public memory in the form of the obituaries of former slaves, where prominent mention was made of the deceased's participation in the annual event.[93] In 1946, a former "town father" provided a form of eulogy for the vanished tradition by fondly reminiscing about Old Slave Day in the pages of the *Pilot*.[94]

There were also ex-slave associations organized by African American community leaders with the aim of providing financial assistance for the elderly. The Florida Project of the FWP documented the Ex-Slave Club of Miami, which had been established in 1932 in the hopes of securing old-age pensions for its twenty-five members.[95] The FWP worker who submitted this short piece observed that memories of slavery would differ based on the age of the ex-slave, for while some had been "very small children,—mere babes who never knew the real meaning of slavery," a few of the oldest members, between the ages of eighty-five and ninety-seven, still possessed "vivid recollections of the emancipation and of their living on the plantation." This writer contrasted the "vivid recollections" of slavery days with the erasure of personal memory and family ties caused by enslavement: "children were separated from their parents while they were so small as to have no recollection of their father or mother."[96]

Like the Florida Project, FWP employees on the Georgia Project also gathered information on ex-slave organizations as part of the material they were collecting on slavery. However, unlike the Florida FWP worker who sought out a personal interview with the head of the ex-slave association, the Georgia Project culled articles from local papers on ex-slave associations. As the Georgia material reveals, the line between ex-slave associations and Old Slave Days could easily become blurred, particularly when the former was dependent on the latter for charitable contributions. An article in the *Atlanta*

Constitution requesting donations for the Christmas Eve party for former slaves organized by the ex-slave association (led by the son of slaves) played up the minstrel trope of the contented slave; using phoneticized dialect it described in detail how former slaves longed for the good old days before emancipation. "Time has dealt unkindly with some of the old southern Negroes and some are wishing they were back in slavery, chopping cotton and eating good victuals on 'marster's plantation . . . Ef Ole Marster was hyah, he wouldn't let us want fur nothin'. . . . They rejoice in recalling the old days—'all of us wukin' dar in de fiel' togedder choppin' cotton and singin'. De plantation smokehouse full of meat, and Marster, he war'nt stingy. Settin in de moonlight at de cabin de playin' wid de chilluns, an' if any of dem git sick, Ole missy she come an' doctor dem.'" This article placed former slaves firmly back in the idyll of an antebellum past, noting that the Christmas festival was a time when "their minds dwell on the days of hard work that paid rewards in warm cabins, plenty to eat and membership in 'de white folks fam'blies,'" and the "things that came after emancipation barely get mention." The article drew a direct link between former slaveholders' generosity and their contemporary descendants, whose largesse permitted ex-slaves to "feast all day, sing the old plantation spirituals, and pray for hours without ceasing, and leave at dusk with new clothes and grocery baskets filled to the brim."[97] Another article from the same paper publicizing the event on December 24 described it in terms familiar to those acquainted with Old Slave Day programs, as an evening of nostalgic entertainment provided by the ex-slaves themselves: "One of the most picturesque Christmas celebrations in the world will be held at noon today when a group of Negroes who served in Slavery get together . . . for their 23d annual Yule festivities . . . [including] a song by the old slave chorus . . . 'Give me that old time Religion.' Later in the program the old men and women will narrate their experiences on the plantation 'befo' de war.' . . . At the close of the entertainment program presents will be given to the ex-slaves."[98]

Competing visions of the past of slavery inevitably complicated the FWP's attempts to include black history, culture, and identity, along with African American voices, in the national narrative. In a number of narratives from the FWP's Ex-Slave Project, the mutually reinforcing tropes of voluntary black servitude and the noblesse oblige of southern paternalism were used to frame economic and social relations between the races, implicitly undermining African American advancement and equality. Some daughters and sons of the "Lost Cause" school of Confederate history employed by the FWP recast the ex-slaves' narratives as faithful slave narratives. Two workers on the

Florida Project, Modeste Hargis and Cora Mae Taylor, were particularly adept at this form of literary memorialization and submitted copy to the state office in Jacksonville featuring stories of slaves who preferred to remain in bondage out of love and fealty to their former masters. These types of faithful ex-slave narratives were selected for circulation in the Florida public school system as part of the WPA contributions to public education in each state, indirectly contributing to the UDC's efforts to immortalize the Old-Time Negro for a new generation of southern children.[99] By memorializing the Old-Time Negro through literature, public monuments, song, stories, stage productions, and historical narratives that blurred the line between history and Confederate heritage, southern loyalists ensured that this trope would not pass away.[100] However, there was another form of Civil War remembrance taking place in the 1930s, one that came from former slaves themselves. "The Civil War is the never-to-be-forgotten date from which many ex-slaves reckon their age," the introduction to the FWP's volume of ex-slave narratives, *The Negro in Virginia*, pointed out.[101] The Civil War and emancipation featured prominently in the ex-slave narratives gathered by the FWP, and many ex-slave narrators recalled markedly different memories of slavery, slaveholders, and even revered figures of the Confederacy, such as Jefferson Davis, from those of southern whites.

The culture of the 1930s was steeped in representations of the nation's past, particularly centering on Civil War remembrance in the form of competing visions and narratives about the antebellum south, slavery, and emancipation. African Americans fought the battle over how black history and identity would be represented on a number of fronts—in debates over historical documents and narratives, in film representations, on the radio, and in folk culture. In so doing, they waged struggles to establish their authority—as historians, folklorists, and as eyewitnesses to the past. Nowhere was the struggle more pronounced than in the New Deal project that promised to reconstruct the national narrative regarding African Americans—the FWP.

CHAPTER TWO

Committing Mayhem on the Body Grammatic

The Federal Writers' Project, the American Guide,
and Representations of Black Identity

Who are the WPA authorities who rule out all manner of school book stories
and emphasize the spuriousness of many anecdotes? . . . Are they recognized
historians, and after all—is it the purpose of the government to write a new
history for us?

—F. E. Turin to Honorable Colgate Darden Jr., February 22, 1936

Of all of the Federal Arts Projects created in 1935, the Federal Writers' Project
(FWP) held the dubious distinction of being considered "the ugly duckling
of the lot."[1] A certain amount of public distrust surrounded a project intended
to benefit the rather ill-defined category of white-collar workers known as
writers, perceived by many as "boondogglers" or slackers on the relief rolls.
Although the FWP aimed to employ seasoned writers of ability and had an
eye for talent, hiring such luminaries as Richard Wright, Conrad Aiken, Carl
Sandburg, and Zora Neale Hurston, the majority comprised a disparate and
largely inexperienced group, many of whom "mixed metaphors and dangled
participles with abandon, and otherwise committed mayhem upon the body
grammatic."[2] A *Time* magazine article described the FWP as "a mazy mass of
unemployed newspapermen, poets, graduates of schools of journalism who
had never had jobs, authors of unpublished novels, high-school teachers,
people who had always wanted to write, [and] a sprinkling of first-rate professional writers who were down on their luck."[3]

Evidence from administrative correspondence appears to support this
critical assessment to some extent; FWP manuscripts were subject to vagaries
in grammar, accuracy, and writing style, as Katharine Kellock, tours editor
for the American Guide, would observe at the project's close in 1940.[4] Each
local office also appears to have hired at least one problem employee: letters
of complaint and dismissals testify to writers who were alcoholics, made
death threats to their coworkers, kept pistols in their desk drawers for bran-
dishing purposes, and stole office funds.[5] Still, given the nearly 6,000 writers
hired by the FWP, it is likely that the overall percentage of these types was
quite low.

In order to justify the first massive federal government sponsorship of the arts to a skeptical public, the FWP desperately needed to be a commercial as well as critical success. Far from being seen as a financial write-off, the FWP was conceived with the intention that initial government intervention and economic investment would eventually lead to manuscripts finding their way into commercial publishing houses or, alternatively, being underwritten by interested investors or local civic organizations. Federal director Henry Alsberg was charged with the problem of inventing a central project for the FWP that could be implemented in all states and, most vitally, not offend anyone's sensibilities. "I can't have a lot of young enthusiasts painting Lenin's head on the Justice Building," President Roosevelt cautioned, acknowledging the political debates surrounding his unprecedented federal innovations.[6] After the FWP, along with the other Works Progress Administration (WPA) arts projects, was targeted for investigation by Martin Dies, chairman of the House Un-American Activities Committee, in August 1938,[7] its directors became particularly sensitive to issues concerning the project's objectivity.

In hope of avoiding potential political minefields, Alsberg decided to first create a series of national guidebooks. The American Guide Series would provide employment for vast numbers of insolvent writers, and it would also stimulate the American tourist industry, which would, in turn, boost local economies.[8] If American tourists could be persuaded to spend their money on domestic instead of foreign travel, Alsberg surmised, "the sum would be bigger than the Roosevelt deficit."[9] Alsberg made it clear that an inquiry of this size and importance could be accomplished and coordinated only by the extensive resources and organization unique to the federal government. He underscored the vast information-gathering network available to this government-sponsored project and the facilities and manpower of government departments and services.[10] The FWP would eventually produce fifty-one state and territorial guides, around thirty city guides, and twenty regional guides, in addition to special theme projects on American life, which included ethnic and "Negro" studies publications.[11]

Alsberg's former occupation as a publicity agent, combined with his extensive journalistic experience abroad as a foreign correspondent for the *New York Times*, the *New York World*, the *Nation*, and the *New Freeman*, made him appear well equipped to oversee a national project to document interesting and unusual cultural traditions and communities at home.[12] However, he little realized how the FWP's attempts to create a new and more inclusive historical narrative for a diverse nation would engender controversy leading some to question whether it was the government's role "to write a new history for us." The challenge of reconciling so many disparate authorial voices and divergent perspectives remained one of the pivotal dilemmas facing FWP directors as they endeavored to create a unified written work in what remains one of the largest literary collaborations ever undertaken. Competing visions of local, state, and national identity plagued the creation of FWP manuscripts and publications and proved particularly problematic when it came to including African American history and culture. Attitudes and perspectives of local staff members, who often embodied the regional and "racial" mentalities that the FWP was attempting to document, led federal directors to attempt to mediate between provincial but often obdurate regional outlooks and the more inclusive and cosmopolitan approach of the federal office. Further complicating the relationship between state and federal offices was the appointment of African American scholar and poet Sterling Brown as the director of the Office on Negro Affairs. The debates that emerged within the FWP over representing black history, culture, and communities illuminate the complexity of this project as race often cut across the lines of federal and state authority. The earliest efforts to collect black folk culture were carried out as part of the American Guide Series, and the rationale, methods, and hiring practices developed for the Guide would shape the Ex-Slave Project's objectives, operations, and personnel.

The American Guide

The American Guide Series was intended to provide more to its readers than the usual Baedeker. As federal relief administrator Harry Hopkins was quick to point out, the series was also designed to acquaint Americans with their own country: "The American traveler gets into his automobile and travels for four days . . . and has the conviction that there is nothing of interest between New York and Chicago. Outside of a few highly advertised [sites] . . . he isn't conscious of what America contains, of what American folk habits are."[13] Ironically, Americans' mobility was blamed for their unfamiliarity with their nation's diverse cultures. "Americans are the most travel-minded people in the world; but their travel is two per cent education and 98 per cent pure locomotion. Speeding through towns whose chain stores look as if they had been turned out on an assembly line, the American motorist is unaware of the infinite variety and rich folklore of the American scene."[14] The FWP viewed the homogenizing forces of modernization as contributing to the disappearance of unique folk traditions and culture.

Hopkins also emphasized a new role for the federal government, as author of a narrative of national identity that was inclusive in its approach to the various ethnic groups, communities, and diverse cultures that comprised the United States: "For the first time, we are being made aware of the rich and varied nature of our country. . . . By producing books that are helping us to know our country, the Writers' Project helps us become better acquainted with each other and, in that way, develops Americanism in the best sense of the word."[15] To achieve these ends, the American Guide needed to be factually correct and historically accurate. Hopkins believed that the treasuring up, on a nationwide scale, of the rich cultural diversity of the United States would serve to increase national pride.

One aim of the American Guide Series was to survey and reveal the obscure and unfamiliar cultures and communities that existed beyond the borderlands of the average American's mental map of the nation. As Hopkins explained: "There is as much variety among the people of America as there is in Europe and South America. There are the Kentucky mountaineers and the Pennsylvania Dutch. The attempt has been made to do the picture of the unknown America and the unusual America, the communities which are little known, the negro, negro life, farm life."[16] Ironically, as part of the mission to familiarize Americans with lesser-known minority cultures and communities, the American Guide also worked to exoticize these cultural pockets in the hope of increasing guidebook sales and domestic tourism. Even in this early conception of forthcoming FWP publications, the intended reader was part of an American majority, a "we" constructed upon a presumed but invisible whiteness, for whom African Americans and black folk culture constituted an unknown and unusual type of human exoticism. Concerns regarding the project's potential for publication would lead the FWP to invert the formula of colonial discourse—the domestication of the exotic—and instead exoticize the domestic by emphasizing the strange and alien cultures and communities that lay within the United States. One publicity article for the Guide elaborated upon this theme: "Of such random phenomena is America made up: of voodoo drugstores and corporation goats; of G-men, borax ski slides, and nudist colonies; of strikes and swing music; of the five-cent hamburger; of Riverpoint, R.I., where the Portuguese population celebrates Labor Day with a Holy Ghost fiesta; and of Riviera, Fla., where a colony of negroid Englishmen lives on sea food and weaves palmetto hats."[17] The search for home-grown exoticism, as this quotation suggests, would lead some FWP writers to draw on stereotypical images of ethnic and "racial" minorities such as Native Americans or African Americans for their entertainment value. In the southern states, "local color" all too often became a euphemism for black exoticism. In order to successfully market both the guides and the locales featured within as tourist destinations, the cultural distinctiveness of places usually overlooked by travelers' itineraries had to be highlighted; where such characteristics seemed to be in short supply, the pedestrian had to be elevated and transformed into something rare and exotic.[18]

Reviewers of the Guide Series frequently reinforced the equation of black communities with the unusual and unexpected by focusing almost exclusively on the "colorful" sections that contained images of black culture as primitive and foreign. In a lengthy article that appeared in the *Prairie Schooner*, the writer directly associated "local color" with the Louisiana Guide's material on the black community. The author praised the Guide for conveying a strong sense of place, but as was quickly made evident, the sense of place came from the copy on African Americans:

> The reader first becomes aware of this strange quality as he peeps into the chapter on Folkways. There he meets . . . blimp-like negresses . . . Voodoo queens and incantations, poorboy sandwiches, lagniappe and haunted houses. Certainly it is these things which have conspired to cast a spell on him. The real New Orleans cannot be like this. It is after all an American city. Still skeptical, the reader turns to a chapter on the Carnival. . . . Here he meets King Zulu, the black, grass-skirted king of the Negro Mardi Gras. . . . So here, too, the spirit of the place is all-pervasive.[19]

FWP officials also contributed to the defamiliarization of African American culture by using such sections in their publicity releases to advertise the books' commercial appeal as entertainment. An official release entitled "Life of New Orleans Negroes Pictured in New Guide Book," which appeared in the *Tampa Bulletin*, focused exclusively on the Louisiana Guide's depictions of African American life, which promised to provide the reader with a scintillating peek: "In a section of The Guide dealing with folkways, Negro street vendors, 'spasm bands,' traditional chimney sweepers, voodoo rituals, 'gris-gris' ceremonials and the chattering Gumbo-French dialect make the backdrop against which the colorful Negro citizens of the Delta State metropolis [stand out]. Quaint 'gun-shot' cottages with their doors opening in a straight line to their distant backyards, and the mysteries of powdered brick sprinkled on the front steps to ward off evil spirits are unfolded in this Writers' Project production."[20] In this way, representations of African American culture were transformed into signifiers for the "special local flavor" of southern culture and became a marketable commodity for the purposes of selling state guidebooks.

The FWP wanted to produce a guidebook that went beyond the merely descriptive. In 1937, a review in the *New Republic* praised the Guide for striking "an admirable balance between interpretation and factual detail."[21] But in order to create a guide that was interpretive, the FWP adopted for its purposes a literary model that was imbued with an authorial point of view. Alsberg was struggling to work out the style he wanted to establish for the FWP's most ambitious and most publicized project; he was looking for a genre that could weave together descriptions of exotic local color and practical advice for the American traveler. In March of 1936, Alsberg invoked a book from the genre of travel literature as an example of the type of writing the FWP guidebook should emulate: "The type of route description desired is a mixture of practical travel guide and running narrative. . . . We would be particularly pleased to have the kind of narrative achieved by Mrs. Anne Lindbergh in her *North to the Orient*, which produced a feeling of exploration of a new world."[22] Lindbergh's 1935 memoir, recounting her travels with her husband by plane from New York to Tokyo, was written in an accessible, conversational style that firmly established an authorial voice and first-person perspective. Through her eyes, the reader could experience the thrills and dangers of traveling abroad and setting foot among strange primitive communities filled with friendly, and sometimes threatening, native inhabitants. As Alsberg hoped to do with the Guide, Lindbergh sought to convey the magical experience of exploring foreign countries and encountering unusual peoples and their ways, before the homogenizing effects of modern technology made such cultural "pockets" obsolete.[23] Taking his cue from Lindbergh, Alsberg envisioned the American Guide as a travel book series that would present communities and locales within the United States as exotic "new worlds" to be explored by Americans unfamiliar with the virgin territories right outside their own backyards.

The genre of travel writing historically alternated between two different (but often mutually reinforcing) modes of sentimental and scientific narration. In the sentimental mode, the authorial voice is embodied in a central protagonist and describes personal interactions with the inhabitants and their customs from the traveler's "outsider" perspective. It described peoples and cultures in a manner that drew the reader vicariously into the adventures of the narrator, while anchoring the authority of the observer in the realistic experience of fieldwork—"I was there." By contrast, the scientific mode effaces the narrator in favor of a disembodied gaze that produces an objective, scientific description of topography, flora and fauna, and natural resources.[24] The FWP guidebook project incorporated both of these narrative styles into a single work because each mode was best suited for a different type of description. The scientific mode worked easily for the impersonal surveying and cataloging of national resources, such as the guides' descriptions of flora and fauna, industry, and education. As the FWP enlarged its sociological perspective with the creation of subprojects on minority cultures, the sentimental mode of narration was increasingly favored. This mode was also recommended for use by FWP interviewers engaged in writing up the ex-slave narratives in order to incorporate the field worker's own experiences with the informant as part of the story. The inclusion of the field worker's observations, however, served to privilege the interviewer's perspective and imbue it with the authority implicit in the authorial voice. The FWP's incorporation of the field worker's perspective, drawn from the literary models of professional ethnography and popular travel writing, seemed to present a solution to the problem of establishing a unified style for the guidebooks. By 1938, Alsberg had become interested in gathering interesting tales of FWP workers' exploits and adventures in the field for the purposes of publishing a special collection tentatively entitled "Guide-Makers and Guide Making."[25] He explained his idea in a memo sent to all state directors: "Workers on the project ... have been in wrecks, have been lost, snowbound, mired and marooned. Their investigations have led them into all sorts of astonishing misadventures."[26] Although nothing seems to have come of this particular proposal, it indicates Alsberg's continuing fascination with the travel narrative form.

Alsberg's interest in adopting the authorial perspective of the protagonist of the travel narrative genre, and the national office's wish to include an interpretive framework within the Guide Series, worked in concert with the FWP's anthropological view of the importance of folklore for understanding a region's people and culture. The FWP would define folklore as "a body of traditional belief, custom, and expression, handed down largely by word of mouth and circulating chiefly outside of commercial and academic means of communication. Every group bound together by common interests and purposes, whether educated or uneducated, rural or urban, possesses a body of traditions which may be called its folklore."[27]

Folk culture could not be studied or understood apart from the societal context of the ethnic or "racial" group that produced it. As the "American Guide Manual for Folklore Studies" explained, "we want to know as much as possible about its source, history, and use, in relation to the past and present experience of the people who keep it alive. This information enables us to understand the function and meaning which folklore has for those who use it and so enhances its interest and significance for others."[28]

The manual noted that the personal interviews and oral histories gathered by FWP folklore collectors would help to provide crucial information about "the living background" necessary for understanding the meaning of folk culture in the life and identity of the ethnic or "racial" group: "by showing how the songs the people sing and the stories they tell grow out of or are adapted to the work they do and the things they know and believe in."[29] As subsequent manual guidelines made clear, however, the FWP interviewer was expected to take an active role in observing and recording sociological information about "the living background" of the informant. In the instruction for interviewers working on a subsidiary project of the FWP's National Social Ethnic Study on the topic "The Lithuanian in America," workers were told to write up their own impressions of the informant's appearance, behavior, and habitat: "While in the presence of your informant's environment, be on the alert to record in your mind as much of the color of the surroundings as possible. By this is meant: any particular action that took place which in your mind is typical of the cultural conduct of the ethnic group; the appearance of the home, its furnishings, etc. Record this *immediately* after the interview on a separate piece of paper and attach it to the schedule [form]."[30]

This directive is similar to the method of participant observation favored by anthropologists and sociologists in the 1930s; given that this particular study was being supervised by Ernest Burgess, a professor in the sociology department at the University of Chicago (where the study of urban sociology was founded and disseminated nationwide under the guidance of Robert Park in the 1920s and 1930s), the similarity is not coincidental. This method was also adopted for use in the FWP's Ex-Slave Project, for which interviewers were encouraged to include their own descriptions of the ex-slave informant's dress, mannerisms, speech, and living conditions. This approach obviously contained serious methodological weaknesses; by asking lay interviewers, who were not academically trained social scientists and who were often unfamiliar with the ethnic or "racial" group being studied, to record whatever seemed to them "in [their] mind" to be typical, or representative of the group, was inviting observations that reinforced the most stereotypical images.

What the American Guide Series essentially promised was to turn average tourists into lay historians and ethnographers by endowing them with the "inside" view. These guidebooks would offer up the kind of anthropological "thick description" of communities and cultures that normally could be obtained only by local residents or professional ethnographers. The ethnographer symbolized knowledgeable authority and, unlike the tourist, through the method of participant observation could uncover secrets previously known only to local inhabitants by living within the community. Under Alsberg's guidance, 5,000 FWP employees were touted as having "covered more than a million miles of American roads by foot or auto, checking . . . every possible point of interest along the way. They have disturbed the deep dust of county courthouse storerooms, interviewed garrulous 'oldest inhabitants,' jotted down millions of notes, assembled thousands of pounds of data."[31] Yet, as an outsider, the ethnographer was also supposed to be capable of maintaining the objectivity necessary for interpretation. The American Guide planned to present local knowledge filtered through the objective editorial pens of FWP writers and federal directors to the American tourist.

As word got out that there were jobs available for state FWP projects, the federal office was inundated with letters from state residents in desperate need of work. Many wrote letters of application directly to Alsberg, listing their qualifications either as writers or as longtime residents or natives of the state who possessed great insider knowledge of local history, geography, and culture.[32] To the majority of these applicants, Alsberg responded with a concise but kind note stating that the national office was not in charge of hiring for those positions and identifying the appropriate contact person. But for applicants who demonstrated the skills prized by the FWP's federal directors, Alsberg and his colleagues were more than willing to use their influence to find them employment on state projects. Both Alsberg and his assistant, Reed Harris, were keen to hire writers who demonstrated familiarity with the increasingly popular genre of travel writing that was beginning to shade into a kind of lay ethnography. Such writing was based on the "real life" adventures of the author's travels through exotic, foreign locales and encounters with the natives.[33]

Applicants with university degrees in history and English received special consideration, and Alsberg and Harris sought out those with work-related experience in keeping with the FWP's emphasis on ethnography in the American Guide Series as well as later spin-off projects, such as the Life History Project, the Folklore Project, "Negro Studies," and the Ex-Slave Project. These projects attracted amateur ethnographers and lay historians who considered themselves "experts" in fields of study on "the Indian" and "the Negro." On behalf of these candidates, Alsberg's office frequently sent letters to state directors encouraging them to find room on their staffs for their employment.[34] The federal office's interference with local hiring policies was a delicate matter, as some of the correspondence attests. State staffs strongly objected to the employment of "outsiders." In a field report to the federal director, tours editor Kellock noted the rancor that had been generated in the Florida office as a result of federal involvement: "Washington's insistence on Mrs. Shelby's hiring is causing a lot of trouble. They resent her being thrust on them—as all Floridians resent an 'outsider' who spends part of her time elsewhere or has come into the state fairly recently."[35] This objection stemmed in part from southern whites' firm belief that they "knew" their "Negroes" far better than northern Yankees ever could. Perpetuating Confederate mythology regarding race relations, southern whites frequently asserted an intimate knowledge steeped in the long past of slavery and the close relationships between slaveholders and their slaves that made them "like family." With few exceptions, FWP staff members were drawn from the native population in each city and state. What these employees lacked in professional writing experience, they made up for in the knowledge they possessed about their own communities; such information was touted by the federal office as indispensable to the preparation of manuscripts pertaining to local and state histories, as well as regional and ethnic cultures.[36] Local experts, as Alsberg's assistant Reed Harris pointed out, would allow "local color and feeling to penetrate into the guides" and could catch the "real spirit" of their locations.[37] Field workers' "local connections" would also help them identify and amiably interrogate local informants in the guise of an "old cook, washerwoman, gardener, or other retainer."[38] These oldest inhabitants, as the American Guide manual pointed out, who are "close to the soil, who because circumstances have cut them off from education and progressive enlightenment, are repositories for local lore, legends, and superstition, would be ideal sources for the field worker."[39]

And yet federal directors realized that there must be some direction in method, some standardizing process, which would come from the top down. As a way of explaining how the intricate chain of command worked for a project in which every city of 10,000 had an FWP office and every one of the nation's 3,000 counties had at least one designated field worker, one article used the analogy of a newspaper office (possibly taking inspiration from Alsberg's former occupation): "In structure, the Writers' Project resembles a big daily newspaper. The Washington office is the city editor, the state offices are the desk men, and the county field workers are the 'leg men.' Most of the actual writing is done in the state office. In Washington, where government bureaus and the Library of Congress offer unlimited checking facilities, every fact is verified at least three times."[40]

But in the interests of accuracy and objectivity, federal and regional directors often found themselves in the uneasy position of questioning and critiquing the material submitted by state project writers. Local staff members could be relied on to take a degree of pride in their communities' traditions and heritage and usually to prevent a patronizing tone from creeping into guidebook copy. However, the federal office also had to be perpetually vigilant when it came to state offices submitting copy that was overly laudatory. An article about the Guide Series in *Pathfinder Magazine* noted that there were "335 cities which claimed to be the crossroads of America. One city ascribed to itself 67 'firsts' and 'bests.'" In addition, a number of towns in the Midwest, apparently, "like Rome, [were] built on seven hills."[41] The "Manual for the American Guide" cautioned FWP employees to be on the lookout for blatantly subjective assumptions: "It is imperative that local bias be avoided in preparing this material for the guide. It should be remembered that when the Chamber of Commerce says Homeville is the loveliest city . . . or has the longest mainstreet in the world, or is the only city in America growing red onions, it may be attempting to boost the city without paying much or any attention to facts. . . . Facts will be checked by regional offices after local offices have recorded them, and by the national office after the regional office has done its work."[42]

In order to correct local boosterism, scholarly experts in relevant fields would lend their services, helping to provide the requisite objectivity that the project's aspirations demanded. The FWP broadcast its success in bringing together local and national experts, amateur and professional researchers and writers, and secured the assistance of prominent individuals to serve as volunteer aides, including the historian Charles Beard, authors John Erskine and Henry Seidel Canby, and the architect Frank Lloyd Wright.[43] Seeking a unified approach and coherent style, federal directors quickly tried to implement certain standard methods and procedures by issuing an authoritative American Guide Manual, the required reference tool for all FWP employees, along with federal guidelines and manuals routinely distributed to all state directors, and by establishing schools "where the preparation of Guide copy could be taught."[44] Alsberg repeatedly emphasized to his state directors the importance of all field workers following the federal instructions as the manuals were "based on [the] actual field experience" of professional anthropologists and sociologists such as Melville Herskovits and Ralphe Bunche, who served as national advisors to the FWP.[45]

Despite these authoritative claims, local community members loudly voiced their opposition to representations of their city or state that failed to meet their expectations. Most notable among the various complaints the FWP received was the controversy that ensued over the Massachusetts Guide's treatment of a cause célèbre of the 1920s, the trial of the Italian-born anarchists Sacco and Vanzetti. Massachusetts's governor Charles Hurley violently objected to the Guide's sympathetic description of the execution of Sacco and Vanzetti (which many had protested against as a miscarriage of justice) as "the classic example of the administering of justice to members of unpopular political minorities."[46] Debates over Guide descriptions were publicized in local newspapers and sometimes led to affronted local residents contacting their political representatives to defend the popular reputations of historical figures, like Captain John Smith, founder of the Jamestown settlement, described in the *Virginia Guide* as a "soldier of fortune" who sold a white boy into slavery. As one Virginian pointed out, if the FWP could rewrite popular history, "many of our national heroes will be branded as renegades or even worse."[47] These protestations could also be marshaled as evidence of the FWP's ability to rise above local loyalties and alliances for the objective portrait. *Fortune* magazine praised the FWP guidebooks for dealing "frankly and in considerable detail . . . with matters which the local boosters' clubs would just as soon omit."[48]

Local versus Federal Views of Black Identity

Many of the bitterest struggles that took place between federal and state offices regarded the inclusion of African American history. Federal director Alsberg and associate director George Cronyn struggled to reconcile the provincialism (at times manifested as racism) that often characterized the state staffs' attitudes toward black history and identity with the more cosmopolitan perspective of the federal office in Washington.[49] As the FWP's editor of Negro Affairs Sterling Brown later recalled, "We had to insist upon proper representation of the Negro in these books. . . . In order to get Negroes in, we had to have an essay on Negroes. For example, Tennessee would send in something about Nashville and not even mention Fisk University. . . . At the start they didn't even count Negroes in the population. They'd give the white population."[50] A variety of competing political perspectives as well as agendas in southern state projects, among white employees as well as black employees, further complicated the work of the Ex-Slave Project (and the FWP). A number of white southern employees were invested in promoting the narrative of the Lost Cause that sought to vindicate the Confederacy, in part through depictions of slavery as a benevolent institution. Ironically, a number of southern whites who found employment through government work-relief programs like the FWP and the WPA still opposed the New Deal and were against the idea of using federal monies to underwrite cultural projects. In Florida, for example, progressive New Dealers worked side by side with ardent anti–New Dealers and the occasional member of the Ku Klux Klan.[51] Alsberg's field supervisor, Katharine Kellock, reporting from Florida on the status of the project in 1936, reminded him that "this is a great states' rights country. Florida is particularly resentful of Washington as you doubtless know."[52]

Correspondence between state directors and the federal office reveals these fundamental fissures. For example, the president of the Florida Division of the United Daughters of the Confederacy (UDC) was quick to contact Florida state director Carita Doggett Corse to express the organization's objection to the term "the Civil War." She emphasized that using "Civil War" instead of the UDC's preferred "War Between the States" could jeopardize the potential audience for FWP publications, and in an interesting choice of words, she argued that this "would be *very* prejudicial to the popularity of the publications in Florida or anywhere in the South."[53] Corse sought guidance from Alsberg, who promptly told her that the phrase "War Between the States" was being used in all state guidebooks for the southern states, and so "it would be satisfactory . . . to use this [phrase] in the Florida State guide."[54]

There was a direct correlation, moreover, between the dearth of African American workers on state projects and resulting treatment of "the Negro" in state Guide manuscripts. The state director of North Carolina explained the difficulty of trying to obtain information on the state's black population from white FWP employees. White racism was so prevalent among staff employees, he observed, that it directly affected the collection of this type of material: "The feeling against any extensive treatment of the Negro is so strong in all larger North Carolina cities . . . that it has been almost impossible for us to make the various district offices dig out and transmit the required material. Furthermore, the failure of the office staffs to collect material has largely depended upon the remarkable ignorance of the white citizenry as to what the Negroes are doing."[55] At the same time, the director had apprehensions about addressing this oversight. "On the other hand," he remarked, "I am sure that extensive treatment of the Negro population, and particularly the mentioning of Negro activities which are overlooked in the case of the whites, will call forth a great deal of resistance when the time for publication arrives."[56]

Other state directors justified their sparse treatment of African American history and communities in their Guide copy in a variety of ways. Some claimed that the small numbers of black Americans in their states were insufficient to warrant mention in the Guide Series. Responding to Brown's request for a progress update on Nebraska's coverage "of Negroes in this state," the state director pointed out that there would be "very little Negro material as the Negro population is considerably less than 1% of the total for the State."[57] Similarly, Nevada's director told the federal office that his state contained "only 600 [Negroes] according to the last census," and therefore "this project has been unable to treat the work of the Negroes as a separate subject."[58] This director's letter also articulates the association that existed in some employees' minds between the FWP's interest in Negro studies and the so-called "Negro problem" and drew a troubling equivalency between the number of African American inhabitants and the "problem." "As we have no Negro 'problem,'" the director went on to explain, "I have been at a loss from the start of this project on how to comply with requests for information as to what Negroes of Nevada are doing. We have so few of them that, in effect, we have none at all."[59]

The blatant racial bias of certain white southern directors and employees made the hiring of black researchers, writers, and editors a clear necessity. If the FWP was to be truly representative, then the inclusion of African Americans, as employees, and not just as informants, was essential. The establishment of the Office on Negro Affairs under the leadership of Sterling Brown was meant to provide, at the federal level, a means of correcting the most obvious oversights and assumptions regarding African Americans in copy submitted by FWP state directors. Brown, a distinguished associate professor of English at Howard University, was hired by Alsberg in the spring of 1936.[60] In addition to sifting out inaccuracies about black history and identity in FWP texts, the creation of such a prominent position for a well-known African American scholar was intended to send the message that the FWP was behaving conscientiously in its preparation of material regarding the black population.

Surprisingly, scholars have not investigated the question of how the Office on Negro Affairs and Brown's position as the national editor came into existence.[61] Neither was it spontaneous nor did the idea originate with Alsberg. Much of the credit for the creation of Brown's position and also the FWP's employment of African Americans in white-collar positions belongs to John

Sterling A. Brown, National Editor of Negro Affairs, Federal Writers' Project. Photo by Addison N. Scurlock, 1944. Scurlock Studio Records, 1905–1994, courtesy of Archives Center, National Museum of American History, Smithsonian Institution.

Preston Davis, a Harvard graduate and an outspoken critic of the limits of New Deal liberalism.[62] Davis's epiphany regarding the urgent necessity for African American representation on New Deal projects occurred in 1933 when he attended hearings on Capitol Hill for the newly established National Recovery Administration (NRA). Davis was outraged to find that white southern mill owners' arguments for their exemption from minimum wage requirements were going unchallenged because no one was scheduled to testify on behalf of the black employees who would be negatively affected if wage differentials based on race as well as region were allowed to continue.[63] Davis "fabricated a representative organization on the spot . . . appointed himself executive secretary, and convinced the NRA hearing administrator to credential him as a consumer advocate for black industrial workers."[64]

Davis quickly set about meeting with Washington government officials but also working to build a broad coalition of African American organizations to serve as a "powerful Negro lobby" that would press for equal opportunity in New Deal relief programs and function as a watchdog reporting discrimination to WPA administrators.[65] He outlined this vision in a document,

"Suggested Plan for Coordination of Negro Organizations for the Purpose of Integrating Interests of the Negro in All Federal Recovery Projects," and circulated it to leaders of civil rights organizations, including the executive secretary of the NAACP, Walter White, and the National Urban League.[66] Successfully soliciting the support of a broad coalition that included the black press, the Federal Council of Negro Churches, the National Association of Colored Women, and the African Methodist Episcopal (AME) Church, Davis created the Joint Committee on National Recovery (formerly the Negro Industrial League) and appointed himself executive secretary.[67]

With the authority of this self-created position, Davis began corresponding with FWP administrators, like Henry Alsberg, as well as the assistant administrator of the WPA, Aubrey Williams, pressuring them to address the racial discrimination running rampant in the hiring practices of southern state projects. In December 1935, Davis pointed out that there were too few black employees in the FWP nationwide and recommended the appointment of a qualified African American to Alsberg's staff in Washington to oversee the portions of the American Guide that would be dedicated to black history, communities, and culture.[68] In a lengthy letter to Williams, Davis also proposed that an "equitable percentage" of the funds for each white-collar project be designated to employ qualified African American white-collar workers. In addition, Davis recommended that each of the major federal WPA projects "Music, Art, Writing, Recreation . . . and scientific studies" appoint African American administrative assistant directors. "It is strange, indeed," Davis wrote, "that of the thousands of employees secured to administer these various projects none is a Negro. I am sure you do not suffer from the illusion that no Negroes are qualified for these posts."[69]

Alsberg promptly wrote to Davis assuring him, as Davis described it, "that regional directors of the Federal Writers' Project are without prejudice in the matter of employing Negroes,"[70] but he simultaneously sent a private interoffice memo to Williams stating he was "sure there is discrimination in the southern states against employment of negroes on the Writers' Projects" and noting his efforts "to ameliorate this situation," which included sending a representative to Georgia to see that a few would be employed on that state project. He also told Williams that it would be "only just if one able negro writer be given a position here in Washington, so that the American Guide will do justice to negroes."[71] That same day, Alsberg sent another letter to Davis telling him that both he and his associate director, George Cronyn, had agreed to appoint "a negro to supervise that part of the work for the American

Guide which will cover the negro population of the country," if Harry Hopkins, the director of the WPA, would fund an additional staff member.[72] By February 1936, Alsberg was soliciting recommendations from Dr. Ambrose Caliver, a member of Roosevelt's "Black Cabinet" in the Department of Education, for the new position of "Negro editor" as part of his staff in Washington to oversee the "Negro section of our Guide."[73] Among those considered before Brown were Professors Allison Davis and Lawrence Reddick of Dillard University, both of whom were unavailable.[74] Reddick, in his earlier position at Kentucky State College, had overseen approximately 250 interviews with ex-slaves, as part of the Federal Emergency Relief Act.

Brown was hired in April 1936. For the WPA press release announcing his appointment, Brown emphasized the important role black employees and prestigious black intellectuals would play in shaping the FWP's representations of African American identity. Brown's commentary articulated his vision of black self-determination in cultural representation: "The Office on Negro Affairs, a unit of the administrative headquarters at Washington, under the supervision of Professor Sterling A. Brown, was set up for the express purpose of helping to present the Negro race adequately and without bias. In this connection Professor Brown has received valuable advice on matters pertaining to Negro life from Horace Mann Bond, Elmer Carter, Ralph Bunche, E. Franklin Frazier, . . . Walter White, Carter Woodson and other prominent members of the race."[75] Brown and his coworkers in the Office on Negro Affairs, Glaucia B. Roberts (a graduate of Howard hired as an editorial assistant in June 1936),[76] Ulysses Lee (of Lincoln University who edited with Brown *The Negro Caravan*), and Brown's colleague at Howard, Eugene Holmes, labored to ensure that the inclusion of African Americans in FWP publications created a more objective portrait. But this endeavor was far from easy and often garnered too little support from the rest of the FWP's administrative officials.

Some of the frustrations regularly encountered by Brown and his small staff were articulated in their report "Existing Conditions in the Office on Negro Affairs" in November 1938. This memo pointed out that in theory, the primary duty of the staff was to read and edit all of "the State, local, and city guidebook copy coming into the office from each of the various States," work for which they were already understaffed. "In general," the memo reported, "the editorial work of these three people entails (1) written criticisms of all of the copy with respect to adequacy, inadequacy, and correctness of the Negro material; (2) library and other research incident to the actual editing; (3) conferences with various supervising and other editors; and (4) *the* writing of material on the Negro to be included in the final copy."[77] However, this last responsibility had overtaken all the others in terms of time expenditure.

> As a result of (1) the disinclination on the part of the writers in the various States, more especially in the South, to include *adequate* or in numerous instances *any* mention of the Negro population constituent in State and city guide copy and (2) the failure on the part of the various writers' projects to employ capable Negro research workers as the most desirable and effective means of uncovering available material on the race, the task of the editors on Negro Affairs is rendered particularly difficult. *Often they are largely or solely responsible for any treatment of the Negro appearing in the final copy.*[78]

Furthermore, the Office on Negro Affairs' ability to influence the states' publications was severely limited. Even though the Office bore the stamp of authority as an official "unit of the national headquarters of the Federal Project in Washington," state directors were apparently loath to extend the same recognition to the Office on Negro Affairs that they regularly acknowledged in their communication with other federal directors.[79] Although other scholars have acknowledged that "it took Brown and his staff almost a year before they could make their editorial weight felt in the Project's field offices" and that "he was not always successful in persuading state editors to include Negro material in the guidebooks or in correcting material that had been distorted," Jerre Mangione suggests that "by and large he and his staff achieved their goal of including honest and accurate material about the Negro in most of the state guidebooks."[80] This is an oversimplification of the difficulties the Office on Negro Affairs encountered. Throughout the duration of his appointment, and well past the first year of the Office's existence, Brown's editorial suggestions were frequently either challenged or ignored by state directors who felt that an African American could not possibly provide an "objective" viewpoint on subjects relating to racial relations. Much of the dialogue (and often disagreement) between federal and state directors over copy concerning African Americans was the direct result of protestations and recommendations made by Brown's office.

Some of the challenges to Brown's authority stemmed from deeply divided, competing ideological visions of the history of slavery and the Civil War. The UDC, an organization founded in 1894 to preserve and memorialize the bloody sacrifice made by Confederate soldiers, had been most active in its endeavors to publicize and promote what it saw as the true history of the southern past, which included the history of slavery as a benevolent institution.

For UDC historian general Mildred Rutherford, the "Old South" was a "template for the southern future," in which the racial order of the past, white supremacy, must be defended against those working to dismantle it.[81]

Surprisingly, scholars have not thought to investigate whether the FWP employed members of the UDC.[82] UDC members did work for the FWP, as field workers and interviewers of former slaves, and at least one state director was also a member of the organization. Alabama state director and UDC member Myrtle Miles[83] wrote several letters to the FWP's associate director, George Cronyn, complaining about Brown's editorial criticism and defending Alabama's State Guide's treatment of slavery and African Americans. Miles plainly found the idea of an African American writer wielding authority over the state of Alabama's achievements very objectionable, regardless of his degree of education. "It is still my feeling," she wrote, "that the general criticism by your Negro editor is biased. . . . I believe Alabamians understand the Alabama Negro and the general Negro situation in Alabama better than a critic whose life has been spent in another section of the country, however studious, however learned he may be."[84] Miles continued to condemn Brown's viewpoint as well as that of the federal office in regard to the South: "We do not believe . . . that the picture [of Alabama] should be painted in black tones. . . . We are well aware that Alabama has faults but is it the only commonwealth in the Union whose faults must be stressed? Must its achievements, even though your Negro editor considers them meager, be damped and its earnest efforts toward improvement be overlooked." Miles concluded her critique by drawing attention to one of the central problems incurred by the FWP's policy of using local writers by pointing out that the viewpoint of the native (white) Alabamian and the viewpoint of the federal office were almost certain to differ: "If, as you say in your letter, we must write the facts as you see them in Washington, our research and experience on the ground has been a wasteful process."[85] She pointed out the inherent difficulty of writing a guidebook that would appeal to the majority of Alabama readers and simultaneously satisfy what she obliquely referred to as "the Washington attitude . . . in regard to a somewhat controversial subject."[86]

Part of "Washington's" objections to the Alabama copy centered on its portrayals of slavery as a benevolent institution. In her defense, Miles emphasized that her staff had exercised restraint: although Alabama's Guide copy "could have stressed the fact that more than a few slave owners actually paid wages to their more accomplished slaves," Miles claimed credit for refraining from including this, as to have done so "would have been no more fair than was Mrs. Stowe's [portrait of the evil slaveholder] Simon Legree."[87] Miles also declared that African Americans had done better under slavery than in the decades following emancipation. "We feel . . . that the Negro, in three or four decades before the Civil War, was economically and spiritually better off than in the 20 years after the war."[88]

As for the Alabama Guide's conclusion "that Negro and white live in amity," another assertion directly questioned by Brown and the Office on Negro Affairs, Miles claimed this was "borne out by facts."[89] Although she admitted that there had been a recent lynching, "it was the first mob action taken in years."[90] Continuing in this vein, she pointed out that "on the other side of the picture" in court cases involving white female plaintiffs charging black men with sexual assault, "there have been more than three acquittals in Jefferson County." In addition, there had been "no attempts made by Negroes through process of law or purchase to infringe on white residential zones."[91] As Miles defiantly concluded her letter: "This explanation is not an apology for our work. It is . . . compiled for the benefit of a view point that may possibly be different."[92]

Associate director George Cronyn replied to Miles's angry defense and tried to reason with her, drawing a historical analogy between the abolition of American slavery and the liberation of the Russian serfs in 1861. "It is also a historical axiom," he wrote, "that *no* master class 'prepares' its chattels for freedom. From the point of view of such a class that would be foolish."[93] Cronyn also took issue with Miles's claim that African Americans had been happier under slavery and tried to call her attention to the importance of maintaining an objective perspective "as dispassionate students of history."[94]

Another point on which Miles and her staff had differed from the federal office was whether Booker T. Washington, the founder of the famed Tuskegee Institute in Alabama, should be treated in the Guide as a "native son." Miles had received this criticism from the federal office: "We must bring to your notice one important point of Alabama history overlooked by you. A History of Alabama that makes no mention of Booker T. Washington has no right to be considered comprehensive."[95] In defense of this oversight, Miles pointed out that Washington "was not a native Alabamian."[96] Cronyn immediately countered with Washington's connection to the Tuskegee Institute and his prominence as a black educator on both the state and national level. Furthermore, he pointed out, "as to a birth requirement, you cannot, or at least should not, limit Alabama's Roll of Honor only to native sons, otherwise you would deny merited notice to many. . . . Alabama was always home to Booker Washington."[97] But Cronyn was also careful to insist that this opinion should not be misinterpreted as liberal bias: "We hold no brief for him, or for the colored 'other million' of Alabama's people. Our interest is merely in the historical record and our aim is to make it comprehensive and true. . . . Further, we say that an Alabama History which does not cover Alabama's colored population with its relative proportion, as well as her white population, cannot be considered as fully representative of Alabama."[98]

Georgia's state director, Samuel Tupper Jr., also wrote to the federal directors to express a difference of opinion with Brown, although he was somewhat more diplomatic than Miles had been. "I have made a sincere endeavor to revise the Negro portion of the Contemporary Scene in accordance with the suggestions of your Negro editor," he told associate director George Cronyn. He refused, however, to take Brown's advice to include "a more expansive treatment of the more prosperous and educated element" as, he claimed, it "would be out of proportion. Savannah is an old fashioned Southern city, and is not a center for Negro education."[99]

Alsberg would lend his clout to Brown's critiques by including them in his own editorial comments to state directors. However, Brown's opinion was often subtly (and perhaps inadvertently) undermined by Alsberg, who continually referred to him in his correspondence as "the Negro editor" rather than by name. This made it easier for state directors to complain of Brown's "bias" because of his racial identity as a "Negro editor." In a letter Alsberg wrote to Virginia's state director, Eudora Ramsay Richardson, he noted specifically that "the Negro editor does not feel that you have given a complete picture in the one sentence about the numerous Negro sections and their ramshackle houses. Nearly half of Portsmouth's population is Negro. These people work at various occupations and professions, and perhaps do not all live in ramshackle houses."[100] Alsberg also suggested that Richardson include in the Virginia Guide a reference to the state's black residents, as they "constitute more than one-third of the population."[101]

Evidence that certain southern state directors often chose to disregard either completely or in part the editorial suggestions made by Brown's office can be seen in a memorandum the Office on Negro Affairs sent to Alsberg protesting the publication of the Mississippi Guide.[102] "There are complete omissions, as well as distortions, and anti-Negro propaganda, some [of] which we were reasonably sure would not be published."[103] The memo was intended to put "on record" the Office on Negro Affairs' objection to the published manuscript "in view of the many adverse criticisms which the treatment of Negroes in the recently published Mississippi Guide will undoubtedly evoke."[104] As proof that their "criticisms and suggestions were almost totally disregarded," the memo cited the Guide's assertions that "it is a . . . State where *everyone* who may vote votes the Democratic ticket," which ignored the large Republican constituency among the state's African American population; the manuscript's condemnation of "the Negro in Reconstruction"; and the claim that the number of black sharecroppers was decreasing while the number of white tenants was increasing, making "the problems of agricultural Mississippi . . . fundamentally economic, without respect to race."[105]

Even more revealing of the racial bias of the Mississippi Guide were the memo's criticisms regarding the section on "Negro Folkways." As Brown's office observed: "For a period of almost two years we have objected to the unsympathetic attitude and the tone of amused condescension characterizing this treatment. As published it appears essentially as originally written under the title 'The Mississippi Negro, His Temperament, Psychology and Culture.'" This section, the memo asserted, abounded with "faulty generalization[s], facetious remark[s] or subjective observation[s]," in which African Americans were represented as obstinate, imitative of "sophisticated whites," and in regard to their religious practice "weirdly African." In addition, black folktales were listed as fact rather than fiction. Brown's office had attempted to correct these views, noting in particular that "anthropologists might not agree that the services are weirdly African; they might find similarities in nearby white 'protracted' and 'camp meetings.'"[106] Despite these extensive editorial corrections, the Mississippi Guide, according to the Office on Negro Affairs, appeared in its published form virtually identical to the pre-final copy to which Brown's office had so strenuously objected. Largely as a result of the racial climate of the 1930s, the Office on Negro Affairs' attempts to positively affect the FWP's published representations of black identity were often sadly ineffectual.

In editorial comments Brown made regarding material submitted for the Florida guidebook, he tried to correct the textual emphasis on the foreign and exotic in African American culture. As he explained: "The account of the Negro is inadequate in its stress upon the quaint and the picturesque in Negro life to the exclusion of less conventional aspects."[107] Instead, Brown instructed, more attention should be given to the ways in which African Americans were contributing members within the Gainesville community: "Emphasis should be placed upon the Negro as an integral part of the city's pattern of life—*he should be shown in relation, rather than as a thing apart.* The space devoted to 'interesting glimpses of his native life and customs' could well be utilized to tell something of where and how the contemporary Negro lives in the city, what he does for a living, his churches, schools and social life. The inclusion of such material, realistically handled, is urged."[108]

Similarly, the Tampa copy covered the black population with a "single sentence describing their queer speech."[109] Brown's comments on the Florida Guide's treatment of African Americans show that he was repeatedly trying to correct stereotypical representations of black culture and identity that were based on older minstrel-tradition models, which concentrated on images of black primitivism in speech and customs and ignored any treatment of African Americans as an integral part of the urban citizenry.

Brown also attempted to maintain in FWP copy a careful distinction between the identity of ex-slaves and more contemporary black Americans. White state and federal directors alike tended to group all representations of black identity together, thereby collapsing diverse black identities into one static group. Brown, on the other hand, obviously (and understandably) wished to distinguish between the ex-slaves' identity as relics of a historical past of slavery and the forward-looking modern black identity of the Reconstruction era. But this distinction between different generations of black Americans, between those who had experienced slavery and those whom one former slave referred to as "late day folks," would be increasingly blurred by white employees at both the state and federal levels working on the Ex-Slave Project.

In the copy resubmitted for the city of Lakeland, Florida, for which Brown had provided editorial comments on a previous draft, he found little evidence of any acknowledgment of his earlier remarks: "The Negro population is not amply described. There is almost no change—only the deletion 'minstrel-minded'—in the original copy. 'Such significant . . . names as Careless Avenue, Jonk Street and Voodoo Corner . . .' is unhappily expressed. Surely this does not apply to all Negroes living in this section. What this group does for a living should be mentioned."[110] In place of these racist stereotypes of black exoticism and backwardness, Brown was trying to incorporate images of African Americans' suitability for the rights and responsibilities of full citizenship. Repeatedly, Brown called for an examination in these city guides of the African American's economic contributions in industry, business, and city life.[111]

Brown remained particularly interested in obtaining information on black entrepreneurs and landowners: "One would like to know . . . the extent of [the Negro's] participation in industry—whether or not Negroes own any citrus fruit lands worthy of mention, etc."[112] Brown's focus on the economic and educational progress of African Americans reflects the black bourgeoisie ideology of "racial uplift," which developed partly in response to the failures of Reconstruction. Coverage emphasizing black-owned businesses and the black middle class over plain laborers was very much in keeping with this ideology, which strove to illustrate upward mobility. One of the central ways in which members of the African American middle class challenged racist assumptions about the nature of black character and identity was through the creation of their own representations of black morality, intellect, and financial savvy. Central to this ideology was an assimilationist ethic; by providing a portrait of black Americans' culture and identity as congruent with the image of the ideal American citizen as hardworking, devout, educated, and economically successful, members of the black elite hoped to provide what Sterling Brown would call "A Portrait of the Negro *as* American."[113] "Racial uplift" was motivated by the instability of black elites' class identity. Middle- and upper-class African Americans' economic position was continually undermined by notions of class status and citizenship inextricably bound up with race. As a result, their racial identity in white circles made them routinely experience the indignities and injustices suffered by all African Americans, regardless of economic position. Thus, "racial uplift" ideology was an attempt by the black bourgeoisie to solidify a class identity based in large part on the recognition of the economic and educational progress of black Americans since Reconstruction. Brown tried hard to promote representations in FWP publications of African Americans' contributions, particularly in education and business. As he proposed to Georgia's state director, Carolyn Dillard: "I should like to recommend some biographical sketches of Negroes who have made their mark in Georgia History, some account of Negro business in Georgia (Atlanta being a focal point of interest insofar as Negro business is concerned) and accounts of the schools and colleges of Georgia."[114]

Brown viewed the FWP's Negro Studies projects as yet another way to promote a more positive image of black American identity, both past and present. In summary of his own pet project, "The Portrait of the Negro as American," Brown referred to the ever-present problem posed to factual accounts of African American history by the "racial bias" exhibited by blacks as well as whites. As Brown explained the predicament:

> The Negro in America has been greatly written about, but most frequently as a separate entity, as a problem, not as a participant. Largely neglected in broad historical considerations, or receiving specialized attention from social scientists, the Negro has too seldom been revealed as an integral part of American life. Many Negro historians have

attempted to counter the neglect, but the result has been overemphasis, and still "separateness." Where white historians find few or no Negroes and too little important participation, Negro historians find too many and too much. This racialistic bias is understandable, but it does not produce the accurate picture of the Negro in American social history at which [my book] aims.[115]

Brown plainly intended to ward off any mistrust that might arise regarding the objectivity of a work on black Americans written by an African American author. As he bluntly stated, this project would "be an essay in social history and biography, not an exercise in race glorification. While I feel that the record of the Negro in America, if accurately presented, will be highly creditable, the propelling force behind the book is not race pride but a wish to see the truth told."[116] Strategically, Brown subtly acknowledged his racial identity to lend authority to his knowledge on the subject matter, and he did it in much the same fashion as white authors in their writings about "the Negro," noting the book would "result from long acquaintance with and study of the subject."[117]

Brown intended this nineteen-chapter work to be a definitive history of African Americans that would include such notable figures as Denmark Vesey, Harriet Tubman, and Frederick Douglass alongside Joe Louis, Father Divine, Bill "Bojangles" Robinson, and the "Scottsboro boys."[118] Brown envisioned it "providing a cross-section of Negro life from the earliest days to the present"[119] and producing an "accurate picture of the Negro in American social history."[120] The unknown multitudes of black Americans—the "sharecroppers, factory workers, students, business men"—would be recognized for their contributions to the nation and as equal members of the Republic. However, Brown left the project closest to his heart—the manuscript that would have been the Office on Negro Affairs' magnum opus—unfinished.[121]

Instead, Brown in 1941, with the help of his former colleague Ulysses Lee from the FWP and Arthur Davis of Virginia Union University, would publish *The Negro Caravan* with Dryden Press without the imprimatur of the federal government. *The Negro Caravan* was meant to fulfill the promise of black cultural authority that "The Portrait of the Negro as American," consigned unfinished to the archives of the Library of Congress, never achieved, providing a record of the richness and complexity of African American life created by African Americans themselves. The case that Brown had originally made for recognizing African Americans "as an integral part of American life" would reappear in the editors' introduction to *The Negro Caravan*, which reads as a manifesto for black self-determination in cultural representation.[122] The "inside view" that only African Americans could provide was "more likely to make possible the essential truth than 'the outside.'"[123]

By deciding to use a literary anthology as the vehicle for conveying African American history, Brown and his fellow editors, Davis and Lee, were staking a radical claim in the field of historical knowledge: that black cultural expressiveness, in all of its varied forms, as poems, novels, slave narratives, autobiographies, speeches, letters, nonfiction essays, songs, folktales, and short stories, could serve as a historical record of the black experience, as well as creating a collective memory, strengthening the black community while directly countering and refuting historical narratives that excluded African Americans through either elision or misrepresentation. Including literary works alongside the black oral tradition without privileging either, *The Negro Caravan* collapsed traditional distinctions between professional historians and common folk, implicitly recognizing that oral traditions had kept black history alive despite all attempts to eviscerate and expunge it.[124] Black folk may not have been professional historians, but they were "nonetheless a watchful people, a people who could not not know; a people of long memory."[125] Yet aside from a brief excerpt from the ex-slave narratives gathered by the Negro unit of Virginia, this 1,082-page compendium contained none of the rich material on black history, culture, and identity gathered through the work of the FWP. The question remains: What happened to Brown and the promise of black cultural authority within the Federal Writers' Project?

From the beginning, the FWP's project to document American culture was animated by an uneasy tension between two desires. Like the other arts projects of Federal One, the FWP intended to improve national morale and edify American citizens through the dissemination of culture; it aimed to produce manuscripts that aspired to the standards of academic scholarship by being historically accurate as well as ideologically instructive about American national identity. The second goal of the FWP was to produce books that would appeal to a wide audience and attract commercial publishers. To achieve these different aims, the American Guide Series strategically adopted the methods associated with one of the most successful genres, the travel narrative, and its literary relatives the academic ethnography and the increasingly popular realist-adventure novel. This would have significant ramifications for the Ex-Slave Project as these models and conventions emphasized the exoticism of "racial" others and simultaneously privileged the view of the outsider to the community being documented. The complex story of the Ex-Slave Project reveals that the conflicts that ensued over how to represent the past of slavery and black identity were not just about federal versus state directors' authority. They also exposed the ways race cut across those lines of authority, challenging African American voices at every level, thus giving rise to black employees' and ex-slave informants' resourceful strategies for turning oral tradition into written history.

CHAPTER THREE

Out of the Mouths of Slaves

The Ex-Slave Project and the "Negro Question"

I don't know how old I was when I saw [Disney's *Song of the South*] ... but I
experienced it as vastly alienating, not only from the likes of Uncle Remus—in
whom I saw aspects of my father, my mother, in fact all black people I knew who
told these stories—but also from the stories themselves; which, passed into the
context of white people's creation, the same white people who, in my real
everyday life, would not let a black person eat in a restaurant or through their
front door, I perceived as meaningless. So there I was, at an early age, separated
from my own folk culture by an invention.

—Alice Walker, "Uncle Remus, No Friend of Mine," 1981

The ex-slave narratives from the Florida Project in 1936 inspired the federal
office to initiate similar projects in other states.[1] In April 1937, associate
director George Cronyn sent a letter to thirteen state directors introducing
the idea for a national Ex-Slave Project: "We have received from Florida a
remarkably interesting collection of autobiographical stories by ex-slaves.
Such documentary records by the survivors of a historic period in America
are invaluable, both to the student of history and to creative writers."[2] There
were a number of earlier projects to collect ex-slave testimony undertaken by
African American scholars. At Fisk University, in the late 1920s, professor of
anthropology Paul Radin supervised graduate student Andrew Watson's
interviews with a hundred former slaves. At Southern University in Louisiana,
in 1929, students of Professor John B. Cade collected eighty-two oral histories
that Cade then drew from as the basis for an article in the *Journal of Negro
History* in 1935.[3]

But it is likely that sociologist Charles S. Johnson had the largest hand in
getting the New Deal administration to undertake the project of interviewing
former slaves. Johnson had studied with Robert Park at the University of
Chicago, where he earned his doctorate. In 1928, Johnson established Fisk's
Social Science Institute; a year later, he encouraged staff researcher Ophelia
Settle Egypt to interview ex-slaves in Kentucky as well as Tennessee. One-
third of these interviews (out of one hundred) were published as the *Unwritten History of Slavery: Autobiographical Account of Negro Ex-Slaves.*[4] In 1934,

Lawrence D. Reddick, who had assisted Settle Egypt with the interviews undertaken at Fisk and was now teaching at Kentucky State College, submitted a proposal to the director of the newly established Federal Emergency Relief Administration (FERA), Harry Hopkins, to collect the testimony of ex-slaves.[5] Under the auspices of FERA, Reddick supervised twelve African American college graduates who conducted 250 interviews in Indiana and Kentucky from 1934 to 1935.[6] Johnson himself would submit a proposal for another federally funded black oral history project, this time under the auspices of the newly created Federal Writers' Project (FWP). This undated document entitled "A Proposal for a Regional (or National) Project under the Federal Writers Project (Utilizing Negro Personnel)" has never been discussed in histories of ex-slave interview projects, nor is it mentioned in the FWP administrative records. In it, Johnson laid out a detailed rationale and plan for a systematic study of racial mores (segregation customs and practices) in the South and across the country, as a means of examining the sociological problem of race. In addition to documenting racial discrimination (what Johnson euphemistically referred to as mores and "racial folkways"), this study would include life "stories of [notable] Negro individuals," both historic figures and contemporary ones, occupational data, and "Negro folkways." Under this last category, which Johnson suggested could be carried out as part of the ex-slave interview project already under way, he included folktales, folk music traditions, ceremonies and rituals, and secular folkways such as "numbers playing, rent parties, frolics, etc."[7] Johnson would serve as a consultant for the FWP's Negro Studies projects.[8]

As the federal directors of the FWP jumped into a national project to collect reminiscences of former slaves, they immediately began to consider how the oral histories might be shaped into publishable material. While submissions of ex-slave narratives poured into the federal office in Washington, D.C., suggestions began to circulate. Although ex-slave narratives had been collected previously for inclusion in the various state guides, after the receipt of the Florida narratives the federal office saw the potential for separate publications based entirely on Ex-Slave Project material.[9] In June 1937, Alan and Elizabeth Lomax were charged with the task of generating a tentative list of books that might be based on the narratives. Their proposals, which fell under three general formats—historical, sociological, and autobiographical—show how the often conflicting approaches to the ex-slave narratives shaped federal guidelines for their collection, content, and form.

Heading the list was a suggestion from Alan's father, John Lomax, that "we put the stories into the mouths of a group of ex-slaves who have gathered from all over the South for a convention,"[10] enabling readers to feel as if they were eavesdropping on an actual event. As the Lomaxes pointed out, this experimental literary device was actually inspired by a real phenomenon as ex-slave associations did hold formal gatherings throughout the South. Human interest would be generated by sociological depictions of ex-slaves in the present. Alan and Elizabeth Lomax did express a reservation, however, that this format "might easily be trite and sentimental."[11]

Another recommendation suggested the narratives might provide the basis for "a serious and careful study of the institution of slavery," but such a project, the Lomaxes noted, would need to balance the slaves' perspective with that of whites: "Against the slaves' testimony could be weighed the testimony of the planters and the abolitionists and others, all of which has been made available in books written about slavery and the Civil War both in the North and the South."[12] However, even this approach would be informed by an ethnographic treatment of the slave experience. The Lomaxes recommended the anthropologist Melville Herskovits's *Life in a Haitian Valley* (1937) "as a working model for this book."[13] The majority of the chapters would be structured around "the life of the slave phase by phase—in chapter headings such as 'Children, Runaways, Patterollers, Work, Living Conditions, Punishment, Birth, Marriage and Death.'"[14] These proposals all emphasized the narratives' "interest as evidence." A compilation of "the hundred best stories from the entire group" along with pictures might be "supplemented by several recording trips in which the entire testimonies of a few slaves should be recorded and transcribed entire."[15]

Evolving visions for the project informed and shaped federal guidelines for how the narratives would be gathered, what types of questions would be asked, and what kinds of information the FWP field workers should try to obtain. Contradictory impulses behind the Project's aims and objectives greatly affected the ways the ex-slaves' oral histories were produced at the state and federal levels. Begun partly as an anthropological salvage project to record and document black history and culture before parts of it disappeared, the FWP's Ex-Slave Project would come to present its ex-slave informants as the object of study themselves. The ethnographic perspective on the ex-slaves' narratives increasingly adopted by the federal and state directors significantly affected the representations of African American culture and identity. Federal directors, such as Henry Alsberg, George Cronyn, John Lomax, and Sterling Brown, helped shape the content as well as the form of the narratives. Conventions they borrowed from ethnography and popular travel writing shifted the emphasis from a project to collect the oral histories of former slaves to one that debated African Americans' racial identity and suitability for full citizenship.

Through a close examination of federal and state directors' administrative correspondence, and the instructions and guidelines federal directors issued to state directors and ex-slave interviewers, this chapter explores the editorial conflicts that ensued over the meaning and significance of African cultural survivals, "Negro folklore," and how to transcribe "Negro dialect." Ironically, guidelines intended to circumscribe a type of literary minstrelsy became a gold standard for determining the authenticity of narratives based on white readers' expectations and reinforced notions of racial difference. Public discourse and scholarly controversy over the legacy of slavery, the significance of African survivals, and the "Negro Problem" informed FWP discussions over how best to collect, interpret, and present ex-slave narratives. Debates arose in part over the application of social scientific methods to interpret African American identity. The Project marked a critical moment when state power, in the form of the bureaucratic and administrative systems of the New Deal, adopted the method of ethnography, the dominant scholarly approach to the subject of racial character and culture. The involvement of numerous contributors to the Project at the local and state level, however, also led to the narratives becoming a site for competing visions of black identity, past and present.[16] The stakes were enormous. Could black Americans ever be full citizens within the American nation? Were they equal? Could they assimilate into the national culture? Ex-slaves became the case study—a metonym—for discussing the possibilities or problems of full integration into the national body. For many FWP employees, varying interpretations of the institution of slavery and African American culture and identity also served as a means of confronting whether emancipation had been a success or a failure.

The Importance of Federal Guidelines

Although each state involved with the FWP had its own director, district supervisors, and staff of local writers, the importance of the federal office's directives cannot be overlooked. Until 1939, when the FWP would be reorganized as the Writers' Project with greater autonomy and involvement at the state level, the visions of federal directors such as George Cronyn, Alsberg, Lomax, Brown, and later Benjamin Botkin did much to shape the outcomes of the various projects. To counteract the difficulties posed by employees who had widely varying writing experience and abilities (discussed in chapter 1), federal directors of FWP projects encouraged state project directors to familiarize themselves and their staffs with the various manuals produced by the federal office. Such handbooks provided workers with an overview of the project, its aims and goals, and instructions on methods and procedures. One of the regional directors for the FWP, William Couch, responded to Virginia state director Eudora Ramsay Richardson's complaints about the incompetency of her staff by reiterating the importance of the instruction booklets in training project workers: "I find that where State directors do not pass our Life History Manual on as it is to members of their staff, they have a great deal of trouble and do not get good copy. . . . If you do not push them into reading and understanding the Manual . . . they won't write, or, if they do, the stuff they turn out won't be any good."[17]

When Mississippi's state director Eri Douglass became interested in having her staff collect ex-slave stories, her first step was to request fifty copies (one for each FWP employee) of the Bulletin and Supplementary Instructions #9-E for the Ex-Slave Project.[18] She also assured Cronyn that Lomax's memo on the ex-slave narratives had been given to the supervisor of assignments, "who in turn has passed on the suggestions to the workers in the field."[19] Arkansas's state director similarly emphasized her staff's compliance with federal guidelines: "These stories are being written according to instructions 9E [and] supplementary notes."[20] State directors relied on constant feedback from the federal office and expected acknowledgment for every submission of ex-slave material. Thus, federal directors were kept busy reading and responding to every batch of ex-slave narratives.[21]

In the three months following the decision to collect ex-slave narratives nationwide, the federal office began to issue further directives. Interviewers were told to record any facts or incidents recalled by the ex-slave; these "should be set down as nearly as possible just as he says them."[22] A supervisor of the Ex-Slave Project in Mississippi dispatched collected narratives to her state director with this comment: "Field workers report that these old Negroes often ramble extensively. Instructions from the Washington office infer that this is permissible if it means more information. Field workers report that they are sending in their slave stories in practically the same order as given by the Negroes. I have made no revision of form as I did not want to risk a stilted, formal, or unnatural narrative. Too, am I not correct in my supposition that Washington wants them this way?"[23] Although state directors were initially encouraged to send the narratives directly to Washington with a minimum of editing and interference at the state level, as they received additional federal guidelines they generated a greater number of drafts before forwarding final copy to D.C. for appraisal. Federal directors began to encourage this, with their criticisms of raw interview copy and suggestions to omit interviewers' questions, comments, and notes.

Florida's Project exemplifies the operation of federal guidelines at the state level, as described by Stetson Kennedy, Florida's director of folklore, life history, and social ethnic studies. As with all other aspects of the FWP, the process was systematized at the federal level and implemented by all state projects using the FWP manuscript flow chart. After the interview, the field worker's notes went through three stages: from preliminary (labeled "FC" for "Field Copy," which referred to a typescript written by a field worker "and as yet untouched by an editor's pencil"), to intermediate (marked "FEC" for "Field Edited Copy," meaning an editor in a district office, Tampa or Miami, had "touched it up and had it retyped"), to final drafts edited in the state office in Jacksonville (labeled "SEC" for "State Editorial Copy"), intended for publication and ready to send on to the federal office.[24] For the ex-slave narratives, editing at the state level followed the project guidelines laid out in the instruction manuals, often eliminating anything that might suggest that the informant had been prompted by specific questions, before forwarding them to D.C.[25]

Lomax and Alsberg periodically sent written acknowledgments for every few stories they received from state directors. These letters were brief but always contained either praise or critique and some suggestions for the field workers.[26] Often they requested more information on a particular narrative. Typical was Alsberg's letter to Georgia's acting state director Samuel Tupper Jr.: "In the interview with William Ward, marked Ex Slave #111, sent in by Ross from District 5, there is a reference in paragraph 5 to a bed known as 'Grand Rascal.' Would it be possible to get some description of the peculiar construction which caused it to be given this name?"[27] Questions such as this had the added advantage of compelling field workers to do a second interview "so as to gather all the worth while recollections that the first talk has aroused."[28] And federal directors were careful to specify the importance of a second interview conducted by the same field worker: "The editor feels that the interview with Rastus Jones . . . is very sketchy. Could he be interviewed a second time with special attention to his memories as cook in Grant's army? He would probably not be any more expansive than the first time if a stranger is sent to interview him but possibly someone could accompany Miss Minor and help suggest questions."[29] State directors promptly responded to inquiries of this nature, providing supplementary interviews with former slaves who were of particular interest to federal directors. Alan and Elizabeth Lomax also emphasized the importance of making more than one visit to ex-slave informants. The repetitive nature of much of the material, they argued, could be solved by FWP field workers' closer adherence to the customary procedures of the ethnographer, namely, by making an effort to befriend the informant to overcome any natural inhibitions: "We realize that it is difficult to get the information you want out of a person seventy or eighty years old, but we still believe that it must be possible for the worker to make friends with at least one informant and revisit him repeatedly."[30]

Questions provided for the field worker initially encouraged the ex-slave to recall the details of day-to-day life on the plantation—what work was done, what the slaves ate, what type of clothes they wore—as well as what the plantation was like—the number of acres and slaves, along with information about the slaveholder and his family. Questions also addressed the various aspects of the slaves' experience regarding punishment, religious services, whether they were taught to read and write, and stories about runaway slaves. But these questions also took a more anthropological turn as interviewers were requested to ask about the culture of the slaves: What took place in the slave quarters, what did slaves do during their leisure time and on holidays, and what happened on special occasions, such as weddings and funerals? John Lomax's proposition that the ex-slave interviews could provide information on Negro folklore was implemented, and questions about children's games, ghost stories, songs, and magical charms and potions were included in the questionnaire.[31]

In a proposed list of additional questions to be added to those already asked of ex-slaves by FWP workers, Alan and Elizabeth Lomax advocated a greater emphasis on the informants' lives after slavery: "What have the ex-slaves been doing in the interim between 1864 and 1937? Have they been hungry? What jobs have they held (in detail) and at what pay? How are they supported nowadays? What is their present monthly or weekly income? What do the ex-slaves think of the younger generation and of 1937? If they don't like the way the world looks, what do they think is wrong?"[32] Stating that the moral of the book should be "not that slavery, but exploitation, is a nasty thing," the Lomaxes explained how they saw the project: "Here, for the first time in the history of literature, so far as I know, a group of poor and despised people are being given a chance to speak their piece, give their side of the picture. . . . The evidence should not stop, therefore, with the war, but with 1937. It is just as important to know how ex-slaves live, as how slaves lived. Rather more is known about slaves than ex-slaves."[33] The Lomaxes were clearly interested in expanding the project's focus to encompass the continued exploitation of ex-slaves; however, in doing so, they were helping to make the ex-slaves, rather than the institution of slavery, the object of study and opening the door for employees who were advocates for the "Lost Cause" version of southern history to make invidious comparisons between the hardship many were experiencing as a result of the Great Depression and the benign paternalism of slavery.

In July 1937, Alsberg sent a memorandum to all state directors with general suggestions for interview methods. Some of these were plainly inspired by Alan and Elizabeth Lomax's proposal for publications using the ex-slave narratives. Field workers were told to "concentrate on one or two of the more interesting and intelligent people, revisiting them, establishing friendly relations, and drawing them out over a period of time."[34] To put informants at ease so they would speak freely and at length, the memo reminded interviewers to "weave the following questions naturally into the conversation, in simple language."[35] Once this had been achieved, "the talk should run to all subjects, and the interviewer should take care to seize upon the information already given, and stories already told, and from them derive other questions."[36]

To avoid subjective bias, the interviewer was instructed to "take the greatest care not to influence the point of view of the informant, and not to let his own opinion on the subject of slavery become obvious. Should the ex-slave, however, give only one side of the picture, the interviewer should suggest that there were other circumstances, and ask questions about them."[37] And just as the Lomaxes had suggested, the instructions placed greater emphasis "on questions concerning the lives of the individuals since they were freed,"[38] including the solicitation of ex-slaves' opinions on "the younger generation of Negroes and . . . present conditions."[39] Alsberg also counseled all state directors to "choose one or two or more of their most successful ex-slave interviewers and have them take down some stories word for word. Some Negro informants are marvelous in their ability to participate in this type of interview. All stories should be as nearly word-for-word as is possible."[40]

State directors took such orders from the federal offices seriously. In a report submitted with a sampling of ex-slave narratives, Ohio's state director directly referred to Alsberg's July memo. The report began with assurances that the narratives were transcribed "word-for-word taken in two interviews, which interviews were long, and had to be in the nature of casual conversations, for these old negroes were only startled by questions, and acted as though they were being cross-examined in court."[41] In addition, Ohio's director took care to explain why the interviews did not include responses to questions regarding freedom and the ex-slaves' lives after freedom: "None of these negroes were old enough at the close of the Civil War to recall just what the negroes generally expected of freedom. They did not even recall their first wages earned after freedom. This may be due to the fact that they have been living so differently here in Ohio for the past forty years."[42] Arkansas's state director also responded positively to Alsberg's memo on method and procedure: "It was a happy thought getting these better stories of ex-slaves. We are getting some of the best material I have ever read."[43]

African "Survivals" and the Culture of Slavery

The folk culture of African Americans and its origins became an object of social scientific inquiry in the 1920s, and questions and debates about cultural "survivals" from Africa informed and shaped the Ex-Slave Project. Until then, theories about African influence on black culture and identity were not subject to much academic scrutiny. Advances in social scientific theory about intercultural contact, however, now made hypotheses about the retention of cultural elements possible. At stake in these theories surrounding black culture was the issue of cultural ownership but also questions regarding black assimilation. A central question was whether black culture was creative and original or merely derivative.[44] Suggestions that it was imitative, rather than original, played on embedded racial stereotypes of black Americans as a race that could ape and mimic but never attain the artistic pinnacles of a white European civilization.[45] The theory that African Americans had retained significant elements of their culture from an African past was widely cited by racial integrationists and segregationists alike. The idea of African cultural survivals was invoked by some white scholars to demonstrate the continuing primitivism of black Americans and their unsuitability for full citizenship. Other scholars, black and white, emphasized the artistic value, strength, and independence of African American culture to promote racial equality.

Central to much of this discussion regarding African survivals were interpretations of slavery's effect on black culture. Because slavery had significantly affected the lives of black people, uprooting initial generations from their homelands, their families, and their communities, the question of whether African cultural elements could have survived the brutalizing system of slavery was crucial to assessing cultural origins. For subsequent generations, the passage of time, new environments, and the institution of slavery all played a role in the formation of black culture and communities. Unfortunately, slavery would come to dominate the dialogue over African survivals, to the exclusion of other important elements in the development of black folk traditions. At the heart of this debate lay the question of whether slavery had eradicated for the African American "all vestiges of a cultural identity, leaving him, tabula rasa, to create or imitate, or both."[46]

One of the most influential histories of slavery written in the early twentieth century, Ulrich B. Phillips's *American Negro Slavery*, published in 1918, was the culmination of the many articles on the subject Phillips had written beginning in 1903. Drawing primarily on plantation records, *American Negro Slavery* painted a sympathetic portrait of the institution, arguing that the racial inferiority of African Americans necessitated a system of paternalism. Because African languages and customs were lost as a result of the sea change, what remained were "the Negro's" racial characteristics, which were as immutable as the pigment of his skin, resulting in future generations who were as unfit for the responsibilities of American citizenship as their ancestors: "Fresh Africans were manifestly not to be incorporated in the body politic; and Negroes to the third and fourth generations were still in the main as distinctive in experience, habit, outlook, social discipline and civilian capacity as in the color of their skins or the contour of their faces."[47]

Phillips's interpretation would influence much of the scholarship on slavery and the Negro character for the next decade.[48] And he was not alone in his assumption that any remnants of African culture had been left behind or destroyed. Prominent sociologist Robert Park, from the University of Chicago, also claimed that "the Negro, when he landed in the United States, left behind him almost everything but his dark complexion and his tropical temperament."[49] The black sociologist E. Franklin Frazier would adopt a similar position on the effects of slavery. In *The Negro Family in the United States* (1939), Frazier asserted, "Probably never before in history has a people been so completely stripped of its social heritage as the Negroes who were brought to America."[50]

One of the first major challenges to Phillips's interpretation of the effects of slavery on black culture would come from Herskovits, whose *Life in a Haitian Valley* (1937) had been recommended by Alan and Elizabeth Lomax as a model for an FWP publication of slave narratives. Herskovits, a student of Franz Boas, had originally supported the idea of complete acculturation as a way of disproving racist arguments about black Americans' inherent inferiority and unfitness for citizenship. In essays published in Alain Locke's Harlem Renaissance anthology *The New Negro* and *Survey Graphic* magazine, Herskovits argued that black Americans had not retained any African cultural elements; complete acculturation had occurred, with the result that African

American communities, such as Harlem, were exactly like white American communities: "The same pattern, only a different shade!" he exclaimed.[51] By the 1930s, however, Herskovits had altered his thinking. *Life in a Haitian Valley* argued, in direct opposition to Ulrich B. Phillips's controversial study, that slaves actively resisted their subjugation through a variety of means, from violent rebellion to the conscious retention of African traditions. His controversial study, *The Myth of the Negro Past* (1941), unequivocally asserted that much of African American culture could be traced back to African traditions; survivals demonstrated the creative and artistic capabilities of black Americans and their contribution to American culture. Herskovits's thesis was rejected by racial progressives and scholars who worried that the less enlightened would argue that these immutable cultural patterns were incompatible with the values of a white majority. The theory of African survivals, Locke pointed out, might "lead to the very opposite of Dr. Herskovits' liberal conclusions, and damn the Negro as more basically peculiar and unassimilable than he actually is or has proved himself to be."[52] In a review of *The Myth of the Negro Past*, the well-known white sociologist Guy Johnson worried that Herskovits's thesis might become "the handmaiden of those who are looking for new justifications for the segregation and differential treatment of Negroes!"[53]

Herskovits and Johnson both served as advisors to the FWP's sole publication focusing on African cultural retentions. *Drums and Shadows: Survival Studies among the Georgia Coastal Negroes* (1940) drew on African parallels to represent black culture as primitive, exotic, and unassimilable. In his foreword to the book, Johnson addressed the debate over "the nature and importance of African heritage in America." Describing the two different schools of thought on the matter, Johnson referred to Robert Park to exemplify scholars who "deny the existence of any significant Africanisms in the U.S." and, on the other side of the spectrum, to Herskovits, "who believes that African heritages are very significant, that they have contributed much to the culture of white America." Johnson placed himself in the middle, as one who acknowledged some African survivals but felt they were largely marginalized and displaced by white culture. As a result, "their influence on the everyday problem of race relations," he concluded, "is relatively inconsequential."[54]

Federal directors' interest in African survivals led to a broadening of the FWP's definition of African American folklore to include the study of folk customs: folk beliefs and traditions such as medicinal cures, superstitions, religious practices, and customs pertaining to the stages of life—birth, childhood and adolescence, marriage, and death. Material relating to these categories was to be included along with the submission of folktales and songs. The Ex-Slave Project would help establish a vital and extensive collection of African American folklore and folk customs for future scholars but also led to representations of black identity and culture that presumed to interpret African American character. Alsberg, for example, expressed interest in this connection. Commenting favorably on some humorous "Negro" stories, he noted their capacity to "illustrat[e] vividly characteristic social attitudes" and requested more of this type.[55]

Some state directors clearly associated the Project's objectives of collecting and gathering information from ex-slaves with the national "Negro Question" or "problem." As Arkansas state director Bernie Babcock confided to Alsberg, "I have given the Negro question a great deal of study the past year and have collected valuable material. But what we are getting now from ex-slaves is extremely valuable."[56] Babcock was also the author of *Mammy*, a play published in 1915, which had won accolades from the president general of the United Daughters of the Confederacy and a member of the United Confederate Veterans for its "graphic picture of the old days of the Old South, true to life (as thousands can testify) . . . bring[ing] back recollections of our own Mammy to each of us who has been so fortunate as to have known one of these faithful and affectionate beings."[57] Brown's Office on Negro Affairs was dismayed to learn that Babock's office was planning a book on "The Negro in Arkansas" "to be written entirely by white writers" and containing "such things as 'loyalty of Negro to masters' interests.'"[58] Some southern directors clearly viewed the Ex-Slave Project in part as an opportunity to memorialize the faithful slave of yore as a counterpoint to the "Negro problem" created by a younger generation intent on challenging the racial hierarchy.

The earliest efforts to collect examples of black folklore had been accomplished under the auspices of the American Guide Series. Brown, as the national editor of Negro Affairs, had entertained the somewhat idealistic hope that the FWP's project to record and document southern black folk culture might improve race relations by laying to rest persistent racial stereotypes. With this goal in mind, he cautioned field workers against accepting without question the opinions of white southerners on African American folklore: "half truth is not enough, however picturesque," he cautioned.[59] In 1936, Brown encouraged state directors engaged in collecting this material to classify it under the headings used by professional folklorists: "What is on hand might be sorted into folk-signs, folk-cures, folk-tales, and folk-songs: children's songs, ballads, blues, dance-songs, convict songs, work-songs and spirituals."[60] He suggested that "where a class seems scanty, more examples might

MRS. BERNIE BABCOCK

Author of the allegorical pageant-drama, "Immortality;" the three-thousand-year-ago drama, "The Bride of King Solomon;" the gorgeous drama, "Pilate's Wife," featuring Claudia Procula, wife of Pontius Pilate; "It Might Be Worse," an optimistic comedy; "Maxa Vodininsky," a drama involving a morality question, and that unique drama in American literature, "MAMMY."

" 'Mammy' stands unique and alone as the greatest drama of the Southland. It is a graphic picture of the last days of the Old South, true to life (as thousands can testify), and brings back recollections of our own Mammy to each of us who has been so fortunate as to have known one of these faithful and affectionate beings. 'Mammy' grips one's very heart-strings and holds them to the end."—*Josie Frazee Cappleman, Poet Laureate Trans-Mississippi Dept., U. C. V.; Poet Laureate Grand Chapter, O. E. S.; Historian Churchill Chapter, U. D. C.; Author of "Heart Songs," etc.*

"I do love your 'Mammy.' She is so human, true and noble—is just the real Mammy."—*Mrs. Cordelia Powell Odenheimer, President General U. D. C.*

"There are humor, tragedy, pathos and the soul of a great humanity in this book."—*Arkansas Democrat.*

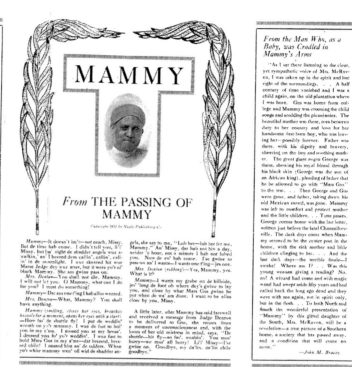

Publicity flier for premier of Bernie Babcock's play *Mammy*, 1917. Redpath Chautauqua Bureau Collection, University of Iowa Libraries, Iowa City, Iowa.

be collected," to ensure that workers gathered materials that reflected the whole range of Negro folklore rather than just those most familiar to white employees.[61] He also suggested another line of inquiry into the area of religion: "I believe it would be interesting also to gather some of the old-fashioned sermons. A propos, I believe a good story of the Heaven Bound Pageant would be a fine assignment."[62]

Some editorial comments Brown made on Georgia's early folklore submissions reveal the ways he was trying to guide FWP representations of black identity. Although Brown began his criticism by complimenting the material as "authentic, sympathetic and sincere," he was clearly worried that workers were extending their analysis to include larger assertions about black culture as a whole.[63] Brown tried to steer workers away from making bald assumptions about black character. As he pointed out, the textual commentary on "the Negro's innate politeness [and] kindly nature" were "dubious generalizations."[64] He specifically objected to the sociological emphasis in the Georgia material on "the picture of social life" to the neglect of "more genuine folklore."[65] Brown also had to tell the Georgia staff to capitalize "Negro."[66] For the origins of African American folklore, Brown wanted the text to emphasize that "Negro superstitions are a composite" rather than purely primitive survivals from Africa: "Many of these beliefs from jungle, many from Scotia's crags, England's moors, and Ireland's bogs."[67] Although Georgia's list of black superstitions "shows many of European as well as African origin," Brown pointed out that the European derivatives were not labeled as such and recommended that they be mentioned.[68] Clearly, Brown wanted black folk superstitions to be viewed not as primitive remnants of an African past but rather as a hybrid creation of European and African civilizations.

By April 1937, John Lomax, as the national advisor on folklore and folkways, would become intrigued by the possibilities presented by the Ex-Slave Project for gathering material related to African American folk customs. Although the questionnaires made up by the federal office and sent to the state directors included extensive questions that concentrated on eliciting historical information about the institution of slavery, the Project under Lomax's direction would gradually begin to place the greatest emphasis on the collection of African American folk customs, folktales, and songs. The questions Lomax provided enabled interviewers to amass an astonishing and substantive array of firsthand information about topics such as folk cures, foodways, marriage practices, clothing, and celebrations, along with personal stories of the experience of slaves, how they learned about freedom, and life after emancipation. This material has enabled scholars to get a more multidimensional picture of slave life and culture. But Lomax would become critical of narratives that concentrated primarily on providing a history of slavery from the ex-slave's point of view. In his commentary on Georgia's early submissions, he impatiently urged the staff to spend more time gathering material of human interest: "While of course we wish the reflections of these old people on the historic details of their experience with slavery, it is their human contacts that will be of far greater interest; the stories current at that time, the gossip of their associates, the small incidents of farm and home life, etc."[69]

Lomax was more interested in concentrating on black folk culture than Brown was, particularly information relating to folk superstition. When he received the Virginia office's essay on the state's folklore for his editorial review, he complained that too much attention had been given to white folklore and songs of English origin. Suggesting that more space be devoted "to the folk beliefs of the Negro," he directed attention to the potential material that might be gathered on voodoo practices: "I question the statement that no belief in voodooism exists among the Virginia Negroes."[70] Having looked over the ex-slave narratives that had been submitted so far from five different states, Lomax was most impressed with those from Tennessee. As Lomax observed in a memo to associate director George Cronyn, "Tennessee is the only [state] in which the workers are asking ex-slaves about their belief in signs, cures, hoodoo, etc. Also, the workers are requesting the ex-slaves to tell the stories that were current among the Negroes when they were growing up." Noting that "some of the best copy that has come to the office is found in these stories," Lomax advised Cronyn to send a special letter on procedure to all the states involved in the Ex-Slave Project recommending them to follow Tennessee's example in routinely asking their informants for material relating to this dimension of Negro folklore.[71] Cronyn immediately sent letters to fourteen state offices in which he quoted Lomax's suggestion directly and added his approval.[72]

Many state directors happily complied with this directive; black folklore of this type was familiar and recognizable to a large white American audience thanks to its popular treatment by writers like Joel Chandler Harris and Mark Twain. Alabama's state director Myrtle Miles immediately responded to this request and assured Lomax that her staff would question ex-slaves about their folk beliefs. Included in the ex-slave stories along with her letter were three titles that indicated that her staff were already pursuing this type of material: " 'The Dead Squinch-Owl's Eye-Sight,' 'A Horn for a Headache,' and 'Alabama Br'er Rabbit Attends a Log Roll.' " The last was also singled out for special mention in her letter to Lomax: "We also have . . . a Br'er Rabbit story . . . told by an ancient Negress last week."[73]

In the weeks following, every batch of ex-slave stories Miles submitted contained some examples of Negro folklore, including some ghost or "hant" stories.[74] The titles also indicate the adoption of Lomax's guidelines for the transcription of "Negro dialect." Stories such as "Ku Klux Rides When De Niggers Starts Trouble," "De Yanks Drapped Outen De Sky," "Us Gwine 'er Wald Dem Gold Streets," "She Seed a Ha'nt," and "Dis Was Dat Long Ago" suggest that the Alabama workers were paying attention to the guidelines and instructions they received from the federal office.[75] Lomax singled out several for special praise and also listed their main attributes: "They show variety, sound authentic, and are treated sympathetically."[76] In keeping with this new emphasis on African American folklore, in the fall of 1937, Alsberg sent a memo to the nineteen states involved in the collection of ex-slave interviews to ask FWP field workers to try to obtain stories that had been passed down from one generation to the next, along with "information about family traditions and legends."[77]

The attention that state directors gave to compiling material relating to black folklore continued to increase. A listing of folklore material submitted by the staff in Arkansas a year later, in July 1938, shows a continuing pattern. The most substantial categories after "Folk songs," which led the group with 353 pages, were topics related to Negro superstition: "Superstitions" had the greatest number of pages with 200; then came "Ghosts" with 123; "Body Marks" (which tended to include superstitions, such as babies born with cauls) followed close behind with 110; and the last grouping to comprise over a hundred pages was "Cures and Magic Remedies" (103).[78] Topics such as "Traditions," "Children's Games," "Expressions," and "Births" each had less than twenty.[79] Certainly the preponderance of these types of materials reflects their vital presence within the slave and ex-slave communities, but they also indicate Lomax's interest in finding folklore and folk customs that would provide color and interest for FWP publications.[80] Following the instructions of the federal office, FWP interviewers included specific questions meant to elicit this type of material, and editors labeled the interviews according to these topical headings.

Associate director Cronyn began to discuss how these stories could be turned into publishable material: "If a volume of such importance can be assembled we will endeavor to secure its publication. . . . While it is desirable to give a running story of the life of each subject, the color and human interest will be greatly enhanced if it is told largely in the words of the person interviewed. The peculiar idiom is often more expressive than a literary account."[81] These phrases, "color," "human interest," and "peculiar idiom," would be invoked every time the issue of publication arose. In this way, representations of the black vernacular would become a central focus of federal and thus state directors who were involved in the process of transcribing the interviews. The FWP's attempts at the federal level to ensure that the slave narrative material would have popular appeal and attract a wide audience strongly affected the ways African American identity was portrayed and led to the widespread adoption of a "Negro dialect" drawn from literary conventions that dated back to the plantation school fiction of the post-Reconstruction era.

"Negro Dialect"

Federal directors' injunction that the slave narratives be written primarily in the words of the person interviewed made the question of how to transcribe the black vernacular of primary importance. Interest in adopting as much as possible an autobiographical style for the narratives placed heavy emphasis on the representation of black folk speech, which would become a key trope of authenticity for the slave narratives approved for publication. Lomax and Brown would both play pivotal roles in establishing the way in which a southern black dialect would be transcribed. Because the attempts to represent a black vernacular were more often a reflection of white interviewers' idiosyncratic (and frequently racist) interpretations, in the interest of uniformity and readability, Brown and Lomax composed guidelines for the transcription of dialect that were sent to all of the state directors in charge of collecting ex-slave narratives.

Pressure to make this material publishable led them to attempt to standardize the ways dialect would be represented by FWP employees. Both Brown and Lomax understood that the black vernacular, like all idiomatic forms of language, was the product of regional variations that often crossed racial lines. "Of course," Lomax wrote, "I understand that there is no norm for Negro dialect. Our efforts will be to preserve as nearly as possible the flavor of this speech and at the same time make it easy for those unacquainted with Negro speech to read the stories."[82] But very often the use of phonetic spelling resulted in stereotypical depictions of African Americans as a provincial folk people, whose racial difference was embodied in their speech. African American author Charles Chesnutt, who often incorporated dialect in his late nineteenth-century fiction, argued that "there is no such thing as a Negro dialect. . . . What we call by that name is the attempt to express, with such a degree of phonetic correctness as to suggest the sound, English pronounced as an ignorant old southern Negro would be supposed to speak it."[83] Dialect writing relies on phonetic spellings and apostrophes to make visible to the eye sounds that cannot be heard in the medium of print. This "eye dialect," as Toni Morrison has observed about representations of the black vernacular, renders the speech of black characters "as an alien, estranging dialect made deliberately unintelligible by spellings contrived to disfamiliarize it. . . . It is used to establish a cognitive world split between speech and text, to reinforce class distinctions and otherness as well as to assert privilege and power."[84] Following their lead, I will be using "black vernacular" to refer to African American oral traditions and "Negro dialect" to refer to Lomax's and other FWP employees' interpretations and literary rendering of black speech patterns.

Although the question of how to transcribe black folk speech had been raised in 1936, early in the FWP's project to collect folklore for the American Guide Series, the initial response of the federal office to this problem suggests that the incorporation of a "Negro dialect" did not originally provoke much interest. When Georgia's state director Carolyn Dillard wrote to Alsberg to suggest that one of her editors, who had "done a great deal of work in the Negro dialect, which she learned from the Negroes themselves and from the personal instruction of Joel Chandler Harris,"[85] might be employed to rewrite FWP copy on black folklore in the "Negro dialect" popularized by the creator of Uncle Remus, Alsberg was quick to scuttle the proposal. "Uncle Remus Negroes do not use the same dialect as do the Negroes of Virginia or Louisiana," he pointed out. "Whenever possible, the interviewer should endeavor to get the stories down in the language of the teller of the stories, being sure to watch for peculiar expressions."[86] Less than seven months later, however, the federal office was ignoring regional variations and directly invoking Joel Chandler Harris's "Negro dialect" in the guidelines and instructions sent to state directors involved with the Ex-Slave Project.

Two weeks after initially suggesting to state directors that the narratives should incorporate, as much as possible, the voice of the ex-slave, Cronyn followed up with a memorandum written by Lomax, "Negro Dialect Suggestions (Stories of Ex-Slaves)," intended to provide some guidance for transcribing "the peculiar idiom" of informants' speech. Significantly, both Cronyn's letter and Lomax's guidelines refer to a race-specific dialect rather than the regional southern dialect prevalent by the 1930s. Emphasizing that all interviews should be written up in "Negro dialect," Cronyn explained the purpose of Lomax's memo as "suggestions for simplifying the spelling of certain recurring dialect words." But, he cautioned, "This does not mean that the interviews should be entirely in 'straight English'—simply, that we want them to be more readable to those uninitiated in the broadest Negro speech."[87] Because Lomax's initial memo was primarily a list of how certain words should not be spelled—the list began with "Do not write"—it was obviously intended to correct the most blatant phonetic misspellings in representations of a black vernacular.

Lomax's cautionary list forbade spellings that exoticized words by writing them phonetically: "Do not write: *Ah* for I, *Hit* for it, *Tuh* for to, *Wuz* for was, *Baid* for bed, *Daid* for dead . . . *Mah* for my, *Ovah* for over . . . *Undah* for under, *Fuh* for for, *Yondah* for yonder . . . *Uz* or *uv* or *o'* for of . . . *Utha* for other . . . *Cot* for caught . . . *Tho't* for thought."[88] For certain words the correction he supplied was merely a different phonetic spelling, which helped create the impression that such words were actual units of a black vernacular. Included among the list of "Do not write" was any substitution of "*Poe* for po' . . . *Wha* for whar . . . *Moster* for marster or massa . . . *Ifn* for iffen . . . *Poar* for poor or po' . . . *J'in* for jine, *Coase* for cose," and "*Gwainter* for gwineter."[89]

These corrections were followed by the English translation in parentheses—"(poor) ... (where) ... (if) and (going to)"—just in case the reader was unable to interpret the unfamiliar derivation.

Furthermore, Lomax and Alsberg made it clear that they were not against phonetic spelling as a matter of principle. To Kentucky's state director, Alsberg reiterated that "exact phonetic transcription is valuable. . . . However, latitude in this direction makes careful typing imperative." Confusion could readily result in cases where "inexact typing is coupled with phonetic spelling."[90] Lomax also encouraged written imitations of black speech, using them himself in his letters to state directors. Suggesting that Texas's interviewers might find some good stories at "a home for aged Negro women in Austin," he concluded "I am sure that some of these old women were alive 'befo' de war.'"[91] Cronyn and Lomax clearly conveyed the expectation of the federal office that all ex-slave narratives be written using a model of dialect in accordance with federal guidelines. In his editorial remarks on the ex-slave stories from Virginia, Lomax told state director Richardson to make sure that all of the narratives were written in the language of the ex-slave: "The story of Charles Grandy, as written out by Mr. David Haggard, contains interesting material, but unfortunately it is told in the language of Mr. Haggard. In every case, so far as possible, the speech of the ex-slave should be recorded."[92] Lomax also suggested that Richardson's staff "get together and agree on the commonly used dialect words." Yet he also cautioned against phoneticized spelling for words "that are pronounced just the same after they are dialectized. For example, in a Virginia manuscript, some of the writers use 'fo'ks' for 'folks,' 'napsack' for 'knapsack,' 'vittals' for 'victuals,' 'bac' for 'back,' and 'wer' for 'were.'"[93] Lomax made it clear that all of the dialect writing samples should be simplified, and he reiterated his list of words that should not be spelled phonetically.

In response to Lomax's criticisms regarding the use of dialect in a sampling of Virginia's ex-slave narratives, Richardson conceded that there were problems apparent to both her and her African American colleague, administrative supervisor Roscoe Lewis: "Much of the dialect was incorrectly written. . . . These interviews were taken in many cases by workers who are inexperienced."[94] She also enclosed a copy of the guidelines Lewis had put together "with some of his field people in an effort to arrive at some standards of Negro dialect."[95] Lewis's notes for Virginia staff workers on "Negro dialect" bore some resemblance to both Lomax's and Brown's guidelines; he stressed simplicity, consistency, and the avoidance of unnecessary phonetic spellings and apostrophes. But he went further than either of them in emphasizing the importance of idiomatic phrasing: "Readable dialect must be uniform; variety of speech is best shown by recording faithfully the individual's peculiarity of idiom and uniqueness of phrasing. Phonetic spelling and apostrophizing do not make speech idiomatic on paper; instead they frequently make it seem artificial."[96] However, he, like Lomax, included a section of over thirty acceptable dialect spellings such as "*haid* for head," "*wid* for with," "*marser* for master," "*keer* for care," and "*nachal* for natural."[97] Lomax's response to Lewis's guidelines was brief: "I was interested in the list of dialect words Mr. Lewis had sent. Any further suggestions from me I should think would tend to be confusing, as this office has adopted no standard dialect for Negro stories."[98]

A more extended commentary on the transcription of dialect was written by Brown and sent on June 20, 1937, to all of the state directors engaged with the Ex-Slave Project. Brown tried to correct FWP workers' apparent penchant for excessive use of phonetic spelling. As he explained, "simplicity in recording the dialect is to be desired in order to hold the interest and attention of the reader. It seems to me that readers are repelled by pages sprinkled with misspellings, commas and apostrophes."[99] In order to illustrate this point, Brown invoked famous literary works as examples of effective dialect writing: "The value of exact phonetic transcription is, of course, a great one. But few artists attempt this completely. Thomas Nelson Page was meticulous in his dialect; Joel Chandler Harris less meticulous but in my opinion even more accurate."[100] Not inconsequentially, Brown's examples were drawn from late nineteenth-century white writers who had helped to popularize a genre of literature steeped in romantic nostalgia for the Old South, rendered largely through the minstrel-type representation of a plantation Negro whose bowdlerized speech was a mimetic portrait of the simple, happy slave. Although he clearly appreciated their technical prowess in representing the black vernacular, Brown voiced serious misgivings, outside of the FWP, regarding the uses to which writers like Page and Harris put their literary facility. Brown was painfully aware that white writers' appropriation of an African American folk idiom often enabled the creation of black literary characters who sounded authentic while articulating their support for southern whites' conservative ideologies regarding slavery and black citizenship. By these means, writers of plantation fiction adopted the black vernacular as a minstrel mask to lend legitimacy to an image of "the Negro . . . as [a] contented slave, entertaining child and docile ward."[101] Minstrel-like stereotypes that helped perpetuate a belief in racial inferiority through tropes of black misspeak (riddled with grammatical errors and malapropisms), superstition, and simple-mindedness had become widely accepted as markers of "authentic" black identity.

Brown drew attention to these misuses by white writers, pointing out that "Page has his three ventriloquist's dummies agreeing upon the blessedness of slavery" and that Harris, through his invention of the character of Uncle Remus, "made [him] the mouthpiece for defending orthodox Southern attitudes."[102] Brown criticized Joel Chandler Harris for fundamentally violating the modus operandi of black folk culture. Because Uncle Remus told traditional folk tales "to entertain a white child," Brown pointed out, Harris's framework ignored a fundamental precept of an authentic African American folk tradition, in which stories were told by the collective "folk for the folk."[103] Similarly, the African American folklorist Arthur Huff Fauset complained that "Harris' variety of the Negro folk tale assumes to *interpret* Negro character instead of simply telling his stories. The result is a composite picture of the ante-bellum Negro that fits exactly into the conception of the type of Negro which so many white people would like to think once existed, or even now exists. . . . Any writing that can be taken as an apologia for a social system, or the idealization of the plantation regime, cannot be taken unsuspiciously as the chronicle of a primitive folk lore."[104]

But whether form could ever be fully separated from the function of "Negro dialect" in plantation fiction to commend slavery and romanticize relationships between slaveholder and slave remained a vexing question. Yet these concerns, discussed at length in Brown's study *The Negro in Fiction* (1937), did not surface in his "Notes on Dialect Usage" written for the FWP that same year, although he was careful to point out that "the values [Page and Harris] sought are different from the values that I believe this book of slave narratives should have."[105] While Brown was keenly aware of the same potential for the misuse of "dialect" by FWP employees busily engaged writing down and writing up the ex-slave interviews, he strategically tempered his remarks, focusing instead on the danger that phonetic spelling of black speech rendered the narratives unintelligible to the contemporary book-buying public. As he remarked: "Present day readers are less ready for the overstress of phonetic spelling than in the days of local color. Truth to idiom is more important, I believe, than truth to pronounciation [*sic*]. . . . In order to make this volume of slave narratives more appealing and less difficult for the average reader, I recommend that truth to idiom be paramount, and exact truth to pronounciation secondary."[106] Brown suggested that more current literary examples of dialect writing be emulated: "Erskine Caldwell in his stories of Georgia, Ruth Suckow in stories of Iowa, and Zora Neale Hurston in stories of Florida Negroes get a truth to the manner of speaking without excessive misspellings."[107]

Trying to be as diplomatic as possible, Brown did not dictate which phonetic spellings were correct. Instead he conceded that the variety of phonetic spellings submitted by FWP workers for the same word were likely the result of local variations: "I appreciate the fact that many of the writers have recorded sensitively. The writer who wrote 'ret' for right is probably as accurate as the one who spelled it 'raght.' But in a single publication, not devoted to a study of local speech, the reader may conceivably be puzzled by different spellings of the same word. The words 'whahfolks,' 'whufolks,' 'whi'folks,' etc., can all be heard in the South. But 'whitefolks' is easier for the reader, and the word itself is suggestive of the setting and the attitude."[108] For frequently recurring words with a variety of spellings such as "paddyrollers," "missis," "massa," and "ter, tuh, teh for to," Brown recommended the adoption of a uniform spelling for the purposes of publication.[109] Citing Howard Odum's observation, Brown also pointed out that the dropped "g" (as in "durin'") was questionable as an example of specifically black speech "since the g is seldom pronounced even by the educated."[110]

Thus, initially, Brown tried to focus FWP field workers' attention on idiomatic expression, encouraging them to record unique expressions and unusual phrases. While he agreed that "words that definitely have a notably different pronunciation from the usual should be recorded as heard," Brown prioritized phrasing over spelling: "More important is the recording of words with a different local meaning. Most important, however, are the turns of phrase that have flavor and vividness." Brown cited some examples he had come across in the submitted narratives: "'durin' of de war ... piddled in de fields, skit of woods, kinder chillish."[111] In this way, Brown was attempting to get FWP employees to avoid the pitfalls of phonetic transcription and eliminate primarily visual depictions of the black vernacular that emphasized the foreignness of black speech and implied the destruction of Standard English pronunciation rather than the linguistic play inherent in the black vernacular.[112]

Brown also attempted to minimize the linguistic intrusion into the narratives on the part of FWP field workers that most often appeared in patronizing descriptions of the informant, in terms of physical appearance, dress, manner, and residence: "I should like to recommend that the stories be told in the language of the ex-slave, without excessive editorializing and 'artistic' introductions on the part of the interviewer. The contrast between the directness of the ex-slave speech and the roundabout and at times pompous comments of the interviewer is frequently glaring."[113] Brown shared Lomax's and Alsberg's concern that linguistic usage not usually associated with whites' established expectations of black speech might mar the narratives' appearance of authenticity. In a revealing statement that exhibits Brown's own strict parameters for a realistic black vernacular, he warned, "Care should be taken lest expressions such as the following creep in: 'inflicting wounds from which he never fully recovered' (supposedly to be spoken by an ex-slave)."[114] Brown also worked to keep out the interviewer's racially biased perspective: "I should like to recommend that the words darky and nigger and such expressions as 'a comical little old black woman' be omitted from the editorial writing. Where the ex-slave himself uses these, they should be retained."[115]

The federal office's creation of a standard for a "Negro dialect" also served to eradicate class distinctions from FWP representations of African Americans. "Race" became the defining linguistic feature in the Ex-Slave Project's adoption of literary renderings of the black vernacular. It suggested that all former slaves spoke English the same way and reinforced their role as icons that recalled the image of the plantation slave. Furthermore, the authoritative guidelines that gave a specific list of phrases with their phonetic spelling provided project workers with a ready-made construction of black speech, one that relied on "eye dialect," a visual defamiliarization of black speech, and a literary means of racial "othering." In the best case, this might influence interviewers' perception of the sound of their black informants and in the worst case might supply a formulaic representation of a black dialect that could easily be plugged into the slave narrative during the write-up stage back at the FWP district office. State directors quickly became aware that the authenticity of their slave narratives would be judged by these standards and that submissions that deviated from Lomax's guidelines would be found wanting by the federal office.

In a letter Lomax wrote complimenting a slave narrative submitted from North Carolina, he conveyed once again the importance of the readers' perception of the slave narratives as stories directly transcribed from the ex-slaves' mouths. "I am very much pleased with your first ex-slave story. . . . The writer of this story has preserved sufficient dialect and peculiar words so as to make the reader feel the Negro is talking. At the same time, the reader has been kept in mind. I have known many people in the North who found difficulty in reading some of our best dialect stories, particularly the work of Thomas Nelson Page."[116] A letter from Alsberg to Tennessee's state director in the following year shows that this policy remained the same. Alsberg criticized the staff's use of dialect and enclosed a copy of Lomax's and Brown's notes on dialect usage for their future reference, recommending it as a "time-saver." He cautioned, "Unless phonetic spelling is extremely carefully done it is better to avoid it."[117] However, the questionable logic of the federal directors' suggestions for dialect transcription clearly remained. Alsberg closed with this illustration of an obvious error in phonetic spelling: "In the interview with Precilla Gray, for example, the verb 'lives' has been written 'libes.' Obviously 'libs' is the correct phonetic spelling."[118]

As states continued to submit ex-slave narratives, the federal office remained steadfast in sending admonitions to the state directors to make sure that "all stories . . . be as nearly word-for-word as possible." Letters from Alsberg, Lomax, and Cronyn all reiterated this point, mentioning specific interviews by the ex-slave informant's and the field worker's name that had failed to follow these guidelines.[119] Ironically, FWP workers could find themselves in the tricky position of following federal directives to take down the accounts "word-for-word" and thereby potentially failing to write the interview in the prescribed dialect. State directors found themselves having to provide explanations for narratives in which the ex-slaves spoke proper English. North Carolina's state director Edwin Bjorkman explicitly defended one interview, fearing that its credibility might be questioned: "Mr. Matthews, who has written the story, calls attention to the fact that the woman interviewed some times talks perfect English and some times a very crude Negro dialect. He says that this is the case with practically every one of the ex-slaves. They will talk good English for a little while and then lapse into their natural dialect, and he has tried to reproduce their speech just as he heard it."[120] Texas's state director also felt compelled to submit a detailed letter of explanation with an interview written predominantly in Standard English: "The almost complete absence of dialect in this story is intentional. He speaks with very little dialect, which is explained by his statement that General Houston impressed upon him that he learn to 'talk right.' His only complete misuse of a word in the course of the interview—'he' (Houston) 'went away and tried to retract his health'—appears on page 5."[121]

The almost apologetic tone of these letters and attempts to rationalize ex-slaves' deviation from the FWP's model of the black vernacular indicates the pressure state directors felt to comply with federal guidelines. The explanations they offered for these apparent anomalies are also telling. North Carolina's anecdotal example of ex-slaves' lapsing into "crude dialect" implied an innate inability to completely master the English language. The fact that they tried to speak Standard English but that they could do it for only short periods of time suggests the contrived quality of their speech; this is contrasted with the easy slippage back into the simpler and more "natural" dialect. The explanation from Texas attributed the ex-slave's proper English to the strict supervision and enforcement provided by his master. But both defenses shared the assumption that Standard English was the sovereign language of southern whites and that the dialect spoken by ex-slaves was an expression of their racial identity.

Another FWP worker also presumed that the dialect of ex-slaves derived from their poor imitation of whites' English. As he explained to his state director in a letter accompanying his submission of ex-slave interviews, "Before Emancipation the slaves had a 'dialect' based upon their hearing the white man's language as spoken and their ability and conception to imitate same." Education, however, had helped to linguistically assimilate black Americans: "After Emancipation the citizens of Nashville sponsored a movement to establish Universities, Colleges and Public schools for both the white and colored. This resulted in the colored race having today the same advantages for education as the white. . . . The Negro dialect of old days, due to education, has been replaced by the use of plain English with the exception, however, of the old slaves who still to a large extent use the old dialect."[122] Other FWP employees also attributed the lack of dialect in their informants' speech to their education. As one interviewer observed about her informant's English: "Minnie is well educated, and she taught school for so long that her speech is remarkably free of dialect."[123]

Mississippi's supervisor of assignments appended an explanation of her staff's transcription of a "Negro dialect" to their submission of ten ex-slave autobiographies to state director Eri Douglass. In it, she attributed the variations in spelling and phraseology that occurred between the narratives not to the individual field workers but to the differences in the ex-slaves' manner of speaking: "Example: if one Negro uses *de* for *the*, we have allowed this throughout the entire manuscript. If another Negro uses *th'* for *the*, *th'* has been used throughout. Note that one Negro says *niver* for *never*, while another uses *neber*. We have tried to avoid too consistent spelling lest we destroy the personality of the story."[124] This supervisor attributed the existence of a "Negro dialect" in part to simple laziness: "Our policy in editing has been to use contractions of words in a number of instances. This is really in line with our Negro's mode of speech. He just does not bother to say all of the letters in a word. Example: he often says *'at* for *that*. He seldom troubles to add his *d's* and *t's*. *Hun'erd* requires much less effort than *hundred*."[125]

The opinion that the black vernacular was largely a result of African Americans' lackadaisical attitude toward everything including pronunciation would remain popular into the 1940s. Bernard Robb's popular dialect tales in *Welcum Hinges* were written completely in the voice of "Uncle Woodson," who had lived out a contented life as a slave on the author's family plantation in Virginia. This book, which was really an updated version of Harris's Uncle Remus tales, contained a prefatory note by the author on his representation of Uncle Woodson's speech entitled "A Word Concerning Negro Dialect." Like Brown and Lomax, Robb acknowledged that the black vernacular was subject to variation based on regional differences as well as changes over time, but Robb explained its genesis as an outcome of African Americans' racial nature: "The Negroes as a race, especially those of the slave period and the years following, were naturally lazy and so took the short cut and the easiest way in the performance of their duties. So, also, in their speech, they followed the path of least resistance and least effort in expressing themselves. They slid over their words and eliminated letters which reduced the number of syllables. They also used very sparingly the letters d, g, and t; especially in words ending in these letters."[126] In this interpretation of black language patterns, Robb was just continuing a school of thought that emerged during Reconstruction. Writers like William Francis Allen concluded that these linguistic differences were the result of an "extreme simplification in etymology and syntax" contributing to a "phonetic decay."[127]

Publishing

Publishing concerns would also contribute to the FWP Ex-Slave Project's growing emphasis on African American folklore and the incorporation of a "Negro dialect." The same month the federal office began encouraging the incorporation of the black vernacular into the ex-slave interviews and issuing guidelines for its transcription, Lomax received a rejection letter from Macmillan regarding the sample of ex-slave stories he had submitted to them. They made it very clear that they were refusing the proposed book because it lacked reader appeal: "Our advisers felt that the material, interesting as it is, is not quite the thing which would make a very saleable book."[128] They advised Lomax to include "additional Negro folk tales," which might make the manuscript "seem more promising to us. If it is possible, perhaps we could see the manuscript then in completed form."[129]

A few days after the receipt of this letter, Lomax wrote up a tentative plan for preparing a new draft of the ex-slave material to submit to publishers. Describing this to Alsberg in a memorandum that was attached to the rejection from Macmillan, Lomax suggested that the first part be devoted to "half a dozen of the most graphic stories, carefully edited and written in an easily understandable Negro idiom, omitting uninteresting detail."[130] Evidently, the demands of making the material competitive on the publishing market encouraged Lomax to focus on the more colorful aspects of the ex-slaves' narratives. With this new emphasis he concluded, "I think a sale of the book could easily be effected."[131]

Another of Lomax's proposals, under the suggested title of "Deep South Folks," was a volume focusing entirely on various elements of African American folk culture, including separate sections on folk stories, folk remedies, folk songs and ballads, and "Voodoo and Hoodoo, Charms, Superstitions, etc."[132] As Lomax observed about the variety and value of African American folk material, they all served to "illustrat[e] the type of people who voice these stories."[133] While Lomax presented his idea to Alsberg as a potentially "significant and noteworthy book" that "would be a valuable and permanent contribution to American Folklore," he also emphasized the publishing opportunities: "I think," he wrote, "that a carefully prepared dummy of this material, edited as we think it should be for publication and including some of our best material, would be certain to find interested publishers."[134] In a handwritten note at the bottom of the page, he concluded: "Moreover, the material could be presented so as to make a wide popular appeal."[135]

In response to Lomax's increasing concern with making the ex-slave material saleable, state directors, at his suggestion, began prioritizing their search for informants who would meet these new demands. Roscoe Lewis, as administrative supervisor for the Virginia project, wrote to Lomax in early June 1937 to inform him of their progress in this direction: "We have directed our other field workers to try 'organizing' their ex-slaves, and list for us interesting and colorful characters." So far they had two possible leads: "'Sweet Ma,'" Lewis mentioned, "is 86 years old, has a colorful personality, and tells some 'tall tales' of slavery days."[136]

Federal directors also expressed special interest in the narratives of ex-slaves who had been owned by or otherwise come into contact with famous historical figures. Lomax told Florida's state director that the narrative of ex-slave William Sherman was particularly intriguing because he had been owned by a nephew of Confederate president Jefferson Davis and that would increase reader interest.[137] State directors took care to bring narratives such as these to the attention of the federal office. In Arkansas, state director Babcock reported that a member of her staff had "found an old woman who was owned by a sister of the famous Jesse James."[138] Texas's state supervisor singled out the "ex-slave story on Jefferson Hamilton" and presented it to

Alsberg, noting that "he was [the legendary Texas governor] Sam Houston's body-servant, [which] seems to me to warrant being sent by itself for special attention."[139]

Plainly the focus of the Ex-Slave Project was gradually shifting from an attempt to gather personal life histories to an effort to collect the most entertaining stories of ex-slaves whom FWP employees saw as colorful characters. Norman Yetman, in his overview of the FWP Slave Narrative Collection, asserts that "despite the large number of interviews obtained by the Writers' Project, less than two percent of the available ex-slaves were interviewed. . . . It has been impossible to determine the processes by which informants were selected."[140] Federal directors' requests that employees focus primarily on the more "colorful" informants, however, suggests one of the criteria.

As the FWP's federal directors began to concentrate on informants who could tell a good story, the ex-slaves themselves increasingly became the primary focus in the narratives. Many of the ex-slave narratives produced under federal supervision, along with some of the images of black identity and culture that would surface in FWP publications, reflected this change from an endeavor to document the black experience in America to a representation of African American culture as an object of colorful interest and amusement for a presumed white readership. This happened in several ways: through the influence of popular theories regarding African cultural survivals; through an increasing emphasis on black folklore, particularly more exotic elements of superstition and voodoo; and through "Negro dialect" as markers of authenticity. The Ex-Slave Project was in many ways a case study of whites grappling unsuccessfully with the past of slavery and the present status of African Americans. It was also a product of the desire of federal directors, like Lomax, to make the material attractive to publishers. With his appointment in June 1936 as the FWP's first folklore editor, Lomax wielded great influence over the project to collect ex-slaves' oral histories. An examination of Lomax's approach to folk collection in the following chapter reveals much about the ways both the form and the content of the ex-slaves' narratives, as well as their value, would be determined by his methods and his philosophy regarding African American folk culture.[141]

CHAPTER FOUR

Adventures of a Ballad Hunter
John Lomax and the Pursuit of Black Folk Culture

Well the world is round and the usa is wrighting to be found[.] there's a lot of
Jimcrow in the movie pitchers shows, why it the rich man got the best go. . . .
There was a man sent from the Holliday magazine to take my picture[;] well
he said he was Huties friend, well so much for nothing. They will sell the
magazine and get money and i get nothing. Well that is the world makes it
go round and round.
—Huddie Ledbetter, New York City, May 22, 1947

In 1937, *Life* magazine published a brief piece on the African American folk
singer Huddie Ledbetter entitled "Lead Belly: Bad Nigger Makes Good Minstrel." The article included a photo of Ledbetter accompanying himself on
his twelve-string Stella guitar, dressed in coveralls and a neckerchief, with his
bare feet resting on some fertilizer sacks. This image, which hearkened back
to the stereotype of the happy plantation slave, was juxtaposed with a close-
up of Ledbetter's hands on the guitar strings with the underlying caption:
"These hands once killed a man."[1] This double image of Leadbelly—the
docile black minstrel superimposed over the bloodthirsty black savage—is
representative of a dominant strain in public discourse on the "Negro problem"
that suggested African Americans could never be fully assimilated into the
"white mainstream" of American society.[2]

The sensationalistic image of Leadbelly as a songster who was also a
"double-murderer" was the creation of the folklorist John Lomax, who discovered the talented musician serving time in a southern penitentiary and
transformed the unknown ex-convict into a celebrity folksinger. Despite
Ledbetter's later objections, this image would be circulated as an integral part
of his commercial persona for the rest of his career. Lomax's inventive marketing strategies presented Ledbetter as a dangerous ex-convict and as a
bandanna-wearing happy southern "darky" by alternately dressing him up in
his former prison uniform and in the outfit he wore in the *Life* photo.[3] *Time*
magazine, in a 1935 article entitled "Murderous Minstrel," also emphasized the
singer's savage nature and Lomax's role in controlling the "wild-eyed" "black
buck," whose "knife bulged in his pocket." Lomax, the article explained, "kept

his hell-raising minstrel locked up in a coat room" until it was time for the performance.[4]

Lomax is still lauded today for the folk music recordings, collected by him and his son Alan, that make up the foundation of the priceless collection held by the Library of Congress. But it is important to consider the dynamics involved in his discovery and promotion of Ledbetter, as well as his approach to other black folk musicians, for they are a vital part of the story of Lomax's impact on the Federal Writers' Project's (FWP) Ex-Slave Project. While Ledbetter's contribution to and complicity with Lomax's construction of the Leadbelly mythology should not be overlooked, the success of the Leadbelly phenomenon relied in large part on Lomax's promotion of himself as Ledbetter's white benefactor and "Big Boss." In media interviews as well as his own writings, Lomax depicted Ledbetter as a black man of uncontrolled primitive impulses whose talent was harnessed only through his pledged loyalty to Lomax and his son Alan, whom Leadbelly referred to as "Big Boss" and "Little Boss." In a *New York Herald Tribune* interview, "Sweet Singer of the Swamplands Here to Do a Few Tunes between Homicides," Lomax recounted the story, which quickly became legend, of how they became partners:

> I told him that as a matter of fact I did need a driver for my car and might be able to use him, but I added, "If some day you decide on some lonely road that you want my money and my car, don't use your knife on me. Just tell me and I'll give them to you. I have a wife and children back home and they'd miss me." Well, at that tears came to his eyes and he said, "Don' talk that way, Boss. Don' talk that way to me. I came here to be your man. You needn' ever tie your shoes again if you'll let me tie them. Boss if you ever get in trouble and some man tries to shoot you I'll jump in front of you and take the bullet before I let you get hurt."[5]

Lomax's creation of Ledbetter's image as a "natural" primitive whose homicidal (and also libidinous) instincts were barely controlled by his white keepers enabled him to present an increasingly savvy and commercial performer in the guise of an artless folksinger.[6] For Ledbetter, in his training and influences, was about as far as one could get from the untutored and isolated folk musicians Lomax built a career out of finding and recording. As his own biographers note, Ledbetter had apprenticed as a twelve-string guitar player under the famous Blind Lemon Jefferson and was an avid consumer of commercial blues records, songs that "became an important part of his repertoire."[7]

The construction of Leadbelly's folk persona, whose raw and natural talent was inseparable from his racial identity, was essential for legitimizing Lomax's own role as the interlocutor for black folk culture. Far from acting as a behind-the-scenes manager for Leadbelly's performances, Lomax himself took central stage interpreting Ledbetter's speech as well as the meaning of his songs. Lomax capitalized on the fact that much of southern black culture was completely foreign to northern white urban audiences, even as he shaped Ledbetter's image to conform to certain audience expectations regarding black "racial" identity. He positioned himself as better equipped to interpret black folk culture than African Americans themselves. And, critically, Lomax also copyrighted the songs he "found," creating a significant financial stake in African American folk culture.

A master of self-invention and presenting himself to the public, Lomax would do more in this era to popularize the role of the folklorist than any other member of that profession. Although Lomax would collect folk music from many ethnic cultures, it was primarily in his descriptions of black folk culture and African American informants that he would construct his own public persona as a great white hunter, modeled on the conventions of the white protagonists of colonial travel writings. Lomax would come to epitomize the image of the folk collector as a hero-adventurer, whose success in tracking down and recording folk cultures was due in large part to his demonstrations of machismo in the field. Eager to dispel notions of folklorists as drier-than-dust, bookish academics, Lomax would adopt many of the tropes of the travel narrative genre in rendering his own career as a self-described "ballad hunter." Journeying into the American equivalent of the dark continent, into the furthermost, isolated regions of the South, penetrating deeply into black communities, risking life and limb, and overcoming tremendous obstacles, Lomax "captured" rare and endangered species of folk culture to preserve them but also market them to white audiences.

In doing so, he would help to legitimize the role of the white folklorist in the collection of black folk culture, at the expense of African American authority. His obsession with this role, along with his theories regarding what constituted "authentic" black folk culture, shaped his direction of the Federal Writers' Ex-Slave Project, and significantly affected how the ex-slaves and their narratives would be represented. Lomax's construction of "authentic" African American folk culture as the vestige of a primitive African past that was in danger of disappearing was directly at odds with long-standing African American vernacular traditions and did not support the project of African American assimilation.

Notes from the Field

The numerous field notes Lomax kept during his recording trips reveal much about his relationship with African American informants and his attitude toward black folk culture; many of these anecdotes appeared with only slight alteration in Lomax's memoir, *Adventures of a Ballad Hunter*, published in 1947, and were also incorporated into a serialized radio program as part of the Library of Congress's wartime Radio Research Project.[8] Traveling through the south with a recording machine and his second wife, Ruby Terrill Lomax, in the winter of 1937, the spring of 1939, and the fall of 1940 (dates that partly overlapped with his appointment as the FWP's national advisor on folklore and folkways), Lomax collected African American folk songs and spirituals for the Library of Congress's Archive of American Folk Song.[9] He also copyrighted many of these songs so that, on publication, he received royalties. Their field notes were rough drafts of material Lomax was clearly hoping to use in his autobiography; written in an engaging narrative style, they included descriptions of the physical appearance and mannerisms of black Americans with whom they interacted. Ruby also wrote letters to her family during the trip that reiterated the most interesting or amusing anecdotes. The correspondence and field notes, along with the autobiography, reveal Lomax's approach to folk collection as an enterprise involving the techniques of stealth, coercion, and domination.

Referring to his peripatetic travel itinerary in a letter to FWP associate director George Cronyn, Lomax explained, "Song Catchers necessarily are uncertain in their movements."[10] Naturalist metaphors were often invoked by folklorists to suggest the collection of raw material in its pristine state, found in its natural environment. It is likely that his mentor, the folklorist Dorothy Scarborough, influenced his approach, pioneering the use of early recording technology in the field to capture live folk renditions.[11] She used the title "song catcher" for her book of folklore from Appalachia.[12] In her introduction to *On the Trail of Negro Folk-Songs*, Scarborough spoke of the difficulties faced by folklorists in the field.[13] Significantly, she referred to the folk songs in zoomorphic terms, which heightened the representation of collecting as an act of entrapment: "Folk-songs are shy, elusive things. If you wish to capture them, you have to steal up behind them, unbeknownst, and sprinkle salt on their tails. Even so, as often as not, they fly off saucily from under your nose. . . . Folk-songs have to be wooed and coaxed and wheedled with all manner of blandishments and flatteries."[14] A proud Texan, Lomax expanded the metaphor from birds to cattle in references to the collection of ex-slave narratives. To Texas's state director, J. Frank Davis, Lomax included this encouraging remark: "I hope you will be able to corral a large number."[15] Such imagery personified the material as separate and in some ways distinct from informants themselves; folklorists spoke primarily about the song or the tale, instead of the singer or the storyteller. As often as not, when they did talk about those who were giving them the material, it was to describe their informants as impediments to be overcome, raising the question of ownership and authorship of black folk culture.

In Lomax's interactions with black informants, their reluctance and uncooperative attitude was a recurring theme. These problematic encounters, which the Lomaxes described as the result of African Americans' defiance, drunkenness, or unreliable nature, provide the dramatic tension for their tales from the field, while underscoring Lomax's ultimate success in capturing valuable material. One of these anecdotes centered on Mike Stephens, whom the Lomaxes had employed in Dallas for help around the house and yard. They also recorded him singing various folk songs. Mike had proved very obliging; he not only recalled the songs his father had sung, but he found other singers for the Lomaxes to record and provided contacts for places they planned to visit. For a trip through Texas and Louisiana, Stephens gave them his brother's address and promised to send ahead word of their project to record local singers. When the Lomaxes arrived, however, they were greeted with wariness and evasion by Mike's sister-in-law, who feared her husband was in trouble with the law. After a circular game of questioning, Mike's brother was finally produced, but for every question about folk songs the reply "was 'No Sir,' with or without amplification."[16]

Stymied, the Lomaxes departed for the next town: "We were amused but also, I suppose, piqued that we found our name unknown to Mike's family."[17] A week later the Lomaxes received a copy of a letter Mike's sister-in-law had written expressing deep concern that Mike was in trouble because of all the questions the Lomaxes had fired at them: "Listen dear what have Mike did in Dallas the man what he is working for. . . . He was at my home yestday he was asking me lots of questions about Mike what is the matter out there plese rite back at once and tell us something . . . please tell me what is the matter. . . . Please rite back at once and tell me something I will look for a letter at once don't delay."[18] This letter is a poignant reminder of the social context that was fraught with fear for many African Americans in the South, into which the Lomaxes were somewhat cavalierly trespassing. It also demonstrates some of the obstacles white folklorists like the Lomaxes regularly encountered.

The racial barrier for white collectors who sought to document and interpret black folk culture was frequently discussed by folklorists such as Dorothy
Scarborough, Lomax's mentor, and Lydia Parrish, who were fond of recounting the difficulties they had encountered but usually in ways that highlighted
their own skills at getting "inside" African American communities.[19] Yet their
own writings reveal, at times, their ignorance of black oral traditions and their
informants' strategies for disingenuous compliance with questioners' demands. Scarborough recalled a conversation she had during her visit to a
black church, where she had invited the congregation to provide her with
some folk songs. Her hosts "expressed the hope that [she] might stay in the
South long enough to get to know the colored folk, and maybe to understand
them and love them a little."[20] But Scarborough quickly denied that there was
any need for further acquaintance in that regard, explaining that she was "a
Southerner born and bred, and . . . had been loving the southern Negroes
ever since I could remember anything."[21] The black preacher's diplomatic
response to Scarborough's queries was given in the form of a tale and, in
keeping with the signifying tradition, masked the fear of interracial contact
under a veil of southern hospitality. Scarborough recorded his remarks, although she failed to fully grasp them:

> Lady, we feel so kind toward you. I feel about you like a colored man I
> once heard of. He and his pardner were working on top of a high, tall
> building, when he got too close to the edge and he fell off. His pardner
> called out to him, "Stop, Jim, you'se falling." But he sang out, "I can't
> stop. I'se done fell." His pardner leaned over the edge an' call out to him
> an' say, "You, Jim! You'se gwine to fall on a white lady!" An' Jim stopped
> and come right on back up. That's the way we feel toward you.[22]

The preacher was clearly making the point, in a humorous manner, that an
African American man would find a way to transcend the laws of physics
rather than risk physical contact with a white woman (almost guaranteed to
lead to violent reprisal in the South), to suggest that his congregation might
be reluctant to speak with Scarborough. But she missed the full import of
the tale, describing the preacher's remarks as "the most chivalrous compli-
ment that anyone ever paid me."[23]

Lomax would also mistake a black preacher's condemnation for praise. In
an anecdote about a visit to a black church in Alabama, Lomax included the
reverend's introduction of the visitors to the congregation: "We are glad to
have with us today these friends of the superior race with their instruments
in their hands. We owe them much. They have learned us everything we

know—everything. They taught us how to steal; and they taught us how to lie and cuss. Yes sir, but thank God, they taught us the way back to Jesus! When I see them sitting here I feel happy."[24] By these means, the reverend slyly managed to belittle Lomax and his wife. Such failures by white folklorists to comprehend their informants' full meaning, and the evasiveness of African Americans in the presence of white questioners, were used by black scholars as an argument for the necessity of black collectors. White folklorists remained unable to see through black subterfuge; as Harold Preece observed, "Negro songs often satirize the white man without the latter's being aware of any mockery."[25] Yet white southerners engaged in collecting black folk culture, like Scarborough, believed that their long acquaintance with "Negroes" meant they were well positioned to understand as well as gather it. Southern paternalism led white collectors to comfortably assume they were in charge of these exchanges.

In keeping with this tradition, the Lomaxes also regarded many of their informants as hopelessly childlike. Bemoaning Leadbelly's lack of business sense, he commented, "If I understood the nature of a Negro, I could perhaps do something with him to the end that I could sell his product. But he is too much of a child to wait."[26] It is evident that Lomax began to view his interactions with black folk informants, in addition to the material he was collecting, as a means of interpreting black Americans' racial character, providing sociological insights into their mentality and behaviorisms. Such experiences and interpretive framework shaped the FWP's ex-slave narratives under Lomax's direction. Anecdotal information, based on the firsthand observation of the informants' appearance, dress, speech, and behavior, became central to framing the folk material in order to imbue it with its proper significance. Lomax instructed state directors and FWP interviewers to include visual descriptions of ex-slave informants in their ex-slave narratives, including physique, dress, and mannerisms. This would lead a number of field workers to place equal or greater emphasis on the character of the ex-slave (as she or he appeared in the 1930s), sometimes at the expense of the narrative's information about the institution of slavery. In this way, field workers' portrayals of black informants worked to authenticate the folk material they provided.

The Lomaxes had an eye and an ear for anything that might serve as colorful copy. Many of their field notes contain representations of African Americans that reinforce minstrel-like stereotypes about black culture and identity. They emphasized the comical nature of their black informants, their tendency toward drunkenness and dishonesty, their malapropisms, their sexuality and superstitions. In a letter to her family, Ruby Lomax reported that one of their informants, Shack, had been firmly instructed by John that "he musn't have liquor on his breath when he came to our room to record. 'Shack' came in reeking with perfume!"[27] One frequently recounted anecdote that appeared in the field notes and in letters to family told of an ex-slave informant, 117 years old, whose remedy "for restoring lost manhood" turned out to be half whiskey: "Two doses a week keeps me potent," he claimed. The Lomaxes also interpreted a tendency to exaggerate as a proclivity for dissembling. From an interview with "Uncle Bob" Ledbetter, Ruby recalled his loose relationship with the truth: "I aint gonna lie to you 'bout dat. I says I don't ever lie 'cep'n when I'se by myself or wid somebody."[28]

Incidents like this that were first recorded in the field notes and then recounted in Ruby's letters to family members often included more dialect. Her insertions of a phonetically rendered "Negro dialect" are indicative of one of the central ways the Lomaxes would create a textual distinction in their writings between themselves and their informants and reflect the same rules for representing black folk speech that Lomax was circulating in the Ex-Slave Project. For example, Uncle Bob Ledbetter was represented by the Lomaxes as a fine, old, dignified "Negro" who expressed proper sentiments of gratitude to the Lomaxes for taking him to Oil City, Louisiana, so he could record songs with his grandson Noah. As Ruby notated it in her field notes: "One of the first things [Uncle Bob] said when he returned home was: 'They sure showed me a good time; that was the first time I ever ate at a white people's hotel in my life.'"[29] But as Ruby described the incident to her family: "When we took him home he told his granddaughter . . . 'I sho' has been treated like a king. This is de fust time I ever et in a white folks' hotel!'"[30]

This distinction through speech, between white interlocutors like the Lomaxes and their black informants, also appears in Lomax's depictions of the latter's inability to fully master the English language. Much of the humor in the anecdotes from the field notes derives from the Lomaxes' application of the black minstrel tradition, where "pathetically comic brutes . . . speak nonsense syllables."[31] This reinforced Lomax's case for the vital role of white folklorists in salvaging and interpreting black folk culture as black folk were not capable of speaking for themselves. Telling of his adventures on the road with the former convict Iron Head (James Baker), who had been paroled into Lomax's custody, he recounted how Iron Head, who was "proud of his ability to read, shouted out the words on billboards" as they drove past: "'Ambassado' Hotel, Grill in Connection.' The word 'Ambassador' floored him. After I prompted, he repeated, 'Ambassador Hotel, Girls in Connection!' Then: 'Dey furnishes girls in dat hotel. Is dat whar we's gwine to stop tonight, Boss?'"[32]

John A. Lomax and Uncle Rich Brown at the home of Mrs. Julia Killingsworth, near Sumterville, Alabama, 1940. Photo by Ruby Terrill Lomax. Lomax Collection, courtesy of the Library of Congress, Prints and Photographs Division, LC-USZ62-56331.

In this instance of black misspeak and misunderstanding, Lomax also managed to humorously highlight his informant's lascivious nature.

The need for white interpreters of black speech, culture, and history was also underscored by the Lomaxes' references to black informants' tendency to get it "wrong." Lomax believed this was even true when it came to informants interpreting their own material. After listening to informant "Uncle Rich," Lomax commented, "At first hearing, Uncle Rich's spirituals sound like jargon. He probably does not know himself what the words all mean."[33]

There was a long-standing belief among whites that blacks' intellectual inferiority caused them to frequently misunderstand English words and the teachings of the Bible, resulting in amusing misinterpretations. Ruby emphasized the critical role her husband played as an interlocutor for the folk, noting that one of their black informants, Alice Richardson, known as "Judge," could perform spirituals but did not understand what they meant: "For two hours Judge sang spirituals and prayed and talked and 'moaned.' . . . One of her songs is 'Roll, Jordan, Roll.' John Avery asked her what that meant. She hesitated and finally replied: 'Well -ll, ef I has to tell you 'zactly today what dat means, I—o' course dat Jurdan, dat means de River Jurdan, yassir, but now dat "roll," dat's what got me stopped. Now I wuz baptized in de River Jurdan, but I didn't see no roll den.' She was stumped."[34] Here, the literal turn of Alice Richardson's mind is made fun of and the point is made: African Americans often do not understand the meaning and significance of their own folk culture; therefore, white collectors must provide correct interpretations of black folk culture.

In a story about his attempts to get Vera, a female black informant, to sing some "sinful" songs, Lomax recounted how he was finally successful in getting her to sing one into the microphone. It began: "When I wo' my apron low, Couldn't keep you from my do', Fare-you-well, Oh honey, fare-you-well." Lomax claimed his informant was unaware of the song's sexual innuendo: "On inquiry I found that Vera Hall had never understood their real significance. She had been carried away by the lyrical beauty of the lines and by the mournful sweetness of the music."[35] It seems much more likely that Vera was aware of the song's real meaning; Lomax had noted earlier that she could be persuaded to sing "sinful" songs only when she was not in the company of her male cousin, and he was not present when she sang this one, which would indicate her understanding of the song's text.

Lomax's self-professed interest in "sinful songs" emanated from his definition of what constituted authentic African American music. Because Negro spirituals "abound in idioms and phrases drawn directly from the Bible and from the older white spirituals," they were comparatively recent expressions of the black experience. In contrast, the newer "sinful songs" took as their subject the secular experiences of black life, "situations as old as the Negro race." Moreover, the content of such songs revealed much about African American attitudes and beliefs: "subjects vital to the Negro's life, every day of the week—his hates, his loves, his earthly trials and privations . . . his physical well-being, his elementary reactions."[36]

However, these types of songs, Lomax noted, had become "taboo, emphatically taboo, to all Negro ministers, all Negro teachers, and to practically all Negroes of any educational attainments whatever."[37] Lomax attributed such restraints to the desire of middle-class blacks to disassociate themselves from their primitive past: these songs, he argued, "definitely connect them with their former barbaric life."[38] But what Lomax refused to acknowledge was that the taboo imposed by educated blacks on "sinful songs" was, in part, a taboo against performing them for white outsiders who might use them as an intellectual weapon against the black community. This taboo was partly an attempt by members of the black bourgeoisie to retain some control over how black culture would be represented and interpreted by white outsiders like Lomax.

Lomax's anecdotes often highlighted the low regard in which black intellectuals and scholars held folk culture in need of preservation and collection. " 'We have grown beyond such crude songs,' said an educated Alabama Negro to me when I asked for help in collecting Negro folk songs."[39] In one particularly telling instance, Lomax asked an African American first-grade teacher if any of the children knew any traditional ring games: "[The teacher] told me that her children knew no ring games except those she was teaching them from a text book. 'Let me ask them,' I insisted. Every little hand went up eagerly when I asked for the songs they sang when they skipped on the playground out of hearing. We recorded five of them."[40] Lomax noted the teacher's lack of enthusiasm: she "languidly expressed surprise at what we discovered among her pupils, though I fear she wasn't really very much interested. Like so many of her race she was not proud of their own creations in the field of folk song."[41] Without white folk enthusiasts like him to collect and record, Lomax believed that black folk culture would eventually disappear.

In fact, while his view of black informants was paternalistic but warm, Lomax saw educated African Americans as a menace to their people. In a successful proposal he wrote to receive funding for his expeditions from the Carnegie Corporation, Lomax clearly identified the major threats to the survival of African American folk culture. Significantly, all of them emanated from within the black population itself. Black educational and religious leaders, Lomax charged, were "making [the Negro] ashamed or self-conscious of his own art." Meanwhile, the more "prosperous members of the community, bolstered by the church and the schools," were "sneering at the naiveté of the folk songs and unconsciously throwing the weight of their influence in the balance against anything not patterned after white bourgeois culture."[42]

He was not alone in this view. Other scholars also accused members of the black bourgeoisie of failing to value and preserve genuine African American folk culture in their rush to assimilate into American society. Professor of English and collector of black folk songs Newman White maintained that "most of the literate and semi-literate members of the Negro race were desirous of forgetting [the spiritual]."[43] There was some truth to these concerns; the emphasis on socioeconomic mobility and the desire to cast off the ignominious legacies of slavery made many members of the emerging black bourgeoisie intent on eradicating folk beliefs and traditions irrevocably associated with the history of oppression and illiteracy. The paradox is profound. Collectors, such as Lomax, were instrumental in preserving black folk culture for the historical record, yet many of them viewed blacks as racially inferior and treated their informants poorly. They spent much of their lives collecting this material and often wrote of the profound and mystical beauty of black folk culture, even as they failed to understand it and fully value the intricate complexities and sophistication of black cultural expressiveness.[44]

Folklorist Lydia Parrish, in her introduction to her collection *Slave Songs of the Georgia Sea Islands* (1942), would draw attention to the "real menace in the scornful attitude of those Negro school-teachers who do their utmost to discredit and uproot every trace of it. Instead of being inordinately proud of their race's contribution to the music of the world, as they have every right to be, too many of them treat it like a family skeleton."[45] Parrish charged that these teachers tried to replace African American musical traditions with English game songs. But she noted that certain African American scholars were also upset about this process: "Carter Woodson, the Negro historian, frankly said that . . . his people are becoming a race of imitators; that not until they study their African background, react to it, and interpret it, can they hope to come into their own."[46]

Other black intellectuals, such as the sociologist E. Franklin Frazier, Zora Neale Hurston, and poet Langston Hughes, would also give voice to this perspective, although their protestations were only rarely recognized by Lomax; he graciously excepted from his critique "great Negro artists [like] . . . Marian Anderson, Roland Hayes, and Paul Robeson," along with "many other intelligent Negroes who are beginning to appreciate the richness of their own racial heritage."[47]

But educated African Americans remained a frequent target; Lomax often made critical references to their ignorance when it came to understanding the value of black folk culture and railed against the willful blindness of the black intelligentsia. "Advanced Negroes," he charged, would only permit representations of black identity that were in keeping with their own ideological vision. Such attempts at revisionist history, he told Alan in an ironic twist that ignored his own creative portrayals of black identity, would never succeed.[48] This attitude would also set him at variance with his FWP colleague, Sterling Brown, national editor of Negro Affairs. Lomax was incensed when, in 1937, Brown claimed publicly that the death of "Empress of the Blues" Bessie Smith could be laid at the door of southern white racism, which had caused a white hospital in Mississippi to refuse the critically injured singer admittance. Lomax went to some lengths to invalidate this theory.[49] But the incident only reminded him that "Brown was an idealist whose notions of blacks focused not on what they were but what Brown wanted them to be."[50] Lomax would continue to warn his son Alan against the influence of educated African Americans and those affiliated with Fisk University, Tuskegee, and "other Negro colleges [that] politely refused to allow me to talk to their students."[51]

Defining Authentic Folk Culture

Lomax saw his work as principally an effort to salvage cultural elements vanishing as a result of the forces of modernization, in the form of mass media such as radio, phonograph recordings, newspapers, and even the telephone.[52] "All these things," he explained, "are killing the best and most genuine Negro folk songs."[53] His main interest was in collecting black folk songs that "in musical phrasing and in poetic content, are most unlike those of the white race, the least contaminated by white influence or modern Negro jazz."[54] Lomax's theories about what constituted "authentic" black folk culture made him particularly interested in gathering material in places where the people were culturally isolated—either by geographical happenstance or by imposed societal codes.[55] He actively searched out communities where the population was entirely African American or plantations in the Mississippi Delta "where in number the Negroes greatly exceeded the whites," as well as lumber camps that employed only black laborers. Recording these songs on location was especially important, Lomax claimed, because it was "nearly impossible to transport Negro folk-singers from the South and keep them untainted by white musical conventions."[56] The greater the contact with white culture, Lomax felt, the quicker genuine African American cultural expression would disintegrate.

Venturing into remote places, Lomax would come across those who remained unacquainted with sound recording equipment. To authenticate the folk music he gathered, Lomax liked to relate incidents where his provincial informants, unfamiliar with modern technology and carried away by their own emotionalism, ruined the recordings he was attempting to make. In a session with Uncle Billy Macree, who "claimed to be 117 years old," which took place over the space of two evenings in Lomax's hotel room, Macree sang "some 'play tunes' from slavery days. He spoiled a record by jumping to his feet and beginning to dance in the most dramatic moment of the song. . . . He was a bit timid of the microphone and talked and sang most freely when we were seated under the shade in front of his cabin."[57] In a letter to his son Alan, Lomax reported: "Your blind Negro preacher, whose jazzing of the spirituals you admired, shot the works for us, though his impossible vociferousness in voice and on the piano made good recording impossible."[58]

The Presto recorder, supplied by the Library of Congress, used a needle to cut a shallow groove directly into an aluminum disc coated with acetate, and while it could easily be disrupted by vibration or even the accumulation of the "rind" extruded by the needle, which had to be carefully blown or brushed away during recording, it had the advantage of immediate playback.[59] Ruby Lomax related a tale about an informant's reaction to the recording machine. Although Harriet McClintock had never seen one before and "was not sure what was happening . . . [she] offered no objection when she saw that there was some relation between her singing in the microphone which John Avery held in his hand as he talked to her, and what I was doing at the machine. She soon caught on, for once when she was relating some amusing personal experience, she turned to me and said, 'Shut off dat ghost!' "[60] But even more pleasing to Ruby Lomax was McClintock's excited response when she heard her voice played back: "If only I had had a movie camera. . . . Aunt Harriet shouted with laughter and cried, 'Sing on, ole lady—Yeah, dat's me. Don't you hear me?' etc., etc."[61]

But even urban dwellers were often unacquainted with the expensive recording technology provided to folk collectors working for the FWP through the Library of Congress. Florida's director of folklore, Stetson Kennedy, recalled using a sixteen-inch acetate disk with a sapphire needle, with instant playback capability: "As a technique I would pretend to be checking the machine and after a few moments of recording would check the machine playback but for the real purpose of letting the informants hear their voices, and it always worked like magic, you know, they may have been shy beforehand but after that they're all ham actors." Recording ex-slaves at the Clara White Mission, where the Negro Writers' Unit (NWU) of Florida was temporarily located, Kennedy also got Eartha White, the daughter of the Mission's founder, to sing, "and after just a few moments after the playback she raised her hand you know, commanding us to stop, stop the machine, and said 'Hold everything right there, we're going to have a little prayer' and she said, uh, 'Lord, this is Eartha White talking to you again and I just wanted to thank you for giving mankind the intelligence to create such a marvelous machine and for giving us a President like Franklin D. Roosevelt who cares about preserving the songs that people sing. Amen.'"[62] These types of stories were used by the Lomaxes to authenticate the value of their collected material in several ways. In the Lomaxes' accounts of their informants' unfamiliarity with the recording machine was evidence of their advanced age and their status as rural "folk." Furthermore, the extreme emotions manifested through physical movement showed the honesty of their performance, as well as documenting the emotional intensity of the "Negro folk."[63]

Lomax also claimed that the recording technology he employed enabled him to create "sound-photographs" of pure, unadulterated folk material, free of any bias or influence on his part as the song catcher, or cowboy, corralling wild subjects. In making this argument, Lomax was cognizant that his own presence as a white listener and interlocutor might make the material he collected suspect of contamination. However, Lomax emphasized his own lack of professional training and academic credentials to prove that the African American songs he collected were completely authentic and had not been tampered with. "I am innocent of musical knowledge, entirely without musical training," he artfully proclaimed. Collectors who were schooled in music, Lomax pointed out, were a liability in the mission to obtain unadulterated specimens. He boastfully related that one of his sponsors, the chief of the Library of Congress's Music Division, had told him before beginning a trip into the field in 1933: "'Don't take any musician along with you. . . . What the Library wants is the machine's record of Negro singing and not some musician's interpretation of it; nor do we wish any musician about to tell the Negroes how to sing.'"[64] The results, Lomax explained, were essentially "sound-photographs of Negro songs, rendered in their own native element, unrestrained, uninfluenced and undirected by anyone who had his own notions of how the songs should be rendered."[65] Nevertheless, Lomax was not quite the purist when it came to folk collecting that he liked to claim he was. His biographer notes that Lomax was not averse to changing sites in order to obtain a better recording and frequently "taught singers the chants he thought they ought to interject in their songs."[66]

In order to find authentic black folk music, Lomax traveled to remote areas "where Negroes are almost entirely isolated from the whites, dependent upon the resources of their own group for amusement; where they are not only preserving a great body of traditional folk songs but are also creating new songs in the same idiom."[67] Southern penitentiaries seemed to Lomax to provide particularly rich places for this type of collection partly because the prisoners were culturally isolated from the rest of society. In Mississippi he happily noted that the convicts hailed from all over the state, "and the best songs of many communities survived among these singing black men."[68] Racial segregation rigorously practiced in the southern prison system also worked to Lomax's advantage. As Lomax pointed out: "Negro convicts do not eat or sleep in the same building with white prisoners. They are kept in entirely separate units; they even work separately in the fields. Thus a long-time Negro convict, guarded by Negro trusties, may spend many years with practically no chance of hearing a white man speak or sing."[69]

Furthermore, Lomax felt, without the corrupting influence of white culture, blacks "would slough off the white idiom they may once have employed in their speech and revert more and more to the idiom of the Negro common people."[70] Prisons, in which "the old songs are kept alive and growing as they are passed along to successive generations of convicts," aided in the preservation of black folk traditions.[71] Black convicts would serve as an apt metaphor for the "pure" and unaffected African American folk culture he was seeking; literally imprisoned in the past without access to the forces of assimilation or contemporary culture, their status as unpaid laborers was reminiscent of slavery. Gang labor kept alive musical traditions used to maintain the pace and make the work go faster: "On the penitentiary farms, where Negro labor must be done in groups, the plantation 'hollers' yet live."[72] On a collecting trip with his son Alan in the summer of 1933, Lomax visited eleven Texas penitentiaries and, in his words, "interrogated" an estimated 10,000 black convicts in the states of Mississippi, Texas, Louisiana, and Tennessee.[73] Here, Lomax claimed, they would record songs that were "practically pure Negro creations, both in words and music. Either that, or the songs have become so encrusted with Negro accretions that any trace of white influence is quite obscured."[74]

Early on in his tenure as national advisor on folklore and folkways, in 1936, Lomax tried to incorporate his own technique for gathering Negro folklore from black prisoners. He suggested to the state director of Virginia that his staff utilize the state prisons as a source for folk material. The response was not particularly favorable.[75] The director went on to undermine Lomax's own method of short prison visits by jokingly remarking, "The most practicable method would be to have some worker committed to the institution."[76] Not surprisingly, Lomax's reply to this refusal was rather terse. As he remarked to Alsberg: "This note reads like a willing surrender to me." Instead, he recommended the use of questionnaires, which would "not require personal visits."[77]

Penitentiaries had other important advantages in addition to the ones Lomax described. Convicts were guaranteed to participate in Lomax's recording sessions, once he had secured the goodwill of the warden, and Lomax could use them as much as he liked during the times scheduled for their meals and their rest periods.[78] In his memoir, *Adventures of a Ballad Hunter*, Lomax proudly recounted a recording session from the 1930s with a black prisoner who was reluctant to sing any "sinful" songs since he had become a religious man: "I'se got religion, boss, an' I'se quit all dat."[79] Lomax told the prison warden that "Black Samson" had a song that they especially wanted, so the warden sent a guard to fetch the man, and "the frightened Negro shuffled up and took his place before the microphone." But Samson managed to have the last word by uttering a prayer into the microphone requesting the Lord's forgiveness for what he was about to sing: "Oh Lord, I knows I'se doin' wrong. I cain't help myself. I'se down here in the worl', an' I'se gotter do what dis white man tell me. I hopes You unnerstan's the situation an' won't blame me for what I gotter do. Amen!" Lomax would also downplay the coercion by claiming that after the session Black Samson was extremely pleased with the results and hoped that it might soften the hearts of "dose big Washin'ton men" who would then "do something to help dis po' nigger." In a letter to Henry Alsberg, the FWP's director, Lomax would refer to this recording as his "prize record."[80] Clearly, Lomax felt that the song that was dearly wrung from an informant was a kind of trophy and testament to his skills as a "ballad hunter."

And yet, the field notes Ruby Lomax kept during their recording trips to penitentiaries in 1939 reveal that in private the Lomaxes recognized when inmates were being poorly treated. In South Carolina, as Ruby reported to her family, "we saw a sight that shocked us all,—eighty Negroes tied by ankle chain to a long large common chain. The fellows were very good-natured about it, and when . . . a singer would say 'this is as close as I kin git to the mike,' the other fellows would shuffle their leg-chains along the big chain until the singer could reach the mike. . . . As guests of the state, John Avery and I, of course, can make no public statement about our reactions."[81] However, after a friend who had accompanied them asked Lomax to send a letter to the governor, protesting the inmates' being chained together, Lomax did so, describing it as "unnecessary and inhumane," but he was careful to praise the courteous conduct of the guards at the Anderson County Prison Camp and describe this incident as an anomaly among his many trips to southern penitentiaries.[82]

On a trip to Arkansas, the Lomaxes questioned the guards about the rags the convicts wore that barely covered them. Although they chose not to say anything to the superintendent, privately, Ruby noted, they felt that more funds should be spent on soap and clothing.[83] In a letter she wrote to her family, Ruby reported that the night after their departure twelve prisoners had tried to escape, and two were killed in the attempt. In a revealing stream of consciousness, she indirectly connected the deaths of the inmates to the deaths of the musical tradition: "We made some pretty good records, but even in the past two years the death rate of old songs has risen."[84]

Former convicts Ledbetter and Iron Head proved to be an invaluable help when it came to persuading current inmates to cooperate with his requests. Lomax had once secured Iron Head's freedom from the governor of Texas and didn't quell rumors that he had also helped Ledbetter obtain a governor's pardon.[85] Many of the prisoners Lomax encountered expressed the hope that he might similarly be able to get them an early release. These efforts, such as they were, were not really acts of altruism. Lomax's main interest in Ledbetter's and Iron Head's parole was so they could serve as traveling companions and help him gain access to black communities. Ledbetter and Iron Head, at Lomax's urging, "sang for me when I met groups of Negroes in or out of the penitentiary, to show the people what kinds of songs I was looking for. Otherwise I could not easily make my hearers understand." But Lomax also relied on them as a foil, to draw attention away from his presence: "Furthermore, the singing of these Negroes always aroused the competitive instinct of the listeners, who would then freely give me their songs to show me how far they could excel those 'niggers from Texas.'"[86]

Part of Lomax's definition of authenticity in African American folk expression turned on its rough, unstudied quality. Lomax presented his black convict informants as less susceptible to the pervasive forces of white society, unwilling to abide by the legal codes. They were lawless and uncivilized and therefore, in Lomax's mind, closer to the primitive impulses he was seeking. Authentic African American folk culture, according to Lomax, was deeply suggestive of a primal, African past. When he heard songs or witnessed expressive black performances that evoked for him stereotypical images of the African jungle and a raw, black primitivism, Lomax felt confident about the genuine nature of the material he was collecting. He once traveled over a thousand miles "to hear the singing of primitive coast Negroes of the Negro Republic on Sandy Island."[87] After hearing a particularly beautiful rendition of an emotional spiritual sung by a mulatto woman, he remarked: "To me and to Alan, there were depth, grace and beauty in this spiritual; quiet power and dignity; and a note of weird, almost uncanny suggestion of turgid, slow-moving rivers in African jungles."[88]

This emphasis on the racial nature of black Americans also enabled Lomax to argue for the existence of primitive traits among African Americans that had survived the collision with white European cultures. Attending a birthday celebration at which many of the guests were dancing, Lomax once again fell into a private reverie about a primitive African past: "As I sat in the car and listened to the steady, monotonous beat of the guitars, accented by handclaps and the shuffle of feet—the excitement growing as time went on, the rhythm deeper and clearer—again I felt carried across to Africa, and I felt as if I were listening to the tom-toms of savage blacks." Emboldened to approach the windows and steal a glance at the revelers, he was rewarded with an even greater sight of the ineluctable racial and cultural difference he was in search of: "The whole house seemed to throb with the movement of the dancers. I saw the grotesque postures and heard the jumbled and indistinguishable cries of jubilant pleasure, and I realized that Alan and I were now enjoying a unique experience amid a people that we really knew very little about."[89] This would affect the instructions he issued to FWP state directors regarding the types of folklore he wanted and led Lomax to place greater emphasis on elements of black folk culture likely to appear to a white readership as unfamiliar and exotic.

For Lomax, the black emotionalism that was the keynote of African American folk music could not coexist with the conscious artistry of the professional performer. Lomax was fond of black folk performers who seemed to lose themselves in their delivery, becoming heedlessly unaware of their audience. "Were it possible," he declared, "for the world to listen to such a group singing, with no vestige of self-consciousness or artificiality, the songs that seem to have sprung full-panoplied with beauty and power from the emotional experiences of a people—I say that the world would stop and listen."[90] Describing Iron Head's moving renditions of prison work songs, he observed that "most of them were dominated by brooding sadness. Here was no studied art. The words, the music, the rhythm, were simple, the natural emotional outpouring of the black man in confinement. The listener found himself swept along with the primitive emotions aroused, and, despite himself, discovered his own body swaying in unison with the urge of Iron Head's melodies."[91] In another description of an informant's untrained ability, he noted its power: "His speaking and singing voice brought chilly sensations along my spine, always tore at my heartstring—deep, vibrant, resonant, tremulous at times from whatever emotions influenced his simple nature."[92] This raw passion, Lomax felt, was inseparable from its source.[93]

Lomax praised the "natural" musicality of black Americans as an intrinsic part of their racial character. "It is well known," he declared, "that the Negro is fond of singing. He is endowed by nature with a strong sense of rhythm. His songs burst from him, when in his own environment, as naturally and as freely as those of a bird among its native trees."[94] As Lomax explained: "The lonely field worker, the gangs building levees and railroads, the cook, the housemaid, all . . . create new songs, new forms of expression while they cheerfully labor. They go singing, singing, all the day even where you would not expect to find music—in the penitentiaries."[95] This description contains overtones of the stereotypical image of the carefree slave of plantation fiction, who was simpleminded enough to be singing even when performing back-breaking labor.

Lomax's definition of authentic black folk music had the added advantage of making it something black performers could not really lay individual claim to, or take credit for, thereby sidestepping any questions of financial compensation. Although unstated, Lomax had another reason for using black convicts. He was in little danger of being sued for ownership claims by those who were completely cut off from the commercial market. Lomax's fast and free approach in utilizing a wide variety of sources for his published work would lead him into legal difficulties over the question of ownership and copyrights. As the publisher of *American Ballads*, Macmillan received many written complaints from those who claimed authorial rights. The publisher would also become embroiled in lawsuits filed by other publishing companies representing the interests of their clients.[96] This experience motivated Lomax to find folk singers who would not be able to demand compensation or recognition for their contribution to his collection. Thus, Lomax's later recruitments would consist of gypsies as well as convicted felons. When he and Alan came across a gypsy camp in Texas in 1934, Lomax saw his escape from legal encumbrances. As biographer Nolan Porterfield explains, "Because the gypsies had no written language (as Lomax happily announced), all their songs were folksongs—that is, none were in print because their language was entirely oral. No copyright problems here."[97]

At the center of these legal difficulties lay the thorny issue of cultural ownership: Who was the rightful owner of the folk material Lomax was gathering and marketing to the public? The answer was complicated by the fact that Lomax was laying authorship claims (solely on the basis of his role as an interlocutor) to cultural expressions that were clearly not part of his identity or heritage. Through his inventive definition of what constituted "authentic" black folk culture, Lomax validated only those black folk performers who did not request financial compensation for their work and delegitimized professional black folk artists. Lomax thus authorized his own appropriation of black cultural expression for his individual profit.

The assumption folk collectors like John Lomax made in the 1930s about their informants' material was that as *folk* material, it did not belong to the informants.[98] Folk culture, for Lomax, was by definition without an author, or artist, who could lay an individual claim upon the product. The informants from whom Lomax gathered his collection were therefore not entitled to any kind of authorship claims for either recompense in the form of financial remuneration or acknowledgment as individual artists. Lomax and other folk collectors thought black folk performers should offer their stuff up freely and gladly. For Lomax, folk culture that was "authentic" did not rightfully belong to anyone, although this putative belief did not keep him from copyrighting as much folk material as he could. He saw his role as primarily that of the presenter of folk songs rather than of folk performers and was pleased when he felt he had been successful in bringing an obscure and deserving song to the public's attention. As he noted happily, "the Rock Island song, found only in the Arkansas penitentiary, has been on the radio throughout the country, while this version of John Henry has a place of honor in Dr. B. A. Botkin's important book, *Treasury of Folk Lore*."[99] Although Lomax would give some recognition in his autobiography to a couple of talented musicians he found in the prisons of the South, generally he was only willing to recognize the quality of the songs themselves rather than the artists who performed them.

But white folklorists' definition of what constituted "authentic" folk culture and folk performers was directly at odds with a long-standing black tradition that drew on black expressiveness for commercial exchange as a means of survival. Lomax's attitude was sharply antithetical to the African American tradition in which material is re-created and thus laid claim to by folk artists who, in altering it, make it their own by placing their individual stamp on it.[100] These opposing views on the role and importance of the individual folk artist would remain a fundamental point of misunderstanding and conflict between Lomax and his black performers.

While the Lomaxes preferred to get their material from black informants for free, they were not above bribing reluctant participants if necessary. In an effort to record a children's song at a "Colored High School" in the spring of 1939, "Mr. Lomax offered twenty-five cents to every child who would sing him a lullaby that he had not already recorded." Although this generous offer met with little response, one boy came forward with a song his grandmother used to sing, but the accompanist didn't want to play anymore, "and so Frank Gallaway could not record his lullaby, was disappointed not only at missing the quarter, but also at failing to 'get on the machine.' A dime helped soothe his feelings."[101]

Although Lomax routinely offered small monetary gifts as incentives with which to bribe his informants, his field notes from the recording trips he made throughout the South reveal his astonishment and anger when an "informant" requested any kind of compensation for their performance, even though Lomax himself profited hugely from this material. However he might represent his own generous nature, Lomax was observed by others as being somewhat stingy in the monetary tips he sometimes gave to his informants. For a day's work of recording, he might bestow a dime on each participant. Another witness claimed that after an all-night session with a group of black prisoners, Lomax gave the warden eighty cents with which to purchase cigarettes for the men.[102] The folklorist Mary Elizabeth Barnicle, an erstwhile friend and colleague of Lomax, would later recall his immense reluctance to pay his informants. When asked if the folklorists of her generation paid "anyone whose material they used—revenues or something?" Barnicle replied: "*I* did. . . . If Lomax wanted anyone he thought was valuable he'd pay them a *little* something. . . . He was the stingiest man on earth. He came from the South and his family was very poor. He didn't have any kind of decent, what we call education—knowing how to act properly and all that. . . . He was a scoundrel."[103] Lawrence Gellert, a fellow folklorist with left-wing sympathies, published an article in *New Masses*, which argued that Lomax "embodies the slavemaster attitude intact . . . [and] failed to get to the heart of contemporary Negro folk lore." Gellert also criticized Lomax's unorthodox collecting methods, which involved bribing prison guards and forcing convicts to sing against their will.[104]

The Lomaxes did make note of African Americans who resented their requests for material and performances when it became clear no compensation would be forthcoming. In one of the revealing anecdotes included in the Lomaxes' field notes, they told of arranging with a black preacher to record some spirituals "at his house where we could get electrical connections."[105] But when the Lomaxes arrived as scheduled, Reverend Johnson wasn't there. Instead, "we found his sister . . . declaring that she was a good songster but didn't propose to sing for nothin' and have some white man makin' a bushel o' money outa her songs."[106] So the Lomaxes "shook the dust of . . . the plantation off our feet and as best we could off the machine and went back to New Roads."[107]

When Lomax encountered Lucious Curtis, "a honky-tonk, guitar picking Negro, living on a precarious income from pick-ups at dance halls," he bought him "a new set of 75 cent strings for his guitar" in order to get him to play. Lomax commented that Curtis "seemed proud of them until I mentioned the expense when dividing the tip between him and Willie."[108] After Curtis and his friend Willie Ford had played their entire repertoire of blues, Lomax could not get him to perform his favorite again: "The best tune, Crawling King Snake Blues, Lucious refused repeatedly to play again. After I begged him I offered a dollar for this one song. Although I promised him that the Library would protect him in his rights he would not be moved. 'I think I can sell it to NBC' he said."[109] The refusal piqued Lomax. He preferred to think of the money he sometimes used to gain an informant's cooperation not as a payment for the material but rather as a "tip" for the performance. If he felt his black informants were becoming overly greedy, as in the case of Lucious Curtis and later with Leadbelly, he used this as evidence that they were not real folk performers. Thus, the connection between money and folk art was a crucial one for Lomax, and he would undermine in various ways folk performers who felt entitled to recompense for their artistic creation.

Repeatedly, Lomax commented favorably on the anomaly of black informants who did not request payment for their services. Remembering his recording sessions with Iron Head, Lomax described him as possessing "the dignity of a Roman Senator. While other Negroes swarmed around us begging for money, even for a penny apiece, he did not ask for a tip. When we paid him something for his time, he thanked us with grave courtesy, saying that he had little use for money except for one purpose."[110] Lomax attributed this noble bearing partly to racial lineage and asked Iron Head if he had Indian blood and received an affirmative nod.[111]

Although Lomax resented it when informants expressed reservations about offering up their material for free, he felt no compunction about using such materials for his personal gain, establishing a lifelong career with prestige and financial remuneration for the folk culture he "collected" and then presented. In a letter to Alan, Lomax mentioned one of his more successful collection attempts: "I wish you could have seen Henry Trevillion when Miss Terrill and I put him behind the microphone . . . and heard him talk and sing for two hours, a lot of it new stuff. I got it all and plan to incorporate it practically entire in my book."[112] Later Lomax referred to the financial profits he and Alan had made from book and radio royalties and other sundries as "cashing in on the folk music we have collected" and "the racket I run with the Ballads."[113]

Perhaps no other source is as illuminating for understanding Lomax's complicated relationship with African American folk informants as the famous and well-publicized affiliation he established with Ledbetter. It was during his travels in 1933 that Lomax encountered this formidable talent at the Angola State Prison Farm in Louisiana. He immediately recognized the star quality of Ledbetter's performance and planned to use it to his own economic advantage; he wrote to Ruby, "He sung us one song which I shall copyright as soon as I get to Washington and try to market in sheet music form."[114] Although Porterfield credits Lomax with "trying to keep [Ledbetter] 'pure' and prevent him from slickening up his act with pop songs and commercial stage business," it is clear that Lomax responded to his potential as a professional performer, for it was Ledbetter whom he chose, out of the thousands of black convicts he heard, to make famous.[115] Although he would secure the convict Iron Head's release as a replacement assistant following Ledbetter's departure, Lomax harbored "no illusions about trying to make him a 'star' in the Leadbelly fashion, for while Iron Head was an able musician with a large repertoire, he lacked Leadbelly's flair for performance."[116] Still, it was a tricky compromise to market a professional like Ledbetter as an example of "authentic" black folk singing. Leadbelly, Lomax worried, was increasingly becoming too much of the consummate performer, and he confided to his wife that he was "disturbed and distressed at his beginning tendency to show off in his songs and talk, when his money value is to be natural and sincere as he was in prison."[117]

In the enduring mythology that surrounds the story of Leadbelly and Lomax, Lomax is credited with securing Ledbetter's release by the governor of Louisiana. That this belief persists is a testament to Lomax's ability to sell a good story to the public and says more about Lomax's self-invention as a heroic white adventurer than it does about the reality of the business relationship they constructed. According to Lomax, his "discovery" of Leadbelly led to the singer recording an original composition for the governor in which he asked for the governor's pardon. Lomax immediately took it to the governor, and a month later, Ledbetter was released: "I was sitting in a hotel in Texas when I got a tap on my shoulder. I looked up and there was Leadbelly with his guitar."[118] Lomax actually made the recording a year after his initial meeting with Ledbetter, and there is no evidence that the governor ever heard it.

Lomax's version, however, supported the image of himself that he was trying to promote as Ledbetter's savior. The grateful Leadbelly, Lomax reported, searched him out and declared his intentions to be a faithful servant to the white man who had rescued him. Lomax's version of his "discovery" of Leadbelly would later be immortalized on film for the *March of Time* documentary series. In 1935, cameramen shot the reenactment of their first meeting using a script written by Alan and John.[119] Ledbetter told Lomax: "Thank you, sir, boss, thank you. . . . I'll drive you all over the United States and I'll sing all songs for you. You be my big boss and I'll be your man."[120] Lomax also had a personal interest in perpetuating the story that he had helped obtain Ledbetter's release. As he told his wife, the singer's belief in Lomax's aid was the best security he could have in traveling with a potentially dangerous ex-convict: "Don't be uneasy. . . . He thinks I freed him."[121]

After Ledbetter's performance at the Modern Languages Association conference in 1934, for which the chairman thanked Lomax for having "your talented aborigine 'nigger' sing for the guests,"[122] Ledbetter quickly became a hot commodity, with appearances at Yale and Harvard and a media blitz that included notices in *Time* magazine and a poetic tribute in the *New Yorker*.[123] Through all of this, Lomax remained in tight control of his protégé. Within a week of their arrival in New York City, Lomax and Leadbelly signed an agreement that made Lomax his manager and agent for five years for a share of 50 percent of all Leadbelly's earnings.[124]

But as Ledbetter's fame increased, so did his aspirations, exacerbating tensions with the Lomaxes. In spite of Ledbetter's demanding performance schedule, the Lomaxes expected him to wash dishes, act as chauffeur, and execute other household chores. As a result, Ledbetter grew increasingly bitter. Lomax perceived the situation as the result of Ledbetter's fame going to his head and making him "uppity."[125] After the business partnership turned sour in 1935, Ledbetter filed several lawsuits against Lomax, claiming ownership rights to the material and demanding appropriate compensation.[126] Some time after this fiasco, in a letter to her family, Ruby undermined Ledbetter's rights to his folk performances. As she noted somewhat derisively, "It was from Uncle Bob [Ledbetter] that Leadbelly learned many of the songs that he 'composed' himself!"[127] When Leadbelly tried to revive his singing career in New York under new management, he discovered that he had turned over all the rights to his songs to Lomax and Macmillan. At the publisher's insistence, Leadbelly was given permission to use his own material with the proviso that he would give up all future claims against them.[128]

Lomax's rise as a commercial success would be accompanied by a corresponding trend toward increasing professionalization among academic folklorists. Even as the American media and public were evincing a greater

interest in folk cultures and creating an opportunity for their further commercialization, the official voice of the American Folklore Society (AFS) was
decrying the pervasive and corrupting influence of market forces on "authentic" folk music and folk artists. Discussions surrounding the annual National
Folk Festival of 1938, held in Washington, D.C., revolved around the potential
commercial hazards that lurked even in this rarefied intellectual atmosphere.
In the official assessment of the festival, which appeared in the *Journal of
American Folklore* (the organ of the AFS), the reviewer congratulated the
festival's director for successfully presenting "authentic" folk performers. Still,
as the *Journal* noted, "it is probably impossible to reproduce a pure folk art
under such artificial conditions."[129] The president of the AFS, Stith Thompson, also recognized the dangers of commercialism: "Even if the festival itself
succeeds in maintaining a thoroughly non-commercial standard, the lure of
the radio may spoil a perfectly good folk singer who learns to give the public
what it wants. All of this may add to the joy of the nation and may bring hillbilly songs to Broadway, but whatever value they have had for the serious
study of folklore has evaporated in the process. Hence it is that many serious
folklorists look with a critical eye on the folk festival."[130] In the AFS's drive
to protect the study of folk cultures from the contaminating and corrupting
influences of the commercial market, they also turned their reproving attention upon the FWP and, more specifically, upon the position John Lomax
held as the FWP's folklore director.

Originally, Lomax's self-characterization as a lay folk collector had been
very much in keeping with the FWP's mission statement to use local amateur
talent. However, the FWP's goals to provide employment for unemployed
writers, and to make its publications intellectually accessible to the average
American while still receiving the blessing of the professional community of
social scientists, created a dilemma: How could projects contribute to current
scholarship while maintaining a popular literary appeal? This difficulty
would appear in Lomax's own publications as he tried to bridge the gap between the academic community and the general reading public. In part, because
of Lomax's fast and free approach to folk material, the AFS discredited Lomax
as an amateur collector and a commercial sellout. Although the AFS would
pay lip service to the important contribution made by lay folk collectors in
the 1937 presidential address entitled "American Folklore after Fifty Years," at
the very same conference, the council of the AFS would pass a resolution that
would lead to Lomax's dismissal from the FWP the following year.

Observing that "the government has entered our field," President Thompson emphasized that the FWP's main contribution had been in the collection

of "good folklore . . . which might otherwise have been lost."[131] Beyond this, Thompson's assessment of the quality of their work was much more circumspect. "When one considers that the collectors were chosen because they were on relief rolls and not because they knew anything about folklore, the work they have done has been far beyond expectations," but ultimately, "it is to be realized that much of the material they gather will be of little value to the serious student."[132]

In their pronouncement on the folklore material collected by the FWP, the council agreed that no endorsement from the AFS would be forthcoming unless "their evaluation, supervision, and continuation were placed under expert guidance" provided in part by the AFS.[133] The amateur collector of folklore still had a place in the AFS, Thompson suggested: "They know their people intimately, and there is individuality to every traditional item they have gathered. There is a personal affection, not only for the people, but also for what these people have uttered."[134] But the amateur was likely to be "unable to evaluate what he has collected," Thompson concluded.[135] Drawing on the same logic that Lomax had used to discredit members of the black folk from interpreting their own cultural expressions, the AFS was casting doubt on Lomax's ability as a professional folklorist. One year after its indictment of the FWP's use of amateur collectors, at the Fiftieth Annual Meeting, the AFS would happily report the appointment of the "trained folklorist, Dr. B. A. Botkin" and state "its willingness to cooperate in [FWP] activities."[136] Ironically, seven years later, Thompson would ask Lomax for advice on his own collection of regional folklore. Lomax suggested that Thompson engage an African American scholar to write the section on Negro folk culture. In a sad testament to the persistent prejudice in and out of academia, Thompson told Lomax that he would be loath to hire any African American for the job, even if qualified, because "the material had to be treated with more objectivity than any black could have."[137]

Thus, the extensive publicity generated by Lomax's popular image of the folk collector as real-life hero adventurer and his successful promotion of Ledbetter would result in his termination from the FWP. Mainly as a result of the ire of the professional academic folklorists affiliated with the AFS, Lomax would be replaced as the FWP's folklore editor by Benjamin Botkin, whose general demeanor and philosophy regarding the collection of folklore was much more conspicuously intellectual. Botkin's appointment also reflected the FWP's increasing desire to rid itself of the growing negative connotations associated with novices, dilettantes, and the provincial attitudes of far-flung employees. Botkin had graduated with honors from Harvard, earned an M.A. from Columbia, and, unlike Lomax, earned a Ph.D., from the University of Nebraska. At the time of his appointment as the FWP's new national folklore editor, he was a professor at the University of Oklahoma and a frequent contributor to prestigious academic journals. He had, in other words, the kind of status and respect within the scholarly community that Lomax had always craved.[138]

Moreover, Botkin's approach to folklore collection appeared to be much more cerebral than Lomax's. Botkin, so it seemed to observers, did not get involved with his informants to the extent that Lomax had. As Jerre Mangione, a colleague of his on the FWP, would recall, Botkin possessed "a quiet and studious demeanor which would have made him inconspicuous in a library." Mangione remembered a telling incident that occurred while they were both on the FWP staff. They had gone to a Chicago nightclub where the evening's entertainment was provided by "the gyrations of a mulatto belly dancer called Lovey." Throughout the performance Botkin remained "hunched over a notebook busily recording his observations of the writhing mulatto, presumably under the heading of living lore."[139] It is hard to imagine such a detached response from John Lomax.

In the end, despite the disapproval of the professionals in the field, Lomax's reinvention of the folk collector as a hero-adventurer would be perpetuated in popular culture representations. Lomax's efforts to sell himself in the role of the white ballad hunter and adventurer achieved its apotheosis: in 1941, the Library of Congress would form the Radio Research Project for which Lomax's stories and songs from his collecting days in the field were serialized; ten different programs were broadcast with great success.[140] A few years later, in 1945, Lomax was profiled in a *Reader's Digest* article and in the *Saturday Review of Literature*. As a result of this publicity, 4,000 initial inquiries were sent to the Library of Congress requesting information on Lomax's recordings housed in the archive, with subsequent letters totaling, in Lomax's estimate, 30,000.[141] The end result of Lomax's risk taking was now that "thanks to John A. Lomax, America will not have to travel half a million miles afoot, by horseback, stagecoach, train, and automobile to hear these songs. All she will have to do is to order the songs she wants to hear."[142]

Even Hollywood became interested in translating Lomax's adventures to the big screen, with Bing Crosby starring as Lomax.[143] Paramount studio heads wrote to Lomax about the idea, claiming they were "extremely enthusiastic."[144] They felt obliged to warn him, however, that he might have to embellish his story in order to provide sufficient drama for the film version; the studio would likely need to "take a few liberties about the actual facts in the lives of yourself and your son."[145] Clearly, they did not know they were dealing with a master of self-invention. Lomax managed to up their original offer by over $17,000 by pointing out the public's great interest in folk songs and in himself as a folk song collector.[146] As a hero who had made such sacrifices just so he could salvage a vanishing folk heritage and present it to the public, surely, he argued, he deserved greater financial compensation.

The suggested film version of Lomax's adventures in the field would never be realized, due in part to Lomax's lengthy delay in writing his own autobiography, and Lomax would receive payment from Paramount only for the option.[147] A much less sympathetic version of his relationship with Ledbetter would reach the silver screen in 1976: *Leadbelly*, directed by African American photographer and former Farm Security Administration employee Gordon Parks. Nevertheless, Hollywood's belief that the moviegoing public would be interested in a film portraying Lomax as a heroic cultural interlocutor, who placed his life in jeopardy by venturing among unknown and potentially dangerous folk communities, is evidence that Lomax's attempts to popularize the figure of the folk collector had succeeded.

But Lomax had triumphed in another way as well. By his authoritative claims that black folk traditions were dying out as a result of the assimilation of African Americans, Lomax suggested that black Americans who were not members of the folk, such as the black bourgeoisie, could not lay claim to their folk heritage. White folklorists' definition of "authentic" black folk culture as preindustrial and precapitalist and as intrinsically tied up with the period of slavery not only served to delegitimize contemporary African American folk artists but, by locating the "black folk" temporally in a premodern past, severed folk traditions from black Americans who were engaged in the process of assimilation into American society. These arguments struck at the heart of the political project of the black intelligentsia to regain the authority to represent African American identity and culture. If John Lomax serves as the case study for the FWP's approach to black folk culture and the success as well as limitations of white folklorists, then the trajectory of Zora Neale Hurston's early career, as a professionally trained ethnographer and employee of the Negro Writers' Unit of Florida, serves as a case study for how much racial identity mattered when it came to representing black culture and identity, and how race, class, and gender identities intersected in the FWP. Hurston's contributions are better understood in the context of African Americans' employment experiences with the Works Progress Administration and the FWP.

CHAPTER FIVE

The Everybody Who's Nobody

Black Employees in the Federal Writers' Project

Who are you? I'm the everybody who's nobody, I'm the nobody who's
everybody.... I am the "etceteras" and the "and so forths" that do the work.
—"Ballad for Americans," FWP musical revue *Sing for Your Supper*, 1939

In 1939, the Negro Arts Committee Federal Arts Council issued a scathing
indictment of the rampant racial discrimination prevailing in the Arts Projects of the Works Progress Administration (WPA). In a brief entitled "The
Negro and Federal Project No. I," the committee critically assessed the WPA's
treatment of African American employees, specifically attacking the dearth
of black artists on the Federal Arts Project: "If a true democratic culture is to
prevail in America, a greater proportion of Negro people should be employed
as artists and artist-teachers in all the arts on the Federal Arts Projects, for
the benefit of both the Negro and white people in this country."[1]

This committee received the endorsement of some of the most prestigious
African American organizations, including the Brotherhood of Sleeping
Car Porters (BSCP), the National Association for the Advancement of Col-
ored People (NAACP), the National Negro Congress, the Congress of
Industrial Organization's United American Artists, and the New York Urban
League, as well as prominent black activists and intellectuals such as the
president of the union of BSCP, A. Philip Randolph, and the author Alain
Locke.[2] The arts projects of the WPA were expected to be demographically
representative of ethnic and racial diversity in their employment practices as
well as their cultural production. The committee's brief speaks to the disillusionment many African Americans experienced after the WPA failed to live
up to its promises.

The committee called for greater representation in the Federal Arts Project
for the "approximately fifteen million Negro citizens [who] constitute the
largest minority group in these United States ... [which] suffers oppression
of various forms: lynching, disfranchisement and Jim-Crow laws in the South,
segregation and discrimination in the North." In their summation, the Negro
Arts Committee concluded "that discrimination has been practiced widely
and flagrantly in the operation of this project."[3] Such inequity, as they pointed

out, was not in keeping "with the principles and ideals of the New Deal Administration." The grievances articulated by this committee are illustrative of the routine discrimination faced by African American employees at all levels of the WPA. They also furnish insight into African American workers' views of the purpose and goals of the WPA and their claims to entitlement.

The Federal Writers' Project (FWP) has a reputation among scholars for being one of the few projects of the WPA that fulfilled its promise to black Americans by providing employment to gifted writers like Richard Wright, Claude McKay, Zora Neale Hurston, and Ralph Ellison and by undertaking projects that aimed to document African American history and folk culture. During the 1930s, publicity for the FWP that focused on black employment prominently featured the names of well-known African American writers such as Wright, McKay, Hurston, and Sterling Brown, to justify inclusive hiring policies and to also encourage support for New Deal programs among black organizations and citizens. A press release on the "WPA Negro Writers" claimed they were already hard at work in the regions of the East, South, Midwest, and far West, although it tactically did not provide exact numbers for black employment. Ten projected publications dealing with "the Negro" were also identified.[4]

At the outset, the FWP projects featuring black history and culture seemed to ensure the employment of African American writers and researchers and promised to provide a forum in which black staff members and black informants could convey the historical experience of African Americans. In particular, the ex-slave oral history project appeared to be one of the few sites where black personnel might strongly influence the FWP's representations of African American history and culture. These special "Negro projects" were intended to reflect the democratic spirit of the New Deal. However, as this chapter will demonstrate, a representative presence on the FWP was never fully realized for African Americans. Many state projects repeatedly demonstrated a reluctance to hire African American workers. When they were pointedly encouraged to do so by federal mandates that established small employment quotas, black employees were the last hired and usually the first to be fired when budget cuts occurred.[5] Decisions on hiring had serious ramifications; during this time of economic desperation for many, employment provided by New Deal projects could hold the key to an individual's and a family's survival. For black researchers, writers, and editors who were successful in obtaining employment with the FWP, their presence did not guarantee that their voices would be recognized or heard. The relationship between African Americans employed by the FWP and the predominantly white personnel that made up most of the state and federal staffs was a deeply ambivalent one.

Race and Hiring Practices in the WPA and FWP

The Negro Arts Committee's report included a chart listing the numbers of black employees compared with the total personnel figures for each division. Although its figures were by necessity estimates, as WPA administrators had refused requests for specific information, they provided clear evidence of racial bias within the hiring practices of the WPA arts projects known collectively as Federal One. Apart from the Music and the Federal Theatre Divisions, which had by far the best ratio for total personnel—for every seven white employees, they had one African American employee—the ratio of black to white employees was poor. The National Service Bureau came close behind Music and Theater with 12.5 whites for every black employee; the Writers' Division was next with a ratio of fourteen to one. However, the Radio Division dropped off sharply with a ratio of fifty-eight white employees for every African American worker. The worst division, not surprisingly, was Administrative Headquarters, where roughly 175 white workers were employed to one African American employee, who was responsible for operating the back-door elevator.[6] The percentage of African Americans employed in supervisory capacities was almost nonexistent. The Music Division again stood out with one black supervisor for every 7.5 white supervisors. The Marionette Division had a total of thirteen supervisory positions, of which one was held by an African American. The Writers' Division came third with one black supervisor in the available fifty supervisory positions. The Federal Theatre Project (FTP) employed five African American supervisors in its total of 350. The rest of the divisions cited had no African Americans serving in supervisory capacities.[7]

To amend this situation, the committee made twelve recommendations for change, including an increase in black personnel on all arts projects, the "promotion of qualified Negroes to supervisory, administrative and technical positions on all projects," the appointment of an African American to serve on the planning board of the FTP, and the creation of projects "dedicated to study and development of the specific culture of the Negro people."[8] Significantly, the committee also called for the establishment of a separate "Negro Theatre" Division, which would enable black playwrights, actors, and directors, who were consistently ignored by the FTP in New York City, to autonomously develop their craft.[9]

New York was not the only city in which African Americans were investigating race discrimination in New Deal projects. A weekly report called the *Negro Press Digest* compiled newspaper articles appearing in the black press across the nation on incidents of discrimination against African Americans within the WPA. With headlines such as "Discrimination Found in New York WPA," "Not One Colored Foreman among 16 on This WPA Project," "Are We the Forgotten Group?," and "WPA Workers File Charges against White DC Foreman," the *Negro Press* articles served as a sentinel for discriminatory practices in the WPA.[10] From the *Cleveland Call and Post* to the *Pittsburgh Courier*, these news articles kept tabs on the experience of black WPA employees: drawing attention to the discriminatory practices in hiring, promotions, and layoffs and the difficulties faced by African Americans who regularly worked under the direction of white supervisors. Also mentioned were cases involving the unlawful diversion of funds specifically designated for Negro personnel and projects that were being filched for white workers and supervisors, along with abuses of power by white supervisors. By drawing attention to the "overt acts of discrimination on WPA projects," the *Negro Press* helped to instigate investigations into acts of racial discrimination in the WPA.[11]

Other articles in the *Negro Press Digest* contained reports on the general unwillingness among WPA officials to promote African American workers. Most black employees were never considered eligible for jobs above menial labor. As the *Cleveland Call and Post* pointed out, in Ohio's WPA, "not a single Negro has a job on the state WPA staff. Not a single Negro, man or woman, has an executive position on the WPA county staff. . . . Out of the hundreds of clerks, etc., employed by WPA at its headquarters, not a one is a Negro. Of the hundreds of foremen on the scores of projects that are being operated by WPA here, there are only two Negroes."[12] Black Americans, the editorial contended, "are equally entitled to all the benefits this government offers on the same basis as they are meted out to other citizens. All of our men are not ditch diggers, neither are all of our women domestics. We have men and women who are capable to hold any of the executive positions WPA has to offer. No one has the right to disqualify them because they are colored."[13] The *Chicago Defender* reported complaints on "the refusal of [WPA] officials to reclassify members of the Race for skilled positions, calling for higher pay."[14] Several cases were mentioned in which black employees worked at assignments in a higher classification without being paid the appropriate increase in salary.[15] Often instead of promotion, these workers' jobs were temporarily terminated and the black employees were laid off, only to have their previous positions mysteriously renewed with the hiring of white employees.[16]

African American civil rights organizations, such as John Preston Davis's Joint Committee on National Recovery and the NAACP, played an important role in policing racial discrimination in the WPA. Thurgood Marshall worked as legal counsel for the NAACP during the 1930s, before winning the landmark Supreme Court case of *Brown v. Board of Education* in 1954. He responded to numerous letters from African Americans who felt they had encountered discrimination in the WPA.[17] The NAACP's executive secretary, Walter White, became directly involved with a number of complaints, such as protests over the unilateral dismissal of black employees in the FTP in Cleveland, Ohio.[18] Most troubling were the reports the NAACP received of African American employees on WPA projects being forced off relief rolls and into the fields to pick cotton in North Carolina.[19] In 1938, White helped black employees on the New York City Writers' Project obtain the promotion of one writer to the position of assistant project supervisor and the hiring of two African American stenographers, "the first engagement of Negroes in this capacity in the entire history of the project."[20]

The FWP's federal director, Henry Alsberg, did try to ensure that most states had employed at least one African American worker. Alsberg's attention to this issue was likely the result of Davis's correspondence to Alsberg and other FWP administrators in early December 1935 expressing concern over racial discrimination in hiring practices within the FWP and his recommendations for addressing it. A month later, in January 1936, Alsberg sent out requests to all state directors asking them to inform him of the number of black employees on their projects.[21] When state directors reported that there were no African American staff members, they were reminded to "give every consideration to qualified persons in various racial groups."[22] As of 1937, the FWP would employ a total of 4,500 workers, 106 of whom were black, constituting roughly 2 percent.[23] By 1938, according to tallies kept by the Office on Negro Affairs, for forty-eight state projects plus the District of Columbia, there were approximately 140 African American employees. New York City and Louisiana were the projects with the largest number of African American workers. Fourteen states, including Kentucky and Mississippi, did not have any black employees on their state projects.[24] Numbers were down slightly from those recorded in 1936, when Brown's position was first established; in that year, the Office on Negro Affairs recorded 155.[25] Budget reductions in 1937 and 1938 led a number of state projects to reduce their staff; very often black employees were the first to be cut from the rolls. As two former employees of the "Negro Project" in Charleston, South Carolina, testified in a letter they sent to WPA administrator Harry Hopkins, the number of black workers had declined from four to two to none in 1937, yet there were still "six white Field workers, two Office workers, two supervisors, and others on [the] Editorial Staff." They begged Hopkins to "see the injustice" and reinstate black representation on the project in Charleston. "We know the whites have to live and as human being[s], may we also live?"[26]

The Office on Negro Affairs worked to make the hiring of greater numbers of black writers a priority for the FWP.[27] In a report from Brown's office regarding the employment of black Americans in the southern state projects, as well as the treatment of African American subject matter, the number of black workers was cited for each state along with the director's explanations for the paucity of such employees. State directors proved to be tenacious in their refusal to hire black workers and made a variety of excuses and explanations for why such hirings were untenable. Ironically, they cited the threat of bad publicity that might result from pursuing a more equitable hiring process. Alabama state director Myrtle Miles rationalized, "It would be unwise to give a Negro this job inasmuch as there might be some feeling engendered against the project itself. There is considerable racial sensitiveness in Tuskegee and vicinity."[28]

Very often state directors claimed that the dearth of black employees was directly attributable to the lack of applicants who were both educationally qualified and properly certified as relief workers in need. Miles explained that her staff in Alabama included only one black employee despite the fact that "frequent efforts have been made to add others." "Educated Negroes," Miles concluded, "are not, to any extent, on relief. The type of Negro available for work on the certified bases is not capable of doing research work or writing. The worker we have in Mobile has never been fully adequate to the task but has been retained for want of better material."[29] New Hampshire's state director asserted that there was only one "colored person" eligible for relief in the state and that he had turned down the position offered to him. However, the director noted, they did have "a Greek, an Armenian, and three French workers" on the staff in Manchester.[30] In a similar vein, a letter from South Dakota's state director tried to make up for the lack of black employees statewide by noting that they had, "however, requisitioned one Indian."[31] Iowa reported only one black employee, but the state director was quick to reassure Alsberg that he "would lean backward in order to employ colored people and that the only reason we have but one worker is that we have found no others competent on the relief rolls or otherwise."[32] And New Mexico's state director explained that the reason "there are no colored persons working on the Federal Writers' Projects" was because "nearly all of the colored people in New Mexico are cooks or chauffeurs."[33]

The Georgia Project also initially claimed a shortage of qualified black applicants. However, this argument was undermined by a letter of complaint sent to Alsberg by the African American director of the Atlanta School of Social Work, who pointed out that this was far from being the case: "In the City of Atlanta a number of qualified unemployed Negro writers are listed as applicants for positions under the Writers' Project. To this day none have been employed. Meanwhile, as you know, many unemployed white writers are now employed in this city on this project. . . . I wish to ask therefore that immediate investigation be made of the failure to employ any Negroes in Atlanta on the Writers' Project."[34] His concern was not merely jobs but practicality, as black writers were better positioned to obtain information regarding the African American community. He noted that at least "one of these white [FWP] writers . . . has been to my office and to the offices of other Negro educational institution heads seeking to secure information for the American Guide. Such information can be more effectively secured by qualified Negro writers."[35] This letter would initiate the expenditure of additional federal funds for the employment of African American researchers and writers.

Bothered by the blatant racial discrimination in the hiring practices of the Atlanta project, Alsberg tried to impress upon Georgia's state director the importance of employing some African American applicants. He was quickly informed, however, that certain state directors would remain unwilling to hire African Americans unless their personnel quotas were increased. Georgia's state directors, who had already filled all of their openings with white workers, were unwilling to let some of them go in order to replace them with black employees.[36] As one of the directors explained: "Naturally, to place additional persons on the project would require either authorization to increase the local personnel or the dismissal of three white employees and the substitution of the colored workers. I do not think such dismissal and substitution would be good policy in this area. Therefore, I am writing to inquire whether you find it feasible to authorize the employment of three colored persons for the Atlanta staff."[37] This seemed to be the only solution to the problem, and a week later, this director made his demand even more unmistakable. "I am still at a loss to know," he wrote to Alsberg, "how we can place additional employees without almost outright dismissal of several white persons. . . . If you deem it advisable to authorize increasing our Atlanta personnel by two or three workers, I can put to work immediately the Negroes I have interviewed and qualified. . . . I will communicate . . . and inform as to our intentions to place colored workers *if* additional funds are authorized."[38]

Alsberg ultimately conceded that the only way to ensure that these state projects would hire African American applicants was by increasing each state's personnel quota specifically for that purpose. He had one of his field supervisors inform Georgia state director Carolyn Dillard "that it would be desirable to get a few Negroes on their projects and that the quota might be extended to include them."[39] Once Georgia state administrators were assured by the federal office that extra federal funds would be made available, they declared their willingness to comply with the hiring of black candidates: "We are ready to place on the payroll of the Atlanta project three Negroes," Dillard wrote to Alsberg. "It is my understanding . . . that we shall be given an additional quota of workers to cover this. As soon as the authorization is received, we can put them to work at once. . . . Is it advisable to place Negroes on any other projects?"[40]

While the federal office may have felt its hand had been forced by recalcitrant state directors, it held the line regarding the purpose of these funds. Alsberg communicated this to Florida's state director, Carita Doggett Corse: "This office . . . does not feel, however, that it can increase your state quota except for the setting up of the negro project you discussed. . . . If you are ready to set up the Negro Writers' Project with not more than ten workers you are authorized to draw up a WPA form 320, and submit it at your first opportunity."[41] At the same time, Alsberg was careful to establish deadlines for the submission of state directors' requests for the extra funds and the subsequent hiring of African American workers: "It appears at this time that we shall not be able to authorize the employment of any persons in addition to those actually working on March 15th. Consequently, you will understand the need to expedite the setting up of the negro project. We are authorizing $2,000 to the State of Florida which we have calculated to provide for employment of ten negroes until May 15."[42] Corse promptly responded to this information and in a follow-up letter to Alsberg, dated March 5, notified him that the "quota of 10 workers allotted the negro unit of the American Guide was filled today and employees are now working."[43] Like Florida, the Virginia project also established a separate black unit; sixteen African American employees under the direction of Roscoe Lewis conducted interviews with more than 300 ex-slaves and contributed to the 1940 publication *The Negro in Virginia*.[44] Virginia held the best record for African American employment; 20 percent of its personnel were black.[45]

However, these additional quotas for the employment of black personnel were a double-edged sword because when the budget cuts came forcing a reduction in staff workers, their status helped to make their jobs

Unnamed African American employee, Federal Writers' Project, Macon(?), Georgia, 1936. WPA Photographs, Basic Skills Projects, courtesy of Hargrett Rare Book and Manuscript Library, University of Georgia Libraries.

vulnerable to dismissal and they were often the first to be let go. The establishment of a separate Negro Writers' Unit (NWU) in South Carolina meant that "when it became necessary for the number of workers on the Federal Writers' Project to be reduced, all of the Negro workers were dropped from the rolls."[46] Budget cuts had also affected the NWU of Florida. As state director Corse regretfully explained, "We were authorized to employ ten Negroes at the start. . . . A reduction in quota forced us to cut the staff to eight and further reduction . . . compelled us to limit the Negro unit to three persons."[47]

NAACP director Walter White was well aware of the drawbacks posed by segregated Negro projects in the WPA. In a letter to the president of the Pennsylvania state branches of the NAACP, he forcefully asserted that "the Association should have . . . taken a definite stand against jim-crow projects, as there is nothing, both in principle and practice, which can be more dangerous to Negroes." Citing the case of the black employees on Ohio's FTP who had been let go while white actors were transferred to other jobs, White observed that had they been "members of a mixed project they could not have been fired as easily nor as completely as they have been. With the retrenchment in WPA projects, this is going to be true right down the line."[48]

African American employees of the FWP working in states that did not have segregated units encountered still other problems. Although the federal office would encourage all state directors to employ at least a few black workers, targeting specifically the southern state projects, federal directors were clearly not interested in challenging Jim Crow. While they repeatedly inquired about the number of African Americans employed on state projects and requested updated information on staff quotas, they accepted the strictly limited capacity in which black applicants could be hired. An early report to Alsberg from a field supervisor in 1935 demonstrates the FWP's sensitivity to southern racial codes. Although Georgia state director Dillard was not opposed to the idea of hiring African Americans, she made it clear that black workers would be considered for positions only outside of the office, specifically as researchers. As the field supervisor explained to Alsberg, "They say that there is a law in Georgia prohibiting Negroes from working in the same office with white people." But the field supervisor also expressed his agreement with this decision, stating, "Even if this were not so I feel that as a matter of policy it would be best to keep Negroes out of the office." As a result, an African American woman who had written to Alsberg looking for a job as a stenographer was turned down, for as an office worker she was "not usable in these delicate circumstances."[49] A newspaper editorial from Youngstown, Ohio, reprinted in the *Negro Press Digest*, drew attention to a similar occurrence at the Ohio State Employment Service. When a young African American woman, who was an excellent stenographer, had tried to apply, she "was told that she could not do so. . . . There was no use registering as there were no calls for colored stenographers."[50]

In many respects, the same "logic" of racial segregation that informed public institutions and public accommodations shaped black employees' experiences with the FWP. Recalling the multiple challenges he faced as national editor of Negro Affairs, Brown related an incident that had occurred with the Oklahoma project. Apparently white staff members were concerned about sharing the drinking fountain with the African American employee and refused to let him use it, "and so I would have to straighten that out . . . [saying] 'Hell, stop this foolishness. A drinking fountain is a drinking fountain is a drinking fountain. Everybody drinks out of the drinking fountain.' "[51] Living and working in Washington, D.C., Brown himself would routinely encounter Jim Crow in the nation's capital, experiences that certainly contributed to the essay he wrote for inclusion in the D.C. guidebook, "The Negro in Washington."[52]

North Carolina's director blamed the complete lack of black employees on a budget deficiency, which had "not permitted the setting up of separate establishments which would be required for such employment."[53] Similarly, Arizona's state director had redirected a well-qualified applicant with newspaper experience to a teaching position "in a colored school" for the WPA Educational Project, because "regardless of competence, it was not the best policy to have one colored man working with twenty-nine white people."[54] South Carolina had ingeniously solved the problem of segregating its six employees from its white staff by the donation of office space from a nearby Negro college. Other southern state projects that wished to maintain the social segregation of Jim Crow in their district offices either relied on local African American organizations to provide space or forced black employees to work at home, rather than come in daily contact with the white employees at the offices. However, this also subjected black employees to greater scrutiny and suspicion by some white supervisors, as they did not punch in. After his field trip to the southern state offices, Benjamin Botkin mentioned this concern on the part of Georgia administrators to Henry Alsberg: "The chief problem with the Negro workers seems to be the difficulty of supervision and time-keeping, since they work at home."[55]

Of course, Alsberg kept these discussions on the hiring of African American workers to himself. When asked by the assistant state director of Florida's National Youth Administration about the hiring procedures for black writers, he assured the director that "I shall do everything to see that there is no discrimination whatsoever," before going on to describe the process by which hiring took place, without any references to racial considerations: "The method of obtaining employment on a writers' project is very simple in the case of writers on relief. If they are properly classified on the local Work Progress Administration files, they will automatically be called upon when local projects are started."[56] Needless to say, the process was considerably more complicated for potential black employees.

Problems with FWP hiring practices still existed when Benjamin Botkin replaced John Lomax as folklore editor in 1938. Botkin, however, proved to be more sensitive to the ramifications of discriminatory hiring practices. As he commented on the lack of black employees on the South Carolina project: "At present, there are no Negro workers on the South Carolina staff. . . . It might be asked, how can the Negro be expected to make a contribution unless he is given more representation in cultural projects? At the same time the Negro is praised for his folklore, and yet the white workers are thought to do a better job of collection because [they are] more 'discriminating' (an unconscious pun)."[57] Even black employees on FWP projects who were working in positions as editors on state projects, jobs that were generally higher-paid positions with greater job security, were subject to bitter struggles over salary and job prestige with white FWP employees who felt that certain distinctions based on race should be respected. Roscoe Lewis, the main editor and writer on *The Negro in Virginia*, came under attack from state director Eudora Ramsay Richardson when federal directors decided to raise his salary in recompense for the additional work he was undertaking for the Washington office as a Negro advisor. Several letters of protest against this promotion were sent by various members of the Virginia staff to Alsberg. William Smith, administrator for the Virginia project, wrote this complaint to Alsberg on behalf of Richardson: "Mrs. Eudora Ramsay Richardson, Director of the project, who is . . . giving of herself freely at all times, is receiving $216 for full time service. . . . If Mr. Lewis' salary is raised as you suggest, it will be out of line with salaries paid all other workers on that project. It will, also, place him out of line with salaries of other project and administrative workers in the State."[58] Alsberg, however, defended Lewis's salary, pointing out that Lewis not only was responsible for his work on the Virginia project but also had responsibilities in Washington. "Therefore," he explained to Richardson, "we feel that the higher salary is justified."[59] When it became apparent that Alsberg would not change his mind about Lewis's raise, Richardson reluctantly accepted Alsberg's recommendation: "Mr. Lewis is a thoroughly nice fellow, with a great deal of ability—though, of course, he is not a seasoned writer. I should be perfectly happy to see him get an increase in salary."[60]

Black Employees, the Ex-Slave Project, and "Negro Bias"

The special projects on African American history and culture had a dual impact on the FWP's hiring of black employees. Such projects simultaneously made the employment of African Americans a necessity in order to establish their "authenticity," while they also provided a ready solution for occupying black workers who had been hired as a result of the federal office's requirements. However, most black employees were only allowed to contribute to FWP topics dealing specifically with African Americans. Brown expressed his hope of expanding the role of black FWP employees beyond their initial assignment as field workers for the Ex-Slave Project by making suggestions to state directors: "If the workers recommended for interviewing the ex-slaves and reconstruction Negroes are secured, perhaps they could do other assignments as well as interviewing."[61] However, in a memo summarizing the employment of blacks in the FWP state projects, it was noted that they were routinely assigned to "subjects pertaining especially to Negroes."[62]

Still, these projects were perceived as one of the few areas in which African American representatives, as employees of NWUs, could make an ineluctable difference by contributing a black perspective. The idea that a direct correlation existed between African American representation on the WPA's cultural projects and their ability to influence representations of black identity was also expressed in the *Negro Press Digest*, which documented the successes of African Americans in the WPA in addition to the setbacks. In particular, the Negro Projects received substantial coverage, and forthcoming FWP publications on culture were discussed. One article stated that "as many as 108 Negro editors, assistant editors, research workers, consultants, typists and office workers have been engaged in the work of the Federal Writers' Project," and projects on black history in Florida, Arkansas, Pennsylvania, and New York were already under way.[63] A lengthy description of *The Negro in Virginia* highlighted its importance as the "first book of its kind to adequately trace the part which the Negro has played in the history of a state." It was praised in the *Negro Press Digest* for its depiction of African Americans as educated, religious, hardworking members of the American South, who had made a substantial contribution to their region's "economic, industrial, civic, and cultural" development. "The book analyzes the Negro as a laborer, a craftsman, an artisan and as a business man."[64]

Regarding the credibility of the book's material on African American history and identity, the article pointed out that black employees were solely responsible for the project—"some fifteen competent Negro workers on the rolls of the WPA gathered, checked and compiled the material for this history"—and that they worked under the direction of a black supervisor; final editing, it was noted, had been done by Brown, the FWP's national editor of Negro Affairs. No mention was made of the input by the white state director of Virginia, Richardson.[65] The article also emphasized the inclusion of African American testimonials by ex-slaves, who had witnessed slavery firsthand. Through the incorporation of a black perspective, which the article referred to as a "unique departure from the usual historical reporting," the book promised to correct the previous historical narratives dominated by a white perspective.

African American interviewers proved to be an invaluable asset to the Ex-Slave Project, as former slaves tended to be much more forthcoming about the horrors and degradations they had experienced than they were in the presence of whites. Scholarship on the FWP slave narratives has long recognized the important role the interviewer's racial identity played in the type of narrative the ex-slave informant told. The social and political codes that governed almost every aspect of race relations in the South of the 1930s greatly affected ex-slaves' oral testimonies. White interviewers, products of Jim Crow, frequently referred to their ex-slave informants by the colloquial titles of the caste system, as "Auntie" and "Uncle."[66] As noted historian C. Vann Woodward aptly describes these encounters, "white interrogators customarily adopted a patronizing or at best paternalistic tone and at worst an offensive condescension. They flouted nearly every rule in the handbook of interview procedure. There were exceptions. . . . But as a rule, the questions were leading and sometimes insulting, the answers routine or compliant, and the insensitivity of the interrogator and the evasiveness of the interrogated were flagrantly displayed."[67] In addition to white interviewers' problematic deportment, a substantial number of ex-slaves interviewed by the FWP were still living on the plantations they had known from their childhood. Many of them had known the relatives of white interviewers as slave owners.[68] As a result, many former slaves were loath to discuss their experiences under slavery candidly. Instead, those who spoke to white interviewers often chose to follow what Paul Escott has referred to as "the ritual of racial etiquette," commenting on the happiness they had known in the "good old days" of slavery and enumerating the kindnesses they had received at the hands of their masters.[69]

While it is possible to compare the ex-slave stories submitted by members of the NWUs of Florida, Virginia, and Louisiana with those submitted by white interviewers, it would be impossible, on the basis of the interviewers' racial identity alone, to either accept or dismiss certain stories as fact or fiction. Individual interviewers fluctuated greatly in their ability to get an informant to speak openly about his or her remembrances of slavery, and they exhibited variations in the ways they wrote the interview material up afterward, although state directors' and editors' preferences can be detected in similarities by state. Some generalizations, however, can be made. For example, white interviewers tended to transcribe the ex-slave stories into a heavy, and often minstrel-like, phonetic dialect, while black interviewers, particularly the members of the NWUs, rarely used dialect, and when they did, they depicted it with a much lighter touch.[70] The slave narratives also exhibit dramatic differences in the portrayal, and the ex-slave's perception, of slavery. Those submitted by white interviewers in states such as Georgia, Texas, and Alabama make many more references to slavery as a beneficent institution and frequently quote ex-slaves referring nostalgically to pre-emancipation years as "the good old days."[71]

The slave narratives of the NWUs of Florida and Virginia, on the contrary, tend to tell more graphic stories of abuse and slave resistance as well as the joy expressed by slaves when they learned of their freedom. Although African American interviewers often differed from ex-slave informants in terms of their class identity and educational background, in the restrictive context of the segregated American South of the 1930s their shared racial identity was important. In this context, African American interviewers were frequently more successful than whites in obtaining information regarding the darker side of slavery, although the veracity of the narratives they collected was often challenged by white employees on charges of "Negro bias."[72]

Black employees of the FWP, along with their ex-slave informants, oper-ated in a social context where their objectivity regarding racial issues was continually being undermined as they were routinely accused of possessing a "Negro bias." The problem of establishing their authority, as either reporters or witnesses of an event as politically charged as slavery, was compounded by the fact that "Negro bias" was widely perceived by whites as having both genetic or racial and cultural bases. This view was partly supported by the belief that African Americans' racial characteristics predisposed them to expressions belonging to the realm of emotions rather than to that of the rational intellect. Music, dance, and storytelling were seen as areas in which African American artists could excel because of the race's emotional primitiv-ism, but such affectivity was considered antithetical to genres dependent on reason and logic. This view was summed up in a 1928 survey of "the Negro's" contribution to the arts, by Elizabeth Lay Green. Written just three years after the publication of Alain Locke's anthology *The New Negro*—a selection of some of the best African American writers of the Harlem Renaissance— Green noted that it was in the mediums of music and poetry that "the Negro so far has found his most natural means of expression." As for primarily liter-ary pursuits such as novel and drama writing, Green observed that it was "the white writer who [had] surpassed the Negro, even in the use of his own materials." The reason for this, according to Green, lay in the fact that these artistic forms demanded "a more *objective* view of their subject matter. But poetry, particularly shorter verse, offers a means of more subjective expression."[73] Thus, "the most valuable attributes of the Negro as artist—his imagination, extreme emotionalism, gift for melodious phrasing" worked best in mediums requiring little intellectual thought and literary effort.[74] Expressing a similar opinion, the white folklorist Dorothy Scarborough would claim, "The Negro is a born dramatist. Who else is capable of such epic largeness of gesture, such eloquent roll of eye, such expressive hesitation in speech?" Furthermore, she noted, these dramatic capabilities were not to be confused with the creativity of artistic genius but rather were part of his "racial" character: "The Negro is by nature a mimetic creature, dramatizing all he knows, his experiences and the life about him, expressing everything in form and motion."[75]

In league with this assumption that African Americans were "natural-born" storytellers was the idea that they so enjoyed telling fictions that they were predisposed to tell lies on almost any occasion. A prominent sociologist of the 1920s, Newbell Niles Puckett, explained that this trait had originated in West Africa as a survival mechanism and that it continued to flourish under the conditions of American slavery. Puckett quoted a nineteenth-century British military commander's observation on the "Negro peoples" of West Africa: "Concealment of design is the first element of safety, and as this axiom has been consistently carried out for generations, the national character is strongly marked by duplicity. The Negro lies habitually; and even in matters of little moment, or of absolute indifference, it is rare for him to speak the truth."[76] Puckett then immediately connected this to similar characteristics exhibited by southern blacks: "May not the organized hypocrisy of the Southern Negro also be an adaptation forced upon him by conditions of life?"[77] Moving quickly from an explanation of "Negro" lies as a method of survival under adverse circumstances, Puckett pointed out that "Negroes" were now as likely to lie about any subject, whether it affected them personally or not. Whether whites attributed blacks' tendency toward untruth to the forces of biology or environment, their steadfast belief in this "racial" characteristic made it very difficult for African Americans to be believed on any subject, least of all one as full of import as the institution of slavery.

FWP interviewers frequently expressed their reservations about the truthfulness of the ex-slaves' narratives and communicated these concerns to state directors. Two frustrated employees on the Georgia Project reported that their attempts to interview Lucius Edwards had been stymied by his lack of cooperation, but they decided this was because "he might be afraid he'd twist his tales and we'd catch him some way."[78] State directors also felt free to use their own judgment in determining the veracity of the ex-slave informants' narratives. In an initial assessment of the ex-slave interview material submitted to the federal office, Ohio state supervisor Miriam Logan summed up: "July 1937 interviews with ex-slaves disclose only two really interesting stories from negroes of an age to remember 'Before the War.' Many stories handed down, one or two 'made up,' to all appearances this is the sum-total of negro ex-slave stories in this county."[79] The report ended with this statement of authenticity: "The stories submitted are to all knowledge, true and are character studies of negroes who have come into the county from the south since 1890."[80] Logan had used the old-age pension list as a means of verifying the informants' identity as aged ex-slaves and justified her omission of several ex-slave interviews in this way: "Reverend Williams, Jesse Wilson, and several others whose names I did not take, because their stories were impossible to make anything out of, were not of the old-age pension list."[81] Many different factors prompted state directors to send testimonials regarding their narratives' authenticity or verifying particular elements of the ex-slave's story. Indiana's state director was repeating a tradition in the slave narrative genre almost a century old when he enclosed a prefatory testimonial with the slave narrative of Sarah Gudger and wrote this statement to George Cronyn: "On account of her unusual claim of 121 years as her actual age, I have included a preliminary statement in support of that claim. We have every reason to believe that her statement is correct, and I think that is also borne out by the two photographs . . . enclosed herewith."[82]

FWP federal and state directors quickly became aware of what a significant factor an interviewer's racial identity could be in eliciting contrasting narratives of slavery. A directive issued by the federal office exposed how the interviewer's persona and point of view could significantly alter the outcome of the ex-slaves' narratives. In responding to the federal office's request for second interviews with the same informant, the Arkansas state director mistakenly sent two different interviewers to obtain the same ex-slave's story. However, when she realized that this had resulted in two dramatically dissimilar narratives, she forwarded both to Alsberg with this note: "I mail you two different stories of the same . . . ex-slave. One of these was written by [an interviewer] of Fayetteville, in which town the ex-slave now resides. The other was written by [an interviewer] in whose family the old negro has lived for many years. The material in these two sketches is entirely different. Both stories are good. So, I sent them both that you may get the slant of different writers on the same rather important negro personage."[83]

But this knowledge was also used to discredit interviews that were obtained by black FWP employees. Some state directors concentrated their efforts on verifying the ex-slave narratives they had received from African American interviewers, particularly when the narratives included stories of slaveholders' abuse and mistreatment. Virginia director Richardson did not believe the narrative submitted by Roscoe Lewis, the director of the NWU, of ex-slave Henrietta King's facial disfigurement, inflicted on her when she was eight or nine years old by her mistress for taking a piece of candy. In order to whip her, the slaveholder had placed King's head beneath her rocking chair and rocked forward, keeping her in one place while she whipped her with rawhide. The weight crushed King's jawbone and made it impossible for her to ever eat solid food again; in King's words, it gave her "a false face. . . . What chilluns laugh at an' babies gits to cryin' at when dey sees me." "Dat's what slave days was like," King concluded.[84] Richardson decided this was a "gross exaggeration" and traveled to King's home in West Point to double-check Lewis's interview. Seeing King in person made Richardson realize the anecdote was true: "She looks exactly as Mr. Lewis describes her and [she] told me, almost word for word the story Mr. Lewis relates."[85] This experience, however, did not stop Richardson from interrogating the rest of the material Lewis wanted to include in *The Negro in Virginia*.

South Carolina state director Mabel Montgomery wrote to her district's director asking him to double-check a particular story: "The enclosed story was sent . . . to our Negro Supervisor. I am wondering whether the statement on page 4, indicated by red pencil, is really true; at least I have never encountered it in any of the other stories of slavery time. Would it be possible for you to personally visit this old Negro and interview her again, as if you had never read the story? I want to see whether she will make the same statement each time. If she does it is probably true, but I should like this check-up before sending it to Washington."[86] Making it clear that she was not pursuing this because of the federal office, Montgomery concluded: "Of course, you recall that Mr. Lomax said to send the stories 'as is,' but nevertheless in my opinion this statement needs verification. Perhaps you can add to it from your store of information about the Negroes."[87] It is evident that Montgomery's suspicions regarding the ex-slave's honesty were fostered by the knowledge that the interview had been conducted by a black field worker. The response of the district director, Chalmers Murray, supported her view. He agreed to check up on this informant because of his opinion "that she made up a great part of the tale out of the whole cloth, apparently being glad of the opportunity to give vent to her bitterness."[88] Citing Woodward's *A New American*

History as an authoritative source on the institution of slavery, he went on to explain to Montgomery that "most of the stories about cruel and inhuman treatment of slaves were sheer propaganda. No one in his good senses would treat a valuable piece of property in this way, slaves costing on an average of from 800.00 up. Woodward also points out, I believe, that the slave owners sometimes preferred to let the negroes remain in idleness when they could be working, rather than run the risk of injuring the health of their slaves. He seems to indicate that very few slaves ever performed a real honest day's work."[89] Murray closed his letter by expressing his complete dissatisfaction with the Ex-Slave Project:

> I have thought from the first that it was rather a mistake to write these ex-slave stories. Such stories are bound to be colored either by the interviewer or the person being interviewed. The general run of negro is only too glad of an opportunity to record his grievances against the white race in black and white. And the sentimental writers of the old school like to paint all pictures of the pre-war south in rosy colors. I have cautioned the district workers to avoid both extremes if possible, but in spite of this prejudice and propaganda will creep in.[90]

His real concern about the Project's potential lack of objectivity was revealed at the very end, when he suggested that the African American field worker had encouraged the racial bias of the ex-slave: "Naturally, an ex-slave will willingly pour out her tales of woe—real or imaginary—to a sympathetic listener like Ladson." To correct this racial bias, Murray planned to have the informant reinterviewed by a white female field worker: "A man, I am afraid, would get little from her."[91] Murray followed through on his promise; this resulted in two dramatically different narratives obtained from the same ex-slave informant. He sent a copy of the interview completed by the white field worker to Montgomery: "I am enclosing a copy of Miss Butler's interview with Susan Hamlin, ex-slave. It is a remarkable story—in fact one of the best of its kind that has been turned in so far. It is doubly remarkable because it flatly contradicts almost all of the statements in the article filed by the negro worker Ladson."[92] Murray jumped to the conclusion that the interview conducted by Ladson had been compromised by the worker's bias: "It is just as I thought; [the black worker] Ladson asked the woman a number of leading questions and literally put the words in her mouth. After all so much depends upon the method used by the interviewer. It is natural, I suppose, for Ladson to feel bitter about the former enslavement of his people, but he should not have allowed his personal feelings to enter into the matter. Miss Butler was perfectly fair in the way in which she put her questions."[93] Interestingly, in this statement, it is only the presumed bias of the black interviewer that is brought into question, not the potential subjectivity of the ex-slave. Murray's assumption rested on his perception of the ex-slave's role in the interview as an entirely passive one; the possibility that the ex-slave actively altered her narrative to suit different audiences was never considered. After consulting with Lomax in the federal office, Montgomery sent both narratives to Alsberg along with this explanation: "When a story came from [an ex-slave] as interviewed by Augustus Ladson, Negro worker on the Writers' Project, I doubted the statement . . . and asked Mr. Murray, then supervisor of the Charleston district to have [the ex-slave] re-interviewed by a white worker in order to test the accuracy of the statement. . . . You, therefore, have the unusual thing of two interviews of the same ex-slave, one by a white and one by a Negro."[94]

As this exchange demonstrates, African American employees' contributions to projects on black history encountered additional challenges and setbacks as white staff members tended to regard all materials submitted by their black coworkers as inherently biased and in need of correction; white objectivity regarding subjects pertaining to race, it was felt, had to be brought to bear on black writers' submissions. Brown later recalled correspondence the federal office received "in which the white supervisors would say 'You see, you can't trust a black interviewer. Look at the lies that are put here; my point of view is really what the truth is.' But the white interviewer was the one that wasn't getting the truth. You had that kind of battle."[95] If Brown, in his authoritative position as director of the Office on Negro Affairs in Washington, frequently encountered objections from state employees who felt that his identity, as an African American, was an insurmountable obstacle to his ability to view their submitted manuscripts pertaining to the history of slavery and black identity objectively, black employees at the city and state level had little hope of escaping white colleagues' and supervisors' scrutiny.

As Robert Stepto has pointed out, even a writer such as the abolitionist (and former slave) Frederick Douglass was continually reminded by his white friends and supporters that he was "better fitted to speak than to write." This emphasis on Douglass's value as an oral narrator was linked to the idea that speech was less consciously constructed than the act of writing and therefore closer to the unadulterated truth. Stepto describes this prejudice that Douglass encountered: "In those days, whenever Douglass strayed from narrating wrongs to denouncing them, Garrison would gently correct him by whispering, 'tell your story Frederick,' and John Collins would remark more directly, 'Give us the facts . . . we will take care of the philosophy.'"[96] Black writers employed by the Ex-Slave Project faced a similar dilemma; thus, the issue of presenting the material gathered from ex-slave interviews became a particularly thorny one for African American workers.

White FWP editors and state directors, who often regarded the material submitted by black employees with a suspicious and patronizing eye, were not reluctant, in the name of upholding the standards of scientific objectivity, to rewrite their submissions so that they might more accurately reflect "historical reality" as it appeared to a white perspective. Virginia state director Richardson, although she considered herself a liberal where racial matters were concerned, expressed this opinion regarding the truthfulness of the ex-slaves' accounts: "The ex-slaves who are quoted have told interesting stories—yet stories that must be taken with the well known grain of salt that Mr. [Roscoe] Lewis [the project's black supervisor] is not administering. I am entirely sympathetic with the Negro's desire for equality of opportunity. So I think I am writing now with the fingers of a liberal. I know the old Negro, moreover. He is a creature of fine imagination who likes to tell his stories after a manner that will be pleasing to his audience."[97] Significantly, Richardson did not restrict her criticism of the subjective (and therefore suspect and inaccurate) nature of the ex-slaves' narratives but included the black supervisor, Lewis, in her indictment. Lewis, who is depicted by Richardson as failing in his editorial responsibilities to administer "the well known grain of salt," does so, according to her letter, because he himself is predisposed to believe these accounts: "The stories Mr. Lewis quotes have been handed down from another generation and have received embellishments through the years. Mr. Lewis apparently takes them in all seriousness. While I think it is quite all right to quote the words of the Negroes interviewed, the author makes himself ridiculous when he does not let the reader know that much that he is quoting should be discounted."[98]

Richardson would take her concerns about Lewis's editorial work on the manuscript for *The Negro in Virginia* directly to Alsberg. In a letter she wrote to him, she brought up the issue of racial bias and the possible repercussions of Lewis's subjectivity:

> I poured out to you my fear that the material for the Negro book is being written with a bias that will react unfavorably upon the project, as well as upon inter-racial relations. . . . You are probably right in suggesting that we wait a while before asking Mr. Lewis to make extensive revisions in his manuscript. Yet I know that SLAVE ROW and parts of other chapters simply must not go to press without radical changes—and I am

a liberal Southerner really! I know, too, that you do want the point of view of liberal Virginians before the book is released.[99]

In this statement, Richardson implied that Lewis, as a black man, could not be representative of the view of liberal (that is, white) Virginians. Although Alsberg told Richardson "that it would be better not to ask Mr. Lewis to make a lot of revisions at this stage of the game," he attempted to placate her: "We very often get copy in here in the early stages that contains material that really could not appear in finished publications, but before the material ever reaches the presses the objectionable matter is removed or revised. . . . We agree in general with the points made in your letter on the subject. It is possible, of course, that when we all read Mr. Lewis' book as a whole we will feel that one chapter explains and balances another so that the complete volume is quite satisfactory."[100] Nine months later, as the project was nearing completion, Richardson again expressed her concerns over the accuracy and objectivity of the manuscript. In a letter to the assistant director of the FWP, Richardson wrote:

I think we should go slowly in the final version of the Negro book, since much is at stake for us all. While Mr. Lewis has done a remarkably fine piece of work, handicapped as he has been by lack of competent assistants, I have detected so many historical inaccuracies that I want to go over the entire script again and call to the task of challenging fact and policy at least two members of my staff. Then I hope some disinterested person, who is not as close to the subject as are those of us who have been going over the material will read the book carefully—this, of course, in addition to the reading that will be given the manuscript by Dr. Howe, President of Hampton Institute, who is the official sponsor.[101]

Why Richardson did not consider Dr. Howe a "disinterested person" is not made clear, but it is likely that she felt that his view might be compromised not only by his position as the publication's sponsor but by his biased perspective as the president of a historic black college. This time Richardson attempted to explain her preoccupation with the manuscript's "historical inaccuracies" as being based in her awareness of the importance of a good reception for a noble cause: "For the sake of Virginia, the Federal Writers' Project, the Works Progress Administration, the New Deal, and the cause of Negroes, this book must be good!"[102]

Failing to achieve the intervention she desired from the federal office, Richardson took it upon herself to correct the "Negro bias" she saw in the manuscript. In an interview given in 1972, Richardson would recall how she attempted to ensure that the material that ended up in *The Negro in Virginia* was accurate and objective. Noting that much of the historical materials gathered by her researchers "was written too soon after the Civil War, and had too much of a Negro bias to be accurate," Richardson claimed that she had spent two weeks alone rewriting the material. In addition, she employed an all-white staff "of people in Virginia who had to recheck everything that the Negroes had researched because we wanted to be sure that it wasn't biased one way or the other."[103]

Confronting the same problem they faced in the nineteenth century, African Americans who wished to speak and write about race relations in the United States in the 1930s were forced to devise ways to imbue their narratives with testimonials of their reliability. As William Andrews has pointed out, African American autobiography emerged as a genre that relied heavily on rhetorical strategies in order to prove that the black narrator was a purveyor of truth—a truth teller: "In the first 100 years of its existence, Afro-American autobiography was a genre chiefly distinguished by its rhetorical aims. During the first half of this century of evolution, most Afro-American autobiography addressed itself, directly or indirectly, to the proof of this proposition . . . that the black narrator was, despite all prejudice and propaganda, a truth-teller, a reliable transcriber of the experience and character of black folk."[104] Black writers employed to collect the oral testimonies of former slaves faced a similar challenge. Although the Ex-Slave Project initially promised to provide a discursive space for the articulation of an African American perspective on the institution and history of American slavery, it too was plagued by assumptions of "Negro bias." African American employees, however, were highly conscious of working within this context of white skepticism and developed a variety of strategies for functioning within these narrowly defined parameters of what constituted "acceptable" discourse on the sensitive history of racial relations in American society. In order to justify and legitimate representations of black history, culture, and identity that often differed sharply from those produced by their white colleagues, black writers, such as those employed by Florida's NWU, resorted to certain types of narrative strategies, which will be discussed in chapter 7. First, however, it is helpful to look at ethnographer and writer Zora Neale Hurston's struggles to gain authority as a black interlocutor to collect and interpret black folk culture, and her experience as an employee of Florida's NWU as a case study of black employees in the FWP.

CHAPTER SIX

Conjure Queen
Zora Neale Hurston and Black Folk Culture

Mouths don't empty themselves unless the ears are sympathetic and knowing.
—Zora Neale Hurston, *Mules and Men*, 1935

Four years before the writer and ethnographer Zora Neale Hurston would be hired in 1938 to work for the Federal Writers' Project (FWP), she submitted an article to the satirically irreverent monthly review *American Mercury*.[1] Using an allegory drawn from the advertising world to illustrate the commodification that lay behind fictionalized representations of black culture, "You Don't Know Us Negroes" argued that the portrayals of African Americans by white writers bore the same resemblance to real black Americans as margarine did to butter: "Margarine is yellow, it is greasy, it has a taste that paraphrases butter. It even has the word 'butter' printed on the label often. In short, it has everything butterish about it except butter. And so the writings that made out they were holding a looking-glass to the Negro had everything in them except Negroness."[2] What Hurston decried most of all was the widespread acceptance of these fictions as ethnographic fact by unsuspecting white audiences: "Show some folks a genuine bit of Negro-ness and they rear and pitch like a mule in a tin stable. 'But where is the misplaced preposition?' they wail. 'Where is the Am it and I'se?'. . . . The rules and regulations of this Margarine Negro calls for two dumb Negroes who chew up dictionaries and spit out grammar. . . . All Negro characters must have pop eyes. The only time when they are excused from popping is when they are rolling in fright."[3]

Hurston's comic depiction of stereotypes drawn from the tradition of blackface minstrelsy was a strategic attempt to undermine white writers' (mis)representations and validate her own collection of black folk culture using the concept of "authenticity." Although she named a few white writers, such as Dubose Heyward, Julia Peterkin, and Paul Green, who "looked further than the too obvious outside," even they could not penetrate to the heart of African American culture. The stereotype of the happy-go-lucky, banjo-picking African American (one thinks of John Lomax's marketing of Leadbelly) "may be very good vaudeville, but I'm sorry to be such an image-breaker and say we just don't live like that."[4]

As her essay suggests, Hurston authenticated her work by drawing a critical distinction between the performances black folk delivered for white audiences (both to folk collectors and for purposes of commercial entertainment) and the "real" stuff of black culture that remained invisible to white outsiders. "I learned," she wrote, "that most white people have seen our shows but not our lives. If they have not seen a Negro show they have seen a minstrel or at least a blackface comedian and that is considered enough. They know all about us."[5] There was more than a bit of voyeurism in white audiences' embrace of these misrepresentations of black culture and identity, but little did whites understand that their peep show was a fiction.

Through her frequent references to rampant commercialism, Hurston indicated, too, that these distortions of African American identity were inseparably linked to the exploitation of black culture as a marketable commodity: "Whenever I pick up one of the popular magazines and read one of these mammy cut tales I often wonder whether the author actually believes that his tale is probable or whether he knows it is flapdoodle and is merely concerned about the check."[6] Hurston was not reticent when exposing the ignorance of white folklorists about black folk culture. In a letter to her mentor, the renowned anthropologist Franz Boas, she criticized even the best known scholars of her day, the regionalists Howard Odum and Guy Johnson, for their gross mislabeling of black folk songs and their greed in capitalizing on the market's interest in "Negro" material: "they could hardly be less exact. . . . Let them but hit upon a well turned phrase and another volume slops off the press."[7]

Because Hurston was a trained ethnographer who had studied at Barnard under Boas, her professional career and impact on the FWP would seem assured. Nonetheless, despite her credentials and considerable talent, she could take nothing for granted because of prevailing assumptions about race as well as gender, which underlay the identity of the professional anthropologist. Hurston continually occupied the interstitial position of one who is both an objective observer and a member of the culture under observation. African American intellectuals who wished to represent their "race" would base their ability to do so primarily on their membership within that racially defined identity. But for Hurston, who was struggling to work as an ethnographer and collector of black folk culture within the Eurocentric, male-dominated field of anthropology, her "racial" identity was seen as conflicting with the requisite objectivity of the social scientist. This necessitated strategies that Lomax never had to employ and required her to continually perform different aspects of her identity, depending on audience and context.

This chapter will focus on Hurston's efforts, using the identities of gender, race, and class as tools, to delicately navigate the challenges she faced as a middle-class, African American ethnographer during an era in which the qualities of the social scientist, membership in the bourgeoisie, and American citizenship were viewed as attributes of whiteness. Hurston and other African American interlocutors for black folk culture regularly encountered the inherent hazards of "going native." By identifying themselves as members of the community under observation, they were risking the invalidation of their professional identity on the basis of that same "racial" identity. The accusations leveled at black Americans—that they were mentally inferior and incapable of being sufficiently objective—were predicated on assumptions about "racial" character. The trick for African American ethnographers such as Hurston was to present themselves as black, but not too black. Thus, educated African Americans who sought to act as cultural interlocutors for black folk culture were placed in the difficult position of simultaneously accentuating and deemphasizing their racial identity. On the one hand, black interlocutors laid claim to a unique "insider" perspective that was invaluable in penetrating to the core of African American culture, while, on the other hand, they argued that their education and middle-class background had sufficiently distanced them from the African American folk, providing them with the objectivity necessary for accurate observation and representation.

Hurston wished to claim for herself both a unique objectivity regarding African American identity and an insider's ability to hear and accurately record the black vernacular. In a segment she wrote while employed by the FWP for the manuscript "The Florida Negro," Hurston identified what she felt had been her primary contribution to literature on black Americans. She wrote:

> Zora Neale Hurston won critical acclaim for two new things in Negro fiction. The first was an objective point of view. The subjective view was so universal that it had come to be taken for granted. When her first book . . . appeared in 1934, the critics announced across the nation, "Here at last is a Negro story without bias." . . . The second element that attracted attention was the telling of the story in the idiom—not the dialect—of the Negro. . . . It gave verisimilitude to the narrative by stewing the subject in its own juice.[8]

This description in 1938 of what she felt she had already achieved invites us to explore how she strove to present black folk culture in ways that were objective but yet immersive, something she claimed other writers, black as well as white, could not accomplish.

Mules and Men

Mules and Men was Hurston's first major work as an ethnographer. Published three years before she joined the FWP, it reveals how she shifted her identity within the same work. It is divided into two parts: part one consists entirely of folk tales and the people who tell them; part two focuses on hoodoo, African American folk medicine traditions and religious practices, and Hurston's apprenticeship with several hoodoo doctors.[9] But textually, Hurston makes three strategic moves in self-presentation that accompany the three different locations she takes the reader as she conducts her fieldwork—from a member of the folk community in her hometown of Eatonville, to professional ethnographer and participant-observer in the labor camps of Polk County, to apprentice of hoodoo in New Orleans. These roles can be viewed as a précis for how she worked to position herself extratextually vis-à-vis her white patrons, white colleagues, black intellectuals, and folk informants, strategically maneuvering and negotiating the lines of race, class, and gender.

In *Mules and Men*, the tensions between Hurston's insider identity and her need to establish her professional authority repeatedly surface. On the first page of her introduction to *Mules and Men*, Hurston carefully delineates her qualifications by emphasizing her dual identity as a member of the black folk and as an objective social scientist:

> I was glad when somebody told me, "You may go and collect Negro folklore." In a way it would not be a new experience for me. When I pitched headforemost into the world I landed in the crib of negroism. From the earliest rocking of my cradle, I had known about the capers Brer Rabbit is apt to cut and what the Squinch Owl says from the house top. But it was fitting me like a tight chemise. I couldn't see for wearing it. It was only when I was off in college, away from my native surroundings, that I could see myself like somebody else and stand off and look at my garment. Then I had to have the spy-glass of Anthropology to look through at that.[10]

By referring to her racial identity and the cultural heritage that came with it through the metaphor of a garment, Hurston suggests her understanding of black folk culture is dyed-in-the-wool. Yet she also indicates that the knowledge and tools of the social scientist—"the spy-glass of Anthropology"—

Zora Neale Hurston in boat, collecting folklore, late 1930s. From Zora Neale Hurston Papers, Department of Special and Area Studies Collections, George A. Smathers Libraries, University of Florida. Courtesy of Jane Belo Estate, Gift of Stetson Kennedy.

enable her to temporarily step outside this racial identity and objectively examine it. Boas, who wrote the foreword for *Mules and Men,* was careful to situate the value of her scholarly contribution to the study of African American folk culture within the unusual perspective granted to her by virtue of her "racial" and regional identity. "It is the great merit of Miss Hurston's work," he wrote, "that she entered into the homely life of the southern Negro as one of them and was fully accepted as such by the companions of her childhood."[11] The problem for white interlocutors regarding the inevitable evasiveness of black informants became for Hurston, as Boas acknowledged, an asset to her chosen avocation: "Thus she has been able to penetrate through that affected demeanor by which the Negro excludes the White observer effectively from participating in his true inner life."[12]

Yet, like her white colleagues, Hurston would discuss the challenges involved in fieldwork, such as reluctant informants, as a way of highlighting her own skills and elevating the value of the collected material: "Folklore is not as easy to collect as it sounds. The best source is where there are the least outside influences and these people, being usually under-privileged, are the shyest." But unlike Lomax and Lydia Parrish, who attributed black informants' reticence to negative qualities, such as plain orneriness or unreliability, Hurston explains the exchange in terms of the value of the material to the informants themselves: "They are most reluctant at times to reveal that which the soul lives by."[13] Next, in a linguistic feat, she underscores her unique position as a black collector of black folk culture by shifting personal pronouns, writing herself within the black community and naming the strategies by which African Americans stonewall white trespassers: "And the Negro, in spite of his open-faced laughter, his seeming acquiescence, is particularly evasive. You see we are a polite people and we do not say to our questioner, 'Get out of here!' We smile and tell him or her something that satisfies the white person because, knowing so little about us, he doesn't know what he is missing. The Indian resists curiosity by a stony silence. The Negro offers a feather-bed resistance. That is, we let the probe enter, but it never comes out. It gets smothered under a lot of laughter and pleasantries."[14] Hurston linguistically "goes native," crossing over the traditional division separating folklorist from informant. For the first part of the statement, she speaks as the ethnographer discussing subjects by using the identifying phrases of "these people," "they," and "the Negro." But in the middle of this observation, she changes from third-person plural to first-person plural, "we," and includes herself along with her subjects as an example of black behavior. Susan Willis is among the scholars who have recognized the symbolic importance of

Hurston's shifts in pronouns. Willis notes that such oscillations "enable Hurston to be both Southern and not-Southern, black and not-black, inferior and not-inferior."[15] Michael Staub also comments on the ways this linguistic strategy allows Hurston to fluidly shift her identity and move between different speech communities and "different worlds, one black and oral and one (presumably in large part) white and literate. Ironically, perhaps, readers accept Hurston's authority as narrator because she writes a 'white' English, while her black informants accept Hurston as native because she speaks a black dialect."[16]

The book breaks significantly from established ethnographic conventions in several ways: by resisting the traditional dichotomous insider/outsider perspective of most ethnographies; by demonstrating the ethnographer's effect on the community under observation; by highlighting rather than effacing the power relationships between reader, author, and subjects; and by adopting a theatrical mode in which Hurston plays the central character.[17] However, many of the conventions Hurston employs for establishing her textual authority as a scientific observer were patterned after familiar conventions found in the companion volumes written by anthropologists and folklorists on their experiences in the field. Published as the popular counterparts to academic works by social scientists, these books centered on the ethnographer as the central protagonist in the narrative and followed him or her through a series of misadventures in the field.

Hurston, like FWP director Henry Alsberg, was influenced by contemporary ethnographic and travel literature; she was an admirer of this type of genre—and a self-admitted fan of such ethnographic travel narratives as W. B. Seabrook's work on Haiti, *Magic Island*, and Sir James Frazer's *The Golden Bough*.[18] The *Saturday Review*, in its notice about Hurston's 1938 study of African Caribbean folk culture, recognized her propensity to merge the conventions of sentimental travel narratives with ethnographic observations. As the reviewer remarked, "'Tell My Horse' is a curious mixture of remembrances, travelogue, sensationalism, and anthropology. The remembrances are vivid, the travelogue tedious, the sensationalism reminiscent of Seabrook, and the anthropology a melange of misinterpretation and exceedingly good folk-lore."[19]

Nonetheless, Hurston would lay the responsibility for the format of *Mules and Men*, consisting of ethnographic material and the in-between conversations and action that took place between her and the informants, so reminiscent of the travel narrative genre, at the feet of her publisher. Although Hurston's own inclinations tended less toward the scholarly and scientific aspects of her material and more toward the aesthetic and theatrical elements, a letter she wrote to Boas shortly before the publication of *Mules and Men* indicates that she was pressured by her publishers at Lippincott to make the material more accessible. Regarding the delay in Boas's receipt of the manuscript, Hurston wrote: "The reason that the publishers did not send the last half of my book on to you, was they were getting me to revise certain parts. They felt that it was too technical for the average reader. I was required to do something more acceptable for public reading."[20] It is evident that the publishers wanted the book to have a wide, popular appeal. Certainly, they were well aware of the potential selling point of having Boas's approval on the first page. As Hurston noted, "they are very, very eager for you to do the introduction."[21]

Hurston noted that it wasn't only Lippincott who had desired such changes in the manuscript. As she reported to Boas, "I have inserted the between-story conversation and business because when I offered it without it, every publisher said it was too monotonous. Now three houses want to publish it."[22] Still, Hurston was concerned that Boas would be put off by the unscholarly approach she had taken and might refuse to lend his endorsement. "I hope," she wrote, "that the unscientific matter that must be there for the sake of the average reader will not keep you from writing the introduction."[23] She went on to assure him that the additional material had also been faithfully recorded from her field experiences: "It so happens that the conversations and incidents are true. But of course I never would have set them down for scientists to read. . . . [They] need no stimulation. But the man in the street is different."[24]

Perhaps because *Mules and Men* begins with Hurston's return to her native town of Eatonville, Florida, scholars have taken this as the embryonic symbol of the entire text as well as of Hurston's identity. It is the most often quoted part of the text, and it is narratively important, for it sets up Hurston's return with "the spy-glass of Anthropology" in hand, to her black roots. Despite her best efforts to play the role of ethnographer, this mantle of scientific authority is stripped from her by the folks who know her best. Although Hurston emphasizes her special ability, as a black ethnographer, to penetrate into the heart of the African American folk community, she notes that her "racial" identity will not be enough to grant her immediate access to any black community: "I knew that even *I* was going to have some hindrance among strangers."[25] Thus, Hurston goes to her hometown first, because "here in Eatonville I knew everybody was going to help me."[26]

But her biographer, Robert Hemenway, and other scholars who have re-iterated Hurston's claims that she was an inside member of the black folk community are much mistaken. Hemenway asserts: "Hurston was not one generation removed [from southern folk culture] . . . and she embodied a closer association with racial roots than any other Renaissance writer. Where they were Los Angeles or Cleveland, she was Eatonville. *She was the folk.*"[27] Hurston had access to African American folk traditions and they influenced her a great deal, but to suggest that she belonged to the folk—the impover-ished and largely uneducated black working class—is to overlook the het-erogeneous and complex hierarchy that existed in African American communities.

Hurston's childhood was solidly middle class until early adolescence, when the death of her mother disrupted the family, leaving Hurston to suffer economic as well as emotional deprivation. Both of her parents were edu-cated; her father, in addition to working as a skilled carpenter, was a successful preacher and had served as the mayor of Eatonville for three terms. Her mother had been a schoolteacher before she was married, and she empha-sized the importance of education by providing her children with additional schooling at home. The Hurstons had six children, but they lived in an eight-room house on five acres of land, and her father took pride in the fact that his wife never had to work to make ends meet.[28]

Although Hurston's mother never tried to inhibit her daughter's active imagination, as an educated woman from one of the better families, Mrs. Hurston held no truck with the prevailing community folk traditions. One of Hurston's most traumatic experiences occurred when she was unable to ensure that her mother's dying request—not to be subjected to the folk rituals associated with death and mourning—be carried out.[29] Although Hurston would note that "the world we lived in required those acts," it is clear that her mother, the most important figure to Hurston in her formative years, took care to raise her children in an atmosphere free of those traditions and superstitions.[30]

In her autobiography and also in the opening to *Mules and Men*, Hurston would recall spending as much time as possible on the porch of Eatonville's main store, Joe Clarke's, listening in on the men—gainfully unemployed as the town's Homers—trading insults and swapping lies. She rightly acknowl-edged a huge debt to this arena in which daily performances of the black vernacular and African American folk culture were offered for free, but as a child, she was a spectator and observer rather than an active member of that vernacular community. "Naturally, I picked up the reflections of life around me with my own instruments, and absorbed what I gathered according to my inside juices."[31] Hurston's father did not like her spending time there: "I was not allowed to sit around there, naturally. But, I could and did drag my feet going in and out whenever I was sent there for something to allow whatever was being said to hang in my ear."[32] And the storytelling skills Hurston so admired and tried to emulate at home were greatly discouraged by her grandmother as well as her father.

According to Hurston's contemporaries, such as Arna Bontemps, much of the material she published as short stories and in *Mules and Men*, had first appeared in her oral performances at parties.[33] When Hurston arrived in New York City in 1925, she quickly established herself as a flamboyant raconteur within social circles that included such luminaries as white writers Fannie Hurst and Carl Van Vechten, and W. E. B. Du Bois, editor of the NAACP's *Crisis* magazine. Drawing upon her Eatonville repertoire, Hurston regaled both white and black listeners with folktales from her youth. Her audiences, including those who took part in the Harlem Renaissance, were largely unfamiliar with southern rural African American culture; Hurston performed her role as an inside member of the folk not only for northern whites but for northern blacks as well. As her erstwhile friend the poet Langston Hughes would later write in his autobiography regarding those years, "Zora Neale Hurston was certainly the most amusing. Only to reach a wider audience, need she ever write books—because she is a perfect book of entertainment in herself."[34]

Hurston's Performances of Blackness

Hurston was quite aware of the performative quality inherent in being black in America. Regarding African Americans' position as the central focus of the national drama of race relations, she commented: "It is quite exciting to hold the center of the national stage, with the spectators not knowing whether to laugh or to weep."[35] Hemenway insightfully observes that Hurston was a mass of personal contradictions as well as a consummate performer. Hurston was viewed primarily in terms of her "racial" identity by many of the white scholars and patrons she came into professional contact with, but she also cultivated such associations in order to further her career and fund her research. While she was a graduate student at Columbia, she worked for the anthropologist Melville Herskovits. He used her not only as a research assistant but as a subject for the work he was doing on African survivals among American Negroes. Examining her gestures while she sang Negro spirituals,

Herskovits noted that although Hurston was "more White than Negro in her ancestry," her "manner of speech, her expressions,—in short, her motor behavior . . . would be termed typically Negro."[36]

Throughout her career, Hurston also proved adept at presenting herself to whites in ways that frequently conformed to their expectations. Hughes would later recall that "she was always getting scholarships and things from wealthy white people, some of whom simply paid her just to sit around and represent the Negro race for them, she did it in such a racy fashion. . . . To many of her white friends, no doubt, she was a perfect 'darkie,' in the nice meaning they give the term—that is a naive, childlike, sweet, humorous, and highly colored Negro."[37] However, many of Hurston's writings, especially those regarding her wealthy white patron, the society matron Mrs. Charlotte Osgood Mason, reveal that she chafed at the economic necessities that compelled these types of performances.

Mason was a benefactor to many Harlem Renaissance intellectuals, not only Hurston, who called her "Godmother," but also Langston Hughes, Alain Locke, and the folklorist Arthur Huff Fauset.[38] But Mason was a firm believer in essentialist notions of black racial identity and frequently chided her protégés if she felt they were betraying their ancestral African roots. She expected American writers like Hughes and Hurston to "be primitive and know and feel the intuitions of the primitive." But as Hughes explained in his autobiography, "I was not Africa. I was Chicago and Kansas City and Broadway and Harlem. And I was not what she wanted me to be."[39]

Like Hughes, Hurston recorded her patron's insatiable desire for performances of black primitivism. As Hurston noted wryly, "Godmother was extremely human. There she was sitting up there at the table over capon, caviar and gleaming silver, eager to hear every word on every phase of life on a saw-mill 'job.' I must tell the tales, sing the songs, do the dances, and repeat the raucous sayings and doings of the Negro farthest down."[40] This quotation lays bare the expectations of white upper-class audiences for the entertainment value of black folk culture. But it also reveals Hurston's double role acting as ethnographer and native informant. Out of financial need, Hurston would don the mask of the black performer for her wealthy white patron, thereby participating in a type of self-commodification. "Godmother" would frequently try to control her by forbidding Hurston to communicate with others besides herself, placing the material Hurston had collected under lock and key, and scolding her for what she perceived as profligate behavior. Such admonishment, Hurston privately related to Hughes, "destroys my self-respect and utterly demoralizes me for weeks."[41]

The insights Hurston gained from firsthand experience, regarding power relationships and performance, inform the first part of *Mules and Men*. The folktales are diagnostic of power relations based on race, class, and gender, but the context in which they are performed is just as important, Hurston indicates, for understanding how oral performance is a vital weapon in the arsenal of the underdog or, in this case, mule.[42] The sexual politics that form the central theme of *Mules and Men* are displayed in the folktales themselves as well as in the informal verbal sparring that occurs between the men and women in social gatherings. Cheryl Wall has recognized the central importance of Hurston's inclusion of her informants' dialogue, for it is one of the few areas in which women can participate in the oral performance.[43] Although a few tales are told by women, women mostly appear as subjects in the misogynistic tales of the men. By recording the impromptu oral performances of the gathering, Hurston provides a forum in which women can and do top their menfolk. However, it is essential to note that Hurston's inclusion of the female voice simultaneously draws attention to the ways in which women's speech is also disempowered in the company of men.

Sexuality is another means by which the women of Eatonville negotiate for male favor. The "toe party" that Hurston attends, so named because the women line up behind a sheet and the men bid on their toes, is illustrative of this negotiation between the sexes. As one of Hurston's informants explains the procedure: "When all de toes is in a line, sticking out from behind de sheet they let de men folks in and they looks over all de toes and buys de ones they want for a dime. Then they got to treat de lady dat owns dat toe to everything she want. Sometime they play it so's you keep de same partner for de whole thing and sometime they fix it so they put de girls back every hour or so and sell de toes agin."[44] Hurston relates with some pride that her toe was sold five times over the course of the evening. But she notes that the system occasionally breaks down, as when "fellows ungallantly ran out of the door rather than treat the girls whose toe they had bought sight unseen."[45] In this way, even black female sexuality is an uncertain and unstable means of leverage in the unequal power struggle between the sexes. It didn't stop Hurston, however, from using it as a tool in her fieldwork. As her FWP colleague Stetson Kennedy recalled of Hurston's folklore expeditions with John Lomax's son, "Alan said that in the field Zora was absolutely magnificent, singing and dancing and acting and cutting the fool, and he put it this way, that she could 'outnigger' any of them, and said she'd butter up and honey the men so they wouldn't ask for money, and she'd honey up to the men sometimes to such a degree that she'd have to jump in that Chevy of hers and run for her life."[46]

Hurston's many anecdotes centering on her easy and successful rapport with her informants serve the same purpose such stories did for white ethnographers, but they are also keen reminders of the distance black middle-class interlocutors could feel between themselves and their uneducated informants. For Hurston, it was just as important to prove her successful infiltration of black communities in order to lend authority to her ethnographic representations as it seems to have been for ethnographers who were estranged from their informants on the basis of "racial" identity. To achieve this central trope of the ethnographic genre, Hurston played up her class difference through an invocation of bourgeois patriarchal gender norms.

Participant-Observer

The second stage of *Mules and Men* commences when Hurston journeys to Polk County, "where they really lies up a mess and dats where dey makes up all de songs and things lak dat."[47] It is here where the difference between Hurston's class and educational background and that of her informants will really reveal itself and where she relies most heavily on standard ethnographic conventions to establish her authority as a participant-observer. Polk County, thus named as the mythical place of origin for African American folk expression and the place where "de water drink lak cherry wine," is set up simultaneously as the ethnographer's dream—to actually locate the headwaters of folk culture—and as the beginning of her descent into the seamier side of the African American community. In this rough section of Polk County, the women fight over their wayward menfolk, and instead of words the weapons are knives and guns.

The gap between Hurston and the inhabitants of the Everglades Cypress Lumber Company is immediately made evident upon her arrival: "Very little was said directly to me and when I tried to be friendly there was a noticeable disposition to *fend* me off."[48] As Hurston points out to the reader, the "featherbed" tactics traditionally employed by African Americans to resist white questioners are now being turned against her; clearly, in this black community, Hurston is an outsider: "I stood there awkwardly, knowing that the too-ready laughter and aimless talk was window-dressing for my benefit."[49] Moreover, it is revealed that she is considered an outsider: "They all thought I must be a revenue officer or a detective of some kind. They were accustomed to strange women dropping into the quarters, but not in shiny gray Chevrolets. They usually came plodding down the big road or counting railroad ties. The car made me look too prosperous. So they set me aside as different."[50] But it is not just the car that is the problem. Hurston's clothes also serve as a giveaway that she is not a member of the folk: "I mentally cursed the $12.74 dress from Macy's that I had on among all the $1.98 mail-order dresses. I looked about and noted the number of bungalow aprons and even the rolled down paper bags on the heads of several women. I did look different and resolved to fix all that no later than the next morning."[51] By relating her initial failure to infiltrate the community and her discomfiture at the realization that she has badly misstepped, Hurston is utilizing one of the ethnographer's oldest tricks to convince her reader of the verity of her later account of this community. Such "fables of rapport," as historian James Clifford refers to them, are "an established convention for staging the attainment of ethnographic authority." Like Hurston's early failure to penetrate the protective mask of these rural folk, such stories "normally portray the ethnographer's early ignorance, misunderstanding, lack of contact—frequently a sort of childlike status within the culture. . . . [Eventually] these states of innocence or confusion are replaced by adult, confident, disabused knowledge."[52]

Realizing her mistakes, Hurston quickly adopts a new persona in order to gain acceptance from the impoverished and lawless community. She claims that she is also, like many of her informants, on the run from the law: "I took occasion that night to impress the job with the fact that I was also a fugitive from justice, 'bootlegging.' They were hot behind me in Jacksonville and they wanted me in Miami. So I was hiding out. That sounded reasonable. Bootleggers always have cars. I was taken in."[53] Hurston proves that she is fluent in speaking the native tongue. When the locals voice their suspicions, Hurston makes up a story to explain her fancy dress and conveys it using the local idiom: " 'Oh, Ah ain't got doodley squat,' I countered. 'Mah man brought me dis dress de las' time he went to Jacksonville. We wuz sellin' plenty stuff den and makin' good money. Wisht Ah had dat money now.' "[54] Hurston juxtaposes her use of white Standard English for the scientific voice of authority in the text with her adoption of the black vernacular as a way of highlighting the two different identities she is operating under: the voice of educated "whiteness" establishes her authority as an ethnographic observer, and the voice of the black folk shows her facility as a "native" speaker.[55]

Such tactics serve more than one purpose. They prove Hurston's worth as an ethnographer who can readily adapt herself to an unfamiliar culture; she manages to obtain access to the inner circle. Hurston revels in her demonstrated ability to "go native" by singing all the bawdy verses to the folk song "John Henry" and by "spreading my jenk"[56] at the local watering hole: "By the time that the song was over, before Joe Willard lifted me down from the table I knew that I was in the inner circle. I had first to convince the 'job' that I was not an enemy in the person of the law; and, second, I had to prove that I was their kind. 'John Henry' got me over my second hurdle."[57] However, in spite of Hurston's success infiltrating this folk community—achieved through her accurate performance of the folk song—the fact that it is a performance highlights the fundamental difference between the black bourgeois identity of Hurston and the black folk of the lumber mill town. In this section of the ethnography, Hurston purposely and repeatedly underscores her essential class difference from the members of this community.[58]

One of the most fundamental ways Hurston conveys that Polk County is, despite "racial" similarities, radically dissimilar to her native community of Eatonville is by emphasizing the extremely violent nature of the community. How violent is it? Hurston demonstrates how far Polk County is from civilized bourgeois values by falling back on an inversion of traditional gender roles. Polk County is so savage that women are the primary perpetrators of brutal acts. Moreover, the barbaric nature of the womenfolk is so commonplace that the law has been modified to suit their heightened criminal nature. As Hurston cracks, "Negro women *are* punished in these parts for killing men, but only if they exceed the quota. I don't remember what the quota is. Perhaps I did hear but I forgot. One woman had killed five when I left that turpentine still where she lived. The sheriff was thinking of calling on her and scolding her severely."[59] The way Hurston tells it, the men of Polk County are the endangered species, and it is the women who threaten Hurston's safety during her stay there. The violent nature of the local women enables Hurston to dramatically contrast them with her own genteel, middle-class, feminine self.[60]

Hurston's gendered identity, like her "racial" identity, was often a performance modulated by the instabilities and tensions of class. Like Hurston, other middle-class women working as documentarians in the 1930s, such as the photographers Dorothea Lange, Marion Post Wolcott, and Margaret Bourke-White, found new opportunities to create representations of their "poorer sisters."[61] However, in breaking previous gender restrictions, finding ways to mark their middle-class identity became indispensable to achieving professional authority. As Paula Rabinowitz has observed: "These women negotiated precarious positions for themselves as artists, documentarians, and commercial photographers by using the signs of middle-class femininity—their supervising eyes"—to examine the lives of working-class women.[62] Hurston would make use of her "supervising eyes," contrasting her bourgeois behavior with that of her Polk County sisters, as a means of establishing her ethnographic authority within the text of *Mules and Men*.

The dramatic climax of this section revolves around the threats made to Hurston's life by Lucy, a jealous member of the community. Hurston would later describe the savage aspect of the community: "That is the primeval flavor of the place, and as I said before, out of this primitive approach to things, I all but lost my life."[63] The final showdown between the two women and the business that leads up to it enable Hurston to bring in yet another convention of the ethnographic travel narrative, the character of the faithful native informant. Just as John Lomax would tell stories about his loyal sidekick, Leadbelly, Hurston related how she cultivated a relationship with Big Sweet. In her autobiography, Hurston recalled how she learned of Big Sweet's reputation. As Hurston's landlady described her: "Tain't a man, woman nor child on this job going to tackle Big Sweet. If God send her a pistol she'll send him a man. She can handle a knife with anybody. . . . She done kilt two mens on this job and they said she kilt some before she ever come here."[64]

On the basis of this report, Hurston, who "felt as timid as an egg without a shell," decides to befriend Big Sweet. She is so successful that Big Sweet swears to protect her: "I loves to friend with somebody like you. I aims to look out for you, too. Do your fighting for you. Nobody better not start nothing with you, do I'll get my switch-blade and go round de ham-bone looking for meat."[65] But Big Sweet's role goes beyond that of protector; she quickly becomes Hurston's devoted native informant, the person with enough status in the community to actively assist Hurston with her collecting. As Hurston would recall: "After that everything went well for me. Big Sweet helped me to collect material in a big way. She had no idea what I wanted with it, but if I wanted it, she meant to see that I got it. She pointed out people who knew songs and stories. She wouldn't stand for balkiness on their part."[66] When Big Sweet hears the rumor that Lucy is going to attack Hurston, she pledges her assistance on the basis of Hurston's genteel nature, carefully articulating the class differences between them. After detailing the best way to stab an opponent to death, Big Sweet tells Hurston: "But don't you bother 'bout no fighting. You ain't like me. You don't even sleep with no mens. I wanted to be a virgin one time, but I couldn't keep it up. I needed the money too bad. But I think it's nice for you to be like that. You just keep on writing down them lies. I'll take care of all de fighting."[67] Hurston has Big Sweet bespeak the contrast between them by emphasizing Hurston's bourgeois values of sexual purity and good breeding.

Hurston tries to head off a showdown between Lucy and Big Sweet by suggesting that they leave early. She contrasts her own civilized nature with her friend's primitive bloodlust: "I knew that Big Sweet didn't mind fighting; didn't mind killing and didn't too much mind dying. I began to worry a bit."[68] The fight is ended before any blood is drawn by the timely arrival of the Quarters Boss, who is carrying two pistols. But as it turns out, the fight has only been delayed. A week later at another big party, Lucy tries to attack Hurston again. Once again Big Sweet comes to her rescue, but this time the brawl turns into a free-for-all and Hurston barely manages to jump in her car and escape. Hurston's depiction of being put in harm's way through her devotion to her work was a standard trope of the ethnographer's encounters with primitive "others." Like Lomax, Hurston would demonstrate a flair for self-dramatization in describing the perils of fieldwork and the lengths to which she had gone for her work: "My search for knowledge of things took me into many strange places and adventures. My life was in danger several times. . . . Primitive minds are quick to sunshine and quick to anger. Some little word, look or gesture can move them either to love or to sticking a knife between your ribs. You just have to sense the delicate balance and maintain it."[69]

Conjure Queen

The third and final stage of the journey story that comprises *Mules and Men* is, like so many journey stories, a spiritual return home, in this case to the roots of African religious practices in New Orleans. It is also the end result of Hurston's own evolution and transformation from outside observer and recorder of black folk culture to inside member, practitioner, and performer of black folk traditions. "Hoodoo" is based on the fieldwork she conducted as a young ethnographer just starting out in 1928 and 1929, while still under Boas's tutelage. Her correspondence with Langston Hughes from the field about her experiences reveals her experimentation with ethnographic methods and the evolution of her thinking on folk culture. Hurston begins by drawing attention to the symbolic meaning of the city; as the headwaters of the practice of hoodoo in America and the native city of the Queen of Hoodoo, Marie Laveau, New Orleans is the spiritual sister homeland of Africa: "New Orleans is now and has ever been the hoodoo capital of America. Great names in rites that vie with those of Hayti [*sic*] in deeds that keep alive the powers of Africa."[70]

Just like the women she documented in her ethnographic studies, Hurston sought out black folk traditions as an alternative means of gaining power. In the secret world of hoodoo, women rely on conjure practices to gain control in their relationships with men. The majority of cases Hurston relates are brought by women and pertain to problems the clients are experiencing in the female-centered world of family. Male infidelity, troublesome in-laws, and domineering husbands are the main reasons for black women to seek help from a hoodoo doctor. But in typical Hurston fashion, she aims to become a hoodoo practitioner and not merely a dependent client.

Apprenticing herself to Luke Turner, a hoodoo doctor who claims he is the nephew of Marie Laveau,[71] Hurston completely undergoes all the rites and initiation ceremonies required of her: she drinks blood, lies nude on a snakeskin for three days, and experiences visions: "For sixty-nine hours I lay there. I had five psychic experiences and awoke at last with no feeling of hunger, only one of exaltation."[72] She achieves such proficiency that Turner asks her to inherit his mantle after his death: "It has been a great sorrow to me that I could not say yes."[73] Thus, Hurston's journey of "going native" is complete. She has come full circle from her place of origin, her birthplace of Eatonville, through negotiating the dangers of black folk whose ways are alien and threatening to her by pretending to be a member of the community, to finally return to the city of her spiritual home of Africa; here, she is initiated into the heart of her ancestral "racial" identity.[74]

Hurston's process of "going native" by becoming a practitioner of hoodoo illustrates her significant break with certain aspects of professional ethnographic theories and methodologies. Hurston's unorthodox methods would lead her into disfavor with some social scientists. Fellow writer and black leader Alain Locke, sensitive to the risk of her writings meeting with disapprobation among academics, tried to steer her toward more traditional research methods. As Hurston explained his suggestions to Hughes: "Now Alain said that I was not definite enough about some of the religious cults of New Orleans so I am thinking of returning there shortly and correcting the errors and closing up the conjure volume too. He said I needed to clinch some of my statements by photostatic copies of documents, plus some more definite information, which I had seemed to take for granted the reader would understand."[75] Despite Locke's and Boas's warnings, Hurston heedlessly chose to disregard the more academic aspects of her fieldwork. In December she confided to Hughes: "I have come to the conclusion that the birth certificate of Marie Laveau is not so important. It is pretty well established about her birth, life and death. I shall photograph her tomb."[76] Hurston's emphasis on the performative nature of African American folk culture tended to over-shadow her interest in its scholarly value. Hurston's correspondence also reveals that she was not above using poetic license with her ethnographic material in order to play up its aesthetic qualities: "Oh, I love my religious material. Some of it is priceless. Know what I am attempting? To set an entire Bapt. service word for word and note for note. The prayers are to be done in blank verse for thats what they are, prose poetry. I have four dandy ones. I dont like my sermon as well, but I shall prop it up on every leaning side. I shall cut the dull spots in the service to the minimum and play up the art."[77] When she engaged to learn these folk practices rather than just observing and recording them, Hurston became caught up in the theatrical aspect of performing them herself: "Oh, honey, I have the most marvellous ceremony. The dance of the nine snakes! Just wait till you see that. You were right again in saying that it would take six months to do the conjure. I am knee deep in with a long way to go."[78]

As Hurston immersed herself more and more deeply in African American folk culture, she began to erase the boundary (always tenuous) between herself and her subject. Earlier, Hughes had jokingly suggested her studies might lead her into going native. Hurston replied in the same spirit, "Dear Langston—I have landed here in the kingdom of Marie Laveau and expect to wear her crown someday—conjure queen as you suggested."[79] But one month later, Hurston infiltrated the inner sanctum. "Things are beginning to go well now," she told Hughes, "I am getting on with the top of the profession. I know 18 tasks, including how to crown the spirit of death, and kill."[80] Taking the practice of participant observation to a new level, Hurston actually became a hoodoo priestess. As she joyfully communicated to Hughes: "Wait till you see my conjure materials. Oh, Langston, my 'crowning' ceremonies were thrilling!"[81] What drove Hurston to immerse herself so completely?

In letters she wrote to Hughes during 1928, Hurston had clearly felt the distance between herself and her informants and was struggling to overcome her feelings of being an outsider. "I am getting inside of Negro art and lore. I am beginning to *see* really and when you join me I shall point things out and see if you see them as I do."[82] This deferential attitude toward Hughes's per-spective on black culture surfaces repeatedly in Hurston's letters and denotes more than just a friendly wish to accommodate his sensibility. On several occasions, Hurston expressed the opinion that Hughes's identity as a member of the black folk community was somehow more legitimate than her own. It is likely that part of her unease stemmed from the discrimination she encoun-tered among some African Americans for her lighter skin tone, which reflected her mixed ancestry. Throughout her life, Hurston would remain sensitive to the intraracial discrimination she experienced as a "high yaller" woman within African American communities. Stetson Kennedy recalled being questioned by a rural black informant about her: "'Who was that colored gal came in here ahead of y'all?' [the informant] asked. 'Zora Neale Hurston,' we replied. 'She was right smart for a colored girl,' he opined. ''Course I figured she's about three-fifths white!' "[83] Hurston's insecurity regarding her mixed ancestry shows up in a letter to a colleague: "I am just as sure that I am going to make history as I am that I am black. (Well, if not really black, of that denomination, so to speak.)"[84]

On a folklore collecting expedition in her native Florida, Hurston emphasized to Hughes that she was establishing a rapport with her informants: "I am truly dedicated to the work at hand and so I am not even writing, but living every moment with the people."[85] In the same letter, she observed that Hughes was "a really great poet for you truly represent your people."[86] Both of these quotations suggest a curious distancing on Hurston's part from her subject, choosing to use "the" and "your" rather than the more possessive form of "my" or "our." It is important to recognize that when Hurston spoke to a white audience, she automatically positioned herself as an insider to the black community by referring to them as "my people." But when she spoke to her friend and confidant Hughes, she referred to them as "your people" rather than the expected "our people."

In 1926, while she was still a student at Barnard, Hurston had expressed some disapprobation regarding what she viewed as Hughes's wholesale appropriation of black folk culture for his own commercial gain. She wrote to Countee Cullen about her concern that Hughes was unethically capitalizing on white audiences' ignorance of African American vernacular culture by passing himself off as the author of well-known folk songs: "By the way, Hughes ought to stop publishing all those secular folk-songs as his poetry. Now when he got off the 'Weary Blues' (most of it a song I and most southerners have known all our lives) I said nothing for I knew I'd never be forgiven by certain people for crying down what the 'white folks had exalted,' but when he gets off another 'Me and mah honey got two days tuh do de buck' I dont [sic] see how I can refrain from speaking."[87] But by the time she entered her fieldwork, Hurston had started using Hughes's poetry as a means of ingratiating herself with her informants and developing a rapport. To do so, she would begin by reading aloud from his most recently published collection. She described this process in detail to Hughes:

In every town I hold 1 or 2 story-telling contests, and at each I begin by telling them who you are and all, then I read poems from "Fine Clothes." Boy! They eat it up. Two or three of them are too subtle and they dont get it. "Mulatto" for instance and "Sport" but the others they just eat up. You are being quoted in R.R. camps, phosphate mines, turpentine stills, etc. . . . So you see they are making it so much a part of themselves they go to improvising on it. For some reason they call it "De Party Book." They come specially to be read to and I know you could sell them if you only had a supply. I think I'd like a dozen as an experiment. They adore "Saturday Night" and "Evil Woman," "Bad Man," "Gypsy Man." They sing the poems right off, and July 1, two men came over with guitars and sang the whole book. Everybody joined in. It was the strangest and most thrilling thing. They played it well too. You'd be surprised. One man was giving the word out-lining them out as the preacher does a hymn and the others would take it up and sing. It was glorious![88]

By sharing Hughes's material with the folk, Hurston was exploring how they used and then interpolated it. This reveals that Hurston was not afraid of tainting the purity of her subjects by giving them "high" print literary culture that they absorbed into their everyday folk culture. It also shows Hurston's wish to have her and Hughes's work adopted by the people they were study-ing; for Hurston, that was the ultimate stamp of approval of their works' authenticity and legitimacy: "Know what, you ought to make a loafing tour of the South like the blind Homer, singing your songs. Not in auditoriums, but in camps, on water-fronts and the like. You are the poet of the people and your subjects are crazy about you. Why not? There never has been a poet who has been acceptable to His Majesty, the man in the gutter before, and laugh if you will, but that man in the gutter is the god-maker, the creator of everything that lasts. . . . Why not think it over?"[89]

Yet another means by which Hurston sought to validate the authenticity of Hughes's material was to provide anecdotes illustrating their subjects' ap-proval: "I read from 'Fine Clothes' to the group at Loughman and *they got the point* and enjoyed it *immensely*."[90] On a postcard she sent with a picture en-titled "Cutting 'Bogalusa Brand' Timber in Logging Operations, Great South-ern Lumber Co." Hurston wrote: "Dear Langston, Read 'Fine Clothes' to enthusiastic bunch of lumber-jacks here Sat. Big colorful jook here. . . . I am full of impressions. Love Zora."[91] This approach was antithetical to the traditional method in which ethnographers kept their observations and notations on the culture a secret from the community's inhabitants. However, it was clearly important to Hurston that her ethnographic research be part of a dialogical process. Hurston told Hughes, "I wanted to let your publishers know what a hit you are with the people you write about. . . . I shall do it as soon as this is over."[92]

Hurston even began hawking Hughes's books at her ethnographic gatherings. "Dear Langston, I sold 7 books and gave 3. Hence the $14.00 Please send me 10 copies of 'Weary Blues.' I could do with some more 'Fine Clothes' too."[93] Earlier she had reported, "Books almost all gone. Check will be forwarded as soon as the last one is in. People like you immensely."[94] Thus, in a quixotic reversal, where white folklorists such as Lomax were engaged in selling the folk to the metropole, Hurston was selling the metropole to the folk. Hurston did not view this entirely as an altruistic endeavor to enlighten the folk; her concern over Hughes's financial situation led her to regularly include checks for the copies he sent. Regarding his latest shipment, she wrote: "The books came O.K. I have had time for no exploiting yet for I have been 'between the snakes.' "[95] However, it is clear that Hurston genuinely felt that members of the folk should not be deprived, on the basis of economic want, of their poet laureate.

Eventually, Hurston began to feel more comfortable with herself as a spokesperson for the black folk she was observing. In April 1929 she told Hughes, "I am just beginning to hit my stride." Significantly, this is one of the first letters in which she referred to her subjects as "my people," and it is evident from her comments that she was beginning to reposition herself as a member of the African American communities she was representing rather than maintaining her identity as a professional social scientist: "I have to rewrite a lot as you can understand. For I not only want to present the material with all the life and color of my people, I want to leave no loop-holes for the scientific crowd to rend and tear us."[96]

Native Informant

In her professional life, Hurston often found herself playing the role of native informant for white folklorists whose collection efforts, particularly in the Deep South, were often hampered by the societal divide that separated blacks and whites. It was imperative for white scholars journeying into the field in the 1930s and 1940s in hopes of gaining access to African American communities to acquire the proper introductions to potential black informants. When anthropologist Jane Belo planned a southern collecting trip, her influential colleagues Margaret Mead and John Dollard could provide her with contacts only in the white communities. Mead noted it would be "essential that [Belo] have discriminating Negro introductions as she would have no direct approach to Negros [sic] at all."[97]

Hurston, on the contrary, in order to facilitate her interactions with her folk subjects, increasingly found accommodations in the very heart of the community under observation. Referring to a change of residence in New Orleans, Hurston explained that she had moved into the center of the Negro conjuring district: "I stayed a week at 834 Orleans, but the bed bugs routed me, so I moved up here. It is better anyway for I am sort of in the lap of the activities."[98] When she was recording the work songs and stories of African Americans who worked in lumber camps and phosphate mines, Hurston would stay on-site at the camp as well: "Living in the quarters of the Everglades Cypress Lumber Co. Please write me."[99] Thus, Hurston, as an African American ethnographer with numerous connections in the South, became indispensable to her white colleagues by supplying the key to the inner sanctum of southern black communities.

Hurston was part of a 1935 recording expedition to Florida, Georgia, and the Bahamas with Alan Lomax and Mary Elizabeth Barnicle. Barnicle, a prominent folklorist who held a position at New York University, would later recall the methods she employed in her attempts to successfully infiltrate black communities in the South. Traveling with Alan, they would rent a room from a white landlord who "lived on the edge of the black section and we were close to the black people then."[100] Barnicle also tried blackening her face in an attempt to pass as African American: "I didn't put very much on my face. They would think I looked rather white but there are so many white Negroes. . . . I had a very Negro hairdo—very creepy."[101] Lomax would claim that it was actually Hurston's idea for both him and Barnicle to "periodically wear blackface so that they could collect without interference from white authorities."[102] It is likely that Hurston, who had a lively and wicked sense of humor, was acting as a trickster figure; when she convinced them to don blackface, she may have received some secret enjoyment from the minstrel pun. Lomax maintained that they did not intend to "fool black folks—who must have been amused by the strange sight—but to present a uniform color to white passersby."[103]

The trip was financed mainly by Barnicle, and it is clear that she viewed Hurston's role primarily as that of guide and facilitator.[104] Lomax was more complimentary; he acknowledged that Hurston was "almost entirely responsible for the success" of the expedition.[105] Hurston unexpectedly left the tour early over a disagreement, one of many, regarding Barnicle's decision to photograph a young black boy eating watermelon.[106] Hurston strongly objected to Barnicle perpetuating such a racist stereotype. Barnicle, however, provided a different version of their parting, claiming that Hurston "stayed down there after me. I came back because I couldn't stand anymore of her. She was so vile. I hated her."[107]

Commenting several years later on the ruin a culturally insensitive colleague could bring to an expedition, Hurston obliquely referred to the debacle she had experienced with Barnicle. Cautioning her friend Belo against the dangers of such companions on difficult assignments, she described a woman she had refused to take with her on a collecting trip to Honduras: "She would be scared of the 'natives' and want to hang around the capitol. . . . Moreover, she is a damned imperialist and would flap her big mouth and turn the Indians and perhaps all the Hondurians against us. I have had that horrible thing happen to me in the field right here in the United States. The wrong person along. One bray, and months of build-up torn down."[108]

Hurston frequently found herself in the position of tolerating others' intentions for the uses of the folk material she found in order to enable her own collecting to continue. Resources, both travel funds and recording equipment, were often hard to come by, and Hurston was adept at interesting sympathetic and well-off people in her ventures. But this meant that she had to remain flexible to the schedules, demands, and budgets set by her white patrons. For example, Hurston accepted the presence of the two white filmmakers her benefactor Belo sent to help record black church services in South Carolina, even though, as Belo made clear, they hoped to profit commercially from the material Hurston found.[109] Speaking to her friend Paul Green, Hurston described her designated assistants as "two sharks" who "want to take the spirituals for *commercial purposes!*" But Hurston had her own savvy strategies of resistance. Although she acknowledged to Green her obligation to Belo to assist them, she privately told him of her plan of ingenuous compliance: "We cant let all that swell music get away from us like that. . . . Of course I am not going to lead them to the fattest and juiciest places nohow."[110]

In her relationships with her white colleagues, Hurston often found her skills, her contacts, and even her materials being pressed into others' service. In addition to serving as liaison and guide, she played the role of "native informant" for them, performing and interpreting the African American songs she had learned from the folk. Hurston allowed Alan Lomax and Herb Halpert to record her singing black folk songs that she had learned on her own collecting expeditions. In addition to her a cappella performances, Hurston would act as a native informant by describing the context and the uses of each song, along with any particular phrases that would be unfamiliar to a white audience.[111] As she dispensed this information, Hurston's speech became more overtly colloquial. In talking about the songs, Hurston emphasized her "insider" identity by speaking not as an academic folklore collector but as a member of the vernacular community. When Halpert, at one point, tried to correct Hurston on the basis of his own information, she immediately contradicted him by speaking from a position of authority based on her intimate and experiential knowledge. Some of the songs she performed, Hurston explained, were part of her own folk heritage: "I heard it sung in my native village when I was a child. I known it all my life."[112]

At times, their exchanges disclose the disparate roles of informant and ethnographer. When Hurston performed a "sinful" song that contained some sexual innuendos and noted that only "jook" women—disreputable women—not ladies, sang this song, Halpert sardonically commented, "I think that's a very valuable contribution to scientific recording," suggesting that Hurston was behaving more like the "jook" than the academic.[113] Hurston laughingly gave the same reply that black informants frequently gave to white collectors to avoid possible censure and embarrassment: "I know some more verses but right now I don't recall." By resorting to this common strategy of black subterfuge, Hurston highlighted the uneasy dynamic that existed between black informants and their white interviewers, one that was too often replicated in her own exchanges with white folklorists.

These recordings reveal that in her collecting methods as well as her singing performances, Hurston's relationship to her informants and the folk material differed dramatically from that of her white colleagues. For almost every song that she sang, Hurston respectfully gave the full name of the person who had given it to her: "I got it at Palm Beach from a fella named Johnny Barden."[114] Instead of describing the process of collection as "hunting" or "capturing," the terms preferred by John Lomax and Dorothy Scarborough, Hurston always referred to it as "gathering" or "collecting."[115] When Halpert asked her how she learned most of her songs, Hurston explained how she took part in a dialogic process: "I learn 'em by just gettin in the crowd with the people and they sing and I just listen as best I can. . . . I keep on and I sing it back to the people till they can tell me I sing it as good as they do, then I sing it to different people till they are satisfied that I can sing it just like them."[116]

Hurston's method of learning the song within the context of its performance and then repeatedly practicing it until she received the approval of the folk themselves was unlike many other collectors' routine of relying solely on one informant's performance and recording it in their notebooks rather than internalizing it to the degree that it became part of their repertoire.[117] Hurston's method is similar to the "call and response" African American musical tradition, one grounded in group participation and performance.[118] Hurston's mastery of her material extended beyond her rendition of the song to her ability to explain the exact purpose each rhythm or line served in work chants or the dialogue that would occur among card players in between verses of a gambling song.

Apparently, Hurston took a similar approach in her collection of African American folktales. She described to Boas the painstaking means by which she attempted to record her informant's idiom and dialect precisely: "I have tried to be as exact as possible. Keeping to the exact dialect as closely as I could, having the story teller to tell it to me word for word as I write it. This after it has been told to me off hand until I know it myself. But the writing down from the lips is to insure the correct dialect and wording so that I shall not let myself creep in unconsciously."[119] Even though Hurston claimed to keep her distance, by learning a story or song so intimately, she inserted herself quite consciously into the material, in the time-honored black folk tradition of oral performance. Black oral traditions focused on the performer's role as an essential component in breathing life into the folk material of song and story. As an apprentice who became a practitioner and transmitter of folk traditions instead of merely a collector, Hurston collapsed the traditional boundaries between collector and informant and transformed herself into an "authentic" representative of the folk community.

Redefining Black Folk Culture

Part of Hurston's contribution to the study of African American folk culture was to dramatically redefine it as part of a living tradition of folk expression that was not dead or dying, as Lomax and other white scholars claimed, but rather vibrantly ongoing in a process of reinvention and modification. While she remained under the tutelage of Franz Boas, her theories regarding folk culture were unremarkably similar to contemporary anthropological views. As Hemenway notes of Hurston's perspective in the late 1920s: "She was dedicated to anthropology, convinced of the need to collect her people's folklore before it was obliterated by the encroachments of modern civilization. In her report to Boas she stressed that material is slowly slipping away: 'The bulk of the population now spends its leisure time in the motion picture theatres or with the phonograph.' "[120] But as early as 1928, Hurston was writing to Hughes from the field about one of her major discoveries: "discovery 7. Negro folk-lore is *still* in the making, a new kind is crowding out the old."[121]

Her belief in the living nature of folk culture would be reflected in her casual approach to taxonomy, which contrasted rather sharply with the professional folklorist's mission to collect and preserve artifacts of a disappearing folk culture. Halpert repeatedly questioned Hurston about the origins of her songs—a classificatory measure—and she continued to refer to their evolutionary nature, that they had evolved over time and were still growing and spreading across communities: "nowhere you can't find parts of this song. . . . I'm gonna sing verses from whole lots of places. . . . It's one of those things that just goes all 'round."[122]

It was precisely Hurston's ability to travel and live throughout many black communities in the South, rather than just relying on the handpicked informants presented to white folklorists, that facilitated her understanding of the living spirit of folk material and its prevalence in everyday communities. Hurston did not subscribe to the theory, so popular among her folklorist contemporaries, that the only valuable examples of the African American folk tradition were those that were recognizably traditional and on the verge of disappearing. As she reported to Boas during a field trip to New Orleans: "Now I find that there is a new birth of creative singing among Negroes. The old songs are not sung so much. New ones are flooding everywhere."[123] In her article "The Characteristics of Negro Expression," Hurston emphatically made her point by positioning traditional folklore tales next to their modern counterparts: "Negro folklore is not a thing of the past. It is still in the making. Its great variety shows the adaptability of the black man: nothing is too old or too new, domestic or foreign, high or low, for his use. God and the Devil are paired, and are treated no more reverently than Rockefeller and Ford."[124]

Hurston, along with Hughes, sought to establish a more embracing and flexible definition of black identity that could allow for modernization and a certain amount of assimilation, while still enabling them to take possession of essential black folk traditions as part of a historic cultural legacy. Instead of accepting dire warnings that the rich African American folk heritage was, along with the traditions of the antebellum South, rapidly becoming obsolete, writers like Sterling Brown, Hughes, and Hurston created their own definitions of what constituted "authentic" black folk culture that were not limited by white folklorists', like Lomax's, definition of "authentic" black folk and culture as "pure," endangered, and precapitalist. In this way, Hurston made black folk culture available as part of a usable past that could be incorporated into her and her contemporaries' construction of African American identity. Through her emphasis on the "characteristics" of black folk expression, and the transformative nature of its continual reinvention, Hurston showed how folk culture was not in opposition to the modernization of black identity; rather, black folk culture was endlessly adaptable. Thus, the connection to an African legacy was never lost, it was just transformed.

Hurston and the FWP

By the time Hurston was hired by the FWP in April 1938, she was a prominent author and a folklorist of some renown. Yet, unlike John Lomax, Hurston would wind up having very little impact on the Project's representations of black culture and identity. She would not be granted sufficient authority to alter the Florida Project, even though her appointment was regarded as a coup by both the state and federal staffs. Hurston's literary reputation was on the rise. Her second novel, *Their Eyes Were Watching God*, published just a year before she was hired by the FWP, received glowing reviews in the mainstream press, although members of the African American literati (whom Hurston jokingly referred to as the "Niggerati") were less impressed.[125]

Initially, Hurston was considered for the position of director of Florida's separate Negro Writers' Unit (NWU).[126] Two years earlier, Hurston's name had appeared on a list Sterling Brown compiled of people who should be consulted in each state for projects pertaining to Negro studies. Brown had identified her as one of the individuals "likely to be most valuable."[127] Two months after she was hired in 1938, federal director Alsberg wrote to Florida state director Carita Doggett Corse with the idea of expanding Hurston's responsibilities, with an accompanying salary increase, to oversee "a book on the Florida Negro."[128] Alsberg commented on Hurston's "considerable experience in collecting" and noted that she "could be gathering material which might be used for another book later."[129] Corse expressed her approval and suggested that Hurston be granted a separate travel fund, equal to her present salary, in order to facilitate her field work.[130] Despite these conversations, Hurston's salary remained commensurate with that of a relief worker with the title of "Junior Interviewer," at the base level of relief salary.[131] Her white coworker, Stetson Kennedy, was hired with the same title, at the pay rate of $37.50 every two weeks; he recalls Hurston's salary as $32.50 "because someone had figured out the cost of living in Eatonville [where Hurston spent most of her time] for a month, or per check, was $5.00 less than living in Jacksonville."[132] It isn't clear from the historical evidence why Hurston didn't end up in a supervisory role until the end of her tenure with the Florida Project, when she included her own essays and material in the "Negro book" and began the process of engaging a publisher. Kennedy surmised, decades later, that "Zora was Zora, and that didn't mean supervising the Negro Unit or editing copy that other Negroes or whites had written. She was, as far as I know, never really an editor, she was Zora the writer, so that the idea of editing other people's work probably did not appeal to her at all." Hurston's friend and patron, the white writer Fannie Hurst, pointed out during a radio town hall meeting on the FWP that "compiling guide books is [not] the average author's dream."[133]

What is clear is that Hurston was busy prioritizing her own writing projects; during her year of employment with the FWP, she published her second major ethnographic study of voodoo, in Haiti and Jamaica, *Tell My Horse* (1938), and she was working intensively on *Moses, Man of the Mountain*, the novel that would be published in November 1939, just five months after she left the FWP. Helping to optimize the time for her own projects was the fact that Hurston was subject to much less scrutiny and accountability than other members of Florida's NWU and that she received certain privileges; for example, instead of working with the segregated unit in Jacksonville, Hurston opted to work out of her lake home near Eatonville. Jacksonville held troubled memories for Hurston; she had moved there from Eatonville as a young adolescent, two weeks after her beloved mother died. In her autobiography, published just four years after her employment with the FWP, Hurston stated that the racial climate in Jacksonville "made me know that I was a little colored girl."[134] She may have also been signifying about her experience there as an NWU employee, although she apparently spent enough time in Jacksonville to decide to marry a young local from the elite Sugar Hill neighborhood, Albert Price III, in June 1939.[135]

While project employees, white and black, had to accept routine oversight of their activities, reporting daily to their field office and submitting timesheets that itemized and dated their written submissions, Hurston mailed her copy to Jacksonville headquarters in a dilatory manner, often doing so only when directly reminded. "She would go off and you wouldn't know where she was and she was supposed to be working by the week," Corse recalled.[136] Kennedy remembered that Corse "would come out into the Editorial room from her office and look around and say 'Anybody heard from Zora?' and everyone would look blank, you know, and Dr. Corse would look at me and say 'Better write her a letter and jog her up.' And I would do that and . . . by return mail we would get a very thick manila envelope postmarked Eatonville. . . . I dubbed it The Mark of Zora, you know, we all got excited by the Eatonville postmark, because inside the envelope there'd be all this fabulous material." Kennedy and the staff at headquarters also "suspected that it was not something she had just done you know, but things she'd collected in bygone years and so when I jogged her up she would stuff some of it in an envelope and send it in."[137] Surprisingly, other scholars have missed the fact that Hurston did indeed recycle much of her own material for the Florida Project; some of the FWP material she included in the 1939 manuscript "The Florida Negro" had appeared four years earlier in *Mules and Men*.[138]

Hurston took care to cultivate a special relationship with Corse, strategically performing the role she'd played before with other white women patrons, writing her intimate letters, alternately calling her "Boss" or just "Dr." and referring to herself as Corse's "pet darkey."[139] While this approach resulted in some concrete gains, such as the additional "travel allowance" for her fieldwork expeditions, and the special loan of an expensive recording machine from the Library of Congress, she still found herself perpetually subjected to racial discrimination, even by colleagues such as Kennedy, who deeply admired her work. Despite the fact that it was Hurston's efforts that brought the machine to Florida, "whites on the project promptly took it away from her," he recalled. On the field recording expeditions she conducted in 1938 and 1939, Hurston was sent ahead as a scout; her white colleagues, Kennedy and John Lomax's son Alan, would follow with a photographer and the recording machine: "only at times would our trails cross, [and] she'd still be on site identifying people when we arrived."[140] This brought both indignity and danger—Kennedy recalled the white bosses at the turpentine camps where Hurston was sent in to collect material from the exploited black laborers scaring her so badly "she was afraid to make full notes."[141] It also brought discomfort, as there were no hotel accommodations for blacks in Florida, "so Zora slept in her car much of the time."[142]

Biographer Hemenway claims that Hurston was almost entirely responsible for the editorial work on *The Florida Negro*, "overseeing the compilation of a two-hundred-page volume,"[143] but Corse and Kennedy maintained that Hurston's work for the Project was largely ignored at the time, even though her submissions had been set aside specifically for inclusion in *The Florida Negro*. Kennedy, who was promoted to become the state editor of folklore, oral history, and ethnic studies, acknowledges that Hurston's contribution was all but eviscerated in the state guide as a result of her unmistakable artistic imprint on all the material she submitted and because she was an African American employee. He later recalled the situation in the Jacksonville office:

There we were, doing our very best to see to it that everything that went into the Guide was couched not only in staid Federalese but also in the specific guidebook jargon set forth in the FWP Style Manual; and there was Zora, turning in these veritable prose poems of African eloquence and imagery! What to do? Inevitably, the inferior triumphed over the superior, and not much of Zora, beyond her inimitable folksongs and tales, got into the Guide. We rationalized this tragedy by reminding ourselves after that, after all, the Guides were meant to be exemplars of the merits of collective authorship.[144]

Corse would eventually express her regret that Hurston's capabilities were not better utilized: "I feel," she later stated in an interview, "that the principle oversight in my direction of the project was my failure to realise [*sic*] that Zora should have written the Negro book . . . but she was forty years ahead of her time."[145]

Hurston's approach to black folklore would also be at odds with some of the views expressed in the earlier drafts of "The Florida Negro." From a comparison of her submitted essays and the only complete draft of the manuscript for "The Florida Negro" (assembled before she was hired), it is clear that Hurston's theories regarding black folk culture and identity were, in some ways, fundamentally unlike those put forth by the other members of the Negro Writers' Unit. They would also place her at odds with Sterling Brown, director of the Office on Negro Affairs in Washington and a staunch and outspoken advocate for portraits of black identity within the FWP that would advance the cause of racial progress.[146] Brown would critique Hurston's novel *Their Eyes Were Watching God* for its lack of realism regarding racial discrimination. Hurston, for her part, after meeting with Brown on FWP business in D.C., would derisively refer to him as Alsberg's "pet darkey." Even Alsberg's patronage, she told Corse, couldn't "make him no new head with inside trimmings."[147]

Although Hurston's essays, such as the ones on folklore and hoodoo, were intended for inclusion in "The Florida Negro," there are indications that Hurston's more colorful and descriptive material was ignored in the editing stage of the state guidebook. Editorial comments from the federal office on material that was submitted six months after Hurston's initial employment noted that "the account of the 'jook' [African American music parties] is quite inadequate in view of the excellent account in the field notes."[148] It is likely that the "excellent account" of the jook found in the field notes was written by Hurston, who demonstrated a special interest in studying and describing this phenomenon; why her notes fail to appear in the manuscript remains a matter of speculation. Pamela Bordelon has identified a number of essays Hurston produced for the Florida Project and asserts that they were intended for inclusion in "The Florida Negro." According to Bordelon, after Hurston left the Project in 1939, the manuscript, under Corse's supervision, was substantially revised by Kennedy and Robert Cornwall, who "deleted all of Hurston's writings from the final manuscript published in 1993" by McDonogh. But there is such a definitive distinction between Hurston's voice, style, and approach to black culture and the approach taken by the core members of the NWU working out of the Mission in Jacksonville, discussed in the following chapter, that it is hard to imagine Hurston's material being readily accepted or embraced by her black colleagues.

During her employment with the FWP as a member of Florida's NWU, Hurston's contribution to "The Florida Negro" manuscript would sit uneasily, side by side, with submissions from her fellow coworkers who wanted to emphasize black racial progress through the process of assimilation and acculturation. In contrast to the rather judgmental viewpoints expressed on black folk culture in "The Florida Negro," Hurston would celebrate the continuation of elements of black folk culture as symbolic of a living, ancestral African past, one that was constantly evolving and adapting to current circumstances. Unlike the members of Florida's NWU, many of whom advocated education and economic advancement at the expense and dismissal of black folk traditions as the best means of "uplifting the race," Hurston sought to create a more flexible definition of black identity that could allow for modernization and assimilation while still actively perpetuating and celebrating African American folk traditions. "The Florida Negro" would languish in the archives for several decades following the close of the FWP, but Hurston drew on much of the material she'd collected as a result of her FWP work for her subsequent novels. If you were a professional author with ambition and great material, you were better off working under your own name than working for the FWP, and Hurston seemed to know that.

The discourse of "authenticity" created by folklorists and writers in the 1930s worked to privilege certain forms of black identity, even as it intentionally undermined others, such as the black bourgeoisie. Chapter 7 will examine the writings and work experiences of Hurston's colleagues in Florida's NWU. Unlike Hurston, most emphasized black respectability and racial uplift and used the life histories of ex-slave informants to construct narratives demonstrating African Americans' readiness for full citizenship.

CHAPTER SEVEN

Follow Me through Florida

Florida's Negro Writers' Unit, the Ex-Slave Project, and The Florida Negro

How many times do we pass through cities and towns in this beautiful state without a single thought of its background and facts in regard to the Negro groups.

—Paul Diggs, "Follow Me through Florida," November 10, 1938

Florida was one of the earliest states to begin collecting personal histories of former slaves, and it was those narratives that gave federal directors the idea for the creation of an Ex-Slave Project in April 1937. Folklore editor John Lomax was so impressed that he decided to introduce the project in other states. As he communicated to Florida's state director Carita Doggett Corse, "I have enjoyed very much reading this batch of reminiscences from ex-slaves. . . . It seems to me they are of very great value and I congratulate you on being the first to open up . . . this field of investigation."[1] Corse, the author of three books on Florida history, had become interested in using slave interviews as primary sources while doing her own research.[2] With a B.A. from Vassar and an M.A. from Columbia University (1916), in 1932 she became one of only seven women to receive an honorary Ph.D. from the University of the South at Sewanee.[3] Corse had also served as the primary writer for a heavily romanticized state guide commissioned by the Florida State Hotel Commission with the aim of promoting tourism. Published in 1930, *Florida: Empire of the Sun* epitomizes the approach federal directors wanted to take to the American Guide Series with its combination of travelogue, history, and colorful descriptive copy.[4] Corse's proven success with state boosterism and her strong local political connections made her well positioned to oversee the Florida Writers' Project.[5] Corse would not become an official member of the United Daughters of the Confederacy (UDC) until the end of 1939, after the Federal Writers' Project (FWP) had been reorganized under state control. However, her connections to the organization were in evidence as early as 1937, when one of her historic essays was published in the UDC's official publication, the *Southern Magazine*.[6] Appointed in the fall of 1935, with an annual salary of $3,292, Corse remained as state director until the official

Carita Doggett Corse,
Florida State Director,
Federal Writers'
Project, ca. 1928.
Courtesy of State
Archives of Florida,
Florida Memory,
http://floridamemory
.com/items/show/399.

end of the Writers' Project in 1942.[7] "Her enthusiasm for uncovering Floridi-
ana kept the morale of the entire staff at fever pitch," recalled former FWP
coworker Stetson Kennedy.[8]

Soon after her appointment, Corse wrote to George Cronyn, associate
director of the FWP, recommending the creation of a separate Negro Writers'
Unit (NWU) to be headed by a Florida native and well-known folklore and
fiction author: "We feel that a State-Wide Negro Project under Zora Hurston
would be of great value. As you realize little cooperation could be expected
in this section from a white district under a negro supervisor or vice versa.
Please advise us if a separate negro project could be set up."[9] At the federal
level, there was increasing support for separate "Negro units" that could penetrate and record the curiously visible yet closed black communities within
the southern states. Alsberg's field supervisor, Katharine Kellock, wrote to
encourage the development of a specifically Negro Project—in terms of its
staff as well as its subject: "I hope you can find a way for the Negro Project
[in Florida and South Carolina]—there is a whole world within a world in

each state."[10] The fact that NWUs were established as a result of the South's segregated society ironically helped guarantee African American involvement in the Writers' Project and constituted one of the few areas in which black personnel could have a strong impact on how materials pertaining to black history and culture would be collected, interpreted, and presented in FWP publications.

These writers tried to maintain a delicate balance as they navigated the ambiguities of race and class in 1930s America. Employees of Florida's NWU were routinely subjected to the same types of discrimination inflicted on ex-slave informants. At the same time, as largely educated, young professionals, black employees belonged to a different class as well as generation than most of their informants and were invested in shaping representations of African American history and culture that would add ballast to arguments for racial equality and the full rights of citizenship. After laying out the details regarding the individuals who made up the NWU and their working conditions, this chapter examines the strategies and methods African American employees on the Florida Project adopted in order to reinscribe their authority over prevailing discourses on black culture and identity, focusing on the contributions of Florida's NWU to the Ex-Slave Project and to the manuscript "The Florida Negro."

Members of Florida's Negro Writers' Unit

The NWU of Florida was founded in February 1936, just five months into Corse's directorship. During its short existence, from 1936 to 1939, it employed sixteen members, although not all at the same time.[11] Zora Neale Hurston would be included on the payroll for only one year in 1938, despite Corse's initial plans to have her supervise the work of the NWU. Unlike many other state directors who dragged their feet when it came to hiring African Americans, Corse quickly hired the maximum number of workers authorized by the federal office. Although she was described by a fellow employee as a "typical southern conservative in matters political, social, [and] economic," she was also praised for her "unconscious liberalism."[12] Corse's interest in black folk culture (and lobbying by local black organizations for more hires) led her to advocate for this separate unit of African American project employees.

Federal guidelines required that 90 percent of FWP staffing come from the ranks of the unemployed, but the Florida Project received permission to hire as many as 25 percent of its staff from applicants who were not on relief, as there was concern that there would not be enough qualified unemployed writers and editors to produce a state guidebook.[13] Initially, the number of state employees was set at 200, including ten African Americans. Corse's progress report submitted to Alsberg in early August 1936 noted that Florida's NWU had ten employees working on the American Guide on "subjects pertaining especially to Negroes" and that one special "Negro study included [the] collection of reminiscences of former slaves."[14] But quota reductions in June and December of that same year shrunk their numbers to eight and then three, respectively.[15] By 1937, one worker had been added, and in the years following, until 1939, five black writers are documented as contributors to Florida's NWU.[16] These slight increases in quota numbers were likely the result of Corse's numerous requests to the federal office for an expansion of the Negro Unit's work.

Florida, like other states, strictly enforced racial segregation on its federal projects. Budgets would not accommodate the establishment of separate professional office spaces, so black employees were forced to work at home or rely on space provided by educational or community institutions within black neighborhoods. Even African American dignitaries, like local heroes Hurston and the educator Mary McLeod Bethune, had to receive special dispensation to visit with white staff members in formal settings. Bethune's visit to Jacksonville's Works Progress Administration (WPA) in her appointed role as director of Negro Affairs for Roosevelt's National Youth Administration presented a dilemma, as an interracial formal reception was unthinkable. Fortunately, someone came up with the idea of a buffet reception, so that white and black attendees would not be "sitting down at the table together."[17] As the celebrated columnist and social critic Harry Golden caustically observed during the Civil Rights Movement, racial integration seemed to work best in public places where there were no seats; he labeled this phenomenon "The Vertical Negro Plan."[18]

A stark contrast existed between the working conditions for black and white FWP employees. Project headquarters were located in Jacksonville, the state's largest city, with a population of 129,459, in modern offices in the Exchange Building constructed in 1930 on West Adams.[19] But to maintain racial segregation, the NWU was housed in the Clara White Mission, a charitable soup kitchen and shelter located in the old Globe Theater at 613 West Ashley Street, between Broad Street and North Jefferson, just south of Jacksonville's black community of Sugar Hill, and less than half a mile from the state office.[20] The Florida Project's director of folklore and social ethnic studies, Stetson Kennedy, recalled that all communication between the

Negro Unit and state headquarters took place by telephone or mail; a delivery boy was sent over every two weeks to pick up the paychecks for black employees. When Hurston signed onto the Project in 1938, Corse made an announcement to her staff at headquarters that Hurston would be paying them a visit, although no member of the NWU had ever made an appearance at that office. As Kennedy recalled, "Dr. Corse went on to say that Zora had already published a couple of books, and been feted by New York library circles and was therefore given to putting on certain airs such as smoking cigarettes in the presence of white folk and that we would have to make allowances for Zora, and sure enough, Zora came, and Zora smoked, and we made allowances."[21]

Working conditions at the Mission were less than ideal, as "there were long lines at meal times out on the sidewalks waiting to get something to eat," spirituals were sung before meals, "and that was the atmosphere in which the Negro Writers' Unit was obliged to work—three meals a day and singing."[22] A short piece about the Mission by an NWU employee in 1938 makes it clear that it was a lively (and noisy) place; in addition to providing accommodations for ex-convicts and homeless individuals, as well as space for WPA arts and sewing projects alongside the NWU, other activities included a day nursery to assist working mothers, a children's music school, an assembly room for regular Bible classes, and a visiting nurse service.[23] There were also a number of ex-slaves living there during the 1930s, and a few of them were recorded on tape by Hurston and Kennedy using the machine that she had wangled from the federal office specifically for the Florida Project.[24]

The majority of employees in the NWU were representative of an educated and aspiring black middle class. Because of the extreme racism African Americans frequently encountered when trying to obtain employment within the FWP, black writers had to possess credentials and skills that would satisfy the most discriminating (pun intended) state director. In addition to the Barnard-educated Hurston, Florida's Negro Unit included members such as Alfred Farrell, a magna cum laude graduate of Lincoln University in 1934. As well as being the salutatorian of his class, Farrell "majored in English and minored in foreign languages."[25] At the time he applied to Alsberg for a job with the FWP, at the age of twenty-two, Farrell was employed as a college instructor in Jacksonville, teaching English and French at the historically black Edward Waters College.[26] After his work for the NWU, Farrell served in the army during World War II. He would later return to Lincoln University as a professor and administrator, after completing his doctorate in English at Ohio State University.[27]

Florida's NWU was also remarkable for the high number of female writers on its staff. Nationwide, women constituted less than 20 percent of WPA employees, and black women who served as WPA staff members made up only 3 percent of all WPA workers. However, half of the NWU staff from 1936 to 1937 was composed of black women.[28] In addition to Hurston, the core roster of contributing black writers included seven women and six men.[29] Overall, the Florida Project had a larger share of female employees; women writers totaled 63 percent in 1936, with more than seventy out of the 127 employees working on the guide project.[30]

Apart from Farrell and Hurston, little is known about most of the NWU members. NWU writer Viola Walker Muse earned her baccalaureate degree in 1925 from Indiana University; as an undergraduate, she was a founding member of a college writing group to which she contributed poetry.[31] Aside from Muse, the remaining female employees working in Jacksonville do not appear to have been as well educated as their male colleagues. Field worker Pearl Randolph completed two years of high school. The remaining three women working out of the Mission office, Rachel Austin, Portia Thorington, and Ruth Bolton, were employed primarily as secretaries, although all three did contribute some writing to the project.[32] Prior to her employment with the NWU, Bolton was working as a stenographer in a law office in Jacksonville.[33] While serving as a typist for the NWU, Bolton also authored several short pieces on contemporary businesses and benevolent organizations. Austin submitted some interviews with ex-slaves, and Thorington provided a folklore essay, but they seem to have possessed less authority to influence the portraits of black identity being churned out by their male coworkers. John A. Simms is identified as editor on much of the copy, beginning in 1936, with the start of the NWU. Simms also edited a magazine called the *Messenger*, published at 1305 Florida Avenue.[34] The greatest amount of copy was produced by Martin Richardson and Paul A. Diggs. Richardson also appears to have served as both a primary contributor and a compiler for the NWU's "Negro book" project, a version of which was published as *The Florida Negro* over fifty years later by Gary McDonogh.[35]

Paul Diggs was the most prolific producer of material for the NWU and the author of more than fifty submissions. After completing college, during the 1930s, he lived with his wife, Louise W. Diggs, principal of the Washington Park High School, and her family in Lakeland, in a close-knit African American community in the northwestern part of the city.[36] Diggs was a civic leader and community organizer and an enthusiastic advocate for racial uplift and racial progress through individual self-improvement and bourgeois respectability.

As a visiting speaker to a sociology class at Southern College in 1938, while working for the NWU, Diggs spoke of "the educational progress of the Negro in Florida" but also regaled the students with a story about winning a collegiate heavyweight boxing match: "The title cost me $50 . . . because I knocked my opponent's front teeth out."[37] Diggs helped organize a separate troop of black Boy Scouts, pushed for a recreational center for black citizens, served as chairman of the Polk County Health Committee for African Americans, and sponsored oratorical contests and school plays.[38] His perspective would greatly influence the portrayals of black identity in *The Florida Negro*.

Kennedy, who also helped edit the manuscript "The Florida Negro," observed of his African American colleagues that their "level of talent was exceptionally high . . . and the quality of copy produced was quite beyond the capacity of the lily-white editorial staff to improve upon."[39] But black employees found that their middle-class status as writers and intellectuals was regularly undermined by white colleagues and supervisors who felt their submissions were marred by "Negro bias." Small wonder, then, that black field workers as well as ex-slave informants looked for ways to inscribe their narratives with built-in testimonials of objectivity in order to preempt questions regarding their veracity.[40]

Members of Florida's NWU resorted to a variety of rhetorical devices to try to ensure that their narratives would be deemed acceptable by white editors and supervisors. Most adopted the same mode of description found in professional ethnographic writing of the 1920s and 1930s by rewriting the ex-slaves' narratives almost entirely in the third person. This was a strategic attempt to appropriate the professional ethnographer's descriptive discourse that establishes scientific authority through the textual self-effacement of the author.[41] They also preferred, when using direct quotations, to present the ex-slaves' speech in Standard English, with very few examples of the black vernacular. This paralleled African American writers of the Harlem Renaissance who, with few exceptions, largely rejected dialect writing and viewed its use by white writers as perpetuating racist stereotypes.[42]

This became an issue for federal directors who preferred that ex-slave narratives be written up in the voice of the ex-slave. In particular, they focused on correcting the Florida staff's deficient employment of the black vernacular. In the same letter congratulating Corse "on being the first to open up . . . this field of investigation," Lomax explained that the workers engaged in rewriting the ex-slaves' stories should "as nearly as possible, quote the exact words of ex-slaves when they are relating incidents in their lives, being sure to include all the peculiar expressions."[43] Just a few days earlier, Cronyn had written a similar letter to Corse: "Mr. Lomax and I have found the stories of the ex-slaves fascinating reading. We feel that these will be valuable for future reference and possible publication. If more stories are gathered, however, ask your interviewer to intersperse the narratives with occasional direct quotations. This has been done to some extent in the present accounts, but a little more of it would greatly increase the color and human interest of the material."[44]

Florida's NWU also incorporated evidence of black objectivity into the subject matter of their narratives, in anticipation of white skepticism, to assure the reader that they were indeed factual accounts. Many field workers emphasized their informants' upstanding characters, youthful appearances, and good health as a way of establishing their accuracy in recalling past events. Viola Muse wrote this description of ex-slave George Pretty: "[He] is a dark complexioned man . . . and looks to be much younger than he is. . . . He does not dissipate, neither does he drink strong drink."[45]

NWU field workers also made an effort to show that their informants had given their stories without unnecessary prompting or interference from the interviewer. In Muse's interview with Pretty, she assured her readers that she had not influenced the information contained within the narrative: "[He] is a ready informant. Having heard that only information of slavery was wanted, he volunteered information without any formality or urging on the part of the writer."[46] Muse even went to such lengths as to provide two citations at the end of the narrative: "1. George Pretty, Vero Beach and Gifford, Florida. 2. Observation of the field worker."[47] But the converse of this method was also used in order to demonstrate the objectivity of the ex-slave informant. Depicting an informant as reluctant to tell of the evils of slavery was often a strategy for proving the truthfulness of the account. After "Prophet" John Kemp had recounted his former master's cruel and abusive treatment, his interviewer Rebecca Baker inserted this observation: "'Prophet' Kemp will tell you that he hates to tell these things to any investigator, because he hates for people to know just how mean his father [sic] really was."[48] The renowned scholar C. Vann Woodward has mistaken this type of truth-telling strategy as indicative of the difficulty with which black interviewers obtained the ex-slaves' narratives by interpreting these types of statements literally: "Even the black interviewers had their problems," he notes. "'It was with difficulty,' reported one of them in Florida, 'that they were prevailed upon to relate some of the gruesome details recorded here.'"[49]

This method of indirectly writing a tale's significance into the way in which the tale is told is common among the slave narratives submitted by the NWU. This strategy comes from the African American tradition of signifying, which developed as a means of communicating information that was either subversive or dangerously unpopular. Very often the connection between sentences is not always direct, but there exists an implied relationship between them. Ex-slave informants took this approach to subtly convey information that might be poorly received if spoken directly. But it was also adopted by members of Florida's Negro Unit to maintain a certain refined bourgeoisie sensibility—a certain delicacy of feeling on the part of the writer and the intended reader.[50]

For example, the narrative of Frank Berry, an ex-slave who claimed he was a direct descendant of the Seminole chief Osceola (famous for leading a bloody attack on Florida's white settlers after they had attempted to drive the Seminoles off of their land), relates that his former master "made no provision for his freedmen as did many other Southerners—usually in the form of land grants—although he gave them their freedom as soon as the proclamation was issued." So that the reader might not wonder why the grandson of such a notorious Indian warrior did not follow his ancestor's example in forcefully demanding recompense from his former master, the sentence immediately following states in an explanatory fashion: "Berry learned from his elders that their master was a noted duelist and owned several fine pistols some of which have very bloody histories."[51] Berry's narrative thus indirectly dispels any potential doubt about Berry's courage that might unfavorably compare with his grandfather's. Black field workers as well as informants employed this rhetorical method of indirection in Florida's slave narratives. After informant Willis Davis related "a humorous incident" about slave children who were promised a reward for whoever managed to pick the most pin feathers and who, in their excitement, overzealously stripped the geese of all of their feathers, the text comments obliquely: "Need we guess what happened to the over ambitious children?"[52]

Various methods of proving the informant's memory reliable were used. Sometimes the ex-slave's excellent memory was established by claims to the accuracy bestowed by the informant's membership in a culture transmitted orally. Reverend Eli Boyd recalled that his Geechee grandmother "used to hold up her hand and look at it and sing out of her hand. She'd make them up as she would look at her hand. She sang in Geechee and also made up rhymes and songs in English."[53] And informant Amanda McCray emphasized that African Americans, even under slavery, had passed along folklore through the generations: "[Children] were duly schooled in all the current superstitions and listened to the tales of ghosts and animals that talked and reasoned, tales common to the Negro today."[54] In other narratives, the opposite proof was invoked, as the informant's education and literacy became central evidence of his or her reliability as an eyewitness. Field worker Rachel Austin wrote this statement about her informant Luke Towns: "Mr. Towns has been noted during his lifetime for having a remarkable memory and has many times publicly delivered orations from many of Shakespeare's works. His memory began failing him in 1936. He is very well-educated and now spends most of his time sitting on the porch reading the Bible."[55]

Because most of the ex-slaves still living in the 1930s had been children when emancipation came, the oral tradition played a key role in maintaining a collective history. Henry Maxwell was "just a tot when the Civil War gave him and his people freedom, [but] Maxwell's memories of bondage-days are vivid through the experiences related by older Negroes."[56] To validate these anecdotes, interviewers sometimes depicted their informants' memory as a recording device. Edward Lyourgas remembered a story his father used to tell him and his siblings when they were children, about purchasing their mother, who was being auctioned off in St. Augustine. Interviewer Pearl Randolph noted in the narrative that "it has been almost 60 years since [they] listened round-eyed to stories they already knew because 'pap' had told them so many times before. These narratives along with the great changes he has seen, were carefully recorded in the mind of Edward."[57] Descriptions like these of African American oral traditions compared them favorably to other modes of preserving the past, such as written forms and recorded sound technology.

In addition to incorporating these truth-telling rhetorical strategies into their ex-slave narratives, NWU interviewers used the life histories of their black informants to challenge the existing views of African Americans that undergirded the sharply segregated society of the 1930s. Like Sterling Brown in the federal office, members of Florida's NWU also tried to produce portraits of African Americans that emphasized "racial uplift" themes. A 1936 progress report regarding the work of Florida's Negro Unit displays the general direction the Project was heading toward in its treatment of African American subject matter. For the local and state guides, "the subjects of literature, art, ethnography, music, religion, education and folklore [had] been completed."[58] Topics listed for future investigation were "Additional slave interviews; Negroes in early Florida politics; Hoodoo practices not yet covered; Unusual Negro enterprises; Negro inventors and inventions; Sketches of successful Negroes; Survey of rural school educational methods and facilities; Survey of effects of Negro fraternal orders on social and economic life of Negroes; Survey of religious trends since 1900 including effect of churches on present life; Survey of economic and social status of Florida Negroes, 1863–1936; Survey of inter-racial good will."[59] With the exception of the reference to hoodoo, all of these subjects were reflective of the focus on education, business and entrepreneurship, religion, upward mobility, and self-help—all themes central to the black middle-class ideology of racial uplift.[60]

The slave narratives submitted by the NWU would repeatedly portray African Americans as the natural possessors of the qualities deemed necessary for citizens of the Republic, namely, the dominance of the rational mind over the instinctual drives and the capability of governing oneself, which might naturally extend to the right to govern others.[61] Moreover, they often tried to demonstrate the informant's possession of these traits by using visual cues. In this way, these slave narratives adopt the same "representational economy" at work in the narrative portraits of former slaves frequently submitted by white interviewers, but used radically different imagery to create a sharply contrasting representation of ex-slaves as fully qualified for the rights and responsibilities of citizenship. NWU field workers described ex-slave informants' physical selves as the site of visible distinctions that could signify important and meaningful character traits. Randolph described Frank Berry in this way: "Berry recalls the old days of black aristocracy when Negroes held high political offices in the state of Florida, when Negro tradesmen and professionals competed successfully and unmolested with the whites. Many fortunes were made by members who are now little more than beggars. To this group belongs the man who in spite of reduced circumstances manages still to make one think of top hats and state affairs. Although small of stature and almost disabled by rheumatism, he has the fiery dignity and straight back that we associate with men who have ruled others."[62] Berry's ancestry was also invoked in connection with the positions of authority that he held with the federal government: "Frank Berry . . . claims to be a grandson of Osceola, last fighting chief of the Seminole tribe. . . . He served variously during his life as a State and Federal Government contractor, United States Marshall (1881), Registration Inspector (1879)."[63] Here, Berry's ability to govern others is demonstrated not only through the various positions he held as a representative of governmental authority but with his genealogical lineage. As the descendant of an Indian chief, Berry's ability to govern is in his blood, just as his noble bearing is revealed in his physical mien.

As this example shows, slave narratives of the Florida NWU created representations of individual ex-slave informants that could then serve as a means for making an argument for African Americans' collective right to self-determination. Representations of ex-slave informants emphasized visual cues of racial ancestry and suggested they were indices of moral character. To represent African Americans as good citizens, narratives of the NWU often highlighted ex-slave informants' contributions to American society as respectable, skilled, economically mobile, members of the Republic: "As State and Federal Government Contractor he built many public structures, a few of which are still in use, among them the jetties at Mayport, Florida which he helped to build and a jail at High Springs, Florida."[64] Lists of achievements frequently emphasized positions of employment or work-related projects that were associated with the authority of the federal government. The narrative of Willis Williams concentrated on his position as a railway mail clerk: "Ten years after the Civil War [he] had advanced in his studies to the extent that he passed the government examination and became a railway mail clerk." Eventually he became the third "colored mail clerk" to be employed by the Jacksonville Post Office. Because he had "filled the position creditably," he retired on a pension.[65]

In addition, some narratives told of how the ex-slave had served his appointment with integrity and honesty. Informant Will Sherman "was at one time Inspector of Elections at Mayport during Reconstruction Days. He recalled an incident that occurred during the performance of his duties there: Mr. John Doggett, who was running for office on the Democratic ticket, brought a number of colored people to Mayport by boat from Chaseville to vote. Mr. Doggett demanded that they should vote, but Will Sherman was equally insistent that they should not vote because they had not registered and were not qualified. After much arguing Mr. Doggett saw that Sherman could not be made 'to see the light' and left with his prospective voters."[66] In this anecdote, Sherman upheld the law when a candidate for political office tried to violate it.

Moreover, in enforcing the law, Sherman prevented his fellow African Americans from voting, a politically charged act in the dual context of the days of the Reconstruction South and the 1930s, when, in both cases, African Americans were routinely disenfranchised through the Jim Crow practices of arbitrarily enforced registration procedures, including gerrymandering, literacy tests, and grandfather clauses. Although Sherman's action in this particular case prevents a clear attempt by a corrupt Democrat to manipulate the outcome of the election by stuffing the ballot box, it demonstrates his color-blindness in following the letter of the law. As discussed earlier, African Americans were routinely accused by whites of "Negro bias." It was therefore all the more important to show that African Americans could place their loyalty to the nation, through strict observance of governmental laws and regulations, over loyalty to their race. Immediately following the relating of this incident, it is noted that Sherman "once served upon a United States Federal jury," further demonstrating his fulfillment of the responsibilities of citizenship.[67]

When discussing an informant's history of employment after emancipation, some ex-slave narratives offered familiar American success stories in which the ex-slave informant went from rags to riches as the result of hard work, thrift, and financial foresight. These individual examples demonstrated the compatibility of African American character with the ethos of American identity, the Protestant work ethic, by showing how easily African Americans as successful entrepreneurs could be assimilated into American capitalism. Field worker Alfred Farrell tried to ensure that this aspect of Henry Maxwell's life history would not be overlooked by directly drawing an analogy between Maxwell's story and a more famous African American success story, that of Booker T. Washington: " 'Up from slavery' might well be called this short biographical sketch of Henry Maxwell. . . . After the Civil War . . . Henry secured work with a farmer for whom he worked for $12 a month. In 1894 he purchased a small orange grove and began to cultivate oranges. Today he owns over 30 acres of orange groves and controls nearly 200 more acres. He is said to be worth around $250,000 and is Titusville's most influential and respected citizen."[68] Referring directly to the autobiography of the founder of Tuskegee, Farrell offered Maxwell's rags-to-riches story as an endorsement of his pragmatic philosophy, promoting economic advancement as the best route for achieving equality.

The narrative of Lindsey Moore, written up by Martin Richardson, captures the main theme in the title: "An Ex-Slave Who Was Resourceful." This didactic tale focuses on how Moore, even during slavery, capitalized on every opportunity to learn a skill or trade. Through the careful observation of the various operations on the plantation—tanning, making cloth and soap— Moore acquired skills that would later become a source of his livelihood. During the Civil War, Moore turned a profit by capitalizing on the Yankee soldiers who were encamping near his plantation by selling cups of water from the nearby spring. After freedom, Moore apprenticed himself to a blacksmith, and at "the end of three years he had become so proficient that his former master rewarded him with a five-dollar bonus for shoeing one horse. . . . He is still . . . recognized as an excellent blacksmith despite his more than four-score years."[69]

Another tale of a former slave's rise to riches through hard work and entrepreneurial know-how, "An Ex-Slave Who Went to Africa," is fascinatingly

reminiscent of colonial travel narratives in which the colonists make good
and then return to the motherland. In a curious reversal of this process,
informant Anna Scott's narrative tells of how her family, following emancipation, returned to Africa as part of a colonization expedition in 1867.[70]
Although her stepfather didn't like any of the ports where they docked, the
group was finally told they had to disembark at Harper Cape, West Africa:
"Here he almost immediately began an industry that would prove lucrative."[71]
Making his own bricks and chopping his own lumber, Anna's stepfather
started a construction business: "One such structure brought him $1100."[72]
But his resourcefulness did not stop there; in addition to the construction
company, he began cashing checks for the missionaries: "Ordinarily they
would have to send them back to the United States to be cashed, and when
he offered to cash them—at a discount—they eagerly utilized the opportunity
to save time; this was a convenience for them and more wealth for Mum-
ford."[73] However, these successes were not without their trials, for "death,
sickness, and pestilence" along with the African ants were part of the native
climate.[74] After eight years of accruing capital, the family returned to the
States "reasonably wealthy."[75] In this narrative, the homeland of Africa, as it
was referred to by those engaged in the colonization effort, is as alien and
perilous to the black protagonists as it ever was to the European colonials,
and it is endured for the same purpose of financial gain. Once the family
fortune was secured, they returned home. This narrative underscores the
point that even for ex-slaves, the true homeland is America.

The Florida Negro

The portraits that emerge in the slave narratives of Florida of African Americans as truthful, hardworking, successful contributors to the American nation
would also appear in the manuscript "The Florida Negro." The Florida narratives, like the ones gathered by the NWU of Virginia, were meant to be used
as part of the primary materials for a book on the black experience in the
state. Although many were originally earmarked for inclusion in the American
Guide Series, when it became clear that there was too much material, they
were later incorporated into a separate manuscript, "The Florida Negro."
However, *The Florida Negro* was not published until 1993, despite Hurston's
attempts to solicit interest from Macmillan and the Christopher Publishing
House in 1939 before she left the project.[76]

In his introduction to the first published edition of *The Florida Negro*, Gary
McDonogh notes that although extensive drafts of the manuscript materials

comprising over 2,500 pages of text (including the ex-slave narratives) exist, his 1993 edition "follows what seems to be both the earliest and the only complete text" from 1937. Martin Richardson seems to have been the primary contributor and editor, but the text also includes material collected and written by Rachel Austin, James Johnson, Samuel Johnson, Viola Muse, and Pearl Randolph, along with some submissions by Cora Mae Taylor, a white folklorist employed by the Florida Project.[77] But it seems clear from the extensive material produced for the "Negro book" project available in "The Florida Negro" manuscript collection that a great deal of work was produced after 1937 and that a fuller iteration was in the works, as many of the topic entries in McDonogh's version are not much more than brief sketches. A table of contents for the manuscript that accompanies a State Editorial Identification Form from June 1939 is much more extensive and includes Hurston's FWP material (material subsequently published by Pamela Bordelon as the "missing" Hurston contributions from "The Florida Negro" manuscript).[78] In an interview Corse gave in 1976, she referred to the manuscript as "a Statewide Study of Negro Activities," which suggests that the central project the NWU was undertaking focused on more contemporary aspects of black life in Florida and helps explain the large number of submissions on black organizations, communities, and businesses.[79]

Much of the portrait that emerges from the 1937 version of the manuscript is one of a decidedly bourgeoisie experience, which emphasizes assimilation, uplift, and respectability. One of Corse's original ideas, proposed to Alsberg in 1935, was a potential study focusing on black progress: "The accomplishments of Florida negroes ranks very high in America. What we have done in the education of the negro and their response are things unrealized by the nation, and even by the people of their own state. This knowledge would do much to remedy the feeling between the two races in Florida, a feeling which is not as good now as it was thirty years ago. I could give numerous reasons for this—economic, social, etc."[80] This motivation helps elucidate in part why the Negro Project took the shape that it did; Corse viewed public recognition of black achievement in Florida as an avenue to improving race relations. In this, Corse's objectives dovetailed neatly with the goals of many of the members of the NWU, who aimed to publicize African American progress as a means of promoting racial equality and whose emphasis on education, business, and racial uplift can be found in the slave narratives as well as the manuscript for "The Florida Negro." The additional essays intended for the book penned by core members of the NWU in Jacksonville, along with the table of contents for a 1938 iteration of the manuscript, indicate that this approach was becoming predominant, overshadowing earlier pieces on black folk culture and negating much of Hurston's "folkloristic image of black life."[81] McDonogh's decision to publish the version that existed prior to Hurston's arrival facilitates a clear comparison between her work for the Florida Project and the other members of the NWU.

Just as in many of Florida's ex-slave narratives, arguments for black self-determination surface in *The Florida Negro*. In a chapter devoted to exploring the capabilities of African Americans for self-government and assimilation into American political institutions, entitled "Unusual Negro Communities," two portraits of black communities are presented, of Eatonville and Pensacola. Best known for being Hurston's hometown, Eatonville is described as "the only town in the state completely owned and governed by the Negroes."[82] Furthermore, the text emphasizes, "this small community has continued through the years to adhere to its regular routine of self-government."[83] Pensacola is presented as a successfully racially integrated city: "Instead of a white section, a colored section, a Jewish section, and so forth, there are no sharp dividing lines at all; in the sections predominantly white, there are usually a number of Negro homes, and in the Negro sections are found many white families living in complete harmony with their neighbors."[84] In addition to racial peace on the domestic front, Pensacola is shown to have incorporated blacks into all areas of city life: "Negroes have always served on the federal juries in the city, and the courts are especially impartial."[85] The story of an African American lawyer who defended white clients and won his cases is presented as evidence of black objectivity.

African Americans who entered the political scene are also covered in this chapter, and the writer notes that "[the Pensacola Negro's] elevation to office was the result of the esteem in which he was held by both races in the community, rather than through the efforts of carpetbaggers and scalawags."[86] Proof of Pensacola's exceptionalism is also provided through blacks' ability to vote even at democratic primaries.[87] The listing of African Americans who served as state legislators, policemen, city marshals, and postmasters offered illustrative examples of African Americans' responsibility and fitness for the demands of American citizenship.[88]

Not surprisingly, the portrayal of slavery days in *The Florida Negro* is much more unfavorable than that found in some of the state projects that employed mostly white writers. The chapter entitled "Slave Days in Florida" by Richardson, which synthesizes evidence from the ex-slave narratives, tells of slave uprisings and resistance, alongside the violent abuses that were part of the system, without mincing words. Bold headings draw attention to the subject matter, for example, "The Paterollers," "Eugenics to Order," and "Thin Dresses and Cold Water."[89] The chapter met with the approval of George Cronyn, associate director of the FWP, as well as Sterling Brown, who called it "a very comprehensive and well-written account" and a testament to "praiseworthy industry on the part of the writer or writers." Brown returned the copy with very few editorial changes marked.[90] The manuscript, however, does occasionally reveal instabilities in the text that are likely reflective of the fact that the material submitted by the Negro Unit was combined with drafts written by white employees on the Project. Although Richardson was the primary compiler and editor for much of the manuscript, white editors such as Kennedy and Corse also helped shape it. In the chapter devoted to ex-slave narratives, there are only two: one was written by Rachel Austin of the NWU; the second, "Mama Duck," was by Jules Frost, a white employee and former journalist; the chapter concludes with "A Slaveholder Speaks," an excerpt from a "good" slaveholder on the harmony that existed between slave and master on his plantation.[91]

Separate chapters were devoted to the themes of education, business, and politics, and discussed current achievements and future progress in a self-congratulatory tone. Many of the gains documented by the NWU were very recent; Lakeland's "Colored City Auditorium" was built in 1937 with WPA funds.[92] Diggs's short piece on the public library in Lakeland noted that the "colored branch" had opened its doors in October 1937, making it only the second library building for African Americans in the state.[93] In the manuscript but also in the written drafts submitted by members of Florida's Negro Unit, the theme of "racial uplift" predominates in essays that moralize about education, economic opportunity, civic duty, religion, and overcoming adversity. These writings commonly referred to successful African Americans as examples of what the race could achieve. "Negro History," by Viola Muse, told of black Americans' contribution to the history of Tampa. Drawn primarily from interviews with prominent black citizens, it was mainly a listing of important members of the black bourgeoisie, including African American state senators, business owners, physicians, and social organizers.[94] Other essays on "Negro history," written by Farrell, Diggs, J. M. Johnson, and Richardson, also centered on African Americans' contribution to various Florida cities, citing examples of black postmasters, businessmen, and civic leaders.[95]

Throughout, words like "elevate," "rise," and "uplift" are used to describe black progress, and the focus is on economic mobility and education. Under a section entitled "Contemporary Life," the proliferation of black middle-class professionals is celebrated as the consummate manifestation of African American progress: "Florida's 462,000 Negroes today present many evidences of the progress they have made in the 250 years they have been in the peninsula. They have businesses ranging from the small bootblack stands and restaurants found in every city to two large insurance companies, one having assets of more than a million dollars. Each city has from one to several undertaking establishments, real estate offices, doctors, lawyers, and other professional men, in addition to a variety of smaller enterprises. Some cities, like Miami, Tampa and Jacksonville, have entire city blocks where Negro businesses are the only ones to be found."[96]

Photographs included in the manuscript depict three main motifs: one picture of a provincial former slave is juxtaposed with a parade of well-dressed students from Bethune-Cookman College, providing a direct illustration of the theme of racial progress—from slavery to education. Other images are of impressive black institutions such as colleges, Masonic temples, and public recreation centers. Two large group photos of separate organizations, the Negro Boy Scouts and the historic black union the National Alliance of Postal Employees,[97] are included, along with several portraits of bourgeois civilized community events: a fancy wedding party and an outdoor festival at Durkeeville.[98]

But there is evidence of certain class tensions in the writings intended for publication in *The Florida Negro*. Part of "racial uplift" ideology was predicated upon class differentiation; members of the black bourgeoisie wanted to have their middle-class identity recognized and chose at times to emphasize their difference in cultural as well as economic terms from the masses of black folk. Such differences helped to de-emphasize the importance of racial identity in determining character and one's place in society, while also proving that African Americans were assimilable into the larger society. Thus, the differences between regular folk and the bourgeoisie could demonstrate that racial identity was meaningless in the face of the "natural law" of capitalism, in which individual achievement naturally separated those who rose to the top from those who remained at the bottom. Stories of successful individuals could simultaneously serve as examples to the masses while underscoring the importance of individual ability, which regardless of race helped one become economically and socially mobile.[99] This aspect of "racial uplift" meant that it was less a vision of complete equality for all than a reiteration of the American capitalistic creed. For the black bourgeoisie, it "affirmed their sense of status and entitlement to citizenship."[100]

The class element inherent in "racial uplift" ideology also appears in the focus on individual "race leaders," members of the black bourgeoisie who could serve as exemplary role models and inspire the lower classes to emulate by example and thereby achieve greatness. Numerous biographies of black Floridians who had been successful in the arts, business, journalism, politics, and civic organizations were written by members of the Negro Unit with the theme of "racial uplift" at the forefront. Many of these were "rags-to-riches" stories with a moralistic bent and would appear in *The Florida Negro* in the chapter "Notable Florida Negroes."[101] Diggs submitted a biographical portrait of the black educator Madame Bethune, which began by introducing the reader to her humble beginnings: "One can picture in his mind a little cabin sitting in the middle of a cotton and rice farm.... It was here that a great woman was born by the name of Mary McLeod Bethune.... There were seventeen of these children born [to] her slave parents.... It is said that she had to walk four miles to and from school."[102] After listing her many accomplishments and professional affiliations, Diggs summed up her legacy as a "race leader": "Today we may find youths who are making good in communities, who have been inspired by her spiritual and educational uplift. Her greatest contribution to the race has been in this field. And Mary McLeod Bethune will go down in history as one of the greatest colored women that the race has ever produced."[103] In another biography on black educators, Diggs wrote on the leadership abilities of Professor William Rochelle, who had instilled his "influence and principles [into his] race members."[104] Throughout, Diggs emphasized the morality and diligence of his subject. In his conclusion, Diggs identified the three traits of the successful man: "These qualities are Industry, Concentration and Self Reliance."[105]

This emphasis on self-help, individual achievement, and class divisions within the race would frequently surface in essays by the NWU. Rebecca Baker explained the process of gentrification that had occurred in Daytona, where "the more energetic and thrifty [members of the black community] took advantage of every opportunity to better their condition; they bought property and built homes.... The thrift of the Negro in this section is indicated by the fact that ... Negroes alone lost $92,000 in the [bank failure of 1927]."[106] By demonstrating black diligence and thrift, descriptions like this also worked to dispel stereotypes of African Americans as financially short-sighted and incapable of looking out for their own interest. The focus on self-improvement, strongly advocated by Booker T. Washington, comes through vigorously in these writings. Richardson's "What the Florida Negro Does" concluded with the factors that "are making the outlook for Negro labor in Florida more optimistic than it has been at any time in recent history."[107] In addition to education, Richardson focused on the black workers' "self-bettering of many conditions." Emphasizing self-reliance, Richardson extolled the "wholesome" virtues of the organization of labor: "Negro labor will soon be able to lift itself, by its own bootstraps, into a position of eminence in the state's economic and social system."[108] This section would appear unaltered in *The Florida Negro* under the heading "The Trend towards Civilization."[109]

Contrasts between the black working class and the black bourgeoisie also appear in the chapters devoted to the discussion of leisure activities. The uplifting of the race relied equally on the cultivation of the health of the body through physical exercise as well as the mind. African Americans were often shut out of educational opportunities because of racial discrimination, but they were also prevented from participating in recreational activities. A section entitled "Organized Recreation" describes tennis tournaments, regattas, and golf clubs, along with their illustrious participants, in glowing terms.[110] After noting that these types of recreation do not play "a large role in the life of the average Negro," the text points out that all of these activities also underwrite black charities. Even the federal government participates in this type of cultural uplift, for the manuscript notes that the WPA provided funding for public band concerts, enabling the "Negroes of Tampa . . . to appreciate the better type of music."[111] A piece on the Lincoln Golf and Country Club, the only recreational club for African Americans, which opened in Jacksonville in 1927, was listed on the table of contents for the 1939 version of the manuscript.

But a tension emerges in the sections describing less "wholesome" amusements, where the author seems torn over how to present them. In addition to providing positive portrayals of contemporary black life, "The Florida Negro" sought to dispel racist stereotypes of black identity. In its educational intent, and its sanctimonious yet sympathetic tone of moral reform, this chapter is representative of the NWU's didactic style of "racial uplift" as opposed to white FWP employees' depictions of black folk amusements as exotic "local color." The folklore chapter takes a critical approach toward black folk traditions, suggesting in the first paragraph that "these old superstitions . . . have contributed to the high Negro death rate" and praising the effects of "concerted health drives and increased educational advantages . . . towards [the Negro's] enlightenment."[112]

In a chapter devoted to a lengthy discussion of the gambling game bolita, Richardson attributed its prevalence specifically to environmental rather than racial factors. Economic insecurity is cited as the main culprit, followed by the corrupting influence of white agents, collectors, and policemen who profit off the gullibility of black as well as white players. Similarly, in a short chapter on the "Conjure Shop," the stereotype of black primitivism and superstition is effaced by the description of the shop's white proprietor. The text also notes that "about half the customers are white, but white or colored, all classes of society are represented."[113] Chapter 6, "Amusements and Diversions," begins with the observation that "in the large cities of Florida, the Negro's diversions are not markedly different from those of his white brother."[114] However, in rural areas at "the turpentine camps, the phosphate mines, and possibly the small saw-mill towns . . . the Negro is thrown upon his own resources for amusement."[115] This section describes "the jooks," communal gatherings where drinking, dancing, and gambling took place. Such lowbrow entertainment was viewed by black middle-class reformers as a means of distinguishing themselves from the folk but also as a site for reform; such public displays of black licentiousness, they feared, could reinforce arguments regarding African Americans' lack of fitness for the rights of citizenship. The politics of respectability necessitated the "reform of individual behavior as a goal in itself and as a strategy for reform."[116]

The politics of respectability were defined in behavioral as well as economic terms, and gendered expectations for men and women were a central component of intraracial class distinctions. Diggs became a local crusader for enforcing middle-class standards of respectability. In 1943, he established the Negro Auxiliary League, a volunteer task force affiliated with the Lakeland Police Department, responsible for patrolling black neighborhoods. While they were authorized to arrest African Americans, they were not permitted to arrest whites. Speaking before the city commission, Diggs asked that they formally approve a midnight curfew for black women "to keep [them] from running around from one jook joint to another at all hours of the night." In addition to cultivating gentility and success through self-discipline and habits of temperance, thrift, and cleanliness, sexual modesty for black women was an essential attribute. "They are running rampant," Diggs asserted.[117] By regulating the boundaries of acceptable conduct for African Americans, NWU members like Diggs invoked but also helped to reinforce what one scholar has termed "a behavioral 'entrance fee,' to the right to respect and the right to full citizenship."[118]

This elitist attitude was one that Hurston lampooned. Unlike her coworkers in the NWU, such as Diggs, Hurston embraced the "jooks" as a loophole for black leisure in the oppressive system and hard labor of phosphate mills and turpentine camps and mined them for folk material. She derided the "well-bred Negro" who "after straining every nerve to get an education, maintain an attractive home, dress decently, and otherwise conform . . . is dismayed at the sight of other Negroes tearing down what he is trying to build up."[119] While she understood the larger context in which aspiring and upwardly mobile black Americans attempted to control as well as distance themselves from the underprivileged, she had no patience for those who "drew color lines within the race."[120] The NWU's emphasis on education, assimilation, and racial uplift was often at odds with black folk culture. Hurston's contribution to the Florida Project tended to celebrate aspects of "the Negro farthest down," as the carrier as well as creator of the wellsprings of black cultural expressiveness. The following chapter will look at the ex-slave narrators for the Florida and Georgia Projects and examine how they drew on those wellsprings of black vernacular traditions to strategically position themselves in relation to white interviewers and create their own narratives of slavery and emancipation.

CHAPTER EIGHT

Rewriting the Master('s) Narrative
Signifying in the Ex-Slave Narratives

Here my Jim Crow education assumed quite a different form. It was no longer brutally cruel, but subtly cruel. Here I learned to lie, to steal, to dissemble. I learned to play that dual role which every Negro must play if he wants to eat and live.

—Richard Wright, "The Ethics of Living Jim Crow," 1937

Never trust the teller, trust the tale.

—D. H. Lawrence

In late August 1938, a white Federal Writers' Project (FWP) interviewer sat down with Minnie Davis at her home in Athens, Georgia, to record her memories of slavery. The interviewer, Mrs. Sadie Hornsby, described Davis's small house as a "tumble-down shack" and noted that an "unsteady wooden box served as a step to the fragment of a porch before the front door." Notwithstanding her impoverished circumstances, the elderly woman was gracious in her reception of the unexpected visitor and invited Hornsby into her bedroom, where she had been resting, for she was in ill health. "Despite the sweltering heat," Hornsby noted, "she wore a pink flannel nightgown, faded and dingy, and a pair of high top black shoes, so badly run over that she hobbled along on the sides of them." When the interviewer explained her purpose, Davis proved reluctant to answer any questions about her remembrances of slavery. The interviewer related their negotiation: "[Davis] explained that she did not care to talk for publication at all. She said she was hungry and had nothing at all in the house to eat. Her nephew . . . would go for food if there was any money. She might feel like talking a little if she had something to eat. The interviewer provided the cash and Ed soon returned with a pint of milk and some cinnamon rolls."[1] Having received the requested payment, Davis related the many kindnesses of her former master, recalling the good food that was plentiful and the dresses she wore with petticoats underneath. The self-conscious way in which Davis then proceeded to construct her story was not lost on Hornsby, who noted that "after her repast, Minnie began to talk, giving the impression that every word was carefully weighed before it was uttered."[2]

"Old Slave," Arkansas, photographed between 1936 and 1938. "Born in Slavery: Slave Narratives from the Federal Writers' Project, 1936–1938," courtesy of the Library of Congress, Manuscript Division, mesnp 021000.

Davis's narrative illustrates the process by which some ex-slaves carefully bargained with FWP interviewers for economic compensation, at times shaping their reminiscences of slavery days to conform to white questioners' expectations.[3] Historically, black Americans were forced to rely on culture and performance as forms of currency in an economic system that sharply delimited their options as wage earners. Out of necessity, African Americans, already aware of the intrinsic personal value of their folk heritage, came to recognize its extrinsic market value.[4] During the Great Depression, rural black folk continued a long-standing tradition of using their oral performances as commodities that could be exchanged for material goods. Ex-slaves, such as Davis, would not likely have expected these negotiations that frame as well as punctuate their stories about "slavery days" to be recorded, yet some Georgia interviewers included them in their write-up of the narratives. Although they appear infrequently in the large collection from Georgia, this type of narrative provides a unique window into the racial dynamics and social context in which these interviews took place. The written record of these exchanges reveals the nexus of two different practices: ex-slaves' commodification of their oral performances and southern whites' paternalistic practice of using charitable gifts to persuade black informants to offer up their stories. It also reveals how these dynamics shaped the content of the narratives, resulting in contradictory views on slavery and emancipation, at times even within a single narrative.

Ex-slaves used their narratives as a form of currency, bartering them for goods and services from FWP interviewers, but they also created their own counternarratives of black identity and experience by drawing on African American oral traditions to exert control over their interviewers as well as the performance of their life histories. Examining the narratives as oral performances helps us reread them as sites of struggle over representation: spaces where ex-slaves exerted some agency over the portrayals of their experiences and identities and where interviewers, although in the very powerful positions of amanuensis and editor, were forced to collaborate with the representations provided by their black informants.[5] Folklorist Gladys-Marie Fry's identification of the performative aspect of oral history is helpful in this regard. As she writes: "Because reminiscences must operate within the natural bounds of a conversational unit, like gossip and rumor, they must appear spontaneous, but are in fact structured by the strict rules of spoken intercourse. While not as stylized as a joke or a folktale, they nonetheless constitute a conversational narrative form which is in fact delivered as a performance while maintaining the appearance of unrehearsed, impromptu dialogue."[6]

Interpreting the ex-slave narratives through the lens of oral performance focuses attention on what ex-slaves chose to recount in the context of the interview dynamic, and there were some, as documented by more than one frustrated FWP employee, who refused to say anything at all.[7] It also reveals how the competing interests and expectations for the Ex-Slave Project played out in direct negotiations between interviewers and informants. As Robin Kelley reminds us, daily acts of resistance employed by oppressed groups serve as a litmus test for the operation of power relations within the social order and should not be overlooked as a viable space for political struggle and negotiation.[8] This chapter focuses on a comparison of some of the slave narratives of Florida and Georgia to illuminate how the context and dynamics of the interviews shaped the stories that got told. White Georgia interviewers posed leading questions, inserted their own impressions of the ex-slaves' character, speech, and mannerisms, and placed their informants' narratives within a broader story of nostalgia for the Old South. Ex-slaves, at times, cooperated with southern whites' agenda by reminiscing about benevolent slaveholders and the benefits of slavery for black folk, but also found ways to covertly contradict these kinds of assertions within their narratives.

When faced with white questioners, African Americans in the South during the 1930s proved to be highly skilled in the tactics of evasion as well as diplomacy. For example, ex-slave Bill Reese explained that his "mother's owner was also her own father, and for that reason I'd rather not tell his name."[9] Black survival during slavery had depended on the ability to feign consent and to dissemble in the presence of whites, veiling sentiments and actions that could otherwise result in severe punishment and often death.[10] In the long era of Jim Crow, these skills were still essential for dealing with whites and particularly when discussing emotionally charged topics such as slavery. Nevertheless, ex-slaves in Georgia still found ways to speak truths about slavery that their white questioners would likely not want to hear, skillfully weaving contrapuntal evidence and perspectives in the warp and woof of their stories through the use of black vernacular traditions, including signifying.[11]

The rhetorical strategy of signifying was one of the principal ways for African Americans to enact the form of resistance known as "disingenuous compliance," or what Zora Neale Hurston so eloquently described as the Negro's "feather-bed resistance."[12] This method protected the speaker by cloaking statements that could be perceived as forbidden or insubordinate and by smothering whites' questions under a blanket of voluble affability and humor. Although signifying may have originated in African vernacular traditions, it quickly evolved under the institution of slavery as a means of survival and a safe form of communication largely because of its inaccessibility to whites.[13] It is a manifest expression of black folk culture and belief, as Claudia Mitchell-Kernan explains: "The Black concept of signifying incorporates essentially a folk notion that dictionary entries for words are not always sufficient. . . . The hearer is thus constrained to attend to all potential meaning carrying symbolic systems in speech events—the total universe of discourse."[14]

Signifying can take a variety of forms, including the use of figurative language, such as tropes and metaphors, indirection, and humor.[15] As Roger Abrahams observes, the term denotes a range of verbal strategies, but it is fundamentally "a language of implication."[16] At the broadest level, it can refer to a speaker's "ability to carp, cajole, needle, and lie" to gain the upper hand, mirroring the central method of the trickster figure found in black folktales.[17] It can also refer to indirect speech acts, including circumlocution (talking "around a subject, never quite coming to the point"), evasiveness and equivocation, as well as euphemisms and other forms of figurative language.[18] Examples of this verbal art form abound in the slave narrative collection and demonstrate how ex-slaves drew on a variety of these tactics when addressing white interviewers.[19] Although Davis's narrative of slavery days affirms the benevolence of her former owner, her double-edged response to a question regarding the punishment of slaves is characteristic of the ways in which ex-slaves accommodated their interviewers' perspective regarding slavery while still maintaining a textual loophole for their own opinion. "I don't recall any certain reason why the slaves were punished," Davis stated, suggesting that slaves were often punished without reason or, conversely, for any reason at all. She quickly followed up with this explanation for slaves' punishment: "They needed it, I'm sure of that."[20]

Given the ways these narratives were shaped by multiple actors, from interviewers to district supervisors and editors, to state and federal directors, it may seem counterintuitive to read these narratives as a record of the dialogue that occurred between interviewers and former slaves. However, this method is essential for recovering ex-slaves' authorship and agency. Examining the collection for evidence of black oral traditions brings to light significant patterns and structures within each narrative, as well as across state projects.[21] It has not been my aim to question the substance of what was said, as recorded in the narratives. In the instructions issued by the federal office for gathering ex-slave stories, FWP interviewers were specifically directed "to write down what was said as accurately as possible in the informant's own words (in the absence of recording equipment), [and] the interviewer was expected not to take sides and not to 'censor any material collected, regardless of its nature.' "[22] As a result, important patterns can be discerned in the questions interviewers asked, as well as the way they asked them, and the observations they made about the ex-slaves' appearance, speech, mannerisms, and abodes. Equally noteworthy patterns can be found in the ways ex-slaves chose to answer their interviewers' questions.

Evidence of signifying occurs throughout the Slave Narrative Collection of the FWP. Florida and Georgia offer striking examples of the different ways ex-slaves used signifying as subtext, depending on their audience. Florida was one of only three states that established a separate Negro Writers' Unit (NWU); African American employees interviewed former slaves and gathered information on black history and communities for an anticipated volume, *The Florida Negro*. By contrast, Georgia did not have an NWU, although it employed five African American writers who contributed to the Ex-Slave Project: Willie H. Cole, Adella S. Dixon, Edwin Driskell, Louise Oliphant, and Minnie B. Ross.[23]

Georgia was a stronghold of the United Daughters of the Confederacy (UDC), the organization dedicated to proselytizing the pro-southern interpretation of slavery and the Civil War. Four employees of Georgia's FWP who worked on the Ex-Slave Project were UDC members; one of them, Sarah H. Hall, served as editor of the Georgia narratives.[24] With white interviewers, ex-slaves frequently used signifying practices to hide their subtext; white employees in Georgia recorded examples of ex-slaves' signifying but usually did so unwittingly. With black interviewers, ex-slaves used signifying practices but expected to be understood by their questioners. Members of Florida's NWU were often aware of the messages ex-slaves were indirectly conveying and actively collaborated with their ex-slave informants, working within the narratives to ensure that these coded messages would be understood by a larger audience. By first examining the slave narratives gathered in Georgia, and then in Florida, this chapter will explore how some ex-slave informants used their performances as a form of currency and self-commodification, and uncover the strategies employed by interviewers as well as ex-slaves to shape the narratives in particular ways.

Georgia's Ex-Slave Narratives—Commodifying Acts

Georgia's district supervisor in Savannah, Mary Granger, likely initiated the practice among FWP interviewers of bringing low-cost items with which to encourage ex-slaves to share their stories. On research trips to gather ex-slave material that the Georgia Writers' Program published in 1940 as *Drums and*

Shadows: Survival Studies among the Georgia Coastal Negroes, Granger's co-workers observed her methods for ingratiating herself with African American informants. She "was always ready to reward cooperative subjects or to persuade reluctant ones to be photographed with an offer of sweet rolls, tobacco, or old but serviceable clothes, all of which Miss Granger seemed to have in endless supply."[25] Georgia interviewer and editor Sarah H. Hall described how she herself had used this method of persuasion after ex-slave Martha Colquitt complained about her cold house: "[I] could not resist the impulse to say, 'Let's make a trade, Aunt Martha! If I give you a little money will you buy wood; then while you enjoy the fire will you think back over your life and tell me about your experiences when I come back tomorrow?' 'Bless de Lord! I sho' will be glad to tell you de truf 'bout anything I can 'member,' was her quick reply as she reached for the money."[26]

Exchanges like these between ex-slave informants and FWP interviewers took place within a context of southern white hegemony, where whites still controlled the social, political, and economic system. Because of their unequal social position, ex-slaves undoubtedly would have been hesitant to directly request compensation from their interviewers. As a result, a carefully structured social discourse surrounds these types of exchanges based on an appeal to southern paternalism and southern whites' sense of noblesse oblige. Ex-slaves could not demand payment for their oral histories, but they could cajole, flatter, and persuade through appeals to southern whites' generosity. Ex-slave Julia Brown, referred to as "Aunt Sally" by her white Georgia interviewer, abruptly "broke off her story" with the explanation that she was too weak from hunger to continue: "Lord, honey, Ah got sich a pain in mah stomach I don't believe I can go on. It's a gnawin' kind of pain. Jest keeps me weak all over."[27] When her interviewer, Geneva Tonsill, returned in a couple of days, she made sure not to arrive empty-handed. As she reported: "I'd put the bag of groceries on the table unobtrusively, but Aunt Sally wasn't one to let such gifts pass unnoticed. Eagerly she tore the bag open and began pulling out the packages. 'Lawd bless you chile, and He sho will bless you! I feels rich seein' what you brought me. Just look at this—Lawdy mercy!—rolls, butter, milk, baloney! You must a knowed what I wanted!' She was stuffing it in her mouth as she talked. 'Honey, you knows God is goin' to bless you and let you live long.' "[28] After expressing her appreciation, Aunt Sally launched straight into a few obligatory ghost stories. Tonsill brought the interview to a close, because "Aunt Sally was beginning to repeat herself and I began to suspect that she was talking just to please me."[29] But the ex-slave's shrewd tactics had not escaped notice; as Tonsill recorded in the narrative,

"My awareness of the obvious fulsomeness in the old woman's praise in no way detracted from my feeling of having done a good deed. Aunt Sally was a clever psychologist."[30]

Because these memories of slavery days were presented to white interviewers as a form of economic exchange, they were often structured in conformity with what ex-slaves surmised were their interviewers' expectations. One of the best examples of this type of narrative from Georgia is an interview with Lina Hunter conducted by white employee Grace McCune and edited by UDC member Hall.[31] Hunter was happy to comply with McCune's request for an interview: "I 'members all 'bout slavery time," she laughed, "cause I was right dar."[32] Hunter began with a favorable portrait of slavery days, focusing on the generosity of her former master. Throughout, she emphasized that "Marster was sho good to his Niggers all de time." When the Yankees came and tried to give the meat that had been stored in the smokehouse to the former slaves, they returned it to "Marse Jack" for "deir bellies was already full and dey didn't need it."[33] Immediately following these tales of benevolent white patronage, Hunter held out the promise of singing some spirituals for her interviewer while subtly making a condition for the continuation of her performance:

> "I kin still hear our old songs, but it's jus' now and den dat dey come back to my mind." For a moment Lina was quiet, then she said, "Honey, I wants to smoke my old pipe so bad I kin most taste it, but how in hell kin I smoke when I ain't had no 'baccy in two days? Chile, ain't you got no 'baccy wid you, jus' a little 'baccy? You done passed de nighest store 'bout 2 miles back toward town," she said, "but if you will pay for some 'baccy for Lina, some of dese good-for-nothin' chillun kin sho go git it quick and, whilst dey's dar, dey might as well git me a little coffee too, if you kin spare de change." The cash was supplied by the visitor and Lina continued her story.[34]

There was clearly more to Hunter's oral performance than just the stories and songs from slavery days she provided for her interviewer. Hunter used the anecdotes regarding her former master's generosity to highlight the similarity between his magnanimous patronage and that bestowed by McCune. To ensure that the comparison did not go unnoticed, Hunter expressed her gratitude vociferously:

> Suddenly the old woman leaped to her feet and began shouting, "Bless God A'mighty! Praise de Lord! I knows de key to prayers. I'se done

prayed jus' dis mornin' for de Lord to send me some 'baccy and coffee, and God is done sont Missy wid de money to answer my prayer. Praise de Lord! . . . I'se gwine to smoke dat damned old pipe one more time. . . . Honey, I jus' feels like prayin' and cussin' too, at de same time. . . . If Old Marster could jus' come back I'd sho have plenty of evvything I needs."[35]

After Hunter's conspicuous display of gratitude for her white benefactors, past and present, she broke into song, providing her interviewer with the words to two African American spirituals. But having done so, Hunter grew visibly anxious for her groceries. As McCune observed: "She stood up and peered down the road, impatient for the return of the children who were to bring her tobacco and coffee. Finally she saw them come over the hill and could hardly restrain herself until they arrived in the yard. Snatching the parcels, as the children came up the steps, Lina called out, 'Callie, come here, gal, fix my pipe quick, and put dat coffeepot on de fire bucket, 'cause Glory to God! I'se gwine to smoke my old pipe and drink me one more good cup of coffee.' "[36] Once she had satisfied herself with the requested items, Hunter proved more than willing to keep her end of the agreement by continuing to talk and sing. Hunter apparently found the transaction satisfactory; as her interviewer made ready to leave, Hunter promised to provide more material if McCune would visit again: "Lina followed her to the veranda and said with much enthusiasm, 'God bless you, Lady. You sho is done made me happy, and I'se gwine to pray for you evvy day and ask de Lord to take keer of you all de time. I'se gwine to do dat, 'cause I wants you to come back and let me sing some more of our good old songs for you sometime.' "[37] As McCune left, "Lina's high pitched voice could be heard singing *My Old Mammy Died A-Shoutin'*."[38]

Exchanges like these, as recorded in the Georgia narratives, are likely to make twenty-first-century readers uncomfortable owing to the abject posturing of ex-slave informants as well as the way their speech was badly rendered in dialect. One might question why Georgia interviewers chose to include these transactions as part of the ex-slaves' oral history that they were charged with faithfully recording. By providing a record of the interview from start to finish, Georgia workers adhered to the dictums of the federal office to write down what was said as completely as possible. Georgia employees often described everything that occurred during their fieldwork, including finding the informant's home, the social preliminaries of the interview and the leave-taking, and all of the in-between bits of action and dialogue. These details provide a wealth of information about the gendered and racial dynamics of the entire interaction between interviewers and ex-slaves. For example, Bill Reese's white interviewer, Sadie Hornsby, noted that when she finally located him at a neighbor's house, he "seemed self-conscious and meticulously mindful of the proprieties" of being alone with her. It was a dangerous risk for an African American man, regardless of his age, to be alone with a white woman in the South, as it could lead to false accusations of rape, often resulting in lynching. Reese requested that Hornsby, if she wished to visit with him, meet him at his sister's house, " 'cause there ain't nobody at my house."[39]

However, Georgia interviewers also used their descriptions of these interactions, particularly ones that involved the gift of goods or services to ex-slave informants, for their own objectives. These framing devices for the ex-slaves' narratives served an overarching agenda—emphasizing African Americans' continuing dependency on southern white paternalism and proving their unfitness for freedom and full citizenship. Members of the UDC, like Georgia editor Sarah Hall, idealized slavery as a mutually beneficial system based on benevolent white paternalism and the loyalty of black dependents, even as they asserted that the "War between the States," as pro-Confederates called it, was fought over states' rights and southern independence, not slavery. The formal aim of the UDC, established in 1894, was to ensure that histories at the local, state, and national level reflected this "true" and "impartial" interpretation of slavery and the Civil War, free from "Negro" as well as northern distortion and bias. Elite southern women played a central role in crafting and popularizing the mythology of the "Lost Cause" as history, and sought public vindication for the Confederacy by strategically rewriting the historical narrative in textbooks for schoolchildren and sponsoring essay contests and college scholarships. These women were brilliant strategists who recognized the powerful role education could play in shaping future generations' views of the nation's past. As Karen Cox observes in her insightful history of the organization, "the UDC left no stone unturned to insure that the next generation was motivated to honor and uphold the values of the Confederate generation."[40] Cox argues that the heyday of the UDC's influence had passed by 1915, but southern white women's involvement with the FWP's Ex-Slave Project suggests otherwise.

The 1930s saw a resurgence of UDC initiatives to sway public opinion on southern race relations. In 1934, the UDC began publication of *Southern Magazine*; a lengthy article from 1936, the year the Ex-Slave Project began, defended the Ku Klux Klan and its methods as necessary for the protection of the South from African Americans and "Negro rule."[41] Back in 1911, the UDC's historian general, Mildred Rutherford, had urged members to engage in the work of historical production that would help to vindicate the noble cause of the Confederacy.[42] In addition to pursuing such topics as notable women of the Confederacy and the reminiscences of veterans, Rutherford encouraged the collection of "Stories of Faithful Slaves."[43] Answering this call over the next three decades, many UDC members and Lost Cause supporters wrote and published biographies of famous Confederate leaders, along with numerous essays on antebellum life and culture emphasizing the loving relationships between slaveholders and their devoted slaves.

A number of southern white women invested in the Lost Cause were also FWP employees working on the Ex-Slave Project. Four years before she was hired as Virginia's state director, for example, Eudora Ramsay Richardson published the definitive biography *Little Aleck: A Life of Alexander H. Stephens, the Fighting Vice-President of the Confederacy*.[44] On the Georgia Project, in addition to Hall, there were at least three other UDC members responsible for interviewing former slaves.[45] In Florida, FWP employee Rose Shepherd was also a UDC member.[46] At the close of the FWP in 1939, Shepherd would endorse Florida state director Carita Doggett Corse for UDC membership.[47] These women recognized that the Lost Cause argument regarding slavery as a benevolent institution would carry more weight if it came from the mouths of former slaves.[48] Instead of the racial ventriloquism used by novelists like Joel Chandler Harris, who invented fictionalized plantation characters such as Uncle Remus, some white FWP employees, including those in Georgia, sought to use actual ex-slaves to help them narrate a version of the past in keeping with Confederate culture and ideology. Through the Ex-Slave Project, the personhood of former slaves and their life histories could be used to make arguments against, as well as for, black citizenship and to envision the future position of black Americans in the body politic.

These southern white women's representations of "faithful slaves," predicated on notions of white paternalism, black dependency, and racial inferiority, and rendered through depictions of black southern speech, folk customs, and quaint mannerisms and dress, converged with FWP federal directors' emphasis on capturing those same elements to lend authority and authenticity to the ex-slave narratives. The FWP's national advisor on folklore, John Lomax, directed interviewers to include descriptions of ex-slaves' residences, physical appearance, dress, and behavior in their narratives. This served to privilege, for readers, the interviewer's perspective. African American interviewers working for Florida's NWU often used this textual authority to make arguments for black citizenship, emphasizing ex-slaves' socioeconomic mobility, noble bearing, and good character. But in the hands of southern white employees, many of whom were supporters of the Old South and its racial hierarchy, these framing devices could become much more demeaning. UDC members who worked on the Georgia Project alternated between complimentary portrayals of the "old darkey" and "Negro mammy" of antebellum days, who embodied "the soul of humbleness and politeness," and more disparaging depictions of black inferiority.[49] These condescending representations of ex-slave informants worked to naturalize a southern hierarchy based on race. Descriptions of ex-slaves' appearance, speech, residence, and behavior became a visual index of "racial" character and helped turn informants' performances into a textual experience of blackness for a presumed white readership. These depictions of black informants, shaped by the minstrel tradition, are as disquieting to readers in the twenty-first century as they were to African Americans in the 1930s forced to challenge these racial stereotypes.[50]

Sadie Hornsby provided the reader with this kind of grotesque exaggeration in her visit with ex-slave Georgia Baker, drawing on the minstrel stereotype of the watermelon-eating "Negro" of base appetites: " 'Now dere you is axin' 'bout dat somepin' t'eat us had dem days! Ida, ain't dere a piece of watermelon in de ice box?' Georgia lifted the lid of a small ice box, got out a piece of melon, and began to smack her thick lips as she devoured it with an air of ineffable satisfaction. When she had tilted the rind to swallow the last drop of pink juice, she indicated that she was fortified and ready to exercise her now well lubricated throat by resuming her story."[51] As this example shows, Georgia narratives submitted by white employees favored the use of phonetic spelling to represent black speech. While federal directors of the Ex-Slave Project cautioned against the overuse (and abuse) of phonetic spelling, they still explicitly instructed FWP employees to capture the voices of former slaves and the flavor of black speech traditions by writing down the interview, word for word, in the voice of the ex-slave. Georgia writers were clearly in thrall to a long-standing tradition of literary minstrelsy that used broad misspellings to authenticate their representations of black speech as a racial, rather than regional, characteristic.

White interviewers' descriptions of the physical appearance of the ex-slaves and their surroundings often resulted in tropes of black identity that seemed to be drawn directly from the plantation literature of the late nineteenth century. Dosia Harris's appearance was described in a manner that emphasized phenotypical traits to underscore racial differences:

Her very black skin, thick lips, and broad nose are typical of her African ancestry . . . and her wooly hair is fast fading from gray to almost white. When she greeted the interviewer, she was wearing a blue striped dress which displayed a large patch of blue print on the front of her skirt. . . . Over her dress a black silk blouse, lavishly trimmed with black beads, was worn for a wrap, and a pair of men's brown shoes, sans laces, completed her costume. Due to illiteracy Dosia has retained the dialect of the old southern darky.[52]

In depictions of their informants' appearance and dress, Georgia interviewers were fond of elaborating on the mismatched aspect of the clothes worn by the former slaves as a way of humorously commenting on their childlike nature. The phrase "a comical little old black woman" commonly used by white interviewers was one that the director of the Office on Negro Affairs, Sterling Brown, had strongly objected to. It appeared in the narrative of ex-slave Jane Smith Hill Harmon, whose interviewer described her as "a comical little old black woman. . . . Her wardrobe consists of out-of-style clothes and hats given her and it is her delight on Saturday afternoons to dress up in her finest and fanciest creations and come strutting along down town proud of the attention she is attracting."[53] These narratives also emphasized the provincial nature of their black informants by recounting their extreme joy and gratitude over the small commodity items they received in return for their stories. Depictions of ex-slave informants' complete reliance on the trade and barter system underscored their inability to understand capitalism, thereby reinforcing the "authenticity" of the folk material interviewers collected. Portrayals of this type of exchange lent credibility to ex-slaves speaking longingly of the days of slavery.

Paradoxically, interviewers' descriptions of these barter and trade negotiations could also serve to cast doubt on the value of the ex-slaves' narratives as truthful accounts of life under slavery. By revealing how the ex-slave's story had been "bought," Georgia workers were playing on a traditional image of blacks as wily performers whose artistic gifts lay in the realm of fiction and storytelling—a people who were such natural entertainers that lies came easily to their lips. In sharp contrast to the slave narratives of Florida's NWU, which emphasized that the ex-slave informants had volunteered their testimonies willingly if often reluctantly, white interviewers suggested to readers that for money and goods, these ex-slave informants would say anything.

Sadie Hornsby's interview with ex-slave Georgia Baker is indicative of how FWP interviewers' representations of these exchanges could paint unflattering portraits of their black informants as mercenary storytellers. After a lengthy description of her carefree days as a slave, at the close of her first interview, Baker reminded the field worker of her promise to bring her a new dress: " 'Good-bye, Honey,' said Georgia, as the interviewer arose and made her way toward the street. 'Hurry back and don't forgit to fetch me dat purty pink dress you is a'wearin.' I don't lak white dresses and I ain't never gwine to wear a black one nohow.' "[54] In her account of the second interview with Baker, Hornsby described Baker's daughter Ida's initial unwillingness to participate. However, "after Ida's eyes had rested on the yellow crepe frock just presented Georgia in appreciation of the three hours she had given for the first interview she became reconciled for the story to be resumed, and even offered her assistance in arousing the recollections of her parent."[55] Baker, in bidding her interviewer good-bye, made it clear that she had traded her story in exchange for the dress: "Now, Miss, I done told you all I can ricollec' 'bout dem days. I thanks you a lot for dat purty yaller dress, and I hopes you comes back to see me again sometime."[56]

Georgia FWP employees accomplished something else with these narratives; they also served as a critique of the New Deal.[57] Depictions of white paternalism, along with the extremity of black poverty and the failures of the federal welfare state in the form of unattainable old-age pensions, can be viewed as an argument against government's inept interference with what the South considered to be its private "Negro" problem. African American interviewers, in contrast, often noted that ex-slaves were supported by pensions and also public welfare.[58] Some ex-slaves were clearly confused about the real purpose of these visits, and assumed the FWP interviewer, as a "gov'mint" employee, was there to assess their eligibility for old-age pensions.[59] Informant Julia Brown focused on the inadequacy of her biweekly stipend of seventy-five cents and the refusal of the government representative, whom Brown described as "a big black 'oman . . . a mean 'oman," to approve her for the old-age pension. "Ah tried to git the ole-age pension," Brown explained to her white interviewer, "fur Ah sho'ly needed it and wuz 'titled to it too. Sho wuz. But that visitor jest wouldn't let me go through. She acted lak that money belonged to her. Ah 'plied when it first come out and shoulda been one of the first to get one."[60] Brown's indignation over the African American agent's attitude underscored her appreciation for the individual generosity of the FWP interviewer, who had provided a bag of groceries. And Brown made sure to draw an unfavorable comparison with the poor quality of the food she received through the relief program: "Ah sho did enjoy the victuals you sent day befo' yistidy. They send me surplus food frum the gove'nment but Ah don't like what they send. The skim milk gripes me and Ah don't like that yellow meal. . . . And that wheat cereal they send! Ah eats it with water when Ah don't have milk and Ah don't like it but when you don't have nothin' else you got to eat what you have."[61]

A similar distinction between government relief and white southerners' generosity was drawn by ex-slave Martha Colquitt. Having traded her story for some wood with which to make a fire, Colquitt ended with a hard-luck tale of the nonexistent old-age pension and the necessity of relying on individual acts of charity: "My neighbors helps me, by bringin' me a little to eat, when dey knows I ain't got nothin' in de house to cook. De storekeeper lets me have a little credit. . . . De white folkses on Prince Avenue is right good to let me have dey clo'es to wash. . . . I sho' is hopin' de old age pension will soon git started comin' to me. . . . I done signed up for mine twict, so maybe it will 'gin to come 'fore I is done plum wore out."[62] Once again, the narrative concludes with a hearty expression of the ex-slave's gratitude for the interviewer's generosity: "When her visitor was ready to leave, Martha hobbled to the door and bade her an affectionate farewell. 'Goodbye, Lady! I prays for you every night. May de good Lord bless you.' "[63]

These depictions of ex-slaves by white interviewers reinforced the myths of the Lost Cause and suggested that white southern paternalism lived on in the post-emancipation era. Just as their slaveholding ancestors had before them, elite southern whites took care of their "Negroes." Such charity implied that ex-slave informants were incapable of caring for themselves.[64] UDC members were wont to describe ex-slaves' narratives that spoke of good treatment and the good old days of slavery as representative: "Followed to its conclusion, Alice's life history is void of thrills and simply an average ex-slave's story. As a slave she was well fed, well clothed, and well treated, as were her brother and sister slaves." These interviewers often mentioned at the end of the narrative that ex-slaves, like Alice Battle and her husband, were now "objects of charity."[65] FWP Arkansas director Bernie Babcock, in a play she published in 1915, wrote that "there is a slavery worse than fetters. . . . It is the slavery of helpless servility."[66] In order to vindicate the Old South, defenders of the Lost Cause argued that slavery was a boon to the enslaved because, in addition to Christianizing them, it provided for their needs. As a slave "the negro [was] housed and fed and cared for when sick," but free he would be "no more able to protect his own interests than cattle or infants."[67]

Not surprisingly, ex-slaves often catered to their white interviewers' expectations; in these narratives, slavery days became happy ones. Former slave owners were remembered as uniformly kind and generous in providing for the material needs and spiritual wants of their slaves: slaves were more than adequately clothed, fed, and cared for. Professional medical attention was always given to slaves who were ailing, slaves attended religious services alongside their owners, and benevolent masters protected their slaves from mistreatment by cruel overseers and patrollers.[68] When the topic of enforced illiteracy was discussed, these narratives often stated that slave owners were not to blame, as they were merely following the law.[69] In some cases, slaves were offered the opportunity by their slaveholders to learn how to read and write but failed to do so. Ex-slave Fannie Jones told her interviewer, "Mistiss used to git a book and say, 'Nig, come here and let me larn you how to read.' I didn't pay no 'tention to her den, but now I sho' does wish I had."[70] When freedom was declared, slaves were reluctant to leave their masters, and many stayed on to avoid the pain of separation. Poverty and want are often described, by both interviewer and informant, as coming after the slaves were freed. Ex-slave Rias Body claimed that "no darky in Harris County that he ever heard of ever went hungry or suffered for clothes until after freedom."[71]

The lengths to which some ex-slave informants went to accommodate their white questioners' expectations did not go unnoticed by some FWP field workers. In a narrative that elaborated on the kindnesses of the informant's former master, the interviewers noted that "Julia [Bunch] kept repeating and seemed anxious to impress upon the minds of her visitors that her white folks were good and very rich."[72] It is unlikely that ex-slaves were unaware of the answers their white interviewers hoped to hear. The questions white FWP employees asked, and the manner in which they asked them, left little doubt. Although a majority of Georgia narratives do not directly include the interviewer's questions, ex-slaves' responses indicate that interviewers were remarkably consistent in the questions they asked, in an order which closely followed the list provided by the federal office.[73] However, white interviewers in Georgia rephrased certain questions to solicit the answers they expected, although they did not always get them.[74] For example, question three from the supplementary instructions provided by federal directors— "What work did you do in slavery days? Did you ever earn any money? How?"—was restated by white employees in this manner: "Did your master ever allow you any spending money?"[75] While several informants answered in the affirmative, when Elsie Moreland was asked this question she replied, "Not me. . . . I sho' don' remember it ef he did."[76] Alec Bostwick expressed greater incredulity at the question's implication: "What you talkin' 'bout Miss? Us didn't have no money. Sho' us didn't."[77]

Many of the ex-slaves' responses reveal that white interviewers often posed the question of the slaves' treatment by their slaveholders in this way: "Were your Master and Mistress good to you?"[78] Maude Barragan was one of the few FWP employees who included her questions along with ex-slave Nancy Boudry's replies. Despite Barragan's push for stories that would soften Boudry's "somber" recollections of brutal whippings and hard conditions, Boudry mostly refused to cater to her listener's leading queries. When Barragan asked, "Nancy, wasn't your mistress kind to you?" Boudry said, "Mistis was sorta kin' to me, sometimes. But dey only give me meat and bread, didn' give me nothin' good—I ain' gwine tell no story. I had a heap to undergo wid." Undeterred, Barragan asked: "But the children had a good time, didn't they? They played games?" Boudry responded evasively, "Maybe dey did play ring games, I never had no time to see what games my chillum play, I work so hard. . . . Never had no frolics neither, no ma'm, and didn' go to none." When Boudry recalled how her family, on learning of their freedom, had "moved right off" the plantation "but not so far I couldn' go backwards and forwards to see 'um," Barragan editorialized, "It was evident that even if Nancy's life had been hard, there was a bond between her and her former owners."[79]

The Georgia narratives, regardless of the race of the interviewer, typically conclude by having ex-slaves weigh in with their opinion on whether slavery days were better or worse than the present day. Instructions from the federal office told interviewers to solicit information on the ex-slaves' current situation, but as reflected in the answers ex-slaves gave, Georgia interviewers often interpolated that by asking their informants if they wished those days of slavery were back again. Interviewers repeatedly asked former slaves to offer their perspectives on slavery; they began with leading questions about how the masters or mistresses had treated the informant, then asked for their views on emancipation, and concluded the interview with a direct question on the benefits of slavery days versus freedom.[80] This made it difficult for informants to diverge from a narrative that eulogized their masters along with the institution of slavery, in order to express a decided preference for freedom. " 'I love my white folks,' said Cora Shepherd, nodding her small turbaned head, 'my marster was a fine one! I wish he was living today, yes ma'am I do. . . . Dey was better times to me."[81] Arrie Binns's narrative asserted that "when freedom came there were sad times on the Sybert plantation," and concluded with this statement: "She is glad she knew slavery, glad she was reared by good white people who taught her the right way to live."[82] Some informants equivocated by trying to accommodate pro-Confederate views while still expressing their gratitude for emancipation. Mary Colbert recalled that "when news came that Negroes had been freed there was a happy jubilee time. Marse John explained the new freedom to his slaves and we were glad and sorry too." She concluded by stating: "I had the best white folks in the world, but it was by God's plan that the Negroes were set free."[83] Easter Brown refused to take a position on whether slavery or freedom was better: "As for slavery days; some of us Niggers ought to be free and some oughtn't to be. I don't know nuttin much 'bout it. I had a good time den, and I gits on pretty good now."[84]

In the process of tailoring their stories to suit their audience, many ex-slaves relied on the African American tradition of signifying in order to retain authorial control of the tale's meaning, through the techniques of "artful evasion and expressive illusion."[85] These narratives testify to ex-slaves' learned versatility—their ability to move fluidly between performances of black identity deemed "acceptable" to southern whites and self-representations of agency and autonomy. Some ex-slaves drew on the African American oral tradition of trickster tales, a central genre of black folk culture in which slaves deceived their masters with guileful performances of ignorance and innocence in order to momentarily gain the upper hand. Using evidence from the FWP Slave Narrative Collection, scholars such as Lawrence Levine and Charles Joyner have demonstrated how slaves emulated the central trickster figures featured in their own folktales, such as Brer Rabbit and John, using their wits "to maneuver as well as they could from their position of weakness."[86] Ex-slaves, I argue, also took on the role of the trickster with their interviewers, providing a strategically comical performance of blackness that often dovetailed with white interviewers' expectations. James Bolton, who had the odd tendency of referring to his former master as his employer (as his interviewer observed), equivocated in this way about the whippings slaves received:

> My employer—I means, my marster, never 'lowed no overseer to whup none of his niggers! Marster done all the whuppin' on our plantation hisself. He never did make no big bruises and he never drawed no blood, but he sho' could burn 'em up with that lash! Niggers on our plantation was whupped for laziness mostly. Next to that, whuppings was for steelin' eggs and chickens. They fed us good and plenty but a nigger is jus' bound to pick up chicken and eggs effen he kin, no matter how much he done eat! He jus' can't help it. Effen a nigger ain's busy he gwine to git into mischief![87]

Bolton also had good words to say about Klan members: "Right soon atter the war we saw plenty of Ku Kluxers but they never bothered nobody on our plantation. They allus seemed to be havin' heaps of fun. 'Course, they did have to straighten out some of them brash young nigger bucks. . . . Mos' of the niggers the Ku Kluxers got atter was'n on no farm, but was jus' roamin' 'round talkin' too much and makin' trouble. They had to take 'em in hand two or three times befo' some of them fool free niggers could be larned to behave theyselfs."[88] Bolton ended his narrative by longing for the good old days: "Now I gwine to tell you the troof. Now that it's all over I don't find life as good in my old age, as it was in slavery time when I was chillun down on Marster's plantation. Then I didn' have to worry 'bout wher my clothes and my somepin' to eat was comin' from or where I was gwine to sleep. Marster tuk keer of all that."[89]

Bolton attributed slaves' acts of running away to their indolence, as opposed to their masters' cruelty: "Most of the time they run away kazen they jus' didn't want to wuk, and wanted to laze around for a spell."[90] During his interview with UDC member Elizabeth Watson, Melvin Smith relied on indirection to discreetly suggest the appeal of the North, and the likelihood of runaway slaves being caught and returned to their owners: "Niggers run away some but they always come back. They'd hear that they could have a better time up north so they think they try it. But they found out that they wasn't no easy way to live away from Marster." With the ambiguous phrase "no easy way to live away from Marster," Smith invoked the often insurmountable obstacles slaves faced in pursuing their freedom. He then laughed and dismissed his own attempt to run away: "I jest got biggity like chillun does now."[91] Ex-slave Tom Hawkins also used humor and indirection when asked about runaway slaves: "Niggers didn't run to no North. Dey run to de South, 'cause dem white folks up North was so mean to 'em."[92] George Brooks, who claimed to be 112 years old, recast his own story of running away as the result of powerful forces beyond his control. Brooks related how, after finishing a chore for his owner's wife, he " 'stepped' to a nearby well to get a drink of water and, impelled by some strange, irresistible 'power jes' kep' on walkin 'til he run slap-dab inter de Yankees.' "[93] Brooks's story of leaving his master to join the Union army presents him as a guileless innocent. His interviewer felt obligated to follow Brooks's anecdote with an editorializing assertion intended to clarify Brooks's actions as involuntary; after running into the Union army, the interviewer noted, Brooks was detained by the Yankees, "who corralled him and kept him for three months."[94]

When speaking to white interviewers, ex-slave informants often employed "third-party signifying," in which "the speaker may realize his aim only . . . if the addressee fails to recognize the speech act as signifying."[95] Indirection was a key strategy for enslaved African Americans, as it enabled them to communicate with one another without whites' knowledge. It remained a crucial skill in the Jim Crow South, as white supremacists' tactics of violence and fear were routinely enacted to keep African Americans "in their place." In her narrative, Minnie Davis tacked back and forth between sharply contrasting statements about slaves' experiences on the plantation. For example, she began her answer regarding medical treatment for slaves with this assertion: "Marse John was grand to sick slaves. He always sent for Dr. Moore, who would make his examination and write out his prescription. When he left his parting word was usually 'Give him a sound thrashing and he will get better.' Of course he didn't mean that; it was his little joke." However, one sentence later, Davis says, "We didn't like Dr. Moore and usually begged for one of the other doctors," suggesting that the doctor was not joking, and raising questions about what she meant by the "grand" treatment of ill slaves by "Marse John."[96]

Davis also moved quickly between stories of African Americans' joy regarding emancipation and more audience-appropriate statements about blacks' fear of the Yankees: "On the day we learned of the surrender, the Negroes rallied around the liberty flag pole. . . . All day long they cut up and there was a song they sung that day that went something like this: 'We rally around the flag pole of liberty, The Union forever, Hurrah! Boys Hurrah!'" But the next morning the new freedmen awoke to discover that "the white folks had cut that pole down." While the insinuation is that white reprisal against the new freedmen was already beginning, Davis instead followed with the observation that "we were mortally afraid of the Yankees when they appeared here a short time after the surrender." But Davis continued, "We were afraid of the Ku Klux Klan riders too." That bold statement was immediately qualified by Davis offering a rationalization for white violence but one that finishes with the cost to the black community: "The Negroes did act so bad; there were lots of killings going on for a long time after the war was supposed to be over."[97]

Eighty-year-old Jasper Battle nostalgically recalled his experience of slavery for white FWP interviewer Grace McCune as the "good old days" and maintained that black folk "would be lucky to have 'em back again," even though his house, as McCune noted, "appeared to be in good condition and the yard was clean and tidy."[98] Battle greeted his visitor warmly, saying, "I'se powerful glad somebody is willin' to stop long enough to pay some heed whilst I talks 'bout somepin. Dem days 'fore de war was good old days, 'specially for de colored folks. I know, 'cause my Mammy done told me so."[99] But Battle drew on central modes of signifying—humor and indirection—in his description of how slave children were treated. "Marster was mighty good to slave chillum," he claimed. "He never sent us out to wuk in de fields 'til us was 'most growed-up, say 12 or 14 years old." However, as Battle explained, slave children grew faster than whites: "A Nigger 12 or 14 years old dem days was big as a white child 17 or 18 years old. Why Miss, Niggers growed so fast, dat most of de Nigger nurses warn't no older dan de white chillun dey tuk care of. Marster said he warn't gwine to send no babies to de fields." By pointing out his former owner's double standard for determining when slave children could be treated as adult workers, Battle slyly managed to subvert his first claim that his owner "was mighty good to slave chillun."[100]

In their responses, ex-slaves sought simultaneously to please their interviewers while remaining truthful about their own beliefs. When asked about their attitude toward famous figures such as Abraham Lincoln and Jefferson Davis, a number of ex-slaves made sure to praise both leaders: "Us would a been slaves 'til yit, if Mr. Lincoln hadn't sot us free. Dey wuz bofs of 'em, good mens."[101] "Aunt" Mary Ferguson's interviewer noted that Ferguson "has never had any particular love for the Yankees, and thinks that they treated the Southern white folks 'most scandalously' after the war, yet she feels that she owes them a debt of gratitude for freeing her people."[102] One informant who had painted a rosy picture of slavery expressed uneasiness at the end of her narrative as to how her tale might be received by a very different audience than her white interviewer. Ex-slave Susan Castle, who told stories of how well her master had treated his slaves and claimed that "in slav'ry time if de Niggers had a-behaved and minded deir Marster and Mist'ess dey wouldn't have had sich a hard time," worried aloud at the end of her interview that her neighbors might have overheard her: "Well, I sho' enjoyed talkin' to you. I hopes I didn't talk loud 'nough for dem other Niggers to hear me, 'cause if you open your mouth dey sho' gwine tell it."[103]

Another means by which ex-slave informants who participated in these exchanges retained their authorial integrity was to frequently include a disavowal of their own "testimony" regarding slavery days. After boldly answering her visitor's question about whether she preferred slavery or freedom with a definitive "Yes Mam, indeed I had rather be free," Minnie Davis ended her ambivalent and contradictory tale with this coy statement: "Now, Miss, I hope I have told you what you wanted to know, but I must admit the things that took place way back there are rather vague in my mind."[104] Here Davis manages to imply that she aimed to please her interviewer with her story, while undermining the truth of her own tale by referring to her own faulty memory—thus, in two ways Davis suggests that her story is not necessarily to be trusted.

Throughout her narrative regarding the fine and generous character of her former master, informant Mary Colbert repeatedly resorted to the strategy of claiming a faulty memory. With statements like "Remember, Dear, when the yankees came through here, I was only ten years old" and "Darling, please get this right: the plantation is a dream to me" and "Honey, don't flatter me. Don't you know a little girl 10 years old can't remember everything that went on that far back," Colbert managed to weave a plantation tale of harmony and plenty while suggesting that this image was far from complete.[105] "I have often considered writing the history of my life and finally decided to undertake it," she told the interviewer, "but . . . I would have to tell too much, so I thought it best to leave it alone."[106] With this observation, Colbert found a way to speak of all that lay unspoken; her history would be too telling and therefore had to remain untold. Using indirection, ex-slave informants in Georgia found ways to speak their mind while avoiding confrontation with southern whites invested in maintaining a romanticized and highly politicized narrative of slavery and white supremacy.

The majority of the narratives submitted by the five African American interviewers on the Georgia Project provide an important contrast to those conducted by whites. While most follow a similar format, they diverge in both content and style in significant ways. With few exceptions, black interviewers wrote up their informants' narratives in the third person, and when they quoted ex-slaves they rarely relied on the heavy dialect favored by their white colleagues.[107] In these stylistic aspects, they bear a striking resemblance to the narratives produced by Florida's Negro Writers' Unit. For example, interviewer Minnie B. Ross's informants related that their owners were generally kind in their treatment, withholding punishment and providing plentiful food;[108] however, these narratives also include evidence of the unequal power dynamics between whites and blacks and the rejoicing of the slaves when those relations were reversed by the war. Sallie Blakely, who impressed Ross with her "youthful looks and sprightliness," spoke of the cruelty of Reverend Murray, whose sermons were "a constant reminder [to slaves] to obey their masters and mistresses." Two events "that brought smiles to the face of Mrs. Blakely" involved the retributions brought about by the Yankee soldiers, including "the day they destroyed Rev. Murray's home."[109] Ex-slave George Washington Browning, in the midst of asserting that his master "never punished his slaves unnecessarily," included a graphic story of a female slave being whipped "until blood ran in streams down her back."[110] Browning's narrative, unlike those customarily submitted by white interviewers, concludes with a critique of the unfair practices of southern whites following emancipation, including the poor treatment of sharecroppers and the Ku Klux Klan's violent acts that forced his family to move to Atlanta.[111]

Isaiah Green, who, according to Ross, possessed a "clear agile mind and intelligent manner," described the treatment of slaves in the manner customarily found in narratives with white interviewers.[112] He noted that slaves were provided with ample food and clothing, frequent slave "frolics," and excellent medical care by kindly slaveholder Colonel Willis, who would not tolerate any cruel punishment.[113] But toward the end of his narrative, Green divulged specific details that revealed the antagonism ex-slaves harbored for their former owner. After emancipation, Colonel Willis ran for office, intending to garner the votes of his former slaves, but all of them refused to support him in the election. Green also related that Colonel Willis's son was an active member in the Ku Klux Klan who set Green's father on fire during an attempted lynching.[114]

Similar to Florida's NWU, African American employees in Georgia usually portrayed ex-slave informants as spry and sound in mind and body, instead of senile and decrepit.[115] These sketches worked to assure readers of the veracity of the ex-slaves' reminiscences. Edwin Driskell's interview with Henry Wright, which, like the others, is written almost entirely in the third person, is an even richer example of the details informants could provide about the experience of being enslaved when speaking with black interviewers. Driskell noted that Wright's "speech and thought indicate that he is very intelligent and there is no doubt that he still possesses a clear and active mind." Wright recalled that when it was cold, his bare feet cracked and bled in the fields, and he remembered how the slaves felt cheated when their master sold the produce they had grown on their own plots.[116] Unlike the narratives submitted by white interviewers, where ex-slaves recalled happily attending church services with whites, Wright specifically mentioned how the preachers, white and black, preached obedience to the slaves. Furthermore, he explained that the slaves did not believe these sermons—they just pretended to do so.[117] Similarly, ex-slave Pierce Cody told black interviewer Adella S. Dixon that slaves became so frustrated with church services where they were segregated and given homilies of submission and obedience that they withdrew and formed a separate church.[118]

Ex-slaves who spoke to black interviewers included numerous examples of slave resistance. Berry Clay told Adella Dixon that his father's position as an overseer necessitated punishing the slaves, "but he was too loyal to his color to assist in making their lives more unhappy. His method of carrying out orders and yet keeping a clear conscience was unique—the slave was taken to the woods where he was supposedly laid upon a log and severely beaten." Instead, Clay's father made the slave "stand to one side and . . . emit loud cries which were accompanied by hard blows on the log," giving "any listener the impression that some one was severely beaten."[119] Ex-slave Henry Wright described the method slaves used to protect themselves when stealing away from the plantation by tying ropes on paths that would knock any pursuers off their horses. He also remembered a mulatto slave who had been promised his freedom; when the master broke his promise, the slave tried to burn his owner's house down, and was hanged for it.[120] The graphic depictions of slave punishment that Wright included in his narrative offer a stark contrast to the majority of narratives given to white employees, which typically asserted that punishment by the slaveholder was rare and usually for the slave's "benefit." Wright offered a vivid description of a whipping he received where he was "spread-eagled" on the ground. After "a severe beating brine water or turpentine was poured over the wounds." Unlike the narratives given to white interviewers that downplayed or dismissed the practice of running away, Wright discussed how he had attempted to escape more than once, including after striking his master, "who had attempted to whip him."[121]

When freedom was declared Wright "was a very happy man." Here the interviewer, Edwin Driskell, inserted a statement intended to forestall any assumption that Wright's happiness stemmed from laziness: "Freedom did not mean that he could quit work but that he could work for himself as he saw fit to." The narrative concluded with Wright's assertion that "he would rather be free than a slave" even though there was less worry "in those days" about having something to eat. The expression "good old days," which was frequently invoked in ex-slaves' narratives with white employees, was here put in scare quotes and only referenced ironically; Wright recalled how, during the scarcity of post-emancipation days, he had used the dirt from the smokehouse floor to flavor his cooking, as it was saturated with drippings from the "meats which had been hung there to be smoked in the 'good old days.' "[122]

Like the interviewers from Florida's Negro Writers' Unit, Driskell made sure to interpret Wright's signifying when necessary, to ensure that the message would be understood. When asked if house slaves were treated any differently than field slaves, Wright drew on a long-standing black folk tradition that used the mule as a metaphor for African Americans' unequal position. As Driskell noted, Wright "replied with a broad grin that 'Old Marster' treated them much the same as he would a horse and a mule." Driskell followed this statement with an explanatory note: "That is, the horse was given the kind of treatment that would make him show off in appearance, while the mule was given only enough care to keep him well and fit for work. 'You see,' continued Mr. Wright, 'in those days a plantation owner was partially judged by the appearance of his house servants.'"[123]

Ex-slaves' memories of Union troops also differed greatly when speaking with black FWP employees. Instead of stories about how the "damyankees" went around "skeerin' de wimmin folks . . . making de folks cook 'em stuff ter eat, den tearin' up an messin' up dey houses,"[124] these narratives told how the Union soldiers had put the power of retribution and vengeance in the hands of former slaves: "When the Yankee troops came through they asked the slaves if their master was mean to them. . . . [If] the answer was 'no' the soldiers marched on after taking all the livestock. . . . [If] the master was mean, all property was burned."[125] These narratives also provided a markedly different portrayal of the Confederate militia. Ex-slave Milton Hammond told Minnie Ross how Confederate soldiers forcibly requisitioned needed supplies from the plantation and "were known to capture slaves and force them to dig ditches." He further recalled that it "was a common sight to see [Confederate] soldiers marching on to Macon, Ga., in the mornings and in the evenings see the same group on their way back running from the 'Yanks.'"[126]

Although these narratives are similar in some ways to those of Florida's NWU, they also share characteristics commonly found in the rest of the Georgia collection, such as statements that characterize slavery as a benign institution. Taken as a whole, they present a quixotic combination of contradictory evidence. They occupy more of what could be characterized as an uneven middle ground, providing a contrast to the pro-South agenda typically found in the interviews with white employees, but also to the more radically subversive presentation of the ex-slave stories found in the narratives produced by Florida's NWU. This affirms the importance of the separate NWUs that put African American editors in charge of gathering submissions and reviewing the copy produced by black writers, even if they ultimately submitted all material to white supervisors at the district, state, and federal level. The Georgia narratives submitted by black employees suggest they were never unaware that they were submitting these narratives for the approval of white editors and supervisors.

Florida—Rewriting the Master('s) Narrative

Ex-slaves in Florida also used signifying, even in conversations with African American interviewers, but here speaker and writer clearly worked in collaboration to craft narratives of black agency and citizenship. For example, informant Ambrose Douglass told interviewer Martin Richardson how he was severely beaten by his master when he was sixteen "because he attempted to refuse the mate that had been given to him—with the instructions to produce a healthy boy-child by her—and a long argument on the value of having good, strong, healthy children." Richardson chose to follow Douglass's statement directly with this observation: "In 1937, at the age of 92, Ambrose Douglass welcomed his 38th child into the world."[127] While this seems, at first glance, an example of a slave being disciplined into obedience, later in the interview it is revealed that by the time emancipation was declared, when Douglass was twenty-one, he had sired only one child. Clearly, the other thirty-seven came after freedom. What this narrative reveals, albeit indirectly, is an ironic tale of a slave taking a master's orders and using them for his own purposes. Once he was no longer a slave, Douglass was happy to comply with his former master's opinion on "the value of having good, strong, healthy children."[128] The crucial theme of free choice is highlighted by the proof of his virility in his numerous offspring. Through the method of indirection, Douglass's narrative demonstrates how he resisted the enslavement of his ability to procreate, doing so only once he was a free man.

Freedom, more than slavery, was often the primary focus of the ex-slave narratives of Florida's NWU. In these, the ex-slave's identity is remade and redefined through personal acts of agency following emancipation. Names, as a signifier of one's own identity as well as genealogical lineage, were freighted with political meaning for the enslaved and for the freedmen and freedwomen. Under slavery, the knowledge of African names, kinship ties, and family lineage was publicly stripped away by traders and slaveholders and replaced with the new nomenclature that designated a slave's ownership by the imposition of the master's surname and often the master's choice of first name upon the birth of a slave. As an act of their own emancipation, many ex-slaves unnamed themselves from these appellations synonymous with enslavement and renamed themselves, often adopting names now synonymous with freedom.[129]

The narrative of William Sherman Jr. is a compelling example of the use of names as tropes to express the symbiotic relationship between naming and identity. William Sherman Jr.'s father was a slave who had purchased his freedom. He renamed himself in honor of William Tecumseh Sherman, the heroic general of the Union army, and passed that name on to his son.[130] His father's choice of names, first and last, was a symbolic act loaded with political implications, given that his previous master, who still owned William Sherman's wife and son, was Jack Davis, a nephew of the president of the Confederacy, Jefferson Davis.

Just as emancipation required a symbolic act of rebirth through renaming, the commencement of a new future of freedom necessitated a new name for the freedman's new life and identity. In his personal narrative, Sherman Jr. tells how, on hearing of his master's plan to kill his slaves in the event of a "Yankee" victory, he and his cousin "slipped off and wended their way to all of the surrounding plantations spreading the news that the 'Yankees' were in Robertsville and exhorting them to follow and join them." The two of them succeeded in acquiring "a following of about five hundred slaves who abandoned their masters' plantations 'to meet the Yankees.'" Thus, ex-slave William Sherman Jr. held his own "Sherman's March," complete with the destruction of Confederate property: "En masse they marched breaking down fences that obstructed their passage, carefully avoiding 'Confederate pickets' who were stationed throughout the countryside."[131]

Sherman's "army" of runaway slaves was so proficient that they managed to take by surprise the Union army, whose lookout was unaware of their approach until "this group of five hundred slaves were upon him." They were then let into the encampment of General Sherman's soldiers and "the guard who had let these people approach so near to him without realizing their approach was court martialled that night for being dilatory in his duties." Here, it is possible that Sherman is signifying on his more famous namesake, for General Sherman's opposition to the Union policy of enlisting black soldiers was widely known. General Sherman did not believe that African Americans could acquire the skills necessary for combat.[132] But in this narrative, self-appointed "General" Sherman Jr. leads his black troops right into the heart of the Union camp without being discovered. Sherman's subtle reference to the punishment inflicted on the guard indicates that this incident did nothing toward changing General Sherman's mind about African Americans' capabilities as soldiers; the organization and skillful stealth of the runaway slaves remained unacknowledged, and the guard was charged with negligence.

The slaves were told that they could either go with the Union army or go on to Savannah, which had already been secured. Sherman was one of the few who decided to go on alone to Savannah. The rest of the slaves, now volunteer soldiers, marched behind the federal troops. It turned out that Sherman's decision saved his life, for "most of these unfortunate slaves were slain by 'bush whackers' (Confederate snipers who fired upon them from ambush.) After being killed they were decapitated and their heads placed upon posts that lined the fields so that they could be seen by other slaves to warn them of what would befall them if they attempted to escape."[133]

This section of Sherman's narrative concludes with the day the war finally ended: "Will . . . says that day was a gala day. Everybody celebrated (except the Southerners). The slaves were free. Thousands of Federal soldiers were in evidence. The Union army was victorious and 'Sherman's March' was a success."[134] The pun on "Sherman's March" is obviously intentional here.[135] General Sherman's March is a success that results in the freeing of the rest of the slaves, but it is not a successful march for the volunteer slaves who followed behind the federal troops. Will Sherman's march, conversely, is triumphant in two ways: first, he succeeds in the role of a general in "enlisting" 500 slaves from neighboring plantations to follow him and surprise the Union army; second, his own personal march to Savannah is victorious, in that it saves him from the gruesome fate of his fellow runaway slaves, and he lives to see the end of the Civil War. On yet another level, this narrative could be viewed as an analogy for the black experience after emancipation. While on the surface the outcome of the Civil War was an opportunity for African American progress, freedmen paid a high price following reunification, as white backlash against black citizenship began. Sherman's narrative can be read as a subtle call for black self-determination in achieving equal rights, for it is Will's leadership, not General Sherman's, that results in a positive outcome.

The revision of personal monikers and tales that punned upon the play of names was not the only means by which ex-slave informants revised the standard historical narrative of slavery. Former slaves invoked personal genealogies as a way of revising racial identities associated with enslavement.[136] Like the symbolic act of naming, the history of an informant's own origins through descriptions of "racial" ancestry sometimes served as a means of reestablishing a personal history and an identity based on kinship ties that transcended the fissures caused by slavery. Native American or "Indian" ancestry, for example, was occasionally invoked to represent the ex-slaves' nobility. While historically there was intermarriage between African Americans and Native Americans, particularly in Florida with the Seminoles, to lay claim to such ancestry was to acquire an identity grounded in freedom and rebellion, rather than enslavement. Identifying Native American ancestry became such a common practice among African Americans that it began to be associated more with wishful thinking and geneaological revisionism than with actual fact. For Zora Neale Hurston, this phenomenon provided grist for her ready wit:

"I am colored," she announced, "but I offer nothing in the way of extenuating circumstances except the fact that I am the only Negro in the United States whose grandfather on the mother's side was *not* an Indian chief."[137]

The narrative of Frank Berry explained his Indian ancestry but also testified to the widespread intermingling of bloodlines between African American slaves and Indians. Berry told his interviewer of his grandmother's abduction by Indians and how she became the squaw of their chief: "She was later recaptured by her owners. This was a common procedure, according to Berry's statements. Indians often captured slaves, particularly the women, or aided them in their escape and almost always intermarried with them. The red men were credited with inciting many uprisings and wholesale escapes among the slaves."[138] Berry's interviewer, Pearl Randolph, also emphasized Native American involvement with slave rebellions and escape. Significantly, William Sherman Jr.'s family tree also possessed Indian branches, which were credited as the source of his good health and longevity: "He is ninety-four years of age, though he appears to be only about fifty-five. . . . The Indian blood that flows in his veins is plainly visible in his features, the color of his skin and the texture of his hair. He gives as his reason for his lengthy life the Indian blood that is in him."[139] Native American ancestry could also be used to explain special gifts. The Reverend Squires Jackson ran away from his master's plantation, and "after four days of wearied travelling being guided by the north star and the Indian instinct inherited from his Indian grandmother, he finally reached Lake City."[140] Here again an NWU interviewer collaborates with an ex-slave informant in their mutual understanding of what Indian blood signifies and its association with individual agency and freedom.

Another form of signifying evident in the narratives from Florida's NWU is the practice of revising dominant tropes as a way of rewriting master narratives. Ex-slaves often retold the history of slavery and emancipation by transposing the symbolic figures of slavery to reconfigure the relationship most fundamentally altered by freedom, that of master and slave. That is, ex-slaves frequently depicted scenes in which the popular antebellum tropes of the childlike, irrational slave and the benevolent, paternal master became inverted, usually when the emancipation of the slaves is made known to the slave owner. This pivotal moment of transition is heavily charged with symbolism, for it marks the transformation of the slave into an American citizen. In these narratives, master becomes child and slave becomes guardian. Mary Minus Biddie described how her former master reacted when he was told of the liberation of his slaves: "Mr. Jamison had never before been heard to curse, but this was one day that he let go a torrent of words that are unworthy to appear in print. He then broke down and cried like a slave who was being lashed by his cruel master."[141]

Ex-slave informants related how, upon hearing the news that the slaves were legally free, slave owners exhibited a variety of irrational and childish behaviors. When Sam and Louisa Everett's master learned that his slaves had been freed, he became uncontrollable:

> "Big Jim" stood weeping on the piazza and cursing the fate that had been so cruel to him by robbing him of all his "niggers." He inquired if any wanted to remain until all the crops were harvested and when no one consented to do so, he flew into a rage; seizing his pistol, he began firing into the crowd of frightened Negroes. Some were killed outright and others were maimed for life. Finally he was prevailed upon to stop. He then attempted to take his own life. A few frightened slaves promised to remain with him another year; this placated him. It was necessary for Union soldiers to make another visit to the plantation before "Big Jim" would allow his former slaves to depart.[142]

In this revision of the master('s) tropes, it is the slaveholder and not the loyal slave who is emotionally devastated and incapacitated by news of emancipation. This tale also provides a new way of interpreting stories of slaves who stayed on with their masters after emancipation, revealing that they did so out of fear and not out of love and fealty.[143] Federal troops were required to intervene to ensure the emancipation of the slaves of "Big Jim."

Moreover, the ex-slaves, once freedom was declared, assumed the roles previously defined as the master's, that of protector, guardian, and provider. Willis Dukes related one such story: "The master did not return after the war and when the soldiers in blue came through that section the frightened women were greatly dependent upon their slaves for protection and livelihood. Many of these black man [sic] chose loyalty to their dead masters to freedom and shouldered the burden of the support of their former mistresses cheerfully. After the war Willis' father was one of those to remain with his widowed mistress. Other members of his family left as soon as they were freed, even his wife."[144] In this quotation, the Confederate theme of the faithful slave who won't leave the plantation even after emancipation is reconfigured, as these former slaves literally take the master's place, becoming surrogate husbands to their former mistresses. The "mammy" figure, so central to the Lost Cause narrative, is replaced with a figure of independent black manhood. Dukes's father ends up symbolically exchanging his wife for the master's, and the role of economic dependent is transferred from slave to slaveholder.

Not insignificantly, the traditional gender roles for men and women remained the same while the racial roles were inverted. But gender roles could be inverted to insult white southern manhood. William Sherman Jr. recalled that when Jefferson Davis, the president of the former Confederacy, was captured, "he was disguised in women's clothes."[145] This may have been a popular "Yankee" myth, but it gained traction with ex-slaves; former slave Elizabeth Keckley, dressmaker for Mrs. Davis, related with seeming relish the experience of seeing at a public exhibition the dress Davis had been captured in and realizing with surprise as well as satisfaction that it was one of her own creations, made while she was in the Davises' employ.[146] Both Sherman and Keckley used the anecdote to underscore how the Confederacy's symbol of courage and heroism was actually so cowardly he literally tried to hide behind a woman's skirts.

Other famous figures of the Civil War were also invoked in the inversion of the tropes of master and slave. Informant Salena Taswell related the memorable occasion when Abraham Lincoln visited her master Dr. Jameson's plantation: "You be sure we knowed he was our friend and we catched what he had t' say. Now, he said this: (I never forget that 'slong as I live) 'If they free de people, I'll bring you back into the Union[.]' (to Dr. Jameson) 'If you don't free your slaves, I'll "whip" you back into the Union.'" Lincoln threatens the slave owner with the whipping usually reserved as punishment for recalcitrant slaves. Taswell then credits Lincoln with saying: "Before I'd allow my wife an' children to be sold as slaves, I'll wade in blood and water up to my neck."[147] Lincoln, formerly speaking from the position of the slave owner, now rhetorically aligns himself with the slaves, making their struggle his own by personalizing the issue of slavery. Furthermore, he suggests that the plight of black slaves is one that could befall his own family. In this retelling, Lincoln speaks first with the authority of the master and then in the language of the slave.

In addition, some stories tell how slave owners refused to comply with the law, often promising the ex-slaves a part of the harvest if they stayed on with them and then refusing to pay. In these narratives, the intervention of the federal government is required to force the former slave owner to pay up. When her former master Mr. Jamison committed this act, Mary Minus Biddie "slipped away, mounted the old mule 'Mustang' and galloped away at a mule's snail speed to Newnansville where she related what had happened to a Union captain. He gave her a letter to give to Mr. Jamison. In it he reminded him that if he didn't give Mary's family what he had promised he would be put in

jail. Without hesitation the old master complied with these pungent orders."[148] This incident highlights the reversal of roles that has taken place: as
the former slave lawfully becomes a citizen, with new rights and responsibilities, the former master is shown to be a transgressor of the laws of the nation.
Just as the slave "required" the constant watch of the master, now the master
is one who requires the vigilant watch of a former slave, who becomes an
agent of the state. In this inversion of antebellum roles, the federal government now assumes the authority for the former slave owner's criminal acts.

Ex-slave informants thus inscribed their new identity as freedmen and
freedwomen through three different, yet interrelated, means of revisionism.
They renamed themselves, often by drawing on appellations associated with
the embodiment of principles of American democracy. By recounting telling
genealogical histories of bloodlines, they gave shape to a multifaceted racial
identity not delimited by the strict southern codes governing miscegenation—a
racial identity that was in itself a history of transgression. And by transposing
the tropes of identity for master and slave, they turned the racial hierarchy of
the Lost Cause on its head. In their strategic counternarratives about the
black experience of slavery and emancipation, ex-slave informants revised
white southerners' master narratives by telling their own life histories.
Ex-slaves in Georgia who were constrained by their white listeners' expectations found it harder to tell a free story. Yet they found ways to make it pay,
and their improvisations drew on black vernacular traditions, enabling them
to tell stories of freedom and African American agency. Harriet Jacobs described in her Civil War slave narrative a "loophole of retreat" where she hid
from her master to attain freedom.[149] Like Jacobs, ex-slave informants in
Georgia made for themselves a figurative loophole of retreat where they could
tell a free story within the confines of the master narrative. Like Jacobs, they
hid in plain sight. It is high time we recovered the evidence they intentionally
left behind.

Epilogue

Freedom Dreams: The Last Generation

We wanted her to tell us about her slave days and she mumbled that, "she done tired of talkin' back there, she live for the future."
—Roberts and Sweet, "Stories of Slaves," interview with ex-slave Sarah Rhodes, August 3, 1937

I am not talking about slavery in my show. . . . I'm talking about modern racism, and I'm talking about modern ignorance. You're an irresponsible person if you don't know American history, because it's connected to politics. It's connected to racism that still exists. It's connected to everything.
—Azie Dungey, 2013

Ninety-one-year-old Sarah Rhodes wasn't the only ex-slave who, in response to Federal Writers' Project (FWP) queries, wanted to focus on the future rather than talk about the past of slavery. In an interview with the aptly named ex-slave "Prophet" John Henry Kemp, Negro Writers' Unit (NWU) worker Rebecca Baker noted that he "does not talk only of the past . . . his conversation turns to the future; he believes himself to be equally competent to talk of the future and talks more of the latter if permitted."[1] Most of the ex-slaves interviewed by the FWP were in their nineties; some were over one hundred years old. That such elderly people would be deeply invested in the future is a striking thing. And yet, this last generation to bear witness to the experience of enslavement would have been slaves for twelve to fifteen years at most, many being freed from chattel slavery at the age of seven or eight; their memories of childhood were memories of slavery, and their experience of slavery was that of children.[2] They had spent seventy to seventy-five years navigating the treacherous and shifting landscape of the black freedom struggle following emancipation. Small wonder, then, that ex-slaves viewed their life histories as encompassing much more than slavery and defined themselves as freedmen and freedwomen. Yet, as the last generation, they found themselves continually being asked to inhabit the past, by folklorists eager to document black folk traditions, by FWP employees instructed to gather folk material and memories of slave days, by a younger generation of African Americans invested in documenting the black experience, by southern whites devoted to maintaining Confederate memory and myths, and, at times, by each other at Ex-Slave Association meetings that were commonly held in various states as well as the nation's capital.[3]

Many African Americans of all socioeconomic levels in the first half of the twentieth century were eager to replace entrenched cultural stereotypes of the "old-time Negro" with a new black consciousness crafted and articulated as the "New Negro." As Martin Favor points out, "the very idea of the 'New' Negro implies an 'Old' Negro who is somehow outdated, inadequate, or insufficient."[4] Members of the black folk community are often not included by scholars as part of the movement to redefine black identity in order to claim the full rights of citizenship or, to use folk idiom, to claim their "entitles."[5] This examination of how ex-slaves used rhetorical practices from black vernacular traditions to challenge pro-Confederate and transregional racist views of black identity shows they were on the front lines of the struggle to rewrite the nation's memories of slavery and freedom. Placing them at the epicenter of debates over black citizenship in the 1930s, both as subject and as agent, demonstrates how hard ex-slaves had to work to claim the "ex" in their identity and how formidable was the opposition they faced from many different quarters that wished to define them solely as former slaves. While Sarah Rhodes wanted to talk of a black future, her interviewers, in their questions as well as their titling of her story—"Stories of Slaves" rather than "Stories of Ex-Slaves"—wanted her to embody slavery.

This history of the Ex-Slave Project reclaims ex-slaves' storytelling as public performance that, similar to the black autobiographical tradition of the nineteenth century, created a space for strategic counternarratives.[6] Seen through this lens, ex-slave informants in conversation with FWP interviewers were engaging in the dissident political culture that the anthropologist James Scott has termed "infrapolitics."[7] As Scott defines it, infrapolitics refers to the "circumspect struggle waged daily by subordinate groups [that exists] like infrared rays, beyond the visible end of the spectrum. That it should be invisible . . . is in large part by design—a tactical choice born of a prudent awareness of the balance of power."[8]

In their narratives, black informants created a space for historical dreaming, not unlike historian Robin Kelley's description of his mother's ability to envision a more optimistic future by "dream[ing] out loud."[9] Ex-slave narratives of the FWP deserve to be considered as part of what Kelley has termed the black radical imagination, not in spite of their circumstances of production but because of them. Former slaves who told their stories to FWP interviewers were aware of the uses of their oral performances as a commodity (that could be used by themselves for barter and trade but could also be commodified by others) and also as a site of potentiality—a dream space where the future (if not the circumscribed present) could be remade by an alternative telling of the past. Because the stuff of memory went into their making, the narratives also exist in the space between recall and dreams—both past and future. By re-envisioning and reclaiming an African American past of resistance to white tyranny and exploitation, even if by encoded means, ex-slaves laid claim to a future free of racial injustice.

Two major events would affect the outcome of the FWP's project to collect the oral testimonies of former slaves: the end of the FWP as a federally controlled project and the onset of World War II. An increasingly conservative bipartisan Congress in 1938 along with waning support for Roosevelt's New Deal programs left the cultural projects of Federal One vulnerable. Although many of the studies that began under the FWP were able to demonstrate their applicability to the war effort by claiming to strengthen national unity by promoting "our democratic heritage,"[10] the threat of war would prompt Congress to reduce funding for Works Progress Administration (WPA) Arts Projects and allow only defense-related programs to survive. In 1938, investigative hearings by the House Un-American Activities Committee (HUAC) began in New York. Its chairman, Martin Dies (a Democrat from Texas), successfully smeared New Deal programs with the tar brush of Communism, which they associated with "the FWP's effort to incorporate excluded groups in a redefined national community."[11] FWP director Henry Alsberg tried to placate Dies, laying the responsibility for the material in the American Guide that Dies deemed objectionable on specific units and state staff members and pointing out the challenge of overseeing a project with so many writers, editors, directors, sponsors, and publishers. Alsberg reiterated what had been the federal directors' goals from the start: to create a national series of guidebooks that was informative, factually correct, and objective in its treatment of various subjects. But the Dies report of Communist propaganda and activity in the projects of Federal One and negative publicity in the press led the House Appropriations Committee to sharply reduce the additional funding for WPA projects Roosevelt had requested; $150 million was cut by the House, and both houses defeated an amendment proposing $22 million for Federal One.[12] The new commissioner of the WPA, Colonel F. C. Harrington, pressured Alsberg to resign, citing poor administration of the FWP, and Alsberg's services were terminated, earlier than he wished, on August 1, 1939.[13]

Federal Writers' Project director Henry Alsberg, explaining to the House Un-American Activities Committee that Communists are no longer a problem in the Federal Writers' Project, 1938. Photo by Harris & Ewing. Harris & Ewing Collection, courtesy of the Library of Congress, Prints and Photographs Division, LC-H22-D-5143.

It was the FWP's writings by African Americans on racial discrimination that provided much of the fodder for the Dies Committee's accusations of un-American activity. Richard Wright's searing autobiographical essay, "The Ethics of Living Jim Crow," published in the FWP's anthology *American Stuff*, was brought forth as proof of Communist infiltration of the project: Democratic representative Joe Starnes of Alabama called it "the most filthy thing I have ever seen."[14] Sterling Brown's essay for the guidebook, "The Negro in Washington," on the history of racial discrimination in the nation's capital, published as part of the guidebook *Washington: City and Capital*, was also singled out as evidence of the "insidious propaganda" penned by "communistically inspired agitators."[15] These accusations, which Brown later referred to as "badges of honor," led the FBI to investigate him until 1945, when it officially concluded he was not a Communist.[16]

For some black employees still struggling against racial discrimination within New Deal projects, the HUAC hearings seemed to offer the opportunity to place these grievances directly before a governmental body with the power and oversight to remedy them. In April 1939, Walter White, executive secretary of the NAACP, consulted with Thurgood Marshall, the organization's legal counsel, regarding the wisdom of using the hearings of the House subcommittee to bring witnesses who could testify to the discrimination they had faced from WPA officials. Both White and Marshall, however, were quick to scuttle this idea as they recognized such testimony would only assist the conservative forces that wished to dismantle the projects that had provided, on the whole, greater opportunities for black employment. White cautioned, "We must keep in mind that this W.P.A. investigation is part of a *smear Roosevelt* campaign, and is backed by all the reactionary forces in the country. . . . The W.P.A. by and large has been as fair in its attitude towards Negroes as any Governmental bureau within recent history." Marshall concurred in a private interoffice memo, noting that those in charge of the investigation had never been in favor of providing "any relief for Negroes," and that the role of the NAACP was to "fight within the WPA set-up" and not to side with those trying to dismantle and "discredit all New Deal legislation."[17]

White had also received an impassioned plea from Sterling Brown to use the authority and connections of the NAACP to intercede on behalf of the FWP. This candid letter written in January 1939 provides perhaps the best insight into Brown's personal assessment of the FWP and its treatment of African Americans in its publications and also as employees. His personal request for support, Brown emphasized, must remain completely confidential. Were it to become known that Brown, still an unpaid advisor to the FWP, asked for NAACP support, his lobbying efforts to reinstate the funding would be undermined.[18] Brown pointed out that much of what the Dies Committee regarded as "subversive, Un-American activities" in the Federal Arts Projects were actually "attempts to record contemporary America honestly, realistically, democratically." The implication that "American democracy is not all it is stacked up to be, seems subversive to the gentleman from Texas and his cohorts." But Brown also privately acknowledged that "as far as the Negro is concerned, these projects . . . still leave something to be desired," given the discrimination in hiring, rank, and salary. And Brown was still annoyed that some state directors had completely ignored the Office on Negro Affairs' extensive editorial critique and suggestions for revising copy pertaining to African Americans. The Mississippi state Guide, which had been published without any of the revisions recommended by Brown, was singled out in Brown's missive for demonstrating "typically Mississippi unfairness to the Negro." Nevertheless, Brown concluded, considering the entire body of FWP publications, "the Negro has received . . . a great deal of sincere and just appraisal." Just as important, the FWP had provided employment "to needy Negroes who otherwise would have had little or no chance to use their training or ability." Furthermore, Brown noted, the very real threat from Congress to discontinue the Writers' Project would leave significant studies on African Americans unfinished, including *The Negro in Virginia*, the first history of the underground railroad written by African Americans, a work on folklore, and a book of ex-slave narratives that would help to counter Lost Cause mythology. "It would be tragic if this work were discontinued," Brown concluded. He urged White to do everything in his power to use the "energies" of the NAACP to protest against any cuts to the FWP. If the public would only read the project's numerous publications, Brown asserted, "they would see that instead of being subversive and un-American, they reflect and inspire the finest sort of patriotism and are written in a true democratic spirit."[19]

White was quick to act on Brown's counsel; in less than two weeks following the receipt of Brown's letter, he sent out a press release.[20] Four months later, he sent a public telegram to the chairman of the House Appropriations Committee, which was then released over the Associated Press wire, urging the committee to immediately restore the $150 million cut to the WPA that threatened the loss of a million jobs: "This is a matter of grave concern to twelve million American Negroes, a disproportionate number of whom are dependent upon relief through their inability to secure employment because of race prejudice."[21] White also urged NAACP members throughout the country to contact their senators to protest the cuts.

As a result of the hearings, Congress curtailed funding, but it is possible that NAACP pressure helped to keep the Writers' Project going, albeit in a fundamentally altered form. Instead of elimination, the FWP was removed from federal oversight and reorganized under the jurisdiction of state governments as the WPA Writers' Program on September 1, 1939. The shift to a state-controlled Writers' Program resulted in the publication of FWP manuscripts that reflected the goals and ideological views of individual state administrators along with the demands of commercial publishing houses and local sponsors. *The Negro in Virginia*, one of the best books to come out of the FWP in terms of its content and style, was largely the result of the contributions of a talented NWU directed by Roscoe Lewis.[22] But state control also led to publications such as Georgia's highly problematic *Drums and Shadows: Survival Studies among the Georgia Coastal Negroes*, the brainchild of Savannah district supervisor Mary Granger. Granger would also oversee the publication of a series of nostalgic plantation histories that appeared in several issues of the *Georgia Historical Quarterly* between 1938 and 1941. These essays glorified the economy and the culture of the slave-owning South by omitting ex-slave testimony.[23]

Drums and Shadows emphasized the retention of "primitive" African practices and behavioral traits by the "modern Negro." For example, the emotionalism of a black church service was offered as a manifestation of "the hungry urge of the jungle," which lurked beneath "the trappings of civilization."[24] The preface to the ex-slave narratives, which were presented in a heavily phoneticized, first-person dialect, worked to invalidate the narratives as historical evidence: "Vain in the same way that children are vain, the [ex-slaves] felt a sense of importance in being sought out for information. . . . Innately creative, they embellished their narratives with exaggerative incidents and irrelevant details in order to impress the questioner."[25] Responses to the manuscript by federal directors and outside readers were unfavorable. Alsberg, Brown, the FWP's national folklore editor Benjamin Botkin, and two prominent sociologists from Howard University, E. Franklin Frazier and W. O. Brown, emphatically objected to the racial stereotypes and arguments regarding black primitivism.[26] Granger refused to make the recommended revisions; instead she found strong allies for the work, the social anthropologist Guy Johnson and Georgia state director Samuel Tupper Jr., and got the University of Georgia Press to commit to publishing it. The dismantling of the FWP in 1939 gave Granger and Tupper hope that the objections voiced by Brown and Alsberg, as well as Botkin, would no longer apply. They wrote to Alsberg's replacement, J. D. Newsom, inquiring whether Brown was still with the Project.[27] He was, but Newsom gave strict instructions to Brown to write a new final report approving publication. Brown did so but included his summation of the federal directors' objections: "What all three editors wished for . . . is hardly likely to be achieved. Long conferences and correspondence have apparently not clarified what the editors want."[28] As a result, *Drums and Shadows* was published without the recommended revisions and retained its emphasis on black primitivism.

Previous scholarship on the FWP has not identified what happened to Brown after the close of the FWP. A WPA job classification form for Brown, dated March 6, 1940, identifies his new position at the Library of Congress Writers' Project as "Senior Editorial Assistant" (starting date October 1939).[29] Brown was now working under Botkin, helping to process the FWP materials for archival acquisition. But Brown experienced discrimination, like many African American employees in white-collar positions on New Deal projects. In a memo he sent to Botkin in April 1940, Brown protested his reduction in salary by $241.92 a year, stating his belief that he was "the only person on the reorganized project to have received a cut in salary."[30] Following his resignation (which indicates that Brown's request was denied), Brown put in a word for his longtime assistant in the Office on Negro Affairs, Glaucia Roberts, suggesting she be promoted to senior editorial clerk. She had worked for the FWP since 1936 "with only one advance in rank and salary. She deserves better."[31]

Due to the termination of the FWP, the ex-slave narratives submitted to the federal office by state projects, over 2,300 of them, were turned over to the Library of Congress.[32] Many ex-slave interviews were not forwarded to the Library of Congress at the close of the FWP but remained in the hands of state employees.[33] From October 1939 to February 1941, Dr. Botkin and his staff subjected the collected narratives to a process of appraisal regarding their authenticity but also their potential publishing value for the commercial market. Botkin had replaced John Lomax in 1938 as the FWP's national folklore editor. But his primary contribution to the Ex-Slave Project would occur after the majority of slave narratives had been collected.

While the American Folklore Society had hoped that this change in leadership within the FWP, from Lomax to Botkin, would yield a more scholarly and scientific approach to the project's folklore collecting, Botkin's unorthodox approach to both the definition of folk culture and its uses was closer to Hurston's. Unlike Lomax, Botkin did not view the continual reinvention of folk culture and its permutations as "inauthentic." And he did not subscribe to the regional bifurcation that drew a clear distinction between rural versus urban, agrarian versus industrial, and transmission face to face rather than through mass media. This perspective allowed the consideration of folk cultures previously dismissed by the purists, elevating the status of the folklore and folk songs of the urban working class. He even coined a new term, "folksay," to connote the literary value of folklore. Unlike folklorists such as Lomax, who viewed technological developments in mass communication (the phonograph, the radio, and the movies) as anathema to the preservation of "authentic" folk cultures, Botkin saw these mediums' potential for transmitting folk cultures, helping them to operate as a unifying force within American life.[34] Collection, Botkin felt, should always move toward publication and popularization. Botkin's flexible approach, however, also allowed greater tampering by editors with the folk materials. Editorial changes that made the material seem more "authentic," or poetic, and accessible to a wide audience were not only tolerated but encouraged by Botkin. Through the adoption and manipulation of folk idioms, Botkin argued, the writer would become "not merely an interpreter but a voice—their voice, which is now his own."[35]

This held enormous ramifications for the assessment of the ex-slave narratives, now under Botkin's authority.

In 1940, he sat down to evaluate the ex-slave narrative collection. In an administrative memorandum, he summarized the challenges the collection posed as a result of the Project's methods: amateur interviewers, aged informants, federal guidelines and manuals, and a lack of information about both the interviewers and the informants. Furthermore, the complex human interaction between two unknown participants, between interviewer and informant, was rife with inherent complications: "In recording oral material, moreover, the only scientific, because objective, medium is the phonographic disc. In the passage from word of mouth and from ear to paper, as in translation . . . much of the scent as well as the sense is lost."[36] The task of weighing their evidentiary value, he ultimately decided, must be "left to the scholars."[37]

Appraisals of the slave narratives per Botkin's criteria were to include three main considerations, which unintentionally undermined black oral traditions and also the narratives of Florida's NWU. First, staff members were to evaluate the reliability and veracity of the information, and hence its value, by considering the source: Was the material based on firsthand experience or hearsay or both? They were also expected to scrutinize the narrative for internal inconsistencies and contradictions, "obvious errors or doubtful points of historical facts," and "confused or ambiguous statements."[38] Second, they were instructed to note the style in which the narrative was presented: Was the narrative told in the first or third person or a combination of both? Was the language conventional, colloquial, or modified or extreme dialect relying on phonetic spelling? Last, appraisers were to assess the narrative's potential merit for publication, and note where interesting passages occurred.[39] But they were also to recommend whether the narrative should be "deposited in the Library or that it not be deposited and express [their] reasons carefully."[40] Because these assessments helped to ascertain which narratives would be put forth for public consumption and which would be relegated to the archives, their determinations about the ex-slave narratives are particularly important.

Botkin strongly favored ex-slave narratives that were written in the autobiographical style, because he felt they conveyed a greater sense of "authenticity," even if it was achieved by the interviewer's sleight of hand. In 1938, Botkin, in his new position as the national editor on folkways, had rejected an ex-slave narrative submitted to the federal office by Jules Frost, a white Florida employee (who had interviewed ex-slave Josephine Anderson). Frost had included his own questions and comments with the testimony of his ex-slave informant. Botkin felt the story was "marred by use of the question and answer method."[41] To please Botkin, Frost rewrote the entire interview as a first-person monologue in heavy dialect. Even more significantly, Botkin would directly criticize the narratives written in the third person, the style favored by members of Florida's NWU, stating that he found them "completely lacking not only in flavor but also in reliability."[42]

A year into the appraisal process, a memo from Botkin's main assistant, Mrs. Wharton, provided a brief overview of the narratives by state. Singled out for praise were the narratives from Arkansas, Mississippi, and Tennessee, because they were written predominantly in the first person.[43] Special censure was given to states such as Indiana and Florida for narratives that "were all third-person accounts; most of them clumsily written, none too clear, and all stressing miscegenation."[44] The narratives submitted by Florida's NWU came under a barrage of criticism by appraisers of the Library of Congress Project for the use of the third person, which was described by Botkin's staff members as "reportorial," "sophomoric," "matter-of-fact," and always "uninteresting."[45] One reader unilaterally recommended the deletion of "all unnecessary comments by the interviewer"; if followed, this instruction would have eliminated black interviewers' textual strategies for inscribing black objectivity and authority within the narratives and the messages of racial uplift, along with the interpretations of ex-slaves' signifying.[46] These narratives also lost "reliability and value" in the eyes of appraisers who felt that they were "impersonal" in their tone and use of conventional English.[47] The use of "conventional language" instead of dialect led appraisers to condemn them for their "reserved manner" and their "lack of human interest and color."[48] By contrast, narratives that incorporated dialect were typically described by appraisers as conveying "warmth and enthusiasm" in language that was "natural and personal," although narratives that relied heavily on phonetic spelling were criticized as artificial; "in the event of publication," such excesses would need to be eliminated.[49]

Appraisals of Georgia's narratives remarked favorably on their inclusion of the interviewer's perspective and picturesque observations of the ex-slave informant. Narratives edited by United Daughters of the Confederacy member Sarah Hall, which contained descriptions of informants' residences, appearances, and behavior, were often singled out for praise by readers who felt the "introductory and interpolated" commentary "show[ed] good observation on the part of the narrator."[50] The narratives were likewise "entitled to a place in the collection" for "the degree of insight into [the ex-slave's] personality afforded by the interviewer's descriptions."[51] Such descriptions could also be used by appraisers to confirm the credibility of the ex-slave's narrative: "Reliability is established," wrote one reader, "by the interviewer's impression of the informant."[52] In such assessments, the ex-slave's word was not enough.

These evaluations of the narratives' reliability clearly reveal the personal biases of members of Botkin's staff. For some, well-rendered dialect was an indicator of the truthful nature of the account. Others relied on the interviewer's personal knowledge of the informant as a testament to the truth of the narrative's content: "The reliability of the comments is attested by the interviewer's long acquaintance with the informant."[53] Ironically, this criterion privileged narratives that were often shaped in conformity with what ex-slave informants presumed were white interviewers' expectations. Very often personal relationships between southern white interviewers and black informants had their origins in slavery; some ex-slaves were interviewed by the direct descendants of their former owners.[54] This inhibited informants from relating anecdotes that would cast the interviewer's family in a negative light. Conversely, a narrative that told of a heroic ex-slave informant who saved his "white folks" by extinguishing a fire was one of the relatively few narratives rejected for deposit into the archives: "Presented . . . without authentication, the tale cannot form part of a collection of slavery narratives."[55]

As these remarks show, appraisers' judgments regarding the narratives' reliability or truthfulness were highly arbitrary and subjective and often based on the reader's own assumptions about the institution of slavery. Happy stories of life under slavery were sometimes deemed to be believable on that basis alone: "The carefree detail and evident earnestness shown in the tellings give the informant's words the ring of truth. It is interesting and valuable as a bright word picture, describing one who was happy as a slave."[56] By the same yardstick, accounts of the injustices of slavery could also be viewed by certain appraisers with skepticism: "Voluble, sensational, sometimes exaggerated. . . . The accounts of punishment are probably somewhat overdrawn," wrote one reader about George Young's oral history of slavery.[57] The assessment of one narrative concluded it was "valuable chiefly for its account of excellent post-slavery relations between a former slave and her owner,"[58] while another was "usable in a social study of plantation life" because "liberal gifts from a master to former slaves should be made of record."[59]

Complicating matters was the consideration by Botkin and his staff of the narratives as useful historical sources but also as material for fiction writers. Appraisers often noted that apart from their value as testimonials of life during slavery, the narratives were rich sources for literature. One such reader enthusiastically suggested that the narratives "might well be the basis for one enormous and 'definitive' novel of the kind currently popular . . . a sort of 'Uncle Tom's Cabin' plus 'Gone with the Wind' plus 'For Whom the Bell Tolls.' "[60] Staff members were also thinking about the commercial possibilities for the narratives in mediums besides literature. Another appraisal summarizing the narratives from Arkansas expressed the opinion that "many of the colloquialisms and much of the dialect can be utilized as source material for fiction, drama, or radio." Representations of slavery in popular film clearly influenced appraisals of the ex-slave narratives. One reader of a narrative from Georgia was reminded of a scene from a Shirley Temple movie, *The Little Colonel*, and on the strength of that association thought that the material might be useful for creative writers.[61] Appraisers were also drawn to examples that demonstrated the informant's ability as a performer. Ex-slave Frank Smith was labeled "A Gifted Liar" and "a born buffoon" on the appraisal sheet, which, with damning praise, compared his "broad comedy and unabashed falsehood" to the "tradition of American humor exemplified by Mark Twain" and suggested that his narrative was "well-worth preserving as an example of natural comedy that gets its effects without too much reliance on dull truth."[62] As the editor in charge of preparing the narratives for archival deposit and eventual publication, Botkin was uniquely situated to have first crack at editing and publishing an anthology drawing on the entire collection; *Lay My Burden Down*, an anthology of the narratives culled from the Library of Congress's collection and other sources, was published in 1945.[63]

The only federal use of the narratives before the end of the war occurred with the Library of Congress's Radio Research Project, the idea for which came from John Lomax's son Alan, who would serve as second-in-command to the librarian of Congress, Archibald MacLeish. Lomax came up with the idea while he was working as an assistant in the Library's Archive of American Folk Song. Established with a special grant from the Rockefeller Foundation on January 1, 1941, the Project sought to use the folk materials gathered by the FWP to produce wartime propaganda about American national identity. Its first foray into radio production was a series called *Hidden History*, intended to showcase the importance of history "found . . . in the minds and the memories of the people."[64] Twenty-six shows of the *Hidden History* series were broadcast over the NBC-Blue network between May and November 1941 to sixty-six stations across the nation.[65] "Follow the Drinking Gourd," written by Joseph Liss and Oscar Saul, introduced listeners to the oral testimonies of former slaves collected by the FWP. Written in heavily phoneticized dialect, with liberal use of "de" and "dat," the story was narrated by the character of Kiziah, a Virginia slave. The only mistreatment he experienced from his slaveholder was depicted in the master's refusal to provide a proper wedding ceremony for Kiziah and his wife. The slaveholder articulated his reasoning in the mildest of terms: "I'm pretty busy right now. Come, join hands and jump the broomstick." Small doses of humor were provided by Kiziah's mistaking the Underground Railroad for a literal train and his quaint folk expressions and naïveté as the story followed his escape to freedom in Canada. The announcer concluded the fifteen-minute show by reminding listeners that the story "was taken from actual interviews with ex-slaves."[66]

One of the most successful Radio Research Projects would be an adaptation of John Lomax's as yet unfinished autobiographical manuscript, "Adventures of a Ballad Hunter." Broadcast as a series of ten fifteen-minute programs under the title *Ballad Hunter*, the shows combined Lomax's stories of "his song-hunting travels" interspersed with field recordings he had made of various types of folk songs.[67] American audiences could hear for themselves "American folk music [as it was] sung by authentic singers" on location, instead of seasoned professionals performing in a sound studio or on stage.[68] The *Ballad Hunter* series, six fifteen-minute programs, was originally free of charge to radio stations, local schools, and libraries across the country.[69] Due in part to Lomax's celebrity, over one hundred advance orders were placed before the scheduled release date in May 1941. By 1942, the series was in its second edition and had garnered almost $600 in sales.[70] John Lomax died in 1948, at age seventy-nine, but his son Alan, who had worked with his father as well as with Hurston in the 1930s, would become even more of a celebrity folklorist than his father had been. His career, like his father's, would be shadowed by accusations of cultural appropriation and plagiarism. Questions about copyright arose during one of Alan's Radio Research Project series, when Harold Spivacke, director of the Library of Congress's Music Division, discovered that required permissions had not been obtained for either the music and lyrics or the folk performers.[71] Fortunately for the Music Division, no one refused to grant their permission, for the records were already being shipped to radio stations. In response to the Library's request for copyright, numerous letters poured in from musicians, all granting the library release of their material, sometimes in exchange for a free copy of the program.[72] Ironically, the mass medium that John Lomax had held responsible for the destruction of "pure" folk material would become the transmitter of these folk materials back into the public realm.

Hurston went to Hollywood. She worked for Paramount Pictures, from October 1941 to January 1942, behind the scenes as an advisor to movie executives interested in capitalizing on the public's fascination with black exoticism in the form of voodoo and zombies.[73] Although it is well known that Hurston did a temporary stint in Hollywood, the connection between Hurston and Val Lewton's cult classic, *I Walked with a Zombie*, released by RKO in 1943, has yet to be recognized.[74] According to Hurston, in a radio interview she did with popular host Mary Margaret McBride, she was employed by the film's screenwriter, Ardel Wray, after Wray read Hurston's book on Haitian voodoo.[75] Not surprisingly, given Hollywood's insistence on stereotypical images of black primitivism and superstition, which conflicted with Hurston's respect for hoodoo as a legitimate religious practice, Hurston left in disgust. Sadly, hers is not a Hollywood ending—Hurston wound up inhabiting two of the roles Hollywood routinely assigned to African Americans onscreen as criminals and servants. After publishing her autobiography to critical acclaim, she was arrested on false charges in 1948 of child molestation of which she was acquitted (having been out of the country during the alleged crime), but not before a firestorm of sensationalistic publicity had all but convicted her. Despite good reviews of her novel *Seraph on the Suwanee*, two years later she wound up working incognito as a black domestic for a white family in Miami in 1950. Hurston passed away ten years later at St. Lucie County Welfare Home for the impoverished, laid to rest in a pauper's unmarked grave.[76]

The Ex-Slave Project illuminates how definitions of black identity in the 1930s were, in the words of Martin Favor, "constantly being invented, policed, transgressed, and contested."[77] This history fits into the larger story of civil rights struggles. A number of scholars, including Nikhil Pal Singh, Patricia Sullivan, and Jacquelyn Dowd Hall, have argued that the New Deal should be viewed as an important interim stage in the long Civil Rights Movement, despite or paradoxically because of its limitations.[78] This look at how the Ex-Slave Project focused on the construction of historical memory and African Americans' place within the national narrative provides a case study of how the goals of black self-representation became so difficult to achieve. The experiences of African American employees with New Deal cultural projects and the resulting portraits of black identity, privileged by FWP directors, too often failed to challenge long-standing myths about racial inequality. To borrow Karen Ferguson's phrasing from her study of Atlanta's black reformer elite, "the New Deal served as an imperfect catalyst for African American liberation."[79]

Most historians agree that the New Deal was not as much of a deal for black Americans as it was for whites. African Americans did not benefit equally from key economic legislation, such as the Agricultural Adjustment Act, the Wagner Act, or even work relief programs, which were frequently segregated and clearly reluctant to hire many African Americans. More glaringly, Roosevelt failed to support efforts by civil rights activists to make lynching a federal crime.[80] As Gary Gerstle has observed, the New Deal's commitment to a type of civic nationalism that gestured toward the inclusion of previously marginalized groups was nevertheless infused with a racial nationalism that curtailed the possibility of a more radical liberal reform.[81] Given the New Deal's poor record on race during the Great Depression, it is evident why a number of historians have come to the conclusion, as David Roediger boldly argues, that the New Deal is about the coming of age of whiteness, about ratifying whiteness.[82] More persuasively, Singh has argued that New Deal liberalism was marred "by a set of ad-hoc, race-specific omissions and adjustments that proved increasingly consequential over time. . . . Because the New Deal failed to actively pursue racial equality, the racial hierarchy continued to serve as an explicit limit within the expanded field of government practice."[83]

Nevertheless, the Federal Writers' Ex-Slave Project was remarkable for enabling African Americans to make a significant contribution to the historical narrative. The greatest achievement of the FWP was its creation of a unique and unprecedented archive of ex-slave narratives as well as folk culture. It remains the largest collection of ex-slave testimony, with arguably a far more extensive and diverse sampling of the experiences of the enslaved than the published autobiographies by former slaves from the nineteenth century. The value of the Ex-Slave Project extended far beyond its short life. Most certainly, without the large body of rich evidence provided by the FWP's Ex-Slave Project, historians' subsequent work on slavery, emancipation, and the African American experience would be severely compromised. These narratives also provide a rich (and, still to date, largely untapped) source of documentation for the African American experience following emancipation, as well as for race relations and race making in the New Deal era.

The FWP also employed African Americans in white-collar positions, as stenographers, researchers, interviewers, writers, and editors, in the midst of an era when the great majority of jobs made available to them were in agricultural labor and domestic service.[84] It is undeniable that many African Americans would have been hard-pressed to make ends meet without the employment opportunities provided by the WPA (not least among them, the FWP). Eloquent testimony on the importance of the WPA for black Americans suffering the deprivation of the Depression comes from the Ex-Slave Project itself; surprisingly, out of all places, it comes from the problematic Georgia Project. Eugenia Martin of Atlanta spoke at length of the personal satisfaction and skills she gained working for the WPA, first gathering information for the "Survey of White Collar and Skilled Negroes," then working as a floor supervisor for the Sewing Project, and finally as a member of the Housekeeping Aid Project. She expressed gratitude for the income that enabled her to keep up the mortgage payments on her home, as well as the work experience she had gained. "I simply could not have held out this long had it not been for WPA." However, the passing of new restrictions on WPA employment by Congress in the fall of 1939, limiting relief work to eighteen months, had once again placed her in financial jeopardy and she was four months behind on her house payment. "There seems so little work for Negroes," she observed. "We have so few places and they are all overcrowded."[85] Relief was vital for individuals like Martin, but perhaps just as important was the sense of self-worth that came from doing useful, skilled work. Thanks to projects like the WPA and the FWP, as Sterling Brown, Walter White, and other black leaders observed, doors essential to African American advancement were opening during the 1930s, creating new opportunities and "a sense of possibility even if, ultimately, many of those possibilities were not realized."[86]

And yet it is important to remember that this was a decade marked by growing frustration among African American intellectuals with the glacial nature of civil rights progress, owing in large part to the longevity of racial attitudes and prejudices that continued to inform and undergird Jim Crow segregation in the North as well as the South and even federal projects like the FWP. W. E. B. Du Bois, who devoted his life's work to dismantling the barriers of segregation, voiced this sentiment in an editorial that appeared in the *Crisis* in 1934, leading to his resignation from the NAACP. Signaling his shift away from integration and toward black separatism as a result of his disillusionment with racial progress, he observed, "Segregation may be just as evil today as it was in 1910, but it is more insistent, more prevalent, and more unassailable by appeal or argument."[87]

The limits of New Deal liberalism left the promise of black self-representation partially unfulfilled, likely contributing to the cultural formation of a more radical black political consciousness—one that increasingly sought to work outside state-sanctioned avenues of institutional authority.

If there was a moment when the federal government might have begun to build a national consensus, not just about the history of slavery but about the incorporation of African Americans as equal citizens, it was the New Deal. But the limitations of the FWP's attempts to include African American voices and history without marginalizing or rewriting them still reverberate today in the controversies over public memory and the legacy of slavery.[88]

In the cult phenomenon that is the web series *Ask a Slave*, actress Azie Dungey impersonates a slave owned by George and Martha Washington. She created the character of Lizzie Mae, lady's maid to Mrs. Washington, based on her experiences as an interpretive docent at the historic site of Washington's plantation, portraying Caroline Branham, a real slave at Mount Vernon. Dressed in period costume, Dungey obeys the same rules for the web series that reenactors at Mount Vernon do: she cannot give any answer that would not be in keeping with the period her character inhabits. Like "Lizzie Mae," ex-slave informants for the FWP often found themselves trapped in the role of a slave and inhabiting a memory not entirely of their own making by FWP interviewers, writers, and editors. Nevertheless, ex-slave informants found creative ways, by talking about slavery, to speak about the racism and racial discrimination they still faced in the 1930s. In a similar manner, Dungey explains that "I am not talking about slavery in my show. . . . I'm talking about modern racism, and I'm talking about modern ignorance." The questions Lizzie Mae fields, based on actual questions posed by tourists to Mount Vernon, suggest that the American public is largely clueless about the history and institution of slavery.[89] Many Americans, irrespective of race, say they are tired of talking about slavery. But the legacy of that past is still very much with us as a nation, and it will continue to haunt political discourse as well as structural inequalities if Americans' historical illiteracy regarding slavery remains.

Appendix
Bibliographical Information Concerning Epigraphs

Introduction

Houston A. Baker Jr., *Blues, Ideology, and Afro-American Literature: A Vernacular Theory* (Chicago: University of Chicago Press, 1984), 7.

Chapter One

Ray Stannard Baker, *Following the Color Line: An Account of Negro Citizenship in the American Democracy* (New York: Doubleday, Page, 1908), 44.
Richard Wright, *Uncle Tom's Children* (New York: Harper & Row, 1938), xxxi.

Chapter Two

F. E. Turin to Honorable Colgate Darden Jr., House Office Building, February 22, 1936, Entry 1, Box 47, File "Virginia S–Z," 1–2, RG 69.

Chapter Three

Alice Walker, "The Dummy in the Window: Joel Chandler Harris and the Invention of Uncle Remus," originally published as "Uncle Remus, No Friend of Mine," *Southern Exposure* 9, no. 2 (Summer 1981): 29–31; reprinted in *Black on White: Black Writers on What It Means to Be White,* ed. David R. Roediger (New York: Schocken Books, 1998), 238.

Chapter Four

This is a transcription of a document handwritten by Huddie Ledbetter, which accounts for the unusual spelling and syntax. Huddie Ledbetter, New York City, May 22, 1947, Folkways Archives, Smithsonian, reprinted in Charles Wolfe and Kip Lornell, *The Life and Legend of Leadbelly* (New York: HarperCollins, 1992), 247–48.

Chapter Five

John LaTouche (lyrics), "Ballad for Americans," music by Earl Robinson, originally titled "The Ballad of Uncle Sam," for the FWP musical revue *Sing for Your Supper,*

1939. First performed as a standalone song by Paul Robeson in 1939; see Denning, *Cultural Front*, 115–16, 128.

Chapter Six

Zora Neale Hurston, *Mules and Men* (1935; repr. New York: Harper Perennial, 1990), 185.

Chapter Seven

Paul Diggs, FWP, "Follow Me Through Florida," November 10, 1938, Florida Negro Papers, Box 3, 1, USF.

Chapter Eight

Richard Wright, "The Ethics of Living Jim Crow," Federal Writers' Project, *American Stuff* (New York: Viking Press, 1937); reprinted in *The Negro Caravan: Writings by American Negroes*, ed. Sterling A. Brown, Arthur Davis, and Ulysses Lee (New York: Dryden Press, 1941), 1059.

Epilogue

Mary K. Roberts and Zelia Sweet, "Stories of Slaves," interview with ex-slave Sarah Rhodes, August 3, 1937, Florida Negro Papers, Box 9, Slavery Interviews, USF.
Azie Dungey, "Azie and Amani: New Movie '12 Years a Slave,'" *Ask a Slave: The Web Series*, https://www.youtube.com/watch?v=mySSx9Pmrio (October 18, 2013), quoted in Soraya Nadia McDonald, "It's Not Slavery; It's Satire," *Washington Post*, November 13, 2013; online as "'Ask a Slave' Talks Race and Gender Issues in the Age of YouTube," http://www.washingtonpost.com/lifestyle/style/ask-a-slave-talks-race-and-gender-issues-in-the-age-of-youtube/2013/11/11/d569124e-4649-11e3-bf0c-cebf37c6f484_story.html.

Notes

Abbreviations

AAFC-LC	Archives of the American Folklife Center, Library of Congress
FB-LC	Franz Boas Papers, Manuscript Division, Library of Congress
FWP-LC	Records of the Federal Writers' Project, Manuscript Division, Library of Congress
LC	Library of Congress
JWJC	Langston Hughes Correspondence, James Weldon Johnson Collection, Beinecke Rare Book and Manuscript Library, Yale Collection of American Literature
MD-LC	Manuscript Division, Library of Congress
MPBRS-LC	Motion Picture, Broadcasting and Recorded Sound Division, Library of Congress
NPD	*Negro Press Digest*
RG 69	Record Group 69, PI 57, National Archives and Records Administration
SSRT-LC	John and Ruby Lomax 1939 Southern States Recording Trip, Archives of the American Folklife Center, Library of Congress
UDC	United Daughters of the Confederacy Collection, Eleanor S. Brockenbrough Library, Museum of the Confederacy, Richmond, Va.
UF	P. K. Yonge Library of Florida History, Special Collections, George A. Smathers Libraries, University of Florida, Gainesville
USF	University of South Florida Libraries, Special Collections, Tampa

Introduction

1. Anderson's narrative was transcribed by her white interviewer in a manner intended to be a written representation of the black vernacular. As I'll discuss at greater length in chapter 3, federal directors of the Ex-Slave Project encouraged project personnel to try to capture the speech patterns of their informants, focusing on idiom but also issuing guidelines on phonetic spelling. See also Levine, "A Note on Black Dialect," in *Black Culture and Black Consciousness*, xv–xvi.

2. Rawick, *American Slave*, Florida, II:17:6, "Hants," informant Josephine Anderson, field worker Jules A. Frost, October 20, 1937.

3. Ibid., 6–7.

4. Yetman, "An Introduction to the WPA Slave Narratives." See also Yetman, ed., *Voices from Slavery*.

5. The history of the Ex-Slave Project has received surprisingly little attention from scholars, especially given its immense potential for helping us to understand the paradoxes of the 1930s. Sonnet H. Retman's engaging study of 1930s constructions of the folk, *Real Folks: Race and Genre in the Great Depression* (2011), is invested, as my book is, in critically examining the ideological work of texts like the FWP's Florida guide but does not mention the Ex-Slave Project. David A. Taylor's informal and celebratory excursion through select writers' experiences working for the WPA, in *Soul of a People: The WPA Writers' Project Uncovers Depression America* (2009), also ignores it completely, while Lawrence Jackson's comprehensive look at African American protest literature, *The Indignant Generation: A Narrative History of African American Writers and Critics, 1934–1960* (2011), treats the Ex-Slave Project only as a footnote in the history of the FWP. Even scholarly monographs that focus specifically on the cultural projects of the New Deal, such as Jerrold Hirsch's *Portrait of America: A Cultural History of the Federal Writers' Project* (2003) and Lauren Sklaroff's *Black Culture and the New Deal: The Quest for Civil Rights in the Roosevelt Era* (2009), give it short shrift, preferring to place their emphasis on the FWP's famous American Guide Series and (in Sklaroff's study) also the Federal Theatre Project and wartime radio and film production.

6. As Shaw has observed in "Using the WPA Ex-Slave Narratives to Study the Impact of the Great Depression," scholars continue to overlook the FWP narrative collection as a potentially rich source for the 1930s.

7. Gordon exhorts us to pay attention to stories of hauntings as an important index of social life and unequal power relations, in *Ghostly Matters*, 17.

8. Kammen, *Mystic Chords of Memory*, 462.

9. Houston A. Baker Jr., *Critical Memory*, 29; Black Public Sphere Collective, *The Black Public Sphere*.

10. As Roediger has discerned, there is a need for more scholarly works on black constructions of whiteness to balance out the plethora of scholarly writings about race and representation that are weighted toward *white* perspectives on blackness. Roediger, *Black on White*, 6.

11. Blassingame, "Using the Testimony of Ex-Slaves," 474–92.

12. Walter Johnson argues that "the rhetorical situation of the interview by a white recorder in the 1930s South [was] a great deal more inhibiting than that which characterized the production of the abolitionist narratives." *Soul by Soul*, 226n24.

13. hooks, *Killing Rage*, 39.

14. Fry, *Night Riders in Black Folk History*, 74–80.

15. For an interesting discussion of how traditional representations of black superstition can be reinterpreted, see Fishkin, *Was Huck Black?*, esp. 79–86.

16. Railroad tracks also evoked for African Americans the possibility of escape from southern segregation to the promised land of the North. During the Great Migration, railroads figured prominently as the primary means by which over half a million African Americans moved northward, and agents for the railroads often assisted this exodus by offering free or heavily discounted fares. See Grossman, *Land of Hope*, 103–4.

But the trains themselves were one of the most strictly enforced sites of segregation. Even when they could afford the fare for first class, African American passengers were forced to ride in the cars (formerly reserved for cattle) designated for "colored" riders. See Giddings, *When and Where I Enter*, 22. See also Barbara Young Welke's insightful study of the evolution of the railroad as a site of contest over public and private space and the intersections of race and gender in constructions of individual liberty, *Recasting American Liberty: Gender, Race, Law and the Railroad Revolution* (2001). For the exploration of the Jim Crow car in literature by black authors, see Smith, *American Body Politics*, esp. 103–11. For a representation on film of the symbolic importance of the train for southern African Americans as an escape to the North, see *Pinky*, directed by Elia Kazan in 1949.

17. On southern racial codes and violence against African Americans, see Wells, Douglass, Penn, and Barnett, *The Reason Why the Colored American Is Not in the World's Columbian Exposition*, and Wells, *Southern Horrors and Other Writings*. See also Bederman, *Manliness and Civilization*. Until the Supreme Court decision of *Loving v. Virginia*, 388 U.S. 1 (1967), many state laws prohibited interracial marriage.

18. Mitchell-Kernan, *Language Behavior in a Black Urban Community*, 97–98.

19. Anderson was certainly also calling attention to the horror engendered by the presence of whites generally in African American experience. Sprigle, *In the Land of Jim Crow*, 101. Ray Sprigle's experiment passing as an African American in the South would later be re-created by the white journalist John Howard Griffin in 1959. Griffin has been mistakenly credited as the original author of this idea, and Sprigle's radical experiment a decade prior has been forgotten in a case of literary amnesia. In a way, Sprigle's book is the ghost text of Griffin's—the animating, but invisible, spirit behind it. See Griffin, *Black like Me*.

20. A notable exception to this is portrayed in the slave narrative of Linda Brent, the nom de plume of Harriet Jacobs. Jacobs's narrative, published in 1861, is unusual for being one of the few authenticated slave narratives to be written by a woman, and even more surprising for its frank and candid discussion of the hidden yet common sexual relationships between white men and enslaved women, which were one of the forms of violence perpetrated on black women under slavery. A key aspect of Jacobs's narrative centers upon her steadfast refusal to submit to her white slaveholder's lascivious demands. Jacobs, *Incidents in the Life of a Slave Girl*.

21. One of the earliest scholars to do so was Woodward, "History from Slave Sources." One of the best examinations of the multiple ways the interviews were shaped by state and federal administrators is Musher's article on the editorial differences between the narratives submitted by Mississippi and Texas to the national office and the ones that remained in the state offices. Musher, "Contesting 'the Way the Almighty Wants It.'"

22. Escott, "The Art and Science of Reading WPA Slave Narratives."

23. Davidson and Lytle, "The View from the Bottom Rail," 187–88.

24. Houston A. Baker Jr., "To Move without Moving," 828–45.

25. *Florida Negro*, Box 8, Slave Interviews, USF.

26. As Fry points out, any one of these interpretations does not necessarily negate or rule out the others. *Night Riders in Black Folk History,* 3–7.

27. This discourse is compellingly traced in Kevin Gaines's *Uplifting the Race.*

28. Blassingame, *Slave Community;* Levine, *Black Culture and Black Consciousness,* xi; Andrews, *To Tell a Free Story;* Charles T. Davis and Gates, *Slave's Narrative.*

29. Blassingame, "Using the Testimony," 487. A number of scholars have called for a more sophisticated method of reading these nuanced and polyphonic texts, including Charles T. Davis and Henry Louis Gates Jr., and most recently Hirsch, in his cultural history of the Federal Writers' Project. Davis and Gates, *Slave's Narrative,* xi–xii; Hirsch, *Portrait of America,* 151–53.

30. For an application of Civil War memory to a more contemporary subject, see Robert J. Cook's revealing study, *Troubled Commemoration,* 14. For the concept of black counter memories as an instrument of civil rights struggles, see Blight, "W. E. B. Du Bois and the Struggle for American Historical Memory."

31. See Blight, *Race and Reunion* and *Beyond the Battlefield;* Jim Cullen, *Civil War in Popular Culture;* Horton and Horton, *Slavery and Public History.*

32. See Brundage, *Where These Memories Grow;* Wallace, *Mickey Mouse History and Other Essays on American Memory.*

33. Scholars wishing to explore the Federal Writers' Project are deeply fortunate that FWP administrators were so careful in preserving the materials submitted by the state projects but also such good record keepers of all administrative correspondence and forms. There is a wealth of documentation available to researchers, the bulk of which resides at the National Archives and Records Administration, Archives II (College Park) in Record Group 69. There is also a substantial collection of FWP print materials in the Library of Congress's Manuscript Division, as well as the many sound recordings, photographs, and films, created under the auspices of the WPA and located in the Library of Congress's Archives of the American Folklife Center, Prints and Photographs Division, and Motion Picture, Broadcasting and Recorded Sound Division. Many of these materials, including the ex-slave narratives and photographs, are now available online at the Library of Congress website, "Born in Slavery: Slave Narratives from the Federal Writers' Project, 1936–1938": www.memory.loc.gov/ammem /snhtml/. However, researchers interested in particular state projects should also travel to state collections as many materials were not forwarded (as instructed) to the federal office at the close of the project; see Rowell, " 'Let Me Be with Ole Jazzbo,' " 301.

34. Butler, in her critique of Bourdieu's theories of social speech acts, notes a critical distinction between "speaking with authority" and "being authorized to speak." As she points out, "It is clearly possible to speak with authority without being authorized to speak. Indeed, I would argue that it is precisely the expropriability of the dominant, 'authorized' discourse that constitutes one potential site of its subversive resignification." Butler, "Performativity's Social Magic," 123–24.

35. The federal arts program approved on September 12, 1935, as WPA-sponsored Federal Project No. 1, consisted of the Federal Art, Music, Theatre, and Writers' Projects and, until October 1936, the Historical Records Survey. Federal One was

terminated on June 30, 1939, but the arts programs continued as a state project, with the exception of the Federal Theatre Project, which was abolished in July 1939. For an excellent history of African Americans' experience with the Federal Theatre Project, see Rena Fraden, *Blueprints for a Black Federal Theatre*. Nicholas Natanson's insightful study of the photographs of the Resettlement Administration/Farm Security Administration, *Black Image in the New Deal*, still remains one of the only works to provide a critical and in-depth analysis of how these images represented African Americans. For African Americans' involvement with the Radio Project, see Savage, *Broadcasting Freedom*. Sklaroff, *Black Culture and the New Deal*, examines African American representation in the FWP's American Guide Series, the Federal Theatre Project, and wartime radio and film production. For representations of gender, see Melosh, *Engendering Culture*.

36. The contribution of the FWP's ex-slave narratives to the historiography of slavery has been enormous, both quantitatively and substantively. See Blassingame, *Slave Community*; Escott, *Slavery Remembered*; Genovese, *Roll, Jordan, Roll*; Glymph, *Out of the House of Bondage*; Gomez, *Exchanging Our Country Marks*; Joyner, *Down by the Riverside*; Levine, *Black Culture and Black Consciousness*; Rawick, *From Sundown to Sunup*; and Deborah Gray White's groundbreaking work on slave women, *Ar'n't I a Woman?*.

Chapter One

1. FWP excerpt, "Passing of Old Time Negroes," n.d., Entry 21, Box 1, File "Tennessee," RG 69.

2. See Jacqueline Jones, *Labor of Love, Labor of Sorrow*, 131.

3. This awareness of the costs of modernization and its homogenizing effects on American culture had much earlier roots in the emerging folk collection movement of the late nineteenth century. The mission to salvage disappearing folk cultures was the raison d'être of the founding of the American Folklore Society in 1888 and its publication, the *Journal of American Folklore*. Bendix, *In Search of Authenticity*, 124–26.

4. Thomas P. Fenner, *Cabin and Plantation Songs*, v–vi, quoted in Filene, *Romancing the Folk*, 30.

5. Herbert A. Miller, *Races, Nations, and Classes*, 149. Ulrich B. Phillips's history of slavery published in 1918, *American Negro Slavery*, helped enshrine this version of the southern past.

6. The United Daughters of the Confederacy's attempt to create a memorial statue of "mammy" in the nation's capital is another example. McElya, *Clinging to Mammy*, 141–59.

7. See Sullivan, *Days of Hope*; Kelley, *Hammer and Hoe*.

8. The robot was designed by Dr. Phillips Thomas and S. M. Kintner, assistant vice president of Westinghouse.

9. For more on images of black servitude in the ready-made food industry, see Witt, *Black Hunger*; and Manring, *Slave in a Box*.

10. "The World's Largest Loud Speaker, and Other Late Devices." *Radio-Craft* 2, no. 8 (February 1931): 468–69, 509.

11. See Blight, *Race and Reunion*.

12. Sterling A. Brown, "The Negro Character as Seen by White Authors," 180.

13. Penkower, *Federal Writers' Project*, 147, cites interviews with Brown, Ralph Ellison, Ted Poston, and Arna Bontemps in support of his assertion that black intellectuals regarded the 1930s as a more important decade for socially realistic and politically aware representations of the black experience, thanks in part to what Bontemps referred to as "the social consciousness of the 'WPA black writers' school" in "Famous WPA Authors."

14. Sterling A. Brown, Davis, and Lee, *Negro Caravan*, 847.

15. Ulysses Lee and Eugene Holmes, both of Howard University, were employed as Brown's editorial assistants; Glaucia Roberts took the lead as editor, filling in for Brown during 1937–38 while he was on a Guggenheim Fellowship. Gabbin, *Sterling A. Brown*, 70, 79; see also Sklaroff, *Black Culture and the New Deal*, 93.

16. See, for example, Natalie J. Ring's excellent study of race, regionalism, and imperialism, *Problem South*.

17. Hirsch, *Portrait of America*.

18. As Robert Cantwell has pointed out, "The Roosevelt administration had simply reached out into what by the 1920s had already become a brisk trade in the representation as well as the commercial, political, and social exploitation, of folk culture." Cantwell, "Feasts of Unnaming," 270. For a comprehensive overview of the pursuit of the "folk" during the 1920s and 1930s, see Kammen, *Mystic Chords of Memory*.

19. Mangione, *Dream and the Deal*, 270.

20. Ibid.

21. Michael Staub and William Stott have made broad claims for the documentary forms of expression that characterize the 1930s. Staub, *Voices of Persuasion*; Stott, *Documentary Expression and Thirties America*.

22. Irr, *Suburb of Dissent*, 234. Irr's comparative study of the uses of the documentary genre by Canadian writers as well as American writers in constructing a more pluralistic national identity is particularly illuminating.

23. Denning, *Cultural Front*, 79, 133–35.

24. For more on the African American left's coalition building and a pan-African movement, see Von Eschen, *Race against Empire*.

25. Penkower, *Federal Writers' Project*, 16–17.

26. There were two strains of folk collecting that emerged from the late nineteenth century and informed the folk movement of the 1920s and 1930s: the literary folklorists who came out of Harvard and who had studied with the ballad scholars Francis James Child and George Kittredge (who would serve as president of the American Folklore Society from 1904 to 1911) and the anthropological folklorists from Columbia who studied with Franz Boas. But both schools shared the common goal of salvaging the vanishing remains of American folklore, as an authentic American cultural form. For more on the development of folk collecting as a professionalizing discipline, see

Zumwalt, *American Folklore Scholarship*. On folk music, see Karl Hagstrom Miller, *Segregating Sound*; Filene, *Romancing the Folk*. For salvage mission and "vocabulary of loss" among folklore collectors dating back to the 1880s, see Bendix, *In Search of Authenticity*. Retman and Hirsch, talking about the 1930s, retrace the lineage of folk collection. Retman, *Real Folks*; Hirsch, *Portrait of America*.

27. Sterling A. Brown, "Negro Folk Expression," 61.

28. Warren-Findley, "Passports to Change."

29. "Black authenticity" is the term Martin Favor uses in his literary study of four writers from the Harlem Renaissance. As he astutely observes, the association of "authenticity" with the folk is a coupling that remains in many contemporary black scholars' projects of black liberation. Favor, *Authentic Blackness*.

30. The Communist Party also perpetuated this connection through the Black Belt thesis of 1928. Jonathan Scott Holloway, *Confronting the Veil*, 3, 11.

31. For an insightful and comprehensive look at the *Amos 'n' Andy* show as illustrative of the complexities of the color line in American culture, see Ely, *Adventures of Amos 'n' Andy*.

32. Cripps, *Slow Fade to Black*, 258–60.

33. For a discussion of black stereotypes in popular culture, see Silk and Silk, "Hollywood's Golden Age and *Gone with the Wind*," chap. 12 in *Racism and Anti-Racism in American Popular Culture*, 134–47.

34. Gaines also discusses the minstrel stereotypes that consigned black identity to preindustrial, agricultural labor and notes that the black bourgeoisie at times "embraced minstrel representations stressing culturally backward, or morally suspect blacks as evidence of their own class superiority. While the ideology of a 'better class' of blacks challenged dehumanizing stereotypes, it also exploited them." Gaines, *Uplifting the Race*, 71–72, 74–75. See also Baldwin, "Mapping the Black Metropolis: A Cultural Geography of the Stroll," chap. 1 in *Chicago's New Negroes*, 21–52.

35. Cripps, *Slow Fade to Black*, 243; also quoted in Silk and Silk, *Racism and Anti-Racism*, 135.

36. Lizabeth Cohen's study of Chicago shows how early mass culture media like the radio and the phonograph initially served to perpetuate traditional immigrant cultures. Cohen, "Encountering Mass Culture at the Grassroots"; see also Cohen, *Making a New Deal*, esp. 155–56.

37. Distribution of these blues artists' recordings in the early years was accomplished through catalogue advertisements designated as "colored" or "race" and through sales in stores catering almost exclusively to black consumers or via Pullman car porters, who sold them along their routes in rural districts. See Angela Y. Davis, *Blues Legacies and Black Feminism*, 141–42; LeRoi Jones [Amiri Baraka], *Blues People*, 98–102; Lewis, *When Harlem Was in Vogue*.

38. Okeh Records' release of the African American vaudeville singer Mamie Smith's "Crazy Blues" in 1920 is often credited with spurring commercial recordings of black musical talent by all the major record companies and helping to start the "race records" and hillbilly music craze of the 1920s. See Filene, *Romancing the Folk*, esp. 34–35.

39. Levine, *Black Culture and Black Consciousness*, 225.

40. LeRoi Jones [Amiri Baraka], *Blues People*, 101–2.

41. Angela Y. Davis, *Blues Legacies and Black Feminism*, 152; see also Filene, *Romancing the Folk*, 34–35.

42. Sterling A. Brown, Davis, and Lee, *Negro Caravan*, 3.

43. Zora Neale Hurston to Langston Hughes, September 20, 1928, Box 76, JWJC.

44. See, for example, Wright, "Blueprint for Negro Writing"; and Hughes, "The Negro Artist and the Racial Mountain." Wright calls for black intellectuals to "possess and understand" folk culture and traditions and to realign themselves with the people.

45. Wright, "Blueprint for Negro Writing."

46. Hughes, *Big Sea*, 228.

47. George Schuyler, author of *Black No More*, quoted in Lewis, *When Harlem Was in Vogue*, 92. This image would actually be made manifest in a French film, *Princess Tam Tam*, released in 1935 and starring the popular African American singer and dancer Josephine Baker.

48. Martin Kilson, "E. Franklin Frazier's *Black Bourgeoisie* Reconsidered"; Holloway, *Confronting the Veil*, 132–41.

49. For a comprehensive study of this phenomenon, see Lewis, *When Harlem Was in Vogue*.

50. Gates, "Trope of a New Negro," 137.

51. From the establishment of an independent black press in the early nineteenth century to the nationwide boycotts by black Americans of minstrel stereotypes in American film and radio in the early part of the twentieth century, African Americans struggled against their misrepresentation in a white-controlled public media. Their "recognition of the sheer ideological force of public media," as Savage astutely observes, led to a prolonged "struggle for access to that marketplace of political ideas, and, ultimately, a fight for the power of self-representation in all forms of public culture." Savage, *Broadcasting Freedom*, 9. See also Elsa Barkley Brown, "Negotiating and Transforming the Public Sphere"; Houston A. Baker Jr., *Critical Memory*. The editors of the *Negro Caravan* identified this "theme of struggle" dating back to the pre-emancipation era not just in print culture and political speeches of abolitionists but in the oral traditions of the enslaved, in folk expression and the spirituals. Sterling A. Brown, Davis, and Lee, *Negro Caravan*, 6.

52. McElya, "The Violence of Affection," chap. 5 in *Clinging to Mammy*, 188–94.

53. See Richard Yarborough, introduction to Wright, *Uncle Tom's Children*, xxix.

54. The Brotherhood of Sleeping Car Porters was the first labor organization of African Americans to receive an American Federation of Labor charter, in 1925.

55. These articulations of the New Negro were circulated in the black press during the race riots of 1919 and laid out by union leader A. Philip Randolph in an essay in the socialist magazine the *Messenger*, titled "The New Philosophy of the Negro," 5. See Gates, "Trope of a New Negro"; and also Huggins, *Harlem Renaissance*, 53–59. Gates, I feel, draws too emphatic a distinction between the term's "radical political connotations"

and what he calls Locke's "co-opting" of the term for an apolitical aesthetic. For a number of black intellectuals, including Du Bois, Locke, and Brown, the creation of a new cultural image for black Americans was a political move with significant implications. In his essay "Criteria of Negro Art," from a 1926 speech delivered at a banquet honoring the historian Carter G. Woodson, Du Bois asserted that "all Art is propaganda and ever must be, despite the wailing of the purists" (published in 1926 in the *Crisis*, 296). As Krasner points out, Du Bois saw art as serving the objectives of historical truth, by using beauty to promote and reveal the truth of black history that had been obscured by minstrel images and the ideology of white supremacy they conveyed. See Krasner, *Beautiful Pageant*, 223–25.

56. Gates, "Trope of a New Negro," 135–36; and Gaines, *Uplifting the Race*, 224. As James Weldon Johnson remarked in 1932, the best way for African Americans to improve their status would be through "a demonstration of intellectual parity by the Negro through the production of literature and art." Quoted in Gaines, *Uplifting the Race*, 248.

57. Minstrel images were emblazoned on toaster, teapot, and sheet music covers, on advertisements, postcards, cigarette boxes, and board games. Gates, "Trope of a New Negro," 150–55.

58. See Wolcott, *Remaking Respectability*; E. Frances White, *Dark Continent of Our Bodies*; Higginbotham, *Righteous Discontent*; and Darlene Clark Hine, *Hine Sight*.

59. Countee Cullen, review of *Uncle Tom's Children*, 2.

60. Sterling A. Brown, Davis, and Lee, introduction to *Negro Caravan*, 5.

61. Ibid., 3.

62. Ibid., 4.

63. Ibid., 4–5.

64. See Robert L. Hall, "E. Franklin Frazier and the Chicago School of Sociology," esp. 55–58; also see Holloway, *Confronting the Veil*.

65. Gilkeson, *Anthropologists and the Rediscovery of America*, 40.

66. For example, the social anthropological study of racial attitudes and mores in Mississippi, *Deep South*, published in 1941, was based on Allison Davis's participant observation of African American residents, while his white coauthors, Burleigh Gardner and Mary Gardner, studied the white inhabitants. Allison Davis, Gardner, and Gardner, *Deep South*.

67. See Yans-McLaughlin, "Science, Democracy, and Ethics." For a useful discussion of how new findings in molecular genetics may contribute to current debates over racial classification and biological difference, see Koenig, "Which Differences Make a Difference."

68. Walter Jackson, "Melville Herskovits and the Search for Afro-American Culture," 95–98. Jackson repeats Stocking's observation that "part of the mission of Boasian anthropology was to give to groups that did not enjoy a sense of antiquity the equivalent of a classical past by collecting texts of myths and folklore and by preserving artifacts." Citing George Stocking Jr., "The Aims of Boasian Ethnography," 4–5.

69. Hutchinson, *Harlem Renaissance in Black and White*, 68.

70. Walter Jackson, "Melville Herskovits," 95.

71. Schuyler, "The Negro-Art Hokum," 662–63, quoted in Holloway, *Confronting the Veil*, 111.

72. Odum, *Southern Regions of the United States*, 479.

73. Ibid., 3–7.

74. Meeting of the Committee on a Study of the American Negro, Division of Anthropology and Psychology, National Research Council, March 19, 1927, Microfilm 1972, Reel 27, FB-LC.

75. Several visits were sponsored for British colonial officers to consult with the white administrators of the South's segregated school system. Moreover, the Julius Rosenwald Fund would bring a Dutch colonial administrator over to study the problem of American minorities. Walter Jackson, "Melville Herskovits," 116.

76. Ibid., 117. W. E. B. Du Bois was another potential candidate for directing the study, later published in 1944 as *An American Dilemma*, but he would lose out on the basis of not possessing the requisite "objectivity" on American race relations. Myrdal, *An American Dilemma*.

77. Lomax, *Adventures of a Ballad Hunter*, 129. For more on folklorists' theories of "authentic" black folk culture as an index to racial character, see Karl Hagstrom Miller's fascinating study, *Segregating Sound*, specifically chap. 3.

78. Kazin and De Voto quoted in Vanderwood, "Introduction," in *Juarez*, 29. De Voto originally published as "Father Abraham," *Harper's*, February 1940, 333–36; Kazin originally published in *New York Herald Tribune Books*, December 31, 1939, 1.

79. Hay, *Lincoln and the Civil War in the Diaries and Letters of John Hay*; Sandburg, *Abraham Lincoln*; Herndon, *Hidden Lincoln, from the Letters and Papers of William H. Herndon*; and Sherwood, *Abe Lincoln in Illinois*, which would become the basis for the film by the same name. Even films that did not appear to be primarily about the Civil War or President Lincoln invoked them. Warner Studio's *Juarez*, directed by William Dieterle in 1939, ostensibly about Mexico's democratic president's struggle to free his country from European imperialism, clearly intended viewers to draw an analogy between the two countries' civil wars and presidents. See also Fahs and Waugh, *Memory of the Civil War in American Culture*.

80. Vanderwood, "Introduction," 29–30.

81. Foster, "Historical Introduction."

82. Woodson, "History Made to Order," 841. Essay originally published in the *Journal of Negro History* (March 1927).

83. Wallace, in *Mickey Mouse History*, 259, lists two films about Lincoln from 1939, *Young Mr. Lincoln* and *Abraham Lincoln in Illinois*; see Chadwick, *Reel Civil War*, esp. chap. 9, "Abe Lincoln in Hollywood," 151–82; Chadwick identifies *Two Americans* from 1929 as the first sound film featuring Lincoln as a central character; D. W. Griffith followed with *Abraham Lincoln* in 1930. However, numerous films about the Civil War from the 1930s would include Lincoln as a stock character, albeit in bit parts. See Chadwick, *Reel Civil War*, 163–66. See also Reinhart, *Abraham Lincoln on Screen*; Guerrero, *Framing Blackness*.

84. *Gone with the Wind*, directed by Victor Fleming (1939; DVD: Burbank, Calif.: Warner Home Video, 1999).

85. *Jezebel*, directed by William Wyler (Warner Bros., 1938). Other films from the 1930s set during the antebellum era that also served to reinforce the image of black racial inferiority included Stepin Fetchit in *Carolina*, directed by Henry King (Fox Film Corp., 1934), and *Steamboat 'Round the Bend*, directed by John Ford (Fox Film Corp., 1935); Shirley Temple vehicles with Bill Robinson that were set on the plantation, *The Little Colonel* and *The Littlest Rebel*, both directed by David Butler for Fox Film Corporation in 1935; and *Swanee River*, directed by Sidney Lanfield (Twentieth-Century-Fox Film Corp., 1939). Dramas such as *Secret Service*, directed by J. Walter Ruben (RKO Radio Pictures, 1931), and *Operator 13*, directed by Richard Boleslavsky (Metro-Goldwyn-Mayer Corp., 1934), were "Civil war spy stories with love and sectional reconciliation themes." Kirby, *Media-Made Dixie*, 70.

86. Kirby, *Media-Made Dixie*, 70.

87. Sterling A. Brown, Davis, and Lee, *Negro Caravan*, 2.

88. For a fascinating discussion of the public rituals of white nostalgia in the form of reunions, ex-slave associations, and obituaries, see Litwack, *Trouble in Mind*, esp. chap. 4, "White Folks: Scriptures," 179–216.

89. See K. Stephen Prince, *Stories of the South*, esp. chap. 5, "Performing Race, Staging Slavery," 166–204.

90. "Old Slave Day," *Pilot*, March 29, 1935, 1, http://newspapers.digitalnc.org/lccn /sn92073968/1935-03-29/ed-1/seq-1/.

91. "Southern Hokum for Northerners," editorial critique from the *Norfolk Blade*, reprinted in Struthers Burt, "Editorial 'Dog Days' Account for Attack on Old Slave Day: Struthers Burt Answers Norfolk Newspaper's Blast against Southern Pines," *Pilot*, May 22, 1935, 1, 4, http://newspapers.digitalnc.org/lccn/sn92073968/1936-05-22/ed-1/seq-1/.

92. Burt, "Editorial 'Dog Days' Account for Attack on Old Slave Day." This method of authenticating ex-slaves' narratives by virtue of the whites who knew them personally dates back to the slave narratives published during the abolitionist movements in Great Britain (see Mary Prince, *The History of Mary Prince*) and in the United States (see Jacobs, *Incidents in the Life of a Slave Girl*; and Douglass, *Narrative of the Life of Frederick Douglass, an American Slave*).

93. "Rev. G. A. Goode, Born in Slavery in 1850, Dies at His Home Here," obituary in the *Pilot*, September 24, 1937, 3, http://newspapers.digitalnc.org/lccn/sn92073968 /1937-09-24/ed-1/seq-3/; "Ex-Slave Passes: Rev. Thomas B. McCain," obituary in the *Pilot*, February 3, 1939, 6, http://newspapers.digitalnc.org/lccn/sn92073968/1939-02 -03/ed-1/seq-6/.

94. "Random Reminuisances of an Ex-Town Father," *Pilot*, August 30, 1946, 2, http: //newspapers.digitalnc.org/lccn/sn92073968/1946-08-30/ed-1/seq-2/.

95. FWP employee Stetson Kennedy conducted interviews with the Ex-Slave Association of Miami. Mormino, "Florida Slave Narratives," 400.

96. Cora Mae Taylor, "Ex-Slave Club of Miami," A876, Folder "Florida Slave Material," FWP-LC.

97. "Ex-Slaves Look back on Old Days of Cotton Choppin' and Good 'Vittles,'" *Atlanta Constitution*, December 5, 1932, clipping in A876, Folder "GA Contemporary Culture—Ex-Slave Association," 2, FWP-LC.

98. "Former Slaves to Take Part Today in Picturesque Christmas Program," *Atlanta Constitution*, December 24, 1932, clipping in A876, Folder "GA Contemporary Culture–Ex-Slave Association," document "Ex-Slave Association (Atlanta)," FWP-LC.

99. For an insightful study of the United Daughters of the Confederacy's impact on textbooks in the 1930s, see Cox, *Dixie's Daughters*, esp. chap. 7, "Confederate Motherhood," 118–40.

100. In fact, as domestic laborers started to organize for better wages and working conditions in the 1920s and 1930s, northern white employers joined southerners in lamenting the "passing away" of the "Old-Time Negroes," who had faithfully and uncomplainingly served their white families. See Ella Baker and Cooke, "The Bronx Slave Market"; and McElya, *Clinging to Mammy*, particularly chap. 6, "Confronting the Mammy Problem," 207–52.

101. Writers' Program of the Work Projects Administration in the State of Virginia, *Negro in Virginia*, 29. The introduction to *Negro in Virginia* was reprinted in Sterling A. Brown, Davis, and Lee, *Negro Caravan*, 847–55.

Chapter Two

1. E. Current-Garcia, "American Panorama—Federal Writers' Project," *Prairie Schooner* 12, no. 2 (Summer 1938), copy in Entry 27, Box 1, File "Incoming Letters," RG 69.

2. Ibid., 6. Current-Garcia's article was a spirited defense of the FWP. In it, he quoted both critics and supporters.

3. "Mirror to America—Political Note: New Dealer's Handbook," *Time*, January 3, 1938, 55.

4. Kellock, in addition to being national tours editor for the Federal Writers' Project, was editor of the Highway Route series of guidebooks. Kellock, "The WPA Writers."

5. "Administrative Correspondence, 1935–39," Entry 1, Boxes 9 and 10, RG 69.

6. Denning, *Cultural Front*, 45.

7. Ibid.

8. "Prospectus: The American Guide," A7 "Manual and Procedural Instructions, American Guide, 1935," 10, MD-LC.

9. Quoted by Edward Angly, "W.P.A. Will Let Public View Samples of Its Huge Guidebook," *New York Herald Tribune*, n.d., clipping in Entry 27, Box 2, File "Material from NY Exhibit," RG 69.

10. Henry Alsberg, "The American Guide," n.d., Entry 2, Box 2, File "Misc. Folder #2," 4, RG 69.

11. Leuchtenburg, *Franklin D. Roosevelt and the New Deal*, 127. It is difficult to identify definitively how many Negro Studies projects were undertaken by various states. Of the state projects planning separate volumes on African Americans, only two were

published at the close of the project in 1940: *The Negro in Virginia* and *Drums and Shadows: Survival Studies among the Georgia Coastal Negroes. Cavalcade of the American Negro* was hastily assembled from the Negro Studies project in Chicago for the American Negro Exposition in 1940. See Mangione, *Dream and the Deal*, 260. Other materials from the Chicago project were recycled in St. Clair Drake and Horace Cayton's *Black Metropolis: A Study of Negro Life in a Northern City* (1945). Roi Ottley, supervisor of the Negro Unit in New York, used many of the FWP materials in *"New World A-Coming"* in 1943 without acknowledgment. In 1940, he gave thirty-five manuscript boxes' worth of FWP materials to the Schomburg Collection of the New York Public Library. Gilbert Osofsky used some of them for *Harlem: The Making of a Ghetto* (1966), and in 1967 a version of the original manuscript materials prepared by the New York Negro Unit was published as *The Negro in New York*. See Mangione, *Dream and the Deal*, 260–62. Benjamin Botkin, at the Library of Congress, oversaw the publication of a small selection of the ex-slave narratives, *Lay My Burden Down: A Folk History of Slavery* (1945). Brown's office kept notes based on reports from state directors on the number of black employees as well as any potential and developing projects on African American studies, but most of these records are undated, and when the FWP was dismantled in 1939 and reorganized under state control, many drafts and materials did not get forwarded (per instructions) to the federal office. A number of manuscript projects have come to light and have finally been published, for example, *The Florida Negro*, edited by Gary W. McDonogh (1993), and *The Negro in Illinois: The WPA Papers*, edited by Brian Dolinar (2013). In various reports from the Office on Negro Affairs, Brown mentioned a "Greater Little Rock, Arkansas Study" (mentioned in "Existing Conditions in the Office on Negro Affairs") and "The History of the Negro in Louisiana from the Earliest Slave Ships to the Present," Microfilm 1366, Reel 1, Editorial Correspondence, 1936–39, Louisiana, RG 69. In the list of projects on African American history that Brown himself planned to undertake and finish in addition to "The Portrait of the Negro as American" were "Go Down Moses: The Struggle against Slavery" (on the abolitionist movement) and "A Selective Bibliography on the Negro." Brown to Walter White, NAACP, December 22, 1937, MD-LC. Brown also mentions: a book of narratives by ex-slaves; "A study of the Underground Railroad"; and a book of Negro Folklore. In a 1938 letter to Jacob Drachler, Brown adds to the list of Negro Studies state projects: a history of the Negro in Louisiana; "The Social and Economic Life of The Negro in Greater Little Rock"; and "Negroes of New York," Entry 27, Box 1, File "General Letters Outgoing by State," RG 69.

12. Manual for *American Guide*, Microfilm Reel 3, Target 2, Entry 12 "Misc. Publicity Materials 1935–41," RG 69.

13. Statement by Harry Hopkins, circa 1936, Entry 2, Box 2, File "Misc. Correspondence Folder #4," 1, RG 69.

14. "Pen Project—America, the WPA, and 20,000,000 Words," *Pathfinder Magazine*, December 17, 1938, A993, copy in File "Publicity—Newspaper Clippings and Statements—Natl. Level," MD-LC.

15. Statement by Harry Hopkins, circa 1936, 5–6, RG 69.

16. Ibid., 1–2.

17. "Pen Project—America, the WPA, and 20,000,000 Words," 1.

18. Leong, "Culture and the State," 363.

19. Current-Garcia, "American Panorama—Federal Writers' Project," 10–11.

20. Press Release, "Life of New Orleans Negroes Pictured in New Guide Book," *Tampa Bulletin*, June 11, 1938, clipping in Entry 27, Box 1, File "Releases and Information on FWP," RG 69.

21. Fall Book Section, *New Republic*, October 20, 1937, 306–7, A993, copy in File "Publicity—Newspaper Clippings and Statements—National Level," MD-LC.

22. Alsberg to G. T. Baker, General Manager, National Airline System, March 20, 1936, Entry 1, Box 10 "Florida–Georgia," File "Florida 'M–Z,'" RG 69.

23. Lindbergh, *North to the Orient*, 10.

24. Pratt, "Fieldwork in Common Places," 35–37.

25. Henry Alsberg to all State Directors, April 5, 1938, Entry 12 "Misc. Publicity Materials 1935–41," Box 3, "Who's Who in American Guide Series," RG 69.

26. Henry Alsberg to all State Directors of the FWP, April 6, 1938, Entry 2 "Records of Henry G. Alsberg, Sept. 1935–June 1937," Box 1, File "Comments," RG 69.

27. "Supplementary Instructions to the American Guide Manual: Manual for Folklore Studies," Summer 1938, Records of the U.S. WPA, A8 "Administrative Files— Procedural Instructions," 5, MD-LC.

28. Ibid.

29. Ibid., 5–6.

30. "Manual for the National Social-Ethnic Study of the Lithuanian in America," 1938, A8 "Administrative Files," File "Procedural Instructions," 3, MD-LC. Emphasis in original.

31. "Pen Project—America, the WPA, and 20,000,000 Words," 1.

32. Letters from people hoping for employment from the FWP were also addressed to President Roosevelt and Eleanor Roosevelt, and these were passed directly on to Alsberg. Entry 1 "Administrative Correspondence," RG 69.

33. Alsberg's and Harris's enthusiastic response to Carl Liddle, the author of *Tunchi*, a travel adventure novel that had been published to some acclaim, is indicative of the literary direction they wished to take with the Guide Series. Alsberg to Carita Doggett Corse, October 30, 1935, Entry 1, Box 9, File "Florida—Carl Liddle," RG 69. See also Alsberg to Liddle, October 30, 1935, Entry 1, Box 9, File "Florida—Carl Liddle," RG 69.

34. See, for example, Alsberg to Eudora Ramsay Richardson, December 21, 1937, Entry 1, Box 47, File "Virginia S–Z," RG 69.

35. Katherine Kellock, Field Report to Henry Alsberg, January 22, 1936, Entry 6, Box 1 "Alab.–Idaho," File "Florida—Kellock," RG 69.

36. Current-Garcia, "American Panorama—Federal Writers' Project," 5.

37. Reed Harris, "Notes on the FWP with Special Reference to the American Guide," September 17, 1936, Entry 5, Box 1, File "1936," RG 69.

38. Manual for *American Guide*, RG 69.

39. Ibid.

40. "Pen Project—America, the WPA, and 20,000,000 Words," 4.

41. Ibid.

42. Manual for *American Guide*, RG 69.

43. "Pen Project—America, the WPA, and 20,000,000 Words," 1.

44. "Selecting Writers for the Federal Writers' Project," Entry 12, RG 69.

45. "Prospectus: The American Guide," 8–10, MD-LC.

46. "Pen Project—America, the WPA, and 20,000,000 Words," 2.

47. F. E. Turin to Honorable Colgate Darden Jr., House Office Building, February 22, 1936, Entry 1, Box 47, File "Virginia S–Z," 1–2, RG 69. See also correspondence regarding the Turin affair and accompanying articles, "John Smith as Slaver," *Norfolk Ledger-Dispatch*, February 22, 1936; "Turin Protests Story Involving John Smith as First Slave Trader: Calls Attention of Senator Byrd to Article Published by Agency of Works Progress Administration," *Norfolk Ledger-Dispatch*, February 20, 1936, copies in Entry 1, Box 47, File "Virginia S–Z," RG 69.

48. Quoted in Current-Garcia, "American Panorama—Federal Writers' Project," 5.

49. A number of scholars have made this observation. See Hirsch, *Portrait of America*; Retman, *Real Folks*; Bold, *WPA Guides*; and Joyner, "Introduction," in *Drums and Shadows*, xiii. For a thought-provoking examination of the relationship of the metropole to the colonies, see Pratt, *Imperial Eyes*.

50. Rowell, "'Let Me Be with Ole Jazzbo,'" 300.

51. Unsigned document, n.d., "The Information Outlined Below represents an attempt to analyze the editorial forces at work within the Federal Writers of the Project," WPA Box 1, 2, USF.

52. Katharine A. Kellock, field report to Alsberg, January 23, 1936, Jacksonville, Fla., WPA Box 6, Correspondence, USF.

53. Mary Branham, Corresponding Secretary, United Daughters of the Confederacy, Florida Division, to Carita Doggett Corse, Florida State Director, Orlando, Florida, August 6, 1938; Editorial Correspondence, 1936–39: Florida; Central Office Correspondence and Memorandums; Records of the Federal Writers' Project, RG 69. Reproduced in Juliet Gorman, "New Deal Narratives: Visions of Florida, Historical Controversies," *Jukin' It Out: Contested Visions of Florida in New Deal Narratives*, Oberlin College Library, May 2001, http://www.oberlin.edu/library/papers/honorshistory/2001-Gorman/default.html (July 29, 2014); also cited in Retman, *Real Folks*, 267n13.

54. Henry Alsberg, Director, to Carita Doggett Corse, State Director, Florida, Washington, D.C., August 18, 1938; Editorial Correspondence, 1936–39: Florida; Central Office Correspondence and Memorandums; Records of the Federal Writers' Project, RG 69. Reproduced in Gorman, "New Deal Narratives."

55. Edwin Bjorkman to Henry Alsberg, December 13, 1937, Entry 27, Box 1, File "Incoming Letters," 1, RG 69.

56. Ibid.

57. J. Harris Gable, Director, to Henry Alsberg, February 25, 1937, Entry 27 "Reports and Misc. Pertaining to Negro Studies," Box 1, Folder 5 "Letters from State Directors," RG 69.

58. David E. W. Williamson to Sterling A. Brown, December 8, 1936, Entry 27, Box 1, File "Letters from State Directors," RG 69.

59. Ibid. Nebraska's director made a similar assertion regarding the black population in his state: "their small number presents no important race problem." J. Harris Gable, Director, to Henry Alsberg, December 17, 1936, Entry 27 "Reports and Misc. Pertaining to Negro Studies," Box 1, File 5 "Letters from State Directors," RG 69.

60. Mangione, *Dream and the Deal*, 258.

61. Hirsch is the only scholar to mention John P. Davis's letter to Alsberg regarding his concerns over black representation on the FWP but doesn't note that Davis proposed the creation of Brown's position. Hirsh, *Portrait of America*, 29.

62. According to the *Crisis*, Davis had earned the title of "Bad Boy Administration Critic." John P. Davis, "Black Inventory of the New Deal," 141.

63. See Hilmar Ludvig Jensen's fascinating dissertation on Davis, "The Rise of an African American Left," 311–13. See also Sullivan, *Days of Hope*, 46–57.

64. Working with his friend from Harvard Bob Weaver, who would become part of Roosevelt's "Black Cabinet" ("He was the Negro; I was the industrial league," Weaver later recalled), they cowrote a brief that proposed an antidiscrimination amendment to ensure that black cotton mill workers would be included in the National Recovery Administration's protective legislation setting minimum wages and maximum hours. Jensen, "The Rise of an African American Left," 313–14.

65. Ibid., 330.

66. Ibid., 330. Initially, Davis received a cool response from both organizations, but early support came from the black press, Hayne's Federal Council of Negro Churches, the National Association of Colored Women, the African Methodist Episcopal and Zion church boards, and the Negro Elks. Ibid., 339.

67. Ibid., 354. Davis would also help cofound the National Negro Congress in 1935 with the help of A. Philip Randolph, the president of the first black labor union, the Brotherhood of Sleeping Car Porters. Sterling Brown would deliver a speech to the National Negro Congress in 1937. See Sklaroff, *Black Culture and the New Deal*, 81. For Davis's role in the National Negro Congress, see Dolinar, *Black Cultural Front*.

68. This appointment, Alsberg reported to Williams, would "cover the part of the American Guide which will be devoted to the negro race." Memorandum from Alsberg to Aubrey Williams, December 16, 1935, Microfilm 1366, Reel 1, Administrative Correspondence, 1936–39, Louisiana, RG 69.

69. Davis to Williams, December 12, 1935, Microfilm 1366, Reel 1, Administrative Correspondence, 1936–39, Louisiana, RG 69.

70. See Davis's letter to Louisiana State Director Lyle Saxon, which he copied to Alsberg and Williams, December 12, 1935; Alsberg letter to Davis, December 16, 1935, Microfilm 1366, Reel 1, Administrative Correspondence, 1936–39, Louisiana, RG 69.

71. Alsberg to Davis and memorandum from Alsberg to Williams, December 16, 1935, Microfilm 1366, Reel 1, Administrative Correspondence, 1936–39, Louisiana, RG 69.

72. Ibid.

73. It should be noted that Alsberg had begun capitalizing "Negro," whereas he had used a lowercase "n" in his earlier correspondence. This was one of many battles waged by African Americans, including Brown, over language. Alsberg to Lyle Saxon, February 1, 1936, Microfilm 1366, Reel 1, Administrative Correspondence, 1936–39, Louisiana, RG 69.

74. See Alsberg to Lyle Saxon, February 1, 1936, and Saxon's telegram to Alsberg, February 10, 1936, Microfilm 1366, Reel 1, Administrative Correspondence, 1936–39, Louisiana, RG 69.

75. Memorandum from Sterling Brown's Office to Dutton Ferguson, Publicity Department, February 8, 1939, Entry 27, Box 2, File "Negro Books," RG 69. Reprinted in WPA Press Release, "American Learns of Negro from Books of the Federal Writers' Project," March 6, 1939, Entry 27, Box 1, File "Releases and Information on FWP," RG 69.

76. See memorandum from Brown to Munson regarding "Information on Personnel," January 9, 1940, 3, Entry 27 "Reports and Misc. Pertaining to Negro Studies," Box 2, File "Negro Studies," RG 69.

77. Memorandum, "Existing Conditions in the Office on Negro Affairs," Office on Negro Affairs, November 1938, Entry 27, Box 2, File "Negro Studies," RG 69. Emphasis in original.

78. Ibid. Emphasis in original.

79. Memorandum from Brown's Office to Dutton Ferguson, February 8, 1939, Entry 27, Box 2, File "Negro Studies," RG 69.

80. Mangione, *Dream and the Deal*, 259. Sklaroff makes a similar argument regarding Brown and the Office on Negro Affairs' influence, *Black Culture and the New Deal*, 119–20.

81. Hale, " 'Some Women Have Never Been Reconstructed,' " 174.

82. It is important to note that UDC membership did not necessarily determine an individual's perspective on race relations or, for FWP employees, determine their approach to collecting and presenting materials related to African American history. Carita Doggett Corse, Florida's state director and advocate for the ex-slave narrative project and Florida's Negro Writers' Unit, for example, would join the UDC in 1939, when the project shifted from federal to state control. Corse's date of admission for membership was November 30, 1939, Jacksonville Chapter No. 1128. Corse joined on the service of her grandfather, Aristides Doggett, Co. A., Third Florida Infantry. She was endorsed for membership by Rose Shepherd, fellow employee on the Florida Project. Information provided courtesy of Teresa Roane, archivist, and Betty Luck, research librarian, UDC, author's site visit (January 14, 2015), and e-mail correspondence with Betty Luck, January 21, 2015.

83. The date of admission was not filled out on Myrtle Miles's application; however, she was registered with the William L. Yancey Chapter No. 722 by the registrar general on October 23, 1920. Her application contains no information, other than that she was the daughter of J. E. Miles, who served in the Montgomery Rifles. Information on UDC membership graciously provided by Betty Luck, research librarian, UDC, e-mail correspondence with the author, January 21, 2015.

84. Alabama State Director Myrtle Miles to Associate Director George W. Cronyn, August 17, 1937, Entry 27, Box 1, File "Incoming Letters," RG 69.

85. Ibid.

86. Miles to Henry Alsberg, March 4, 1937, Entry 27, Box 1, File "Incoming Letters," RG 69.

87. Ibid.

88. Ibid.

89. Ibid.

90. Ibid.

91. Ibid.

92. Ibid.

93. Cronyn to Myrtle Miles, August 26, 1937, Entry 27, Box 1, File "General Letters," RG 69. Emphasis in original.

94. Ibid.

95. Ibid.

96. Miles to Cronyn, November 3, 1936, Entry 27, Box 1, File "Incoming Letters," RG 69.

97. Cronyn to Myrtle Miles, November 5, 1936, Entry 27, Box 1, File "General Letters," RG 69.

98. Ibid.

99. Samuel Tupper Jr. to George Cronyn, October 20, 1937, Entry 13, Box 9, File "Georgia State Guide—Cities," RG 69.

100. Alsberg to Eudora Ramsay Richardson, May 15, 1939, Entry 27, Box 1, File "General Letters," 4, RG 69.

101. Ibid.

102. A field report telegram from Miller to Alsberg, March 12, 1936, identified the state directors from Mississippi (Eri Douglass), Arkansas (Bernie Babcock), and Alabama (Myrtle Miles) as problematic and "completely ignorant of Guide Instructions." Microfilm 1366, Reel 1, Field Reports, 1935–37, "Wallace Miller File," RG 69.

103. Memorandum from Sterling Brown's Office to Henry Alsberg, Re: *Mississippi: A Guide to the Magnolia State*, May 24, 1938, Entry 27, Box 1, File "General Letters," RG 69.

104. Ibid.

105. Ibid.

106. Ibid.

107. Sterling Brown, Editorial Criticism, Florida State Guide—Gainesville, September 28, 1937, Entry 13, Box 9 (Florida), File "Florida, July 1937–Feb. 1939," RG 69.

108. Ibid. Emphasis mine.

109. Sterling Brown, Editorial Criticism, Florida State Guide—Tampa, September 27, 1937, Entry 13, Box 9 (Florida), File "Florida, July 1937–February 1939," RG 69.

110. Sterling Brown, Editorial Criticism, Florida State Guide—Lakeland, September 25, 1937, Entry 13, Box 9 (Florida), File "Florida, July 1937–February 1939," RG 69.

111. Sterling Brown, Editorial Criticism, Florida State Guide—Tampa, September 27, 1937, RG 69.

112. Sterling Brown, Editorial Criticism, Florida State Guide—Lakeland, July 14, 1937, Entry 13, Box 9 (Florida), File "Florida, July 1937–February 1939," RG 69.

113. Emphasis mine. Gaines discusses the assimilationist theme in *Uplifting the Race*, 76–77.

114. Brown to Carolyn Dillard, August 31, 1936, Entry 21, Box 1, File "Georgia," RG 69.

115. Memorandum from Sterling Brown to [Gorham] Munson, "Description of Writers' Project Activity Concerning the Negro," January 9, 1940, Entry 27, Box 1, File "Negro Books," RG 69.

116. Ibid.

117. Ibid.

118. Gabbin, *Sterling A. Brown*, 79–80. The Scottsboro case of 1931 became a cause célèbre among leftist groups of the Popular Front. The case involved nine young African American men charged with raping two white women and convicted without evidence and without appropriate legal counsel. The involvement of the International Labor Defense (Communist Party) and tension with the NAACP created fissures in the Popular Front coalition that continued to erode over the course of the decade. See Denning, *Cultural Front*, 333; Jensen, "Rise of an African American Left," 296–97; Robin D. G. Kelley, "Case of the 'Scottsboro Boys,'" July 18, 2007, http://www.writing.upenn.edu/~afilreis/88/scottsboro.html (January 10, 2015).

119. Quoted in Sklaroff, *Black Culture and the New Deal*, 110.

120. Memorandum from Sterling Brown to [Gorham] Munson, "Description of Writers' Project Activity Concerning the Negro," January 9, 1940, RG 69.

121. There is some dispute regarding when and why Brown left the FWP. Penkower claims that teaching responsibilities led to Brown's departure from the FWP, *Federal Writers' Project*, 146. Sklaroff cites a letter Brown wrote in January 1939 to Charles Jones of the Urban League in which he stated that he was "no longer on the pay-roll, unfortunately"; Sklaroff, *Black Culture and the New Deal*, 270n147. Sklaroff suggests that the congressional investigations under the Dies Committee made Brown realize that "Congress would eventually abandon the Federal Arts Project, making it impossible for him to achieve his goals for ["The Portrait of the Negro as American"] under federal auspices." Ibid., 114. However, Brown's biographer, Joanne V. Gabbin, cites an office memorandum Brown sent regarding the manuscript as late as the spring of 1940, after the FWP had been renamed the Writers' Project and reorganized under state, as opposed to federal, direction. Gabbin, *Sterling A. Brown*, 79–80, 84nn36–38. My research documents that Brown was working for the reorganized Writers' Project in 1940 at the Library of Congress: a WPA job classification form for Brown, March 6, 1940, identifies his job responsibilities as "Editorial Supervisor of Negro Studies of Writers' Unit." Entry 32, Box 3 "Records of the Library of Congress Writers' Unit, 1939–1941," Folder "Personnel File: Sterling Brown," RG 69. Friends suggest that Brown's generosity with other people's book projects often led to his own never reaching completion. "Interview with Michael S. Harper, by Graham Lock, at Yaddo, June 2003," in Tidwell and Tracy, *After Winter*, 375.

122. Memorandum from Sterling Brown to [Gorham] Munson, "Description of Writers' Project Activity Concerning the Negro," January 9, 1940, RG 69.

123. Sterling A. Brown, Davis, and Lee, *Negro Caravan*, 4.

124. Interestingly, there was an earlier model for *Negro Caravan*; in 1900, Booker T. Washington, Fannie Barrier Williams, and N. B. Wood edited *A New Negro for a New Century: An Accurate and Up-to-Date Record of the Upward Struggles of the Negro Race*. Like "The Portrait of the Negro as American," it was an ambitiously conceived project with eighteen chapters, totaling 428 pages and sixty portraits of important black Americans, and included excerpts drawn from black historical scholarship, biographies, journalism, and slave narratives. It also emphasized black military service in American wars and sought to correct the plantation tradition's version of slavery. See Gates, "Trope of a New Negro," 136–40.

125. Fabre and O'Meally, *History and Memory in African-American Culture*, 5.

Chapter Three

1. Initially all such correspondence was labeled under the subject heading of "Folklore."

2. Cronyn to Eudora Ramsay Richardson (this letter was also sent to North and South Carolina, Georgia, Alabama, Louisiana, Texas, Arkansas, Tennessee, Kentucky, Missouri, Mississippi, and Oklahoma), April 1, 1937, Entry 21, Box 1, File "Ex-Slaves," RG 69.

3. Cade, "Out of the Mouths of Ex-Slaves," 295.

4. Charles Perdue Jr., introduction to Perdue, Barden, and Phillips, *Weevils in the Wheat*, xi–xii. Perdue notes that Settle Egypt's book was reprinted in 1972 as volume 18 of George Rawick's *American Slave* series of ex-slave narratives drawn primarily from the FWP Collection at the Library of Congress. For other discussions of earlier ex-slave interview projects undertaken by researchers at Historically Black Colleges and Universities (HBCUs), see Yetman, "The Background of the Slave Narrative Collection"; and Musher, "Contesting 'the Way the Almighty Wants It,'" 6–7.

5. On June 14, 1934, Reddick submitted to Harry L. Hopkins, director of the Federal Emergency Relief Administration, a proposal to gather the oral histories of former slaves. Perdue, introduction to Perdue, Barden, and Phillips, *Weevils in the Wheat*, xiii. See also Benjamin Botkin's "The Slave as His Own Interpreter," *Library of Congress Quarterly Journal*, November 1944.

6. Perdue, introduction to Perdue, Barden, and Phillips, *Weevils in the Wheat*, xiii.

7. Charles Spurgeon Johnson, "A Proposal for a Regional (or National) Project under the Federal Writers Project (Utilizing Negro Personnel)," Department of Social Science, Fisk University, [193?], Schomburg Center for Research in Black Culture, New York Public Library.

8. Eugene C. Holmes, Assistant Editor, Office on Negro Affairs, to Editor of the *Spokesman* (California), April 10, 1938, Entry 27, Box 1 "Reports and Misc. Records Pertaining to Negro Studies, 1936–40," File "General Letters Outgoing by States," RG 69.

9. Virginia state director Eudora Ramsay Richardson expressed her hearty approval of such an endeavor, noting that she was in possession of sixty ex-slave interviews that were worthy of publication as they were "told in the dialect of the old Negroes and . . . full of historical value and human interest." However, because they could not be used fully either in the anticipated volume "The Negro in Virginia" or the state Guide, Richardson was "delighted to know that you are looking toward a publication that can incorporate them." Richardson to George Cronyn, April 5, 1937, Entry 22, Box 3, File "Virginia—Folklore," RG 69.

10. This idea was illustrative of John Lomax's general approach to the slave narratives, as I will demonstrate in the next chapter. Memorandum, "Ex-Slave Stories," from Alan and Elizabeth Lomax to Henry Alsberg, n.d. (circa June–July 1937), Entry 21, Box 1, File "Ex-Slaves Correspondence," 1, RG 69.

11. Ibid.

12. Ibid.

13. Ibid.

14. Ibid.

15. This would seem to indicate that the Lomaxes were sensitive to the possible differences in accuracy between a transcription from the memory of an FWP field worker or a recording machine and that such discrepancies were important enough to warrant the publication of both types of narratives. However, suggestion number seven indicates a different conclusion: "Print three or four hundred stories almost 'as is' and consider we've done a fine bit of unbiased evidence-gathering." Ibid., 2.

16. It is important to note that the New Deal's early application of anthropological knowledge was used in conjunction with policies pertaining to Native Americans. Under the Indian Reorganization Act of 1934, anthropologists were asked to help compose constitutions for the tribal nations. See Kelly, "Why Applied Anthropology Developed When It Did."

17. Couch to Eudora Ramsay Richardson, January 3, 1939, Entry 1, Box 46, File "Virginia—Misc. 1937–38," RG 69.

18. Clara Stokes, Mississippi Assistant State Director, to George Cronyn, May 7, 1937, Entry 21, Box 1, File "Mississippi," RG 69. Cronyn promptly sent several, with the promise of additional copies as soon as they were available. Cronyn to Eri Douglass, May 12, 1937, Entry 21, Box 1, File "Mississippi," RG 69.

19. Douglass to George Cronyn, May 24, 1937, Entry 21, Box 1, File "Mississippi," RG 69.

20. Bernie Babcock to Henry Alsberg, August 13, 1937, Entry 21, Box 1, File "Arkansas," RG 69.

21. See, for example, Henry Alsberg to Alabama State Director, Myrtle Miles, July 8, 1937, Entry 21, Box 1, File "Alabama," RG 69.

22. John Lomax, Instructions and Questionnaire labeled "Stories from Ex-Slaves," sent to fifteen states, n.d. (circa Spring 1937), Entry 21, Box 1, File "Maryland," RG 69.

23. Burnette Yarbrough, Mississippi State Supervisor of Assignments, to Eri Douglass, July 19, 1937, Entry 21, Box 1, File "Mississippi," RG 69.

24. Kennedy, "Florida Folklife and the WPA, an Introduction."

25. T. Lindsay Baker and Julie P. Baker, *WPA Oklahoma Slave Narratives*, 6–7.

26. See Entry 21, Box 1, State Files, RG 69.

27. Alsberg to Samuel Tupper Jr., September 8, 1937, Entry 21, Box 1, File "Georgia," RG 69.

28. John Lomax, Instructions and Questionnaire labeled "Stories from Ex-Slaves," n.d. (circa Spring 1937), RG 69. Lomax would continue to exhort FWP field workers to make more than one visit, repeatedly insisting to state directors on the value of a second visit. See, for example, Lomax to Myrtle Miles, May 18, 1937, Entry 21, Box 1, File "Alabama," RG 69.

29. Alsberg to Samuel Tupper Jr., September 8, 1937, RG 69.

30. Memorandum, "Ex-Slave Stories," from Alan and Elizabeth Lomax to Alsberg, n.d. (circa June–July 1937), 2, RG 69.

31. Perhaps significantly, a mention of ghost stories appeared twice in the questionnaire: once as an inquiry about stories the informant might know about ghosts and hants and again as not a question but a directive based on an assumption that any ex-slave would have such information: "Tell about the ghosts you have seen." An assumption was also made in the questions dealing with the ex-slaves' religion: "Tell why you joined the Baptist Church and why you think all people should be religious." John Lomax, Instructions and Questionnaire labeled "Stories from Ex-Slaves," n.d. (circa Spring 1937), 2, RG 69.

32. Memorandum, "Ex-Slave Stories," from Alan and Elizabeth Lomax to Alsberg, n.d. (circa June–July 1937), 2–3, RG 69.

33. Ibid.

34. Memorandum from Henry Alsberg to State Directors of Alabama, Arkansas, Florida, Georgia, Kentucky, Louisiana, Maryland, Michigan, Missouri, North Carolina, South Carolina, Oklahoma, Tennessee, Texas, Virginia, West Virginia, Ohio, Kentucky, and Indiana, July 30, 1937, Entry 21, Box 1, File "Ex-Slaves Correspondence," RG 69.

35. Ibid.

36. Ibid.

37. Ibid.

38. Ibid.

39. Several questions were also devoted to the subject of slave rebellions and resistance. Ibid.

40. Ibid.

41. Report on Ex-Slave Interviews, Submitted by Miriam Logan, State Supervisor, Warren County, Ohio, to the Federal Office, n.d. (after July 30, 1937), Entry 21, Box 1, File Unnamed, 1, RG 69.

42. Ibid.

43. Babcock to Alsberg, August 13, 1937, RG 69.

44. Seward, "The Legacy of Early Afro-American Folklore Scholarship," 50. One of the areas of African American culture that engendered the most heated debate over

national origins was black music. Some scholars, such as the ethnomusicologist Erich von Hornbostel, claimed that Negro spirituals were mainly of European origin, being primarily derivative of European folk songs. See Walter Jackson, "Melville Herskovits and the Search for Afro-American Culture," 106.

45. Walter Jackson, "Melville Herskovits and the Search for Afro-American Culture," 95.

46. Seward, "The Legacy of Early Afro-American Folklore Scholarship," 50.

47. Ulrich B. Phillips, *American Negro Slavery*, quoted in Elkins, *Slavery*, 17n21.

48. Indeed, the first major challenge to Phillips's thesis is often considered to be Kenneth M. Stampp's revisionist history, *Peculiar Institution: Slavery in the Ante-Bellum South*. For a list of scholars influenced by Phillips's work, see Elkins, *Slavery*, 15–16.

49. Robert Ezra Park, "Education in Its Relation to the Conflict and Fusion of Cultures: With Special Reference to the Problems of the Immigrant, the Negro, and Missions," quoted in Seward, "The Legacy of Early Afro-American Folklore Scholarship," 49.

50. E. Franklin Frazier, *Negro Family in the United States* (1939), quoted in Joyner, "Introduction," xvii.

51. Herskovits, "The Negro's Americanism," 353.

52. Locke, "Who and What Is 'Negro'?," 83–84.

53. Guy B. Johnson, Review of *Myth of the Negro Past*.

54. Guy B. Johnson, "Foreword," xxxv. For Herskovits's evolving views, see also "Some Next Steps in the Study of Negro Folklore," 3.

55. Alsberg also asked workers to specify "whether the persons interviewed were white or colored." Alsberg to Carolyn Dillard, October 20, 1936, Entry 22, Box 1 "Alabama–Miss.," File "Georgia—Folklore," RG 69.

56. Babcock to Alsberg, August 13, 1937, RG 69.

57. "Mrs. John McRaven: Premier Presentation of the Drama 'Mammy'" [circa 1917], Redpath Chautauqua Collection, University of Iowa Special Collections Department, http://apps.its.uiowa.edu/libsdrc/details.jsp?id=/mcraven/1 (July 24, 2014).

58. "Interesting Developments," undated report, 8, Entry 27 "Reports and Misc. Pertaining to Negro Studies," Box 1, RG 69. Babcock also managed to make a bad impression on the field supervisor with a "tirade against Newspapermen" at a meeting with six state directors in 1936. Telegram from Miller to Alsberg, March 12, 1936, Microfilm 1366, Reel 1, "Field Reports—Wallace Miller File," RG 69. Reed Harris, assistant director of the FWP, asked Louisiana state director Lyle Saxon to go and supervise Babcock because she was such a problem, June 10, 1936, Microfilm 1366, Reel 2, "Field Reports," RG 69.

59. Reprinted in Joyner, "Introduction," xxiii. See Hirsch, "Portrait of America" (PhD diss.), 49, 301, 388.

60. Brown to Carolyn Dillard, August 31, 1936, Entry 21, Box 1, File "Georgia," RG 69.

61. Ibid.

62. Ibid.

63. Sterling Brown, "Georgia Folklore—Criticism," December 7, 1936, Entry 22, Box 1 "Alabama–Miss.," File "Georgia—Folklore," RG 69.

64. Ibid.

65. Ibid.

66. Ibid.

67. Ibid.

68. Ibid.

69. Lomax to Carolyn Dillard, May 24, 1937, Entry 22, Box 1 "Alabama–Miss.," File "Georgia—Folklore," RG 69.

70. John Lomax, Editorial Comments "Virginia—Folklore and Folk Music," March 30, 1937, Entry 22, Box 3, File "Virginia—Folklore," RG 69.

71. Memorandum from Lomax to Cronyn, May 3, 1937, Entry 21, Box 1, File "Ex-Slaves Correspondence," RG 69.

72. These fourteen states were North and South Carolina, Georgia, Alabama, Louisiana, Texas, Arkansas, Kentucky, Missouri, Mississippi, Oklahoma, Florida, Virginia, and Kansas. See, for example, Cronyn to Edwin Bjorkman, State Director, North Carolina, May 3, 1937, Entry 21, Box 1, File "Ex-Slaves Correspondence," RG 69.

73. See Correspondence from Alabama State Director Myrtle Miles to John Lomax, May, June, and July 1937, Entry 21, Box 1, File "Alabama," RG 69.

74. Ibid.

75. Ibid.

76. This is only one of several such letters. See also correspondence in this file for the months of May and June 1937. Lomax to Myrtle Miles, June 3, 1937, Entry 21, Box 1, File "Alabama," RG 69.

77. Memorandum from Alsberg to State Directors in Alabama, Arkansas, Florida, Georgia, Kentucky, Louisiana, Maryland, Michigan, Missouri, North Carolina, South Carolina, Oklahoma, Tennessee, Texas, Virginia, West Virginia, Ohio, Kentucky, and Indiana, September 8, 1937, Entry 21, Box 1, File "Ex-Slaves Correspondence," RG 69.

78. A general category for "Folk Customs" had 110 pages' worth of material. "Folk Lore from Files of Federal Writers' Project," Little Rock, Ark., July 1, 1938, Entry 21, Box 1, File "Arkansas," RG 69.

79. "Folk Lore from Files of Federal Writers' Project, Arkansas" submitted to Washington office, July 12, 1938, Entry 21, Box 1, File "Ex-Slaves Correspondence," RG 69.

80. In keeping with this interpretation, I must acknowledge the possibility that ex-slave informants also consciously contributed to this numerical outcome; they may have provided their questioners with the kind of information they felt the latter wished to hear. However, FWP interviewers did guide the informants through the use of specific questions meant to elicit this type of material, and FWP editors assigned the interviews to these topical headings.

81. Cronyn to Eudora Ramsay Richardson (also sent to North and South Carolina, Georgia, Alabama, Louisiana, Texas, Arkansas, Tennessee, Kentucky, Missouri, Mississippi, and Oklahoma), April 1, 1937, Entry 21, Box 1, File "Ex-Slaves," RG 69.

82. Lomax to Eudora Ramsay Richardson, May 1, 1937, Entry 22 "Correspondence Pertaining to Folklore Studies," Box 3, File "Virginia," RG 69.

83. Houston A. Baker Jr., *Modernism and the Harlem Renaissance*, 42.

84. Morrison, *Playing in the Dark*, 52.

85. Dillard to Henry Alsberg, October 31, 1936, Entry 22, Box 1 "Alabama–Mississippi," File "Georgia—Folklore," RG 69.

86. Alsberg to Carolyn Dillard, November 6, 1936, Entry 22, Box 1 "Alabama–Mississippi," File "Georgia—Folklore," RG 69.

87. Cronyn to North Carolina State Director Edwin Bjorkman, with enclosure, also sent to South Carolina, Georgia, Alabama, Louisiana, Texas, Arkansas, Tennessee, Kentucky, Missouri, Mississippi, Oklahoma (with reference to a special letter sent to Florida, April 15), April 14, 1937, Entry 21, Box 1, File "Ex-Slaves Correspondence," RG 69.

88. John Lomax, "Negro Dialect Suggestions (Stories of Ex-Slaves)," sent to North and South Carolina, Georgia, Alabama, Louisiana, Texas, Arkansas, Tennessee, Kentucky, Missouri, Mississippi, and Oklahoma, April 1937, Entry 21, Box 1, File "Ex-Slaves Correspondence," RG 69.

89. Ibid.

90. Alsberg to Dr. U. R. Bell, August 2, 1937, Entry 21, Box 1, File "Kentucky," RG 69.

91. Lomax to Texas State Director J. Frank Davis, May 3, 1937, Entry 21, Box 1, File "Texas," RG 69.

92. Lomax to Eudora Ramsay Richardson, May 1, 1937, Entry 22, Box 3, File "Folklore—Virginia," RG 69.

93. Ibid.

94. Richardson to John Lomax, May 5, 1937, Entry 22, Box 3, File "Folklore—Virginia," RG 69.

95. Richardson to John Lomax, May 18, 1937, Entry 22, Box 3, File "Folklore—Virginia," RG 69.

96. Roscoe Lewis, "Negro Dialect," copy sent to John Lomax by Eudora Ramsay Richardson, May 18, 1937, Entry 22, Box 3, File "Virginia—Folklore," RG 69.

97. Ibid.

98. Lomax to Eudora Ramsay Richardson, May 25, 1937, Entry 22, Box 3, File "Virginia—Folklore," RG 69.

99. Sterling A. Brown, "Notes by an editor on dialect usage in accounts by interviews with ex-slaves. (To be used in conjunction with Supplementary Instructions 9E)," sent June 20, 1937, to Alabama, Arkansas, Florida, Georgia, Kentucky, Louisiana, Maryland, Michigan, Missouri, North Carolina, South Carolina, Oklahoma, Tennessee, Texas, Virginia, and Ohio, Entry 2, Box 2, File "Misc. Correspondence Folder #4," RG 69.

100. Ibid.

101. Sterling A. Brown, *Negro in American Fiction*, 50. As William Taylor has noted, many of these qualities of slave characters in plantation literature, "the stock characters of Uncle Tom fiction—the kind but crochety old mammies . . . and the 'banjo-picking, heel-flinging, hi-yi-ing happy jacks' of minstrelsy," had appeared a century earlier, in novels of the 1830s. William R. Taylor, *Cavalier and Yankee*, 300–303.

102. Sterling A. Brown, *Negro in American Fiction*, 51, 54.

103. Although Brown observed that Harris "lost something authentic when he adopted this framework," he also admired the literary creation, saying, "Uncle Remus is worth gaining . . . [as] one of the best characters in American literature." Sterling A. Brown, *Negro in American Fiction*, 53.

104. Fauset, "American Negro Folk Literature."

105. Sterling A. Brown, "Notes by an editor on dialect usage in accounts by interviews with ex-slaves. (To be used in conjunction with Supplementary Instructions 9E)," 1, sent June 20, 1937, RG 69.

106. Ibid.

107. In George Rawick's version of Brown's "Notes," the text reads as quoted above with the regional specification of "Florida" modifying the noun "Negroes." However, in the numerous copies of this essay that I found in the files of RG 69 (see note 99), not one included the specification of "Florida" before "Negroes." Although the reason for this change remains undiscovered, it is significant that the copy that state directors received did not include the regional specification for Hurston's writings. This removal (besides doing an injustice to Hurston's careful attention to the regional differences in the black vernacular) implies a universal dialect located within a racialized identity of blackness. Sterling A. Brown, "Notes by an Editor on Dialect Usage in Accounts by Interviews with Ex-Slaves," in *American Slave*, Vol. 1.

108. Sterling A. Brown, "Notes by an editor on dialect usage in accounts by interviews with ex-slaves. (To be used in conjunction with Supplementary Instructions 9E)," 1, sent June 20, 1937, RG 69.

109. Ibid.

110. Ibid.

111. Ibid.

112. Henry Louis Gates Jr. has also criticized representations of the black vernacular that rely on a purely visual difference, rendered through inconsistent phonetic spellings. Gates, "Dis and Dat," 188–91.

113. Sterling A. Brown, "Notes by an editor on dialect usage in accounts by interviews with ex-slaves. (To be used in conjunction with Supplementary Instructions 9E)," 3, sent June 20, 1937, RG 69.

114. Ibid.

115. Ibid.

116. Lomax to North Carolina State Director Edwin Bjorkman, May 8, 1937, Entry 21, Box 1, File "North Carolina," RG 69.

117. Alsberg to Charles Elder, January 5, 1938, Entry 21, Box 1, File "Tennessee," RG 69.

118. Ibid.

119. Alsberg to Indiana State Director Gordon Briggs, September 9, 1937, Entry 21, Box 1, File "Indiana," RG 69. Briggs received another letter of this type one week later in response to additional ex-slave narratives he had submitted. Alsberg to Briggs, September 14, 1937, Entry 21, Box 1, File "Indiana," RG 69.

120. Bjorkman to George Cronyn, June 1, 1937, Entry 21, Box 1, File "North Carolina," RG 69.

121. J. Frank Davis to Henry Alsberg, October 7, 1937, Entry 21, Box 1, File "Texas," RG 69.

122. Harry Argo to Tennessee State Director Charles J. Elder, December 22, 1937, Entry 21, Box 1, File "Tennessee," RG 69.

123. Rawick, *American Slave*, Georgia, II:12:1:253, informant Minnie Davis, field worker Sadie B. Hornsby, ed. Sarah H. Hall and John N. Booth [1938].

124. Burnette Yarbrough to Eri Douglass, July 19, 1937, Entry 21, Box 1, File "Mississippi," RG 69.

125. Ibid.

126. Robb, *Welcum Hinges*, 19–20.

127. William Francis Allen, introduction to *Slave Songs of the United States* (1867), reprinted in Gavin Jones, " 'Whose Line Is It Anyway?'," 20.

128. Assistant to the President, Macmillan Company, to John Lomax, May 13, 1937, Entry 22, Box 3, File "Folklore 1936–37, Misc.," RG 69.

129. Ibid.

130. Memorandum from Lomax to Henry Alsberg, "Publication of Ex-Slave Stories," May 18, 1937, Entry 22, Box 3, File "Folklore 1936–37, Misc.," RG 69.

131. Ibid.

132. Memorandum from Lomax to Henry Alsberg, May 24, 1937, Entry 22, Box 3, File "Folklore 1936–37, Misc.," RG 69.

133. Ibid.

134. Ibid.

135. Ibid.

136. Lewis to John Lomax, June 11, 1937, Entry 22, Box 3, File "Virginia Folklore," RG 69.

137. Lomax to Carita Doggett Corse, April 6, 1937, Entry 21, Box 1, File "Florida," RG 69.

138. Babcock to Henry Alsberg, August 13, 1937, Entry 21, Box 1, File "Arkansas," RG 69.

139. Davis to Alsberg, October 7, 1937, RG 69.

140. Yetman continues, "There appears to have been little concern in the Writers' Project for systematic sampling procedures or for obtaining a representative sample of the former slaves." Yetman, "Ex-Slave Interviews and the Historiography of Slavery," 188.

141. Although Lomax would be replaced by Benjamin Botkin in 1938, Botkin's main contribution to the slave narratives would occur after the collection had been completed, when he supervised their preparation for publication and deposit into the Library of Congress's archives in 1939.

Chapter Four

1. "Lead Belly: Bad Nigger Makes Good Minstrel," *Life*, April 19, 1937, 38–39.

2. These tropes date back to the nineteenth century; see, for example, "Water-Millions Is Ripe," and "A Zulu Scout," *Harper's Weekly*, August 23, 1879, 672–73.

3. The photo was actually a reprint of a $250 photo that had been made to serve as the frontispiece of Lomax's 1936 book on Ledbetter, *Negro Folk Songs as Sung by Lead Belly*. Wolfe and Lornell, *Life and Legend of Leadbelly*, 195–96.

4. "Murderous Minstrel," *Time*, January 14, 1935, 50.

5. "Lomax Arrives with Leadbelly, Negro Minstrel: Sweet Singer of the Swamplands Here to Do a Few Tunes between Homicides," *New York Herald Tribune*, January 3, 1934, reprinted in Wolfe and Lornell, *Life and Legend of Leadbelly*, 141.

6. As Hazel Carby has observed, "it is the Lomax-invented black folk persona of Leadbelly as a mean and dangerous 'nigger' who has to be tamed by his white male patron that is elaborated into the cultural fiction which, in turn, legitimates and authenticates his music." Carby, *Race Men*, 108–9.

7. Wolfe and Lornell, *Life and Legend of Leadbelly*, 91.

8. A colleague, S. B. Hustvedt at the University of California, Los Angeles, attending Lomax and Ledbetter's session at the Modern Languages Association's conference in Philadelphia in 1934, encouraged him to write up a manuscript based on his collecting expeditions. See Lomax, *Adventures of a Ballad Hunter*, viii–ix. An earlier and considerably shorter version titled "Adventures of a Ballad Hunter: Iron Head and Clear Rock" had appeared a few years earlier in the magazine *Southwest Review*. The concept of "Adventures of a Ballad Hunter" would later be transformed into a serialized radio program as part of the Library of Congress's wartime Radio Research Project.

9. Ruby had had her own career as the dean of women at the University of Texas until her retirement in 1936.

10. John Lomax to George Cronyn, February 4, 1937, Entry 22, Box 3, File "Folklore 1936–37, Misc., John Lomax," RG 69.

11. Scarborough used a dictaphone.

12. Scarborough, *Song Catcher in Southern Mountains*, was published posthumously two years after her death.

13. Lomax would reprint several songs from this collection in his *American Ballads and Folk Songs*, which would receive a favorable review from Scarborough. Porterfield, *Last Cavalier*, 335.

14. Scarborough, *On the Trail of Negro Folk-Songs*, 3. Scarborough's books, like Lomax's, were also part of a 1930s resurgence in the travel narrative genre.

15. John Lomax to J. Frank Davis, May 3, 1937, Entry 21, Box 1, File "Texas," RG 69.

16. This and all of the following quotations regarding Mike Stephens are from Ruby Lomax's field notes, No. 3946–3947, AFS 3942–4087, SSRT-LC.

17. Ibid.

18. Ibid.

19. A fascinating discussion of the ways in which female anthropologists of the early twentieth century, such as Margaret Mead and Ruth Benedict, navigated the terrain between their identities as women and their identities as intellectual scholars in a field dominated by men appears in Newman, "Coming of Age, but Not in Samoa."

20. Scarborough, *On the Trail of Negro Folk-Songs*, 30.

21. Ibid.

22. Ibid.

23. Ibid.

24. Lomax, *Adventures of a Ballad Hunter*, 205.

25. Preece, "Negro Folk Cult," 364.

26. Porterfield, *Last Cavalier*, 333.

27. Ruby Lomax to her family, New Roads, La., October 14, 1940, AFS 3942–4087, SSRT-LC.

28. Ruby Lomax to her family, n.d., AFS 3942–4087, SSRT-LC. On lying, see also field notes of John Lomax, informant Richard Amerson, Livingston, Ala., n.d., AFS 3942–4087, SSRT-LC.

29. Ruby Lomax's field notes, "Bob Ledbetter and Noah Moore," AFS 3992–3995, SSRT-LC.

30. Ruby Lomax to her family, n.d., AFS 3942–4087, SSRT-LC.

31. Houston A. Baker Jr., *Modernism and the Harlem Renaissance*, 22.

32. Lomax, *Adventures of a Ballad Hunter*, 170–71.

33. Field notes of John Lomax, informant Richard Brown, Sumterville, Ala., n.d., AFS 3942–4087, SSRT-LC.

34. Ruby Lomax to her family, Natchez, Miss., October 19, 1940, AFS 3942–4087, SSRT-LC.

35. Field notes of John Lomax, informants Vera Hall and Dock Reed, n.d., AFS 3942–4087, SSRT-LC.

36. All quotations in this paragraph from John Lomax, "'Sinful Songs' of the Southern Negro," 183.

37. Ibid.

38. Ibid.

39. Lomax, *Adventures of a Ballad Hunter*, 114.

40. Field notes of John Lomax, No. 3981, AFS 3942–4087, SSRT-LC.

41. Ibid.

42. Lomax, *Adventures of a Ballad Hunter*, 129.

43. Newman Ivey White, *American Negro Folk-Songs*, 14.

44. I am indebted to Larry Levine for insisting on the paradoxical nature of white folklorists in his response to early drafts of this work.

45. Parrish, *Slave Songs of the Georgia Sea Islands*, 10.

46. Ibid., 11.

47. Lomax, *Adventures of a Ballad Hunter*, 114.

48. Porterfield, *Last Cavalier*, 434–35.

49. Porterfield claims that later evidence supported Lomax's view that Smith's death could not be blamed on a white hospital's discriminatory admission policy. See *Last Cavalier*, 542–43n7.

50. Ibid., 434.

51. Ibid., 299.

52. Lomax, "'Sinful Songs' of the Southern Negro," 184.

53. Lomax, *Adventures of a Ballad Hunter*, 129.

54. Lomax, "'Sinful Songs' of the Southern Negro," 181.

55. For more on Lomax and other folklorists' definition of "authentic" folk culture versus commercial music, see Karl Hagstrom Miller, *Segregating Sound*.

56. Lomax, "'Sinful Songs' of the Southern Negro," 182.

57. Field notes of John Lomax, Jasper, Tex., informant Uncle Billy Macree, n.d., AFS 3942–4087, SSRT-LC.

58. John Lomax to Alan Lomax, Shreveport, La., October 8, 1940, AFS 3942–4087, SSRT-LC.

59. "Lomax the Songhunter"; also Stephanie A. Hall, "Preserving Sound Recordings."

60. Ruby Lomax to her family, October 29, 1940, regarding an interview with informant "Aunt Harriet McClintock near Sumterville, Alabama," AFS 3942–4087, SSRT-LC.

61. Ibid.

62. Personal interview conducted by the author with Stetson Kennedy at his home, Beluthahatchee, in St. Johns, Florida, October 2005.

63. For another example, see Lomax, *Adventures of a Ballad Hunter*, 158–59.

64. Lomax, "'Sinful Songs' of the Southern Negro," 181.

65. Ibid.

66. Porterfield, *Last Cavalier*, 435.

67. Ibid.

68. Lomax, *Adventures of a Ballad Hunter*, 139.

69. Ibid., 113.

70. Ibid.

71. Lomax, "'Sinful Songs' of the Southern Negro," 182.

72. Lomax, *Adventures of a Ballad Hunter*, 171.

73. Lomax, "'Sinful Songs' of the Southern Negro," 181. This estimate would balloon in his autobiography to 25,000 convicts. Lomax, *Adventures of a Ballad Hunter*, 113.

74. Lomax, "'Sinful Songs' of the Southern Negro," 182.

75. H. J. Eckenrode to Henry Alsberg, October 24, 1936, Entry 22, Box 3, File "Virginia—Folklore," RG 69.

76. Ibid.

77. Lomax to Henry Alsberg, October 27, 1936, Entry 22, Box 3, File "Virginia—Folklore," RG 69. Alsberg relayed these suggestions to Eckenrode, emphasizing that "Mr. Lomax feels that this prison material is of extreme value." Alsberg to H. J. Eckenrode, November 25, 1936, Entry 22, Box 3, File "Virginia—Folklore," RG 69.

78. Porterfield, *Last Cavalier*, 302.

79. All quotations from Lomax, *Adventures of a Ballad Hunter*, 149–51.

80. According to Porterfield, this letter from Lomax to Alsberg is undated, but it is likely from 1936 or 1937. Porterfield, *Last Cavalier*, 389, 536n24.

81. Ruby Lomax to her family, Clemson, S.C., n.d., AFS 2589–2728, SSRT-LC.

82. John Lomax to Honorable Burnet R. Maybank, Governor of South Carolina, n.d. (after June 27, 1939), AFS 2589–2728, SSRT-LC.

83. Ruby Lomax, field notes, May 21, 1939, Varner, Ark., Cummins State Farm, Camp #1, John A. Lomax Recording Trip, AFS 2589–2728, SSRT-LC.

84. Ruby Lomax to family, May 1939, AFS 2589–2728, SSRT-LC.

85. Ledbetter's release was really the result of a reduction of his sentence by five and a half years for "good behavior." Porterfield, *Last Cavalier*, 330–31.

86. Lomax, *Adventures of a Ballad Hunter*, 294–95.

87. Ibid., 208.

88. Ibid., 117.

89. Ibid., 117–18.

90. Ibid., 124.

91. This description was originally published in 1934 in Lomax's " 'Sinful Songs' of the Southern Negro," 177, and then was reprinted almost exactly in Lomax, *Adventures of a Ballad Hunter*, 166.

92. Field notes of John Lomax, informant Doc Reed, Livingston, Ala., n.d., AFS 39424–087, SSRT-LC.

93. Always one to be thinking of the potential commercial value of such distinctive material, Lomax concluded: "A play built around the imprisoned black and the songs he has made about his life and work would probably have more appeal than [the Broadway hit and Hollywood film] 'Green Pastures.' " Lomax, *Adventures of a Ballad Hunter*, 125.

94. Lomax, " 'Sinful Songs' of the Southern Negro," 184.

95. Lomax, *Adventures of a Ballad Hunter*, 300.

96. Porterfield, *Last Cavalier*, 338–39.

97. Ibid., 340.

98. This is an assumption that continues today. See Levine, *Black Culture and Black Consciousness*. For a critique of Levine's approach to the concept of "folk culture," see Kelley, "Notes on Deconstructing 'the Folk.' "

99. Lomax, *Adventures of a Ballad Hunter*, 149. Lomax's son and fellow collector Alan showed greater signs of wishing to recognize and give due credit to individual informants' artistry. For more on the differences between father and son, see chapters 3 and 4 of Mullen, *Man Who Adores the Negro*.

100. For more on the artistic tradition of revision of which jazz is a classic example, see Gates, *Signifying Monkey*, and writings by LeRoi Jones (Amiri Baraka).

101. A year and a half later, Frank Gallaway did get to record his grandmother's song, for Lomax remembered him and gave him the long-awaited quarter. Field notes of John Lomax, Wiergate, Tex., September 1940, AFS 3942–4087, SSRT-LC.

102. These incidents are noted in Porterfield, *Last Cavalier*, 442–43.

103. Mary Elizabeth Barnicle Interview, January–February 1977, Zora Neale Hurston Collection, MPBRS-LC.

104. See Wolfe and Lornell, *Life and Legend of Leadbelly*, 194.

105. Field notes by Ruby Lomax, Alma Plantation, near New Roads, La., October 1940, AFS 3942–4087, SSRT-LC.

106. This theme is explored from an African American perspective in the short story "Nineteen Fifty-Five" by Alice Walker, in which a female black folk artist's material is

appropriated and exploited by an aspiring white male singer who, on the strength of her songs, becomes a huge commercial success. In Walker, *You Can't Keep a Good Woman Down*, 3–20.

107. Field notes by Ruby Lomax, Alma Plantation, near New Roads, La., October 1940, AFS 3942–4087, SSRT-LC.

108. Field notes of John Lomax, Natchez, Miss., n.d., AFS 3942–4087, SSRT-LC.

109. Ibid.

110. Lomax, *Adventures of a Ballad Hunter*, 122.

111. Lomax, " 'Sinful Songs' of the Southern Negro," 177–78.

112. John Lomax to Alan Lomax, Shreveport, La., October 8, 1940, AFS 3942–4087, SSRT-LC.

113. Porterfield, *Last Cavalier*, 397.

114. Ibid., 300.

115. Ibid., 347.

116. Ibid., 375.

117. Lomax quoted in Wolfe and Lornell, *Life and Legend of Leadbelly*, 145.

118. Lomax quoted in "Lomax Arrives with Leadbelly," reprinted in Wolfe and Lornell, *Life and Legend of Leadbelly*, 141.

119. Porterfield, *Last Cavalier*, 354n28.

120. *March of Time* transcript, reprinted in Wolfe and Lornell, *Life and Legend of Leadbelly*, 166. All the principal characters involved, along with a film crew, traveled to locations in Connecticut that could serve as facsimiles of the original locale. Scenes included their first encounter, Lomax's recording of Leadbelly's plea to the governor, and Leadbelly pledging his fealty to Lomax and swearing his eternal gratitude. The short film is now available for viewing online, "The March of Time: Folk Legend Leadbelly," Time, Inc./HBO archives, http://content.time.com/time/video/player /0,32068,30862122001_1918195,00.html (July 29, 2014); HBO licensing information, http://www.hboarchives.com/apps/searchlibrary/ctl/marchoftime (July 29, 2014).

121. Porterfield, *Last Cavalier*, 332.

122. Ibid., 342.

123. William Rose Benet, "Ballad of a Ballad-Singer," *New Yorker*, January 19, 1935, 40; notices in *Time*, January 14 and January 28, 1935.

124. This arrangement would later be revised to include Alan in the take, with each of the three involved receiving an equal third of the profits. Porterfield, *Last Cavalier*, 349.

125. Ibid., 352–53.

126. Ibid., 364–67.

127. Ruby Lomax to her family, n.d., AFS 3942–4087, SSRT-LC.

128. Porterfield, *Last Cavalier*, 365–67.

129. Beckwith, "National Folk Festival, Washington."

130. Thompson, "American Folklore after Fifty Years," 1.

131. Ibid., 5.

132. Ibid.

133. "Forty-Ninth Annual Meeting of the American Folk-Lore Society," 103.

134. Thompson, "American Folklore after Fifty Years," 1.

135. Ibid., 2.

136. "Fiftieth Annual Meeting of the American Folklore Society," 209.

137. Melville Herskovits would recommend that Thompson collaborate with Professor Richard Waterman of Northwestern University. However, Waterman primarily drew on Lomax's writings for his sections on African American culture, and Lomax ended up receiving a payment for granting permission to Waterman and Thompson to publish his material. Porterfield, *Last Cavalier*, 475.

138. "Fiftieth Annual Meeting of the American Folklore Society," 209.

139. Mangione, *Dream and the Deal*, 276–77.

140. "Report of the Library of Congress, 1941," Radio Research Project Box, Recorded Sound Division, LC.

141. Porterfield, *Last Cavalier*, 475–76.

142. Day, "John Lomax and His Ten Thousand Songs," 5.

143. Wolfe and Lornell, *Life and Legend of Leadbelly*, 234.

144. Porterfield, *Last Cavalier*, 476.

145. Ibid.

146. Ibid., 476–77.

147. Ibid., 478.

Chapter Five

1. "The Negro and Federal Project No. I (WPA Arts Projects) for New York City: A Brief," prepared by the Negro Arts Committee Federal Arts Council, Entry 21, Box 1, File "Miscellaneous," 2, RG 69.

2. Ibid., 1.

3. Ibid., 4.

4. Work of the WPA Negro Writers, n.d. (prior to the publication of *The Negro in Virginia* and after the employment of Hurston), Entry 21, Box 1, File "Misc.," RG 69.

5. Yetman, "The Background of the Slave Narrative Collection," 534–53.

6. The committee noted that WPA administrators had "refused to cooperate . . . in furnishing figures necessitating a most difficult research." As a result, the figures are estimates. "The Negro and Federal Project No. I," 3, RG 69.

7. Ibid.

8. Ibid., 15.

9. Ibid., 12–15.

10. *Negro Press Digest*, ed. Edward Lawson (hereafter abbreviated as NPD), various dates, Entry 27, Box 1, RG 69.

11. NPD, March 19, 1938, Entry 27, Box 1, RG 69.

12. Editorial, *Cleveland Call and Post*, reprinted as "Are We to Have A Scandal," NPD, Week ending March 26, 1938, 4–5, Entry 27, Box 1, RG 69.

13. Ibid.

14. *Chicago Defender,* article reprinted as "Launch Probe into Discrimination on WPA Projects," NPD, Week ending March 19, 1938, 1, Entry 27, Box 1, RG 69.

15. Ibid.

16. Editorial, *Cleveland Call and Post,* reprinted as "Are We to Have A Scandal," NPD, Week ending March 26, 1938, 4–5, Entry 27, Box 1, RG 69.

17. Records of the NAACP, Series I, C Administrative File, Box 286, Subject file: Discrimination, MD-LC. These files contain an enormous treasure trove of handwritten letters from all over from African Americans who felt they were being discriminated against in seeking WPA positions; many were very personal and revealing of circumstances and different forms of discrimination.

18. Walter F. White, Secretary, NAACP, to Hallie Flanagan, Director of the Federal Theatre Project, November 28, 1936, NAACP, Box 286, Folder "WPA 36–37," MD-LC.

19. Records of the NAACP, Series I, C Administrative File, Box 386 "Peonage," Folder "Oct. 6–Dec. 14, 1937," MD-LC. This case was investigated by the attorney general; see Assistant Attorney General Brien McMahon to Walter White, Exec. Sec of the NAACP, October 6, 1937, NAACP Series I, C Administrative File, Box 386 "Peonage," Folder "Discrimination," MD-LC. See also "WPA Officials Probe Cotton-Picking Charge, Oct. 8th," NAACP Series I, C Administrative File, Box 386 "Peonage," Folder "Discrimination," MD-LC. There is a report to Alsberg from the state director of Mississippi on black employees in the FWP, which states that one worker was dropped because "he was needed to haul cotton and gather crops in the Delta." This might indicate that the practice of forcing black employees off of WPA projects during picking season may have been more widespread. See letter from Mississippi state director Eri Douglass to Henry Alsberg, December 23, 1936, Entry 27, Box 1 "Reports and Misc. Pertaining to Negro Studies," File 3 "Incoming Letters," RG 69.

20. Dorothy Kaufman, Executive Secretary, Federal Writers' Local, Worker's Alliance of Greater New York, to Walter White, NAACP, August 30, 1938, NAACP Series 1, C Administrative File, Box 298, Folder "Federal Theaters Writers Project, July–Dec. 1938," MD-LC.

21. Alsberg to State Directors, January 7, 1936, referred to in letter from Charles Morgan, Arizona State Director, to Alsberg, January 14, 1936, Entry 27, Box 2 "Reports and Misc. Pertaining to Negro Studies," File "Negroes—Employee Letters on Negroes," RG 69.

22. P. C. Gilbert, "Notes on Negro Material in State Guides," August 11, 1936, Entry 27, Box 1, File "Memos," RG 69.

23. Penkower, *Federal Writers' Project,* 67. Referred to in McDonogh, *Florida Negro,* xiv.

24. "Number of Negro Workers," 1938, 2–4, Entry 27 "Reports and Misc. Pertaining to Negro Studies," Box 1, File 2 "Memos," RG 69.

25. Untitled list of black employees by state, 1936, Entry 27 "Reports and Misc. Pertaining to Negro Studies," Box 1, File 1 "General Letters—Outgoing by State," RG 69.

26. Laura L. Middleton and Augustus Ladson, Charleston, S.C., to Harry L. Hopkins, July 13, 1937, Entry 27 "Reports and Misc. Pertaining to Negro Studies," Box 1, File 5 "Letters from State Directors," RG 69.

27. Mormino, "Florida Slave Narratives," 402; Mangione, *Dream and the Deal*, 123–27, 255–65; Penkower, *Federal Writers' Project*, 66–67, 147.

28. Miles to Henry Alsberg, January 9, 1936, Entry 27 "Records and Misc. Pertaining to Negro Studies," Box 1, File "General Letters," RG 69, partially quoted in the Office on Negro Affairs, "Report on the Status of the Negro in Alabama, Florida, Georgia, North Carolina, South Carolina, Virginia, and Tennessee," to Couch, October 19, 1938, Entry 27, Box 1, File "General Letters," RG 69.

29. Miles to Henry Alsberg, December 9, 1936, Entry 27, Box 1, File "Incoming Letters," RG 69.

30. New Hampshire State Director Charles Ernest White to Henry Alsberg, January 13, 1936 (replying to Alsberg's letter of January 7), Entry 27 "Records and Misc. Pertaining to Negro Studies," Box 2, File "Negroes—Employee Letters on Negroes," RG 69.

31. South Dakota State Director Lisle Reese to Henry Alsberg, January 13, 1936, Entry 27 "Records and Misc. Pertaining to Negro Studies," Box 2, File "Negroes—Employee Letters on Negroes," RG 69.

32. Iowa State Director Jay Du Von to Henry Alsberg, January 13, 1936, Entry 27 "Records and Misc. Pertaining to Negro Studies," Box 2, File "Negroes—Employee Letters on Negroes," RG 69.

33. New Mexico State Director Ina Sizer Cassidy to Henry Alsberg, January 13, 1936, Entry 27 "Records and Misc. Pertaining to Negro Studies," Box 2, File "Negroes—Employee Letters on Negroes," RG 69.

34. Forrester B. Washington to Henry Alsberg, December 31, 1936, Entry 1, Box 10, File "Georgia—'A–J,'" RG 69.

35. Ibid.

36. Georgia State Director Carolyn Dillard to Henry Alsberg, August 1, 1936, Entry 21, Box 1, File "Georgia," RG 69.

37. William O. Key to Henry Alsberg, January 7, 1936, Entry 1, Box 10, File "Georgia—Employment, 1935–36," RG 69.

38. Emphasis mine. William O. Key to Henry Alsberg, January 13, 1936, Entry 1, Box 10, File "Georgia—Employment, 1935–36," RG 69. In February, Key's replacement, Carolyn Dillard, followed up with Alsberg, noting that the death of a white employee had opened up a spot for one black worker, but because Alsberg did "not mention the possibility of enlarging our quota, we have not added other negroes to our list." Georgia State Director Carolyn Dillard to Alsberg, February 7, 1936, Entry 27 "Records and Misc. Pertaining to Negro Studies," Box 2, File "Negroes—Employee Letters on Negroes," RG 69.

39. Darel McConkey, Acting Field Supervisor, Field Report on Georgia to Henry Alsberg, December 26, 1935, Entry 6, Box 1 "Field Reports, 1935–37," File "McConkey—Georgia," 2, RG 69.

40. Carolyn Dillard to Henry Alsberg, January 22, 1936, Entry 1, Box 10, File "Georgia—Employment, 1935–36," RG 69.

41. Alsberg to Carita Doggett Corse, February 20, 1936, Entry 1, Box 9, File "FL—Employment, 1935–36," RG 69.

42. Ibid.

43. Corse to Henry Alsberg, March 5, 1936, Entry 1, Box 9, File "FL—Forms 330 and 320," RG 69.

44. Writers' Program of the Work Projects Administration in the State of Virginia, *Negro in Virginia.*

45. "About the WPA Life Histories Collection," Library of Virginia, Richmond, n.d., http://www.lva.virginia.gov/public/guides/opac/wpalhabout.htm (July 29, 2014).

46. Office on Negro Affairs, "Report on the Status of the Negro in Alabama, Florida, Georgia, North Carolina, South Carolina, Virginia, and Tennessee," to Couch, October 19, 1938, Entry 27, Box 1, File "General Letters," RG 69.

47. Corse to Henry Alsberg, December 16, 1936, Entry 27, Box 1, File "Incoming Letters," RG 69.

48. Walter White to Dr. James A. Gillespie, President, [Pennsylvania] State Conference of NAACP Branches, November 25, 1936, NAACP Series I, C, Box 286, Folder "WPA 36–37," MD-LC.

49. McConkey, Field Report on Georgia to Alsberg, December 26, 1935, 2, RG 69.

50. "Are We the Forgotten Group?," editorial from the *Buckeye Review*, NPD, Week ending March 26, 1938, 5, Entry 21, Box 1, RG 69.

51. Rowell, "'Let Me Be with Ole Jazzbo,'" 300.

52. It was the publication of this essay that would contribute to the House Un-American Activities Committee's charges of Communist subversion with the FWP and the Federal Bureau of Investigation's inquiry of Brown for Communist activity. See the Epilogue for this discussion.

53. Office on Negro Affairs, "Report on the Status of the Negro in Alabama, Florida, Georgia, North Carolina, South Carolina, Virginia, and Tennessee," to Couch, October 19, 1938, RG 69.

54. Arizona State Director Charles M. Morgan to Henry Alsberg, Jan. 14, 1936, Entry 27 "Records and Misc. Pertaining to Negro Studies," Box 2, File "Negroes—Employee Letters on Negroes," RG 69.

55. Memorandum from Benjamin Botkin to Henry Alsberg, "First Field Trip to the South, October 27–November 5, 1938," November 14, 1938, Entry 22, Box 3, File "Folklore—Misc.," RG 69.

56. Alsberg to Edward Rodriguez, October 14, 1935, Entry 1, Box 10, File "Florida M–Z," RG 69.

57. Memorandum from Botkin to Alsberg, "First Field Trip to the South," November 14, 1938, RG 69.

58. William Smith to Henry Alsberg, November 29, 1937, Entry 1, Box 47, File "Virginia K–R," RG 69.

59. Alsberg to Eudora Ramsay Richardson, December 6, 1937, Entry 1, Box 47, File "Virginia K–R," RG 69.

60. Richardson to Henry Alsberg, December 8, 1937, Entry 1, Box 47, File "Virginia K–R," 2, RG 69.

61. Brown to Georgia State Director Carolyn Dillard, August 31, 1936, Entry 21, Box 1, File "Georgia," RG 69.

62. Memorandum, September 19, 1936, Entry 27, Box 1, File "Letters from State Directors," RG 69.

63. "WPA Federal Writers' 'The Negro in Virginia' Regarded as Most Revealing Book of Its Kind," NPD, Entry 21, Box 1, RG 69.

64. Ibid.

65. Ibid.

66. Woodward, "History from Slave Sources," 51.

67. Ibid.

68. See, for example, Georgia editor Sarah H. Hall's interview with Emmaline Kilpatrick. Hall, whose work on the Ex-Slave Project is discussed in chapter 8, was a granddaughter of Kilpatrick's slaveholder, Judge William Watson Moore. Library of Congress, American Memory, "Born in Slavery," Georgia Narratives, Volume IV, Part 3, 9, informant Emmaline Kilpatrick, field worker Sarah H. Hall, May 8, 1937, Library of Congress Manuscript Division, Digital Collection. See also Davidson and Lytle, "The View from the Bottom Rail," 187.

69. Escott, "The Art and Science of Reading WPA Slave Narratives," 42.

70. One of the few narratives submitted by the Florida Project that uses a phonetically spelled dialect and is completely written in the first person was produced by white field worker Barbara Darsey. Rawick, *American Slave*, Florida, II:17:190–93, informant Cindy Kinsey, field worker Barbara Darsey, n.d.

71. For a fascinating look at competing representations of slavery in the Mississippi ex-slave narratives, see Musher, "Contesting 'the Way the Almighty Wants It.'"

72. See, for example, the disagreement in the Virginia Project between Roscoe Lewis and state director Eudora Ramsay Richardson over the narrative of Henrietta King, whose disfigured face testified to the brutality of the whipping she received from her former slaveholder. In Perdue, Barden, and Phillips, *Weevils in the Wheat*, 190–92; Brendan Wolfe, "She'll Be Wid Ole Missus One o' Dese Days," *Encyclopedia Virginia* blog, April 15, 2013, http://blog.encyclopediavirginia.org/2013/04/15/shell-be-wid-ole-missus-one-o-dese-days/ (July 29, 2014); Kenra Hamilton, "The Negro in Virginia (1940)," *Encyclopedia Virginia*, last updated June 13, 2013, http://www.encyclopedia virginia.org/Negro_in_Virginia_The_1940 (July 29, 2014).

73. Emphasis mine. Green, *Negro in Contemporary American Literature*, 7.

74. Ibid.

75. Scarborough, *On the Trail of Negro Folk-Songs*, 65.

76. A. B. Ellis, *Ewe-Speaking Peoples*, quoted in Puckett, *Folk Beliefs of the Southern Negro*, 9–10.

77. Ibid.

78. Library of Congress, American Memory, "Born in Slavery," Arkansas Narratives, Volume II, Part 2, 234, informant Lucius Edwards, field worker Irene Robertson, n.d., Library of Congress Manuscript Division, Digital Collection.

79. Report on Ex-Slave Interviews, submitted by Miriam Logan, State Supervisor, Warren County, Ohio, to the Federal Office, n.d. (after July 30, 1937), Entry 21, Box 1, File Unnamed, 2, RG 69.

80. Ibid.

81. Ibid.

82. Edwin Bjorkman to George Cronyn, May 15, 1937, Entry 21, Box 1, File "Indiana," RG 69.

83. Bernie Babcock to Henry Alsberg, October 19, 1937, Entry 21, Box 1, File "Arkansas," RG 69.

84. Henrietta King, excerpted from Perdue, Barden, and Phillips, *Weevils in the Wheat*, 190–92.

85. Wolfe, "She'll Be Wid Ole Missus One o' Dese Days"; Hamilton, "Negro in Virginia (1940)."

86. Mabel Montgomery to Chalmers Murray, June 28, 1937, Entry 21, Box 1, File "South Carolina," RG 69.

87. Ibid.

88. Chalmers Murray to Mabel Montgomery, July 1, 1937, Entry 21, Box 1, File "South Carolina," RG 69.

89. Ibid.

90. Ibid.

91. Ibid.

92. Chalmers Murray to Mabel Montgomery, July 8, 1937, Entry 21, Box 1, File "South Carolina," RG 69.

93. Ibid.

94. Mabel Montgomery to Henry Alsberg, July 30, 1937, Entry 21, Box 1, File "South Carolina," RG 69.

95. Rowell, " 'Let Me Be with Ole Jazzbo,' " 301.

96. Stepto, "Storytelling in Early Afro-American Fiction."

97. Richardson to Henry Alsberg, November 27, 1937, Editorial Correspondence Pertaining to Ex-Slave Studies, Virginia, RG 69, reprinted in Perdue, Barden, and Phillips, *Weevils in the Wheat*, xxii.

98. Ibid.

99. Richardson to Henry Alsberg, December 8, 1937, Entry 1, Box 47, File "Virginia K–R," RG 69.

100. Alsberg to Richardson, December 6, 1937, Entry 1, Box 47, File "Virginia K–R," 2, RG 69.

101. Richardson to Clair Laning, August 30, 1938, Entry 1, Box 46, File "Virginia," RG 69.

102. Ibid.

103. Richardson to Alsberg, November 27, 1937, RG 69, reprinted in Perdue, Barden, and Phillips, *Weevils in the Wheat*, xxiii.

104. Andrews, *To Tell a Free Story*, 2. See also Starling, *Slave Narrative*; Foster, *Witnessing Slavery*; and Yellin, "Text and Contexts of Harriet Jacobs' *Incidents in the Life of a Slave Girl.*"

Chapter Six

1. This piece would never appear in print, having been "killed" in 1934 by the editorial staff for unknown reasons. There is a holograph note on the proofs of the article that reads: "Dr. G.—Not printed. I don't remember why? C. [N? R?]"

2. Zora Neale Hurston, "You Don't Know Us Negroes," unpublished article for *American Mercury*, killed 1934, 1. Lawrence Spivak Papers, Container 37 "Subject File," Folder "American Mercury—Articles Killed," MD-LC.

3. Ibid., 2.

4. Ibid., 3.

5. Ibid., 2–3.

6. Ibid.

7. Hurston to Franz Boas, October 20, 1929, "Professional Correspondence of Franz Boas," Microfilm 1972, Reel 30, 2, FB-LC.

8. Hurston, "Art and Such," written for the Florida Federal Writers' Project, "The Florida Negro" (unpublished), 1938, reprinted in Hurston, *Folklore, Memoirs, and Other Writings*, 910.

9. "Hoodoo" is the preferred term used by African Americans, while "Voodoo" is the nomenclature used by whites. Zora Neale Hurston, "Florida Folklore—Negro Customs and Folklore," Box A591 "Folklore Project—FL," File "FL—Negro Lore," MD-LC.

10. Hurston, Introduction, *Mules and Men*, 1.

11. Franz Boas, Foreword, in Hurston, *Mules and Men*, xiii.

12. Ibid.

13. Hurston, Introduction, *Mules and Men*, 2.

14. Ibid., 2–3.

15. Willis, *Specifying*, 27–28.

16. Staub, *Voices of Persuasion*, 92–93.

17. Ibid., 80–81. Retman in her insightful study of Depression-era documentary texts has coined the phrase "signifying ethnography" to refer to Hurston's methods of self-reflexively critiquing concepts of "authentic" and "folk." See Retman, *Real Folks*, 5–6 and chap. 4, "Ah Gives Myself," 152–88.

18. Hurston would favorably mention both books in *Tell My Horse*, 132–33. To Seabrook's description of the isle of La Gonave, she attributed her own desire to travel there.

19. Harold Courlander, "Witchcraft in the Caribbean Islands: Review of *Tell My Horse*," *Saturday Review*, October 15, 1938, 6–7.

20. Hurston to Franz Boas, October 23, 1934, "Professional Correspondence of Franz Boas," Microfilm 1972, Reel 37, 1, FB-LC.

21. Ibid.

22. Ibid. It is very possible that the publishing houses were also speculating about what would appeal to a primarily white audience.

23. Ibid.

24. Ibid.

25. Hurston, Introduction, *Mules and Men*, 3.

26. Ibid.

27. Emphasis mine. Hemenway, *Zora Neale Hurston*, 62.

28. This biographical information is drawn from Hurston, *Dust Tracks*, 12–17; Hemenway, *Zora Neale Hurston*, 14–15.

29. Hurston, *Dust Tracks*, 65–67.

30. Ibid., 66.

31. Ibid., 45.

32. Ibid., 46.

33. Hemenway, *Zora Neale Hurston*, 22–23, 61–62, 79.

34. Hughes, *Big Sea*, 238–39.

35. Zora Neale Hurston, "How It Feels to Be Colored Me," 827.

36. Walter Jackson, "Melville Herskovits and the Search for Afro-American Culture," 107.

37. Hughes, *Big Sea*, 239.

38. Lewis, *When Harlem Was in Vogue*, 152.

39. Hughes, *Big Sea*, 325.

40. Hurston, *Dust Tracks*, 145.

41. Hurston to Hughes, n.d., New Orleans, La., Box 76, JWJC.

42. For an interesting examination of the folktales' emphasis on economic structures and black alterative economic strategies, see Willis, "Wandering: Zora Neale Hurston's Search for Self and Method," chap. 2 in *Specifying*, 26–52.

43. Wall, *Women of the Harlem Renaissance*, 163–65.

44. Hurston, *Mules and Men*, 15.

45. Ibid.

46. Oral history interview with Stetson Kennedy in Beluthahatchee, circa 1985, videotape, American Folklife Center, LC. Also see Kennedy, "What Alan Lomax Meant to Me and This World," cultural equity [2002], http://www.culturalequity.org /alanlomax/ce_alanlomax_remembering_sk.php (August 29, 2014).

47. Hurston, *Mules and Men*, 55.

48. Ibid., 60.

49. Ibid., 62.

50. Ibid., 60–61.

51. Ibid., 63.

52. Clifford, *Predicament of Culture*, 40–41. Michael Staub has also made this observation about Hurston's text.

53. *Mules and Men*, 61.

54. Ibid., 64.

55. But there may be more here than even meets the eye. In her attempts to formulate some of the laws under which the black vernacular operated, Hurston noted that in the use of pronouns, such as "you" and "I," application of the dialecticized form "yuh" and "Ah" varied depending on the placement in the sentence. As she observed: "The same form is not always used. Some syllables/words are long before or after certain words and short in the same positions. Example: You as subject gets full value but is shortened to yuh as an object." Hurston to Langston Hughes, April 12, 1928, quoted in Hemenway, *Zora Neale Hurston*, 114–15. When Hurston addresses the reader, she uses "I"; when speaking to informants, she invariably used "Ah." Since "I" stands for the subject, and "Ah" is used as an object, Hurston may be making a symbolic political statement about race and gender relations through the rules of linguistic usage: "Ah" as the object of a sentence is always acted upon, whereas "I" is always the actor.

56. Hurston coyly provides a definition for this idiomatic expression for her presumed white readership as "having a good time." Hurston, *Mules and Men*, 65.

57. Ibid.

58. Ibid., 63–65.

59. Ibid., 60.

60. Hurston is also playfully invoking a black stereotype of darker-skinned women who are always depicted as less feminine and more pugilistic and bad-tempered than lighter-skinned African American women: "White, yellow and brown girls dreamed about roses and perfume and kisses. Black gals dreamed about guns, razors, ice-picks, hatchets and hot lye." Hurston, *Dust Tracks*, 184.

61. Rabinowitz, *They Must Be Represented*, 57.

62. Ibid., 66.

63. Hurston, *Dust Tracks*, 152.

64. Ibid., 154.

65. Ibid.

66. Ibid., 154–55.

67. Ibid., 155.

68. Hurston, *Mules and Men*, 150.

69. Hurston, *Dust Tracks*, 146.

70. Hurston, *Mules and Men*, 183.

71. Ibid., 191–92.

72. Ibid., 199.

73. Ibid., 205.

74. Karla F. C. Holloway, *Character of the Word*, 103.

75. Hurston to Hughes, October 15, 1929, Miami, Fla., JWJC.

76. Hurston to Hughes, December 10, 1929, JWJC.

77. Hurston to Hughes, April 30, 1929, Eau Gallie, Fla., JWJC.

78. Hurston to Hughes, November 22, 1928, New Orleans, La., JWJC.

79. Hurston to Hughes, August 6, 1928, Algiers, La., JWJC.

80. Hurston to Hughes, September 20, 1928, JWJC.

81. Hurston to Hughes, April 3, 1929, JWJC.

82. Hurston to Hughes, March 8, 1928, Eatonville, Fla., JWJC. Emphasis in original.

83. This quotation also reveals that among black folk communities, the privileges of education and learning were considered to be attributes of whiteness. Kennedy, "Way Down Upon . . . ," 25.

84. Hurston to Dr. Harold Spivacke, Music Division, Library of Congress, August 21, 1945, Vertical Files, Correspondence—Zora Neale Hurston, American Folklife Center, LC.

85. Hurston to Hughes, March 8, 1928, Eatonville, Fla., JWJC.

86. Ibid.

87. Hurston to Countee Cullen, March 11, 1926, Barnard College, Vertical Files, Correspondence—Zora Neale Hurston, American Folklife Center, LC.

88. Hurston to Hughes, July 10, 1928, Magazine, Ala., JWJC.

89. Hurston to Hughes, November 22, 1928, New Orleans, La., JWJC.

90. Hurston to Hughes, March 8, 1928, Eatonville, Fla., JWJC. Emphasis in original.

91. Hurston to Hughes, November 19, 1928, Bogalusa, La., JWJC.

92. Hurston to Hughes, July 10, 1928, Magazine, Ala., JWJC.

93. Hurston to Hughes, August 16, 1928, New Orleans (Algiers), La., JWJC.

94. Hurston to Hughes, August 6, 1928, Algiers, La., JWJC.

95. Hurston to Hughes, September 20, 1928, JWJC.

96. Hurston to Hughes, April 30, 1929, Eau Gallie, Fla., JWJC.

97. Northern "Yankee" anthropologists also required letters of introduction to the elite southern white social circles. Belo's letters to members of the upper echelon in Natchez, Mississippi, emphasized her non-Jewish ancestry and her impeccable family connections. As Margaret Mead somewhat wryly observed, "she has all the requisite Junior League Background." Mead to John Dollard, March 14, 1940, Margaret Mead Papers, Container C5 "General Correspondence," Folder "1940-D," MD-LC. As this quotation makes clear, constructions of whiteness in the 1930s did not generally include Jews. See Jacobson, *Whiteness of a Different Color.*

98. Hurston to Hughes, October 15, 1928, New Orleans, La., JWJC.

99. Hurston to Hughes, January 31, 1928, JWJC.

100. Mary Elizabeth Barnicle, interview, January–February 1977, Zora Neale Hurston Collection, MPBRS-LC.

101. Ibid.

102. Hemenway, *Zora Neale Hurston,* 211.

103. Ibid.

104. Mary Elizabeth Barnicle, interview, January–February 1977, Zora Neale Hurston Collection, MPBRS-LC.

105. Alan Lomax quoted in Chronology by Cheryl A. Wall, in Hurston, *Folklore, Memoirs, and Other Writings,* 971.

106. Hemenway, *Zora Neale Hurston,* 212.

107. Mary Elizabeth Barnicle, interview, January–February 1977, Zora Neale Hurston Collection, MPBRS-LC.

108. Hurston to Jane Belo, October 14, 1944, Vertical Files, Correspondence—Zora Neale Hurston, 2, American Folklife Center, LC.

109. Belo to Hurston, April 29, 1940, Margaret Mead Papers, Container O20 "Correspondence—Jane Belo," 2, MD-LC.

110. Hurston to Paul Green, May 3, 1940, reprinted in Kaplan, *Zora Neale Hurston,* 458–59.

111. Hurston recorded by Alan Lomax in Petionville, Haiti, December 21, 1936; also, Hurston recorded by Herb Halpert, Folk Arts Committee, WPA, Jacksonville, Fla., June 1939, MPBRS-LC.

112. Hurston recorded by Herb Halpert, Folk Arts Committee, WPA, Jacksonville, Fla., June 1939, MPBRS-LC.

113. Ibid.

114. Ibid.

115. Ibid.

116. Ibid.

117. Hurston would acknowledge that this technique did have its drawbacks in her request for the use of a recording machine while she was working for the FWP in Florida. As she explained to state director Corse: "It is hard to set [folk songs] down correctly at one sitting, and the informant usually grows self conscious if asked to sing them over and over again so that they may be set down so that one does not secure the same thing as when they are sung naturally. The answer is a recording machine." Hurston to Carita Doggett Corse, June 16, 1938, Entry 22, Box 1, File "FL—Folklore," RG 69.

118. Sale, "Call and Response as Critical Method," 41–50.

119. Hurston to Boas, October 20, 1929, "Professional Correspondence of Franz Boas," Microfilm 1972, Reel 30, FB-LC.

120. Robert E. Hemenway, "Zora Neale Hurston and the Eatonville Anthropology," manuscript notes, 1972, Box 2, Folder 30, page 15, JWJC.

121. Hurston to Hughes, April 12, 1928, Maitland, Fla., JWJC.

122. Hurston recorded by Herb Halpert, Folk Arts Committee, WPA, Jacksonville, Fla., June 1939, MPBRS-LC.

123. Hurston to Boas, October 20, 1929, "Professional Correspondence of Franz Boas," Microfilm 1972, Reel 30, FB-LC.

124. Hurston, "Characteristics of Negro Expression," 836–37.

125. Reviews include Sterling Brown, "Luck Is a Fortune," *Nation* 145, no. 16 (October 16, 1937): 409–10; Sheila Hibben, "Vibrant Book Full of Nature and Salt," *New York Herald Tribune Weekly Book Review,* September 26, 1937, 2; Alaine Locke, "And Now Zora Neale Hurston and Her Magical Title: *Their Eyes Were Watching God,*" *Opportunity,* June 1, 1938; George Stevens, "Negroes by Themselves," *Saturday Review of Literature,* September 18, 1937, 3; and Lucille Tompkins, "In the Florida Glades," *New York Times Book Review,* September 26, 1937, 29.

126. WPA Box 6, Correspondence, Field Report—Florida, Darel McConkey, Acting Field Supervisor, "Negroes," April 22, 1938, USF. He mentions that she received two Guggenheim fellowships, authored three or four books, "is greatly interested in all the Project is doing and will probably furnish us with valuable new Florida folklore."

127. Brown to Regional Supervisor Darel McConkey, May 25, 1936, 1, Entry 27 "Reports and Misc. Pertaining to Negro Studies," Box 1, File "General Letters—Outgoing by State," RG 69.

128. Alsberg to Carita Doggett Corse, June 21, 1938, Entry 1 "Administrative Correspondence," Box 9 "Florida," File "Florida—Employment," RG 69.

129. Ibid.

130. Corse to Alsberg, June 23, 1938, Entry 1 "Administrative Correspondence," Box 9 "Florida," File "Florida—Employment," RG 69.

131. See Mangione, *Dream and the Deal*, 257; personal interview conducted by the author with Stetson Kennedy at his home, Beluthahatchee, in St. Johns, Fla., October 2005.

132. Kennedy, interview by the author, October 2005.

133. Minutes and transcript from WPA Nationwide Radio Staff meeting, June 22, 1936, submitted by C. H. Ward, Asst. State Editor, American Guide, approved by Dr. Corse, State Director, WPA Box 1 F1, [Part 2], USF.

134. Hurston, *Dust Tracks*, 70.

135. Bordelon, *Go Gator and Muddy the Water*, 48.

136. Ibid., 20.

137. Kennedy, interview by the author, October 2005.

138. Examples include "The White Man's Prayer," "Big John de Conqueror," and "John and the Persimmon Tree."

139. Hurston to Corse, December 3, 1938, Box 2, 56a, Zora Neale Hurston Papers, UF.

140. Kennedy, interview by the author, October 2005.

141. Leland Hawes, "Author Recorded Voices of the Downtrodden," page 2d from (1–3d), clipping from WPA Box 1, Folder 1, "Articles," USF.

142. Kennedy, interview by the author, October 2005.

143. Hemenway, *Zora Neale Hurston*, 252–53.

144. Stetson Kennedy, quoted in McDonogh, Introduction, *Florida Negro*, xix.

145. Interview with Dr. Carita Doggett Corse by Nancy Williams, New Smyrna Beach, Fla., March 18, 1976, transcript, page 10, UF.

146. McDonogh suggests that most of the published version of the manuscript was completed prior to Hurston's arrival on the Project. This would seem to be the case; however, a section that appears in the chapter "Workaday Songs" is strikingly reminiscent of not only Hurston's unique way of learning a song's lyrics but her ability to re-create the in-between sounds and context of the song in use by workers. See "Workaday Songs," chap. 5 in McDonogh, *Florida Negro*, esp. 51–53.

147. Hurston to Corse, December 3, 1938, Box 2, 56a, Zora Neale Hurston Papers, UF.

148. Editorial Criticism for "Florida—Racial Elements and Folklore," Federal Office, October 13, 1938, Entry 13, Box 8, File "Florida State Guide: Essays," RG 69.

Chapter Seven

1. Although Virginia was also engaged at this time in a similar collection process, in an editorial report on the copy that had so far been received from the state FWP offices, Florida's slave narratives were officially credited with initiating the Ex-Slave Project. John Lomax to Carita Doggett Corse, April 6, 1937, correspondence pertaining to Folklore Studies, 1936–41, Florida, Federal Writers' Project, Box 192, RG 69. See also Editorial Report on State Copy, n.d., Entry 21, Box 1, File "Florida," RG 69.

2. Florida contributed almost 3 percent of the interviews for the slave narrative collection, even though only 1 percent of the ex-slave informants interviewed for the project had experienced slavery in Florida. Mormino, "Florida Slave Narratives," 402–5. Corse's books are *Dr. Andrew Turnbull and the New Smyrna Colony of Florida* (Jacksonville, Fla.: Drew Press, 1919), *The Key to the Golden Islands* (Chapel Hill: University of North Carolina Press, 1931), and *The Fountain of Youth* (St. Augustine: C. D. Corse, 1933).

3. "Nine Lady Doctors," *The Sewanee News*, March 1970, 4, http://www.mocavo.com/Sewanee-News-March-1970-Volume-36/965847/44 (July 29, 2014); *Florida Women's Hall of Fame: The Lives and Works of Florida's Historical Women*, 2009/2010, Florida Commission on the Status of Women (March 2010), 44, http://edocs.dlis.state.fl.us/fldocs/commissions/women/halloffame/websitefinalhalloffamebrochure2010.pdf (July 29, 2014); Matt Schudel, "During the Depression, A Corps of Writers Working for the New Deal Program Took the Pulse of the Nation. They're Still Teaching Us What It Means to be American," [Fort Lauderdale] *Sun Sentinel*, January 30, 2000, 4, http://articles.sun-sentinel.com/2000-01-30/features/0002010364_1_library-american-guide-series-federal-writers-project/4 (July 29, 2014).

4. *Florida: Empire of the Sun* (Tallahassee, Fla.: Florida State Hotel Commission, 1930) in USF. This book is typically overlooked by scholars who identify Corse primarily as the author of *Dr. Andrew Turnbull* and *Key to the Golden Islands.*

5. WPA Box 6, Correspondence, USF. This commercial publication was later used by members of the advisory committee to try to smear Corse's reputation as a historian and undermine her relations with federal directors. See Kellock Field Report to Alsberg, January 25, year unknown, "Subject: Hanna, Davis and others referred to by Ballou as objecting to Mrs. Corse as historian." Kellock reported to Alsberg, "Mrs. Corse is very strong politically and could not be removed without trouble and also damage to the project." Kellock also described Corse as having "delusions of grandeur. I find that she is off in the state driving with her secretary, if you please—10 day swing around the circle with stenog. Receiving $5 per diem, etc." Kellock Field Report to Alsberg, January 21, 1936, Jacksonville, Fla., WPA Box 6, Correspondence, 1, USF. In another report, Kellock sarcastically notes, "Mrs. Corse is a Florida 'lady' with no idea of

arithmetic or expenses." Kellock Field Report to Alsberg, January 22, 1936, Jacksonville, Fla., WPA Box 6, Correspondence, 2, USF.

6. Carita Doggett Corse, "Treatise on Andrew Jackson," *Southern Magazine* 4, no. 1 (April–May 1937): 12. Corse's date of admission for membership was November 30, 1939, Jacksonville Chapter No. 1128. Information provided courtesy of Teresa Roane, archivist, and Betty Luck, research librarian, UDC, author's site visit (January 14, 2015) and e-mail correspondence with Betty Luck, January 21, 2015.

7. Salary information from Kennedy, "Florida Folklife and the WPA, an Introduction"; *Florida Women's Hall of Fame*, 44.

8. Kennedy, "Florida Folklife and the WPA, an Introduction."

9. Corse to George Cronyn, October 19, 1935. Katharine Kellock notes in a letter to Alsberg in January 1936 that Corse was very interested in a "negro project" and that "there is a good deal of pressure from negro organizations" for such a project. Kellock report to Alsberg from Jacksonville, Fla., January 23, 1936, WPA Box 6, Correspondence, USF. Mary McLeod Bethune was going to serve as a volunteer "negro supervisor" for the project, according to Kellock's report of January 25, 1936, WPA Box 6, Correspondence, USF.

10. Kellock to Henry Alsberg, January 26, 1936, Entry 6, Box 1 "Alab.–Idaho," File "Florida—Kellock," RG 69.

11. *The Florida Negro*, edited by Gary McDonogh, lists sixteen African Americans who were employed during various years, although the racial designation of Ruth Bolton, who appears on the list, is noted as unknown. See Appendix C of *Florida Negro*. Stetson Kennedy identifies Bolton as a member of the NWU but recalled only twelve members in total, including Hurston (he doesn't mention Paul Diggs, Portia Thorington, and Rachel Austin). See Kennedy, "Florida Folklife and the WPA, an Introduction."

12. Katharine Kellock, Field Report to Henry Alsberg from Florida, January 26, 1936, WPA Collection, Box 6, Folder "Correspondence," 1, USF. Kellock is quoting Mrs. Shelby, who assisted Corse with the Florida Project, after Corse advocated for her hire. Kellock was also not impressed with Corse's editorial abilities, but she appreciated Corse's ability to surround herself with a good team and to delegate responsibility; she also noted Corse's enthusiasm for local history. There was brief consideration in April 1938 of trying to shift Corse over to direct the state's archaeological project, which Rolla Southworth, director of the Women's Professional and Service Division of Florida's WPA, thought her talents would be better suited for, but Corse refused to acknowledge that this new responsibility would remove her from her position as state director for the FWP; Kellock also noted that Corse was too well connected politically to be removed. See Darel McConkey, Acting Field Supervisor's Report to Alsberg, April 22, 1938, WPA Collection, Box 6, Folder "Correspondence," 1, USF.

13. Kennedy, "Florida Folklife and the WPA, an Introduction."

14. Corse's Progress Report for Florida to Alsberg, August 18, 1936, Entry 1, Box 9, File "Florida—Misc.," RG 69.

15. Figures and dates listed in letter from Corse to Henry Alsberg, December 16, 1936, Entry 13, Box 8, File "Florida Editorial—Misc., 1935–36," RG 69.

16. McDonogh, Introduction, *Florida Negro*, xxii.

17. Stetson Kennedy, interview by the author, at Beluthahatchee, his home in St. Johns, Fla., October 2005.

18. Harry Golden, "How to Solve the Segregation Problem," *Carolina Israelite* (May–June 1956), reproduced in "Race and Education in Charlotte," University of North Carolina—Charlotte Library, Special Collections Unit, http://speccollexhibit.omeka.net/items/show/74 (July 25, 2014).

19. U.S. Census, 1930; Diggs, in "Follow Me through Florida," cites Jacksonville's population as 150,000. November 10, 1938, Florida Negro Papers, Box 3, 1, USF.

20. A field report from Stella Block Hanau to Mr. Newsome, January 1941, describes the Jacksonville office as "adequately housed in seven rooms in a modern office building, provided by the city for WPA projects, NYA, etc." WPA, Box 6 Correspondence, 1, USF. When Hurston contacted publishing houses in New York regarding the manuscript for "The Florida Negro," she used a return address identifying the Exchange Building but listing the street address where the NWU was housed without naming the Clara White Mission. May 11, 1939, from Associate Editor Lois Dwight Cole, Macmillan Company, to Miss Zora Neale Hurston, Works Progress Administration of Florida, Exchange Building, Jacksonville, Fla.; May 10, 1939, from Arthur J. Christopher, Christopher Publishing House, to Miss Zora Neale Hurston, 611 West Ashley Street, Exchange Building, Jacksonville, Fla., FN, Box 8, Folder "Notes of Z. N. Hurston," USF. Florida's WPA was very reluctant to provide funds for FWP administrative setup; housing the NWU at the Mission was probably financially expedient as well; see Kellock's field reports, WPA Collection, Box 6, Folder "Correspondence," USF.

21. Kennedy, interview by the author, October 2005; Kennedy made a nearly identical statement in an interview conducted by Pamela Bordelon in 1988. See Bordelon, *Go Gator and Muddy the Water*, 20.

22. Kennedy, interview by the author, October 2005. Clara White's daughter, Eartha White, became owner of the building in 1932. The Mission also offered work training for African American women in typing and stenography and in nontraditional occupations, such as taxi drivers and elevator operators during World War II. Eartha White also managed a Negro baseball team during World War II. The Mission was still feeding 400 to 500 people a day in 2005 and also houses the Eartha M. M. White Historical Museum and Resource Center; tour of building and museum exhibits given to the author by Michelle Ditch, October 2005.

23. Paul Diggs, "Little Angel of Ashly Street—Miss Eartha M. M. White," October 14, 1938, Lakeland, Fla., WPA, Box 5, Folder 7, USF. Over time, the Clara White Mission became home to a number of black businesses as well as labor and political organizations. See Antoinette T. Jackson and Allan F. Burns, "Ethnohistorical Study of the Kingsley Plantation," 37–38. See also "100 Years in the Making," Clara White Mission, http://www.clarawhitemission.org/About/History.aspx (July 29, 2014).

24. Kennedy, interview by the author, October 2005. Some of these recordings made at the Clara White Mission are now available online, for example, "Plantation Recording," Jacksonville, Fla., June 6, 1939, sound recording, AFC 1939/005; AFS 03140 A01 DLC-AFC, American Folklife Center, LC, http://www.loc.gov/item/flwpa.3140a1/ (August 29, 2014).

25. Alfred Farrell to Henry Alsberg, January 8, 1936, Entry 1, Box 9, File "Florida A–L," RG 69.

26. Kennedy notes that the office of the assistant state director of the National Youth Administration, Edward R. Rodriguez, was located at Edward Waters College and that Rodriguez had written to Alsberg on October 7, 1935, requesting that he ensure that African American applicants receive equal consideration, as many had been summarily told it was too late to apply. Kennedy, "Florida Folklife and the WPA, an Introduction."

27. In 1999, Farrell recalled what it was like to arrive at Lincoln University for the first time in 1930 "during the Depression, as a poor 16-year-old from Reading [Pennsylvania]." Noted in obituary of H. Alfred Farrell, *Philadelphia Inquirer*, October 16, 2005, B07, Newsbank, America's Obituaries and Death Notices.

28. Mormino, "Florida Slave Narratives." There were eight women and eight men, although not all of them overlapped: Rachel Austin, L. Rebecca Baker, Ruth D. Bolton, Paul A. Diggs, H. Alfred Farrell, Zora Neale Hurston, James M. Johnson, Samuel Johnson, Viola B. Muse, Pearl Randolph, Wilson R. Rice, Martin Richardson, John A. Simms (editor), Robert T. Thomas (assistant supervisor), Grace Thompson, and Portia Thorington.

29. Rachel Austin, L. Rebecca Baker, Ruth D. Bolton, Paul A. Diggs, H. Alfred Farrell, James M. Johnson, Samuel Johnson, Viola B. Muse, Pearl Randolph, Wilson R. Rice, Martin Richardson, Grace Thompson, and Portia Thorington. McDonogh, Introduction, *Florida Negro*, xxi–xxii.

30. "Writers for 'American Guide,' WPA Project, Visit in City," *Panama City Herald*, April 14, 1936, 5.

31. "Campus Literary Lights Form New Organization," *Bloomington* [Indiana] *Daily Student*, April 8, 1922, 1; "Literary Society Adopts Constitution," *Bloomington Daily Student*, April 28, 1922, 4. There is a discrepancy of four years in the records for Viola Walker Muse's birth date: the Social Security Death Index lists it as April 11, 1894, whereas the Florida Death Index lists it as April 11, 1898.

32. Kennedy identifies Ruth Bolton as a typist; Austin and Thorington are identified on their submissions as "Secretary." Kennedy, "Florida Folklife and the WPA, an Introduction." McDonogh also notes the secretarial status of Rachel Austin and Portia Thorington in *Florida Negro*, xxii.

33. U.S. Census, 1930, Bolton, Ruth. Married at 17, and widowed by 23, Bolton would be living with her mother, Katharyn Daniels, on Eighth Street in 1940, according to the 1940 census.

34. Paul Diggs, Lakeland, Fla., October 28, 1938, "Negro Newspapers and Periodicals in the United States," 5, WPA, Box 23, Folder "Negroes," USF. According to the 1940

census, there was a John A. Simms living in Jacksonville in 1935 who would have been forty-three years old in 1936 when the NWU was created. He and his wife Margaret both completed four years of college.

35. McDonogh describes Richardson as main author and compiler of the 1937 draft of the manuscript. *Florida Negro*, xvii.

36. U.S. Census, 1930 and 1940; the census lists four years of college as the highest educational level for Diggs. Information on Diggs's neighborhood from "The African American Experience," City of Lakeland Library, Special Collections, http://www .lakelandgov.net/libraryspecialcollections/Exhibits/AfricanAmericanExperienceinL akeland.aspx (July 24, 2014). An area of Lakeland was later named for him. In an essay from 1938 for the NWU, Diggs identifies three "colored" communities in Lakeland: "Teaspoonful Hill," "Morehead," and "Babylon." "Follow Me through Florida," November 18, 1938, USF.

37. "Diggs Tells Negro Educational Work; Is Former Fighter," *Southern* [Florida Southern College] 21, no. 11 (November 26, 1938): 3.

38. LaFrancine K. Burton, "Teaspoon Hill Became Black Commerce Center as Lakeland Expanded," *Ledger*, August 24, 2002; information on Diggs reproduced in "Paul A. Diggs, Chairman, Polk County Health Committee for Blacks," ZoomInfo, http://www.zoominfo.com/p/Paul-Diggs/234285480 (August 20, 2014).

39. McDonogh, Introduction, *Florida Negro*, xxi.

40. For nineteenth-century antecedents of this practice, see William Andrews, *To Tell a Free Story*.

41. A glaring exception to the NWU's general avoidance of the first person and the use of the black vernacular comes in the form of slave narratives submitted by Rachel Austin. Although she submitted several narratives to the collection, Austin's primary job was as the secretary for Florida's NWU. One can only speculate about factors that may have affected the way she wrote her interviews. See, for example, Austin's interview with Margrett Nickerson, Rawick, *American Slave*, Florida (Negro Writers' Unit), II:17:250–56, December 5, 1936.

42. For an excellent discussion of the adoption of the black vernacular by white writers and artists in search of a modernist style at the moment when black writers were distancing themselves from it, see North, *Dialect of Modernism*.

43. Lomax to Carita Doggett Corse, April 15, 1937, Entry 21, Box 1, File "Florida," RG 69.

44. George Cronyn to Carita Doggett Corse, April 1, 1937, Entry 21, Box 1, File "Florida," RG 69.

45. Rawick, *American Slave*, Florida (Negro Writers' Unit), II:17:277, informant George Pretty, field worker Viola B. Muse, November 9, 1936.

46. Ibid.

47. Ibid., 278.

48. Baker also noted in her submission that "Prophet" was unclear about whether his master was just called "father" or was really his father by blood. Rawick, *American Slave*, Florida (Negro Writers' Unit), II:17:185–86, informant "Prophet" John Henry Kemp, field worker L. Rebecca Baker, January 11, 1937.

49. Woodward, "History from Slave Sources," 52. Quotation from Rawick, *American Slave*, Florida (Negro Writers' Unit), II:17:131, informants Sam and Louisa Everett, field worker Pearl Randolph, ed. John A. Simms, October 8, 1936.

50. Morrison, "The Site of Memory," 109–13.

51. Rawick, *American Slave*, Florida (Negro Writers' Unit), II:17:27, informant Frank Berry, field worker Pearl Randolph, ed. John A. Simms, August 18, 1936.

52. Rawick, *American Slave*, Florida (Negro Writers' Unit), II:17:122–23, informant Willis Davis, field worker Pearl Randolph, January 20, 1937.

53. Rawick, *American Slave*, Florida (Negro Writers' Unit), "Dade County, Florida, Folklore: Ex-Slaves," II:17:40, informant Reverend Eli Boyd, n.d.

54. Rawick, *American Slave*, Florida (Negro Writers' Unit), II:17:212, informant Amanda McCray, field worker Pearl Randolph, November 13, 1936.

55. Rawick, *American Slave*, Florida (Negro Writers' Unit), II:17:345, informant Luke Towns, field worker Rachel Austin, November 30, 1936.

56. Rawick, *American Slave*, Florida (Negro Writers' Unit), II:17:218–19, informant Henry Maxwell, field worker Alfred Farrell, ed. John A. Simms, September 25, 1936.

57. Rawick, *American Slave*, Florida (Negro Writers' Unit), II:17:204, informant Edward Lyourgas, field worker Pearl Randolph, December 5, 1936.

58. "Progress Report, Negro Unit, Federal Writers' Projects," December 16, 1936, Entry 13, Box 8, File "Florida Editorial Misc., 1935–36," RG 69.

59. Ibid.

60. "Hoodoo" is the preferred term used by African Americans, while "Voodoo" is the nomenclature used by whites. Zora Neale Hurston, "Florida Folklore—Negro Customs and Folklore," Box A591 "Folklore Project—FL," File "FL—Negro Lore," MD-LC.

61. See Takaki, *Iron Cages*; and Wiegman, *American Anatomies*.

62. Rawick, *American Slave*, Florida (Negro Writers' Unit), II:17:29, informant Frank Berry, field worker Pearl Randolph, ed. John A. Simms, August 18, 1936.

63. Ibid., 27.

64. Ibid., 28.

65. Rawick, *American Slave*, Florida (Negro Writers' Unit), II:17:354, informant Willis Williams, field worker Viola B. Muse, March 20, 1937.

66. Rawick, *American Slave*, Florida (Negro Writers' Unit), II:17:297–98, informant William Sherman, field worker J. M. Johnson, ed. John A. Simms, August 28, 1936.

67. Ibid., 298.

68. Rawick, *American Slave*, Florida (Negro Writers' Unit), II:17:218–19, informant Henry Maxwell, field worker Alfred Farrell, ed. John A. Simms, September 25, 1936.

69. Rawick, *American Slave*, Florida (Negro Writers' Unit), "An Ex-Slave Who Was Resourceful," II:17:229–32, informant Lindsey Moore, field worker Martin Richardson, January 13, 1937.

70. Rawick, *American Slave*, Florida (Negro Writers' Unit), II:17:279, informant Anna Scott, field worker Viola B. Muse, January 11, 1937.

71. Ibid., 282.

72. Ibid.

73. Ibid., 282–83.

74. Ibid., 283.

75. Ibid., 284.

76. Correspondence to Hurston was sent to the Exchange Building: May 11, 1939, from Associate Editor Lois Dwight Cole, Macmillan Company, to Miss Zora Neale Hurston, Works Progress Administration of Florida, Exchange Building, Jacksonville, Fla.; May 10, 1939, from Arthur J. Christopher, Christopher Publishing House to Miss Zora Neale Hurston, 611 West Ashley Street, Exchange Building, Jacksonville, Fla., FN, Box 8, Folder "Notes of Z. N. Hurston," USF.

77. McDonogh, Introduction, *Florida Negro*, ix, xvi. He also notes that there is very little information available regarding Martin Richardson.

78. State Editorial Identification Form—The Florida Negro, July 14, 1939, Florida Negro, Box 8, Folder 1, USF.

79. Carita Doggett Corse, interview by Nancy Williams, transcript, March 18, 1976, New Smyrna Beach, Fla., UF.

80. Corse to Henry Alsberg, October 30, 1935, Entry 1, Box 9, File "Florida—Misc.," 1, RG 69.

81. McDonogh notes this shift toward a middle-class emphasis in the materials collected in 1938, which is when, as he observes, Paul Diggs and Hurston both began work and contributed extensively.

82. McDonogh, *Florida Negro*, 88.

83. Ibid.

84. Ibid., 89.

85. Ibid.

86. Ibid., 91.

87. Ibid., 93.

88. Ibid.

89. Ibid., 26–27.

90. Sterling Brown, Editorial Report on State Copy "Slave Days in Florida," June 7, 1937, and Cronyn, accompanying cover letter to Corse, June 9, 1937, FN Box 9, Folder 8, USF.

91. McDonogh, *Florida Negro*, 37–38.

92. Paul Diggs, "Colored City Auditorium—Lakeland," October 7, 1938, WPA Box 23, Folder "Negroes," USF.

93. Paul Diggs, "Lakeland Public Library," November 18, 1938, WPA Box 23, Folder "Negroes," USF.

94. "Negro History," Viola Muse, Negro Writers' Unit, June 2, 1936, A 879, File "Florida—Historical Material, 1936–39," MD-LC.

95. Ibid.

96. McDonogh, *Florida Negro*, 13–14.

97. The National Alliance of Postal Employees would play an instrumental role, along with the NAACP, in persuading President Roosevelt to abolish the Civil Service application photograph requirement that was used to establish Jim Crow post office branches by screening out African American applicants. Rubio, " 'Who Divided the Church?,' " 174.

98. McDonogh, *Florida Negro*, photos appear between pages 68 and 69.

99. See, for example, Paul Diggs, "Negro Newspapers Influence on Public," NWU, October 28, 1938, A879, File "Florida Historical Material, 1936–39," 1, MD-LC.

100. Gaines, *Uplifting the Race*, 4.

101. "Notable Florida Negroes," in McDonogh, *Florida Negro*, 97–106.

102. Paul Diggs, "Negro Educator—Mary McLeod Bethune," Negro Writers' Unit, July 8, 1938, A877, File "Florida Biographical Sketches," 1, MD-LC.

103. Ibid., 3.

104. Paul Diggs, "Negro Educator—Prof. William A. Rochelle—A Florida Pioneer School Teacher," Negro Writers' Unit, July 15, 1938, A877, File "Florida Biographical Sketches," 1, MD-LC.

105. Ibid., 6.

106. L. Rebecca Baker, "Negro Ethnography," Negro Writers' Unit, May 27, 1936, A879, File "Florida—Historical Material, 1860–1938," 1–2, MD-LC.

107. Martin Richardson, "What the Florida Negro Does," Negro Writers' Unit, n.d., A879, File "Florida—Historical Material, 1860–1938," 46, MD-LC.

108. Ibid., 46–49.

109. "What the Florida Negro Does," in McDonogh, *Florida Negro*, 42–43.

110. McDonogh, *Florida Negro*, 59–61.

111. Ibid., 60–61.

112. Ibid., 71.

113. Ibid., 85–86.

114. Ibid., 56–58.

115. Ibid.

116. Higginbotham, *Righteous Discontent*.

117. "Lakeland Negroes Recommend Curfew," *St. Petersburg Times*, September 30, 1943, 14.

118. Harris, "Gatekeeping and Remaking," 213.

119. Hurston, "My People, My People," in *Dust Tracks on a Road*, 177–78.

120. Ibid., 189.

Chapter Eight

1. Rawick, *American Slave*, Georgia, II:12:1:253, informant Minnie Davis, field worker Sadie B. Hornsby, ed. Sarah H. Hall and John N. Booth, [1938].

2. Ibid.

3. The phrase "the mastery of form and the deformation of mastery" is Houston Baker Jr.'s designation for the two different methods by which African Americans appropriated and subverted the mask of black minstrelsy as a strategy for survival. See Houston A. Baker Jr., *Modernism and the Harlem Renaissance*. For examples of goods and services provided by Georgia interviewers, see Rawick, *American Slave*, Georgia, II:12:1:230, informant John Cole, ed. Edward Fichlen, n.d.; Rawick, *American Slave*, Georgia, II:12:1:343, informant Carrie Nancy Fryer, field worker Maude Barragan, n.d.;

and Rawick, *American Slave*, Georgia, II:12:1:46–47, informant Alice Green, field worker Sadie B. Hornsby, ed. Sarah H. Hall, n.d.

4. My observations on this aspect of the narratives have been shaped by Houston Baker Jr.'s essay on Trueblood's narrative in Ralph Ellison's *Invisible Man*, where he describes this practice. See Houston A. Baker Jr., "To Move without Moving," 243.

5. Another creative form of African American agency, deployed in encounters with New Deal photographers, is documented by a Florida interview conducted by a white employee. According to informant Susie Lee, black female cotton pickers shielded themselves from photographers wanting to take their picture: "Because they are too proud to [be] seen in the old clothes they wear in the fields, the negro women always turn their backs and stoop over when a photographer goes into the fields to take pictures of the crew." As Lee explained this practice in her own words, "That's one thing we don't have to do, let 'em take our pictures and show us in the newspapers with our old dirty clothes on." Statewide Writers' Project, field worker Gladys Buck, "The Florida Negro," interview with Susie Lee, "negress," April 29, 1940, A878 "Negro Studies Project—Florida," Folder "FL—Folklore, Lifestyle," FWP-LC.

6. Fry, *Night Riders in Black Folk History*, 7n12.

7. Library of Congress, American Memory, "Born in Slavery," Arkansas Narratives, Volume II, Part 2, 234, informant Lucius Edwards, field worker Irene Robertson, n.d., Library of Congress Manuscript Division, Digital Collection.

8. Kelley, *Race Rebels*, 8–9. Kelley's work draws on that of the anthropologist James Scott and the ethnographer Lila Abu-Lughod. For works on resistance as it manifests itself through black cultural expressiveness, see also Angela Y. Davis, *Blues Legacies and Black Feminism*, and Krasner, *Beautiful Pageant*. For a thoughtful and engaging discussion of the variety of factors affecting the FWP narratives, see Davidson and Lytle, "View from the Bottom Rail."

9. Reese observed that "things like that was common in slavery time. Masters often had children by their slave women." Rawick, *American Slave*, Georgia, Supplemental Series I (SSI):4:2:512, informant Bill Reese, field worker Sadie B. Hornsby, ed. Sarah H. Hall and John N. Booth, July 13, 1939.

10. See, for example, Levine, *Black Culture and Black Consciousness*, 99–101.

11. Scholars whose work I draw on to discuss and identify the use of signifying in the ex-slave narratives include Mitchell-Kernan, *Language Behavior in a Black Urban Community*, and Henry Louis Gates Jr., *Signifying Monkey*; Gates's work builds on that of Roger Abrahams and Thomas Kochman, as well as Mitchell-Kernan.

12. Hurston, *Mules and Men*, 18. In his critical analysis of theories of colonial discourse, scholar Nicholas Thomas lists "disingenuous compliance" as one of the key elements that constitutes colonial encounters and mediates colonialist discourse. Thomas, *Colonialism's Culture*.

13. Both Alan Dundes and Henry Louis Gates Jr. suggest this origin. See Henry Louis Gates Jr., "The Signifying Monkey and the Language of Signifyin(g)," in *The Henry Louis Gates, Jr. Reader*, 241.

14. Mitchell-Kernan, "Signifying," in *Language Behavior in a Black Urban Community*, 314.

15. Mitchell-Kernan, *Language Behavior in a Black Urban Community*.

16. Abrahams quoted in Gates, "Signifying Monkey and the Language of Signifyin(g)," 242.

17. Abrahams quoted in Mitchell-Kernan, "Signifying," in *Language Behavior in a Black Urban Community*, 311. The most famous animal trickster in the black folk tradition, discussed by scholars of signifying, is the monkey, but other trickster figures, such as Brer Rabbit, as well as John, the slave trickster in black folktales, also use the verbal art of signifying to come out on top. Hurston documents many of these tales in *Mules and Men*. For further discussion of the trickster tradition and its importance to black folk culture, see Levine, *Black Culture and Black Consciousness*, and Joyner, *Down by the Riverside*.

18. Abrahams quoted in Mitchell-Kernan, "Signifying," in *Language Behavior in a Black Urban Community*, 311.

19. Much of the evidence for ex-slave narrators' use of signifying practices is lost to us. Important aspects of signifying that can signal a speaker's change in meaning and involve physical gestures, such as "changes in posture, speech rate, tone of voice, and facial expression," were not recorded in written form, with the few exceptions of brief observations made by the interviewer. Mitchell-Kernan, "Signifying," in *Language Behavior in a Black Urban Community*, 327. Nevertheless, other aspects of signifying are embedded in the speech acts themselves; it is possible, I contend, to find examples of this verbal art form in the slave narrative collection.

20. Rawick, *American Slave*, Georgia, II:12:1:257, informant Minnie Davis, field worker Sadie B. Hornsby, ed. Sarah H. Hall and John N. Booth, [1938].

21. Narratives from the Florida and Georgia collections may be of particular value for this approach, as both state projects were generally held in high regard by federal directors, and comparisons of the ex-slave material held in state archives with that sent to Washington indicate consistency in most narratives' progression from field notes to revised copy to final submission to the federal office. With the Georgia Project, George Rawick found that "no attempt was made to destroy material, significantly alter it, or bury it," unlike in Mississippi and Texas. Rawick, *American Slave*, Georgia, Supplemental Series I (SSI):3:xvii. For an illuminating look at the ways Mississippi and Texas significantly revised the narratives, not just stylistically, but substantively in terms of censoring content, see Musher, "Contesting 'the Way the Almighty Wants It.'"

22. See Supplementary Instructions No. 9-E to the American Guide Manual, Folklore, Stories from Ex-Slaves, April 22, 1937. B. A. Botkin, "Answers to Questions," attachment to letter to Terry O'Neill, December 3, 1966, Botkin Corporate Subject File, AAFC-LC. See also Memorandum from Henry Alsberg to State Directors of Alabama, Arkansas, Florida, Georgia, Kentucky, Louisiana, Maryland, Michigan, Missouri, North Carolina, South Carolina, Oklahoma, Tennessee, Texas, Virginia, West Virginia, Ohio, Kentucky, and Indiana, July 30, 1937, Entry 21, Box 1, File "Ex-Slaves Correspondence," RG 69. Alsberg provides suggestions on collecting ex-slave material: "All stories should be as nearly word-for-word as is possible." While interview-

ers were responsible for writing down what informants said without the benefit of recording equipment, the act of transmitting oral to print culture was widespread in the 1930s, in a way that is hard for twenty-first-century audiences to understand given the ubiquity of audio and visual recording devices. The broad category of "writer" used by the FWP for employment purposes drew on a wide array of people trained in writing down accurately what was said; newspaper reporters and clerical workers all possessed skills of shorthand and transcription.

23. Monty Noam Penkower in his early definitive history of the FWP asserts that Georgia did not hire any black employees, based on his correspondence with state director Carolyn Dillard, who did not recall any "Negro representation" on her staff, and Gary McDonogh reiterates Penkower's claim. "Out of 4,500 workers employed by the [FWP] in 1937, only 106 were black—slightly over 2 percent. Penkower notes that blacks were mostly employed in New York, Illinois, and Louisiana, while other states hired none, including southern projects such as Georgia." McDonogh, *Florida Negro*, xiv, citing Penkower, *Federal Writers' Project*, 66–77. Rawick, in his introduction to the supplemental series 1, identifies only four African American interviewers from the Georgia Project: Willie Cole, Edwin Driskell, Louise Oliphant, and Minnie B. Ross (p. xli); he does not include Adella S. Dixon, although she is identified on one narrative by a handwritten note as "colored." Rawick, *American Slave*, Georgia, II:12:1:125, informant Della Briscoe, field worker Adella S. Dixon, n.d. However, Brown's report on state projects' number of black employees suggests that Georgia hired five, although it is not clear what positions they held or what their responsibilities were. Another report from Brown's office from August 26, 1936, notes that in Savannah and Macon, black employees were "already at work interviewing ex-slaves." Notes from the Office on Negro Affairs, Entry 27 "Reports and Misc. Pertaining to Negro Studies," Box 1, File 5 "Letters from State Directors," RG 69. In an inventory of submissions from Georgia in 1937, there are three employees identified as "Negro": Minnie Ross, Mildred Sneed, and W. H. Cole. Cole is the only one identified as an ex-slave interviewer. Inventory of Files, sent by Kathryn Hook, Assistant State Director, Georgia, to Alsberg, December 3, 1937, Entry 1 "Administrative Correspondence 1935–1939," Box 10, File "Georgia," RG 69.

24. It is important to note that although the Georgia Project had a strong UDC connection, Sarah Hall's name also appears on a number of narratives that speak of the evils of slavery. Sarah Hall is listed in the Georgia Division of the Daughters of the Confederacy Ancestor Roster, 1895–1995, Georgia Historical Society, Savannah, Ga. Other FWP employees on the Georgia Project confirmed as UDC members are Mrs. Annie Lee Newton, Mrs. Mattie B. Roberts, and Elizabeth Watson. Information provided courtesy of Teresa Roane, archivist, and Betty Luck, research librarian, UDC, author's site visit, January 14, 2015.

25. Muriel Barrow Bell and Malcolm Bell Jr., "Photographers' Note," in *Drums and Shadows*, xxx.

26. Rawick, *American Slave*, Georgia, II:12:1:238, informant Martha Colquitt, field worker Sarah H. Hall, ed. John N. Booth, July 8, 1938.

27. Rawick, *American Slave*, Georgia, II:12:1:148, informant Julia Brown (Aunt Sally), field worker Geneva Tonsill, July 25, 1939.

28. Ibid., 149.

29. Ibid., 153.

30. Ibid.

31. Athens, Georgia, where Hunter lived, was also home to Mildred Rutherford, who had served as president of the Georgia Division of the UDC, as well as historian general for the national organization.

32. Rawick, *American Slave*, Georgia, II:12:2:253, informant Lina Hunter, field worker Grace McCune, ed. Sarah H. Hall and John N. Booth, September 21, 1938.

33. Ibid., 263.

34. Ibid., 264.

35. Ibid., 264–66. This depiction of Hunter resembles Lomax's humorous representations of what he perceived to be the curious mix in African American culture of the sacred and the secular.

36. Ibid., 269–70.

37. Ibid., 272.

38. Ibid.

39. Rawick, *American Slave*, Georgia, SSI:4:2:510–11, informant Bill Reese, field worker Sadie B. Hornsby, ed. Sarah H. Hall and John N. Booth, July 13, 1939.

40. Cox, *Dixie's Daughters*, 140.

41. Walter Henry Cook, "Secret Political Societies in the South during the Period of Reconstruction."

42. Cox, *Dixie's Daughters*, 103–4.

43. McElya, *Clinging to Mammy*, 54.

44. Richardson, *Little Aleck*. Richardson's membership in the UDC does not seem likely, but her biography of an important figure in the Confederacy aligns her with one of the missions of the UDC. A search by UDC research librarian Betty Luck in the membership database and all nine chapters in the Richmond area in the vertical files did not locate Richardson. Identifying UDC membership presents researchers with a number of challenges. Minutes for both the annual and state conventions are not widely available, and they list only the names of officeholders. The UDC membership database, directly accessible only by UDC members, currently contains 227,494 names, spanning the years from the start of the UDC in 1894 to 2015. The UDC began transferring names of members into the computer database in 1988 but did not initially include any women who were unmarried, as it was erroneously assumed that they would not have descendants; however, to qualify for membership, one does not have to be a direct descendant. Information on UDC membership database provided by Teresa Roane, archivist, onsite research consultation with the author, January 14, 2015. The vertical (paper) files containing completed applications for UDC membership are arranged by chapter; a state like Florida, for example, by 1927 had forty-six chapters with a total enrollment of 2,354 members statewide. Mrs. Townes Randolph Leigh, "History of the Florida Division, United Daughters of the Confederacy," Vol. II, Section 2, Gainesville, Florida, 1927, UDC.

45. See note 24.

46. Rose Shepherd to Dr. Carita Doggett Corse, correspondence on the United Daughters of the Confederacy notecard, [April 26, 1946], Florida Writers' Project, Papers of Dr. Carita Doggett Corse, Special Collections, Carl S. Swisher Library, Jacksonville University. Rose Shephard (misspelled) is identified as the recording secretary in the 1936 UDC Annual Convention Minutes. Sarah H. Hall is identified as the recording secretary for the Marietta Kennesaw Chapter 241 in the 46th Annual Convention Minutes of the United Daughters of the Confederacy from 1939, UDC.

47. The date of admission for Carita Doggett Corse was November 30, 1939, showing she joined on the service of her grandfather, Aristides Doggett, Co. A, Third Florida Infantry. Information on UDC membership provided by Betty Luck, research librarian, UDC, e-mail correspondence with the author, January 21, 2015.

48. For a fascinating account of white women's impersonations and performances of the faithful "mammy" figure in amateur and professional theatrical productions across the country, see McElya, "Anxious Performances," in *Clinging to Mammy*, 38–73. See also illustration (#4): the Redpath publicity flier for Bernie Babcock's play *Mammy* on the Chautauqua circuit that featured the white actress Mrs. John McRaven, in blackface in the eponymous role.

49. Rawick, *American Slave*, Georgia, SSI:4:2:453, informant Elsie Moreland, field worker Elizabeth Watson; and Library of Congress, American Memory, "Born in Slavery," Georgia Narratives, Volume IV, Part 3, 136, informant Bob Mobley, field worker Elizabeth Watson, 1937, Library of Congress Manuscript Division, Digital Collection.

50. For more on the racial stereotypes of blackness emerging from the minstrel tradition and marketing ploys based on claims to authenticity, see K. Stephen Prince, *Stories of the South*, esp. chap. 5, "Performing Race, Staging Slavery," 166–204.

51. Rawick, *American Slave*, Georgia, II:12:1:40, informant Georgia Baker, field worker Sadie B. Hornsby, ed. Sarah H. Hall and John N. Booth, August 4, 1938.

52. Rawick, *American Slave*, Georgia, II:12:2:104, informant Dosia Harris, field worker Sadie B. Hornsby, ed. Sarah H. Hall, Leila Harris, and John N. Booth, n.d.

53. Rawick, *American Slave*, Georgia, II:12:2:98, informant Jane Smith Hill Harmon, field worker Minnie Branham Stonestreet, n.d.

54. Rawick, *American Slave*, Georgia, II:12:1:52, informant Georgia Baker, field worker Sadie B. Hornsby, ed. Sarah H. Hall and John N. Booth, August 4, 1938.

55. Ibid., 53.

56. Ibid., 57.

57. There is a startling exception in the narrative of Eugenia Martin, identified as a "WPA Worker–Housekeeping Aide," who was interviewed by Geneva Tonsill in November 1939. Martin speaks at length of the personal satisfaction and skills she gained during her WPA employment and emphasizes that she wouldn't have survived without government relief, as "there seems so little work for Negroes." This interview is not labeled as a submission for the Ex-Slave Project, nor was it edited by Sarah Hall. It is

free of dialect, and Martin emphasizes her father's "great desire . . . to see his race share the blessings of other people, equal rights, similar working conditions, decent living conditions, and educational advantages." "I Managed to Carry On," Eugenia Martin, WPA Worker–Housekeeping Aide, November 1939, Box A713, "Folklore Project, Life Histories, 1936–40," File "Georgia-Geneva Tonsill," FWP-LC.

58. See Rawick, *American Slave*, Georgia, II:12:2:56, informant Isaiah Green, field worker Minnie B. Ross, January 25, 1937; Isaiah Green is described as "fairly contented" and living in a shelter provided by public welfare. See also Rawick, *American Slave*, Georgia, II:12:1:125, informant Della Briscoe, field worker Adella S. Dixon, n.d.; Library of Congress, American Memory, "Born in Slavery," Georgia Narratives, Volume IV, Part 4, 37, informant Phil Towns, field worker Adella S. Dixon, n.d., Library of Congress Manuscript Division, Digital Collection; Library of Congress, American Memory, "Born in Slavery," Georgia Narratives, Volume IV, Part 2, 243, informant Bryant Huff, field worker Adella S. Dixon, April 28, 1937, Library of Congress Manuscript Division, Digital Collection.

59. See, for example, Rawick, *American Slave*, Georgia, II:12:2:352–55, informant Fannie Jones, field worker Emily Powell, ed. John Booth, September 1, 1938; Rawick, *American Slave*, Georgia, SSI:3:277, informant John Harris, field worker Grace McCune, July 27, 1939; Rawick, *American Slave*, Georgia, II:12:1:112, informant Alec Bostwick, n.d.: "I don't want to talk no more. I'se disappointed, I thought sho' you wuz one of dem pension ladies what come for to fetch me some money. I sho' wish dey would come."

60. Rawick, *American Slave*, Georgia, II:12:1:152, informant Julia Brown (Aunt Sally), field worker Geneva Tonsill, July 25, 1939.

61. Ibid., 150.

62. Rawick, *American Slave*, Georgia, II:12:1:250, informant Martha Colquitt, field worker Sarah H. Hall, ed. John N. Booth, July 8, 1938.

63. Ibid.

64. Holographic notes in which the informants are referred to by Georgia's FWP workers as "clients"—a nomenclature associated most closely with the history of the professionalization of welfare beginning in the late nineteenth century—also suggest that ex-slaves were viewed as objects of charity rather than oral history subjects. See, for example, the note appended to the narrative of Mary Colbert in Georgia. Rawick, *American Slave*, Georgia, II:12:1:213, informant Mary Colbert, field worker Sadie B. Hornsby, ed. Sarah H. Hall and John N. Booth, n.d. For more on gender, Jim Crow, and constructions of white womanhood, see Hale, *Making Whiteness*.

65. Rawick, *American Slave*, Georgia, II:12:1:58, informant Alice Battle, field worker Elizabeth Watson, 1936; longer version in Rawick, *American Slave*, Georgia, SSI:3:39–44, n.d.

66. Babcock, *Mammy*, 28.

67. Ibid., 27.

68. See, for example, Rawick, *American Slave*, Georgia, II:12:1 and 2, the narratives of informants Wheeler Gresham, Callie Elder, Julia Bunch, Fannie Jones, Jasper Battle, Georgia Baker, Mary Colbert, and Martha Colquitt. See also Rawick, *American Slave*,

II:12:1:81–83, informant Henry Bland, field worker Edwin Driskell, n.d.; Rawick, *American Slave*, Georgia, II:12:1:263, "Plantation Life as Viewed by an Ex-Slave," informant Minnie Davis, field worker Sadie B. Hornsby, ed. Sarah H. Hall and John N. Booth, [1938].

69. Informant Minnie Davis explained that "white folks didn't teach their slaves to read and write because it was against the law." Rawick, *American Slave*, Georgia, II:12:1:257, informant Minnie Davis, field worker Sadie B. Hornsby, ed. Sarah H. Hall and John N. Booth, [1938].

70. Rawick, *American Slave*, Georgia, II:12:2:354, informant Fannie Jones, field worker Emily Powell, ed. John Booth, September 1, 1938.

71. Rawick, *American Slave*, Georgia, II:12:1:87, informant Rias Body, field worker unknown, July 24, 1936. "Uncle" Dave also doubted "very seriously if the 'Niggers' were benefited by freedom," given that the slaves "were well-fed, given plenty of meat to eat, and furnished" with good shoes and clothes. Rawick, *American Slave*, Georgia, SSI:4:2:497, informants "Uncle" Dave and "Aunt" Lillian Ramsay, field worker J. R. Jones, July 1936.

72. Rawick, *American Slave*, Georgia, II:12:1:157, informant Julia Bunch, field worker Leila Harris, ed. John Booth, n.d.

73. Supplementary Instructions No. 9-E to the American Guide Manual, Folklore, Stories from Ex-Slaves, April 22, 1937. B. A. Botkin, "Answers to Questions," attachment to letter to Terry O'Neill, December 3, 1966, Botkin Corporate Subject File, AAFC-LC. Questions focused on these topics: Where were you born?; Overseers and slave patrols or "pattyrollers"; Work that the slaves did; Medical treatment for slaves; Food (fishing and hunting) and clothing and living quarters; Holidays like Christmas, Easter, and frolics; Churchgoing/religious training; Funerals; Slave sales/auctions; Runaways; Folk beliefs and superstitions; Slave punishment (including jails); Feelings about the war and freedom; Memories of the Yankees; Views on Lincoln and Davis (and sometimes Booker T. Washington); Ku Klux Klan; Courtship and marriage; and Life now.

74. One narrative that provides a rare glimpse into the uneasy dynamics of the interview process includes a comic rendering of the interviewer's struggles throughout to gain the upper hand in his encounter with ex-slave George Carter: "I have listened to lawyers ask leading questions; I must try that method. 'George,' I ask, 'wasn't Doctor Arnold good to you?'" Rawick, *American Slave*, Georgia, SSI:3:157, informant George Carter, n.d.

75. Two interviews from the Georgia collection that were not sent to the federal office are typed up in question and answer format, enabling a comparison to the questions provided by the federal office. One narrative in the supplemental series for Georgia, volume 3, and one in volume 4 are typed up as a list of numbered questions with the answers given by the ex-slave; they follow the content of the narratives written up without the questions. Rawick, *American Slave*, Georgia, SSI:3:1:118–30, informant Queen Elizabeth Bunts, n.d. (Question: "Did your master ever allow you any spending money?" Answer: "Yes."); Rawick, *American Slave*, Georgia, SSI:4:2:561–70, informant

Mary Jane Simmons, n.d. (Numbered question 37: "Did your master ever allow you any spending money?" Answer: "Yes.")

76. Rawick, *American Slave*, Georgia, SSI:4:2:456, informant Elsie Moreland, field worker Elizabeth Watson.

77. Rawick, *American Slave*, Georgia, II:12:1:107, informant Alec Bostwick, n.d.

78. Rawick, *American Slave*, Georgia, II:12:2:208, informant Laura Hood, September 23, 1936.

79. Rawick, *American Slave*, Georgia, II:12:1:113–17, informant Nancy Boudry, field worker Maude Barragan, n.d.

80. "When asked if he has been happier since he was freed, he replied: 'In a sense the niggers is better off since freedom come. Ol' Marster was good an' kind but I like to be free to go whar I please. . . . It ain't that I didn't love my Marster but I jest likes to be free.'" Library of Congress, American Memory, Born in Slavery, Georgia Narratives, Volume IV, Part 2, 293, informant Melvin Smith, field worker Elizabeth Watson, July 15, 1937, Library of Congress Manuscript Division, Digital Collection.

81. Rawick, *American Slave*, Georgia, SSI:4:2:551, informant Cora Shepherd, field worker Velma Bell, May 14, 1937.

82. Rawick, *American Slave*, Georgia, II:12:1:78–79, informant Arrie Binns, field worker Minnie Branham Stonestreet, n.d.

83. Rawick, *American Slave*, Georgia, II:12:1:223, 225, informant Mary Colbert, field worker Sadie Hornsby, n.d.

84. Rawick, *American Slave*, Georgia, II:12:1:140, informant Easter Brown, field worker Sadie Hornsby, n.d.

85. These are Houston A. Baker Jr.'s words used in his essay "To Move without Moving," 243.

86. Levine, *Black Culture and Black Consciousness*, 121.

87. Rawick, *American Slave*, Georgia, II:12:1:96, informant James Bolton, field worker Sarah H. Hall, n.d. This narrative of Bolton's is written by UDC member Sarah Hall and edited by Miss Maude Barragan. It has less phonetic spelling and interviewer's editorializing removed to make it all in the first person. The Bolton narrative in Rawick's supplemental series contains the same information; this one is also written and edited by Hall and dated September 10, 1937, and it includes the interviewer's description of informant. Rawick, *American Slave*, Georgia, SSI:3:1:76–90, informant James Bolton, field worker Sarah H. Hall, September 10, 1937.

88. Rawick, *American Slave*, Georgia, II:12:1:102–3, informant James Bolton, field worker Sarah H. Hall, n.d.

89. Ibid., 104.

90. Ibid., 96.

91. Library of Congress, American Memory, "Born in Slavery," Georgia Narratives, Volume IV, Part 2, 290, informant Melvin Smith, field worker Elizabeth Watson, July 15, 1937, Library of Congress Manuscript Division, Digital Collection.

92. Rawick, *American Slave*, Georgia, II:12:2:131, informant Tom Hawkins, field worker Sadie B. Hornsby, n.d.

93. Rawick, *American Slave*, Georgia, II:12:1:133, informant George Brooks, August 4, 1936.

94. Ibid.

95. Claudia Mitchell-Kernan, quoted in Gates, *Signifying Monkey*, 85.

96. Rawick, *American Slave*, Georgia, II:12:1:261, "Plantation Life as Viewed by an Ex-Slave," informant Minnie Davis, field worker Sadie B. Hornsby, ed. Sarah H. Hall and John N. Booth, [1938].

97. Ibid., 262.

98. Rawick, *American Slave*, Georgia, II:12:1:61, informant Jasper Battle, field worker Grace McCune, ed. Sarah H. Hall, Leila Harris, and John Booth, n.d.

99. Ibid., 62.

100. Ibid., 64.

101. Rawick, *American Slave*, Georgia, II:12:1:111, informant Alec Bostwick, n.d.

102. Rawick, *American Slave*, Georgia, II:12:1:329–30, informant "Aunt" Mary Ferguson, December 18, 1936.

103. Rawick, *American Slave*, Georgia, II:12:1:178–83, quote on page 182, informant Susan Castle, field worker Sadie B. Hornsby, ed. Sarah H. Hall and John Booth, n.d.

104. Rawick, *American Slave*, Georgia, II:12:1:264, informant Minnie Davis, field worker Sadie B. Hornsby, ed. Sarah H. Hall and John N. Booth, [1938].

105. Rawick, *American Slave*, Georgia, II:12:1:216, 218, 222, informant Mary Colbert, field worker Sadie B. Hornsby, ed. Sarah H. Hall and John N. Booth, n.d.

106. Ibid., 219.

107. There are some narratives submitted by black employees that do favor the first person and are written using dialect; see, for example, Rawick, *American Slave*, Georgia, II:12:1:28–31, informant Celestia Avery, field worker Minnie B. Ross, n.d.

108. See, for example, Ross's interviews with Hannah Austin, Sarah Gray, Camilla Jackson, and G. W. Patillo. Rawick, *American Slave*, Georgia, II:12:1 and 2, and also II:13:3.

109. Rawick, *American Slave*, Georgia, SSI:3:1:65–66, informant Sallie Blakely, field worker Minnie B. Ross, January 25, 1937.

110. Rawick, *American Slave*, Georgia, SSI:3:1:114, informant George Washington Browning, field worker Minnie B. Ross, January 25, 1937.

111. Ibid., 116–17. See also Berry Clay's narrative in which he describes persecution by the Ku Klux Klan and the Black Horse Cavalry but relates how a well-trained group of ex-slaves were successful in defending themselves, and killed a number of whites who tried to attack them. Rawick, *American Slave*, Georgia, II:12:1:193–94, informant Berry Clay, field worker Adella S. Dixon, n.d.

112. Rawick, *American Slave*, Georgia, II:12:2:49, informant Isaiah Green, field worker Minnie B. Ross, January 25, 1937.

113. Ibid., 51–53.

114. Ibid., 54–56.

115. See, for example, Minnie B. Ross's interviews with Hannah Austin, Sarah Gray, Camilla Jackson, and G. W. Patillo. Rawick, *American Slave*, Georgia, II:12:1 and 2, and also II:13:3.

116. Library of Congress, American Memory, "Born in Slavery," Georgia Narratives, Volume IV, Part 4, 191, 197–98, informant Henry Wright, field worker Edwin Driskell, n.d., Library of Congress Manuscript Division, Digital Collection.

117. Ibid., 201.

118. Rawick, *American Slave*, Georgia, II:12:1:197, informant Pierce Cody, field worker Adella S. Dixon, n.d.

119. Rawick, *American Slave*, Georgia, II:12:1:189–90, informant Berry Clay, field worker Adella S. Dixon, n.d.

120. Library of Congress, American Memory, "Born in Slavery," Georgia Narratives, Volume IV, Part 4, 200–201, informant Henry Wright, field worker Edwin Driskell, n.d., Library of Congress Manuscript Division, Digital Collection.

121. Ibid., 202. For another example of slaves' brutal punishment, see Rawick, *American Slave*, Georgia, II:12:2:11–14, informant Leah Garrett, field worker Louise Oliphant, ed. John N. Booth, n.d., and Louise Oliphant's "Compilation Richmond County Ex-Slave Interviews—Mistreatment of Slaves."

122. Library of Congress, American Memory, "Born in Slavery," Georgia Narratives, Volume IV, Part 4, 203, informant Henry Wright, field worker Edwin Driskell, n.d., Library of Congress Manuscript Division, Digital Collection.

123. Ibid., 196.

124. Rawick, *American Slave*, Georgia, II:12:1:58, informant Alice Battle, field worker Elizabeth Watson, 1936; Library of Congress, American Memory, "Born in Slavery," Georgia Narratives, Volume IV, Part 3, 196, informant Fanny Randolph, field worker Mattie Roberts, March 29, 1937, Library of Congress Manuscript Division, Digital Collection.

125. Library of Congress, American Memory, "Born in Slavery," Georgia Narratives, Volume IV, Part 4, 203, informant Henry Wright, field worker Edwin Driskell, n.d., Library of Congress Manuscript Division, Digital Collection; see also Rawick, *American Slave*, Georgia, II:12:1:192–93, informant Berry Clay, field worker Adella S. Dixon, n.d.

126. Library of Congress, American Memory, "Born in Slavery," Georgia Narratives, Volume IV, Part 2, 95, informant Milton Hammond, field worker Minnie B. Ross, January 25, 1937, Library of Congress Manuscript Division, Digital Collection.

127. Rawick, *American Slave*, Florida (Negro Writers' Unit), II:17:101, informant Ambrose Douglass, field worker Martin D. Richardson, n.d.

128. Ibid.

129. Benston, "I Yam What I Am," 153.

130. Rawick, *American Slave*, Florida (Negro Writers' Unit), II:17:286, informant William Sherman Jr., field worker James M. Johnson, ed. John A. Simms, August 28, 1936. Gates's theory of "signifyin(g)" as a black tradition based on "repetition and revision, or repetition with a signal difference" is applicable to William Sherman's act of renaming, for at the start of the narrative, field worker J. M. Johnson notes that Sherman is usually pronounced as "Schumann." See Gates, *Signifying Monkey*, 46.

131. Rawick, *American Slave*, Florida (Negro Writers' Unit), II:17:294, informant William Sherman Jr., field worker James M. Johnson, ed. John A. Simms, August 28, 1936.

132. John F. Marszalek, *Sherman: A Soldier's Passion for Order* (New York: Free Press, 1993), 270–71, 314–15. See also William L. Barney, "William Tecumseh Sherman," in Foner and Garraty, *Reader's Companion to American History*, 987–88.

133. Rawick, *American Slave*, Florida (Negro Writers' Unit), II:17:294–95, informant William Sherman Jr., field worker James M. Johnson, ed. John A. Simms, August 28, 1936.

134. Ibid., 296–97.

135. Frederick Douglass employs a similar play on names in "The Heroic Slave" when he evokes the image of George Washington, the statesman, to indirectly refer to his slave protagonist of the same name: the state of Virginia's other famous son. Stepto, "Storytelling in Early Afro-American Fiction," 180.

136. Ellison poignantly suggests the crucial interrelationship for African Americans between names and family histories of bloodlines in *Shadow and Act*, 148.

137. Hurston, "How It Feels to Be Colored Me," 826.

138. Rawick, *American Slave*, Florida (Negro Writers' Unit), II:17:28, informant Frank Berry, field worker Pearl Randolph, ed. John A. Simms, August 18, 1936.

139. Rawick, *American Slave*, Florida (Negro Writers' Unit), II:17:298, informant William Sherman Jr., field worker James M. Johnson, ed. John A. Simms, August 28, 1936. A Georgia narrative submitted by a black employee also draws this connection. See Rawick, *American Slave*, Georgia, II:12:1:194, informant Berry Clay, field worker Adella S. Dixon, n.d.

140. Rawick, *American Slave*, Florida (Negro Writers' Unit), II:17:179, informant Rev. Squires Jackson, field worker Samuel Johnson, September 11, 1937.

141. Rawick, *American Slave*, Florida, "Florida Folklore: Slave Customs and Anecdotes," II:17:36, informant Mary Minus Biddie, n.d.

142. Rawick, *American Slave*, Florida (Negro Writers' Unit), II:17:130, informants Sam and Louisa Everett, field worker Pearl Randolph, ed. John A. Simms, October 8, 1936.

143. This narrative provides ample evidence of the slaveholder's terrifying and barbarous behavior, including forcing sexual relations between slaves while he watched. The FWP interviewer, Pearl Randolph, framed their testimony with this statement regarding its veracity: "Sam and Louise [*sic*] Everett have weathered together some of the worst experiences of slavery, and as they look back over the years, can relate these experiences as clearly as if they had happened only yesterday." Ibid.

144. Rawick, *American Slave*, Florida (Negro Writers' Unit), II:17:122, informant Willis Dukes, field worker Pearl Randolph, January 20, 1937.

145. Rawick, *American Slave*, Florida (Negro Writers' Unit), II:17:297, informant William Sherman Jr., field worker James M. Johnson, ed. John A. Simms, August 28, 1936.

146. Keckley, *Behind the Scenes*, 54, 58–59; for an account of the capture of Davis, see Julian G. Dickinson, "The Capture of Jeff. Davis," in Military Order of the Loyal Legion of the United States (MOLLUS), Michigan Commandery, War Papers (Detroit, Mich.: Ostler Print Co., [1889]), transcribed for MOLLUS Internet Published War Papers, http://suvcw.org/mollus/warpapers/MIv1p179.htm (July 29, 2014); description and unsigned cartoon from *Harper's Weekly*, May 27, 1865, HarpWeek,

http://www.harpweek.com/09Cartoon/BrowseByDateCartoon.asp?Month=May
&Date=27 (July 29, 2014).

147. Rawick, *American Slave*, Florida, "Dade County, Florida Ex-Slave Stories," II:17:372–73, informant Salena Taswell, June 30, 1938.

148. Rawick, *American Slave*, Florida, "Florida Folklore: Slave Customs and Anecdotes," II:17:36, informant Mary Minus Biddie, n.d.

149. Jacobs, chap. 21 of *Incidents in the Life of a Slave Girl*, 114–17.

Epilogue

1. Rawick, *American Slave*, Florida (Negro Writers' Unit), II:17:184, informant "Prophet" John Henry Kemp, field worker L. Rebecca Baker, January 11, 1937.

2. Many scholars have discussed the possible impact of the informants' age (as children during slavery and elderly citizens asked to recall early memories). See Charles T. Davis and Gates, *Slave's Narrative*.

3. See, for example, "Slaves Reunion. Annie Parram, Age, 104; Anna Angales, Age 105; Elizabeth Berkeley, 125; Sadie Thompson, 110," photograph, Harris & Ewing, 1917, Prints and Photographs Division, Library of Congress, http://www.loc.gov/pictures/item/hec2008001617 (August 15, 2014).

4. Favor, *Authentic Blackness*, 3.

5. Benston, "I Yam What I Am," 153. In Polk County, Hurston was politely asked for her "entrimmins" and her "entitlum"; Hurston, *Mules and Men*, 63.

6. As Paul Gilroy observes regarding black cultural production in the nineteenth century, "the particular styles of autobiographical self-dramatization and public self-construction [could be] formed and circulated as an integral component of insubordinate racial countercultures." Gilroy, *Black Atlantic*, 200.

7. My knowledge of Scott's work comes from Robin Kelley's application of the concept of infrapolitics to his study of the black working class. See Kelley, *Race Rebels*, 1–13.

8. Scott, *Domination and the Arts of Resistance*, 183.

9. Kelley, *Freedom Dreams*, 1.

10. J. D. Newsom, Director, WPA Writers' Program, "Project Reservoir Plan: The Social Contribution of the WPA Writers' Program to American Democracy," April 12, 1941, A9, Folder "Proposals," LC; Florence Kerr, New Release "WPA Writers Map Interesting Program for Coming Months," Federal Works Agency, Work Projects Administration, August 30, 1941, A994, Folder "Publicity—Press Releases, 1936–42," LC; "Fourteen Selected Book Projects of a Regional or National Scope," Part III "USA—A Democracy Looks at Itself: A Book Designed for Circulation in Latin America," Entry 27, Box 1, File "B. Botkin," RG 69.

11. Hirsch, *Portrait of America*, 198.

12. Penkower, *Federal Writers' Project*, 202.

13. "Alsberg Ousted as Director of Writers Project," *New York Herald Tribune*, August 10, 1939, copy in Records of the NAACP, Series I, C Administrative File, Box 286,

Folder "June–Dec. 1939," MD-LC. Harrington had replaced Harry Hopkins when Hopkins, on the advice of Roosevelt, left to become secretary of commerce in order to improve a bid for the presidency; see Penkower, *Federal Writers' Project*, 202. NAACP executive secretary Walter White sent Alsberg a short but personal note of condolence, expressing his profound regret that Alsberg would no longer be associated with the FWP, asking whether there was anything "any of your friends can do?" and reminding him to take pride in the fact that the "material which has been dug up under your direction concerning American history is going to loom larger and larger in importance as the years and decades go by." Walter White to Henry Alsberg, August 10, 1939, Records of the NAACP, Series I, C Administrative File, Box 286, Folder "June–Dec. 1939," MD-LC.

14. Penkower, *Federal Writers' Project*, 197.

15. For details on the specifics of Wisconsin Republican representative Frank Keefe's objections, Brown's response to the charges, and the subsequent FBI investigation, see ibid., 203–5.

16. For a discussion of Brown's essay, see Gabbin, *Sterling A. Brown*, 81–82.

17. Memorandum from White to Marshall, April 3, 1939, referring to letter from C. T. Williams of March 28, and Memorandum from Marshall to White, April 13, 1939, Records of the NAACP, Series I, C Administrative File, Box 286, Folder "June–Dec. 1939," MD-LC.

18. Sterling Brown to Walter White, January 14, 1939, Records of the NAACP, Series I, C Administrative File, Box 286, Folder "WPA Jan.–May 1939," MD-LC.

19. Ibid. Brown lists the number of FWP publications as 160.

20. See Walter White to Brown, January 16, 1939, assuring Brown that he will be sending out a press release and also notifying all NAACP branches as well as other organizations and leaders of the crisis, Records of the NAACP, Series I, C Administrative File, Box 286, Folder "WPA, Jan–May 1939," MD-LC.

21. White to Hon. Edward T. Taylor, Chairman, House Appropriations Committee, May 17, 1939, Records of the NAACP, Series I, C Administrative File, Box 286, Folder "WPA, Jan–May 1939," MD-LC.

22. Writers' Program of the Work Projects Administration in the State of Virginia, *Negro in Virginia*.

23. Slaves were only either referred to in these histories as part of the financial assets of the plantation or identified along with emancipation as the reason for economic decline. All the plantations were located in Chatham County, Georgia. See, for example, Savannah Unit, Georgia Writers' Project, "Colerain Plantation," *Georgia Historical Quarterly* 24 (1940): 343–73; 25 (1941): 35–66, 120–40, 225–43; "Richmond Oakgrove Plantation," *Georgia Historical Quarterly* 24 (1940): 22–42, 124–44; "Drakies Plantation," *Georgia Historical Quarterly* 24 (1940): 207–35; "Whitehall Plantation," *Georgia Historical Quarterly* 25 (1941): 341–63; 26 (1942): 40–64, 129–55.

24. Manuscript Studies of Negro Survival Types in Coastal Georgia, Entry 27 "Records and Misc. Pertaining to Negro Studies," Box 2, File "Savannah, GA Unit," RG 69.

25. "Introduction to Interviews," Manuscript Studies of Negro Survival Types in Coastal Georgia, Entry 27 "Records and Misc. Pertaining to Negro Studies," Box 2, File "Savannah, GA Unit," RG 69.

26. Sterling Brown to District Supervisor Mary Granger, February 24, 1938, Entry 27, Box 2, File "Georgia," RG 69; W. O. Brown, Critique of "Study of Negro Survival Types in Coastal Georgia," to Sterling Brown, Entry 27, Box 2, File "Georgia," 1, RG 69; E. Franklin Frazier, Critique of "Study of Negro Survival Types in Coastal Georgia," to Sterling Brown, February 1, 1938, Entry 27, Box 2, File "Georgia," 1, RG 69; Memorandum from Henry Alsberg to Sterling Brown, Re: "Studies of the Negro Survival Types in Coastal Africa," February 16, 1938, Entry 27, Box 2, File "Georgia," RG 69.

27. Samuel Tupper Jr., to WPA Writers' Program Director, J. D. Newsom, September 22, 1939, Entry 27, Box 2, File "Georgia," RG 69.

28. Sterling Brown, "Synthesis of the Three Memoranda" on "Georgia, Drums and Shadows," April 4, 1940, Entry 27, Box 2, File "Drums and Shadows," RG 69.

29. WPA job classification form for Brown, March 6, 1940, Entry 32, Box 3 "Records of the Library of Congress Writers' Unit, 1939–1941," File "Personnel File: Sterling Brown," RG 69.

30. Memorandum from Sterling A. Brown, Editorial Supervisor, Negro Studies, to Dr. B. A. Botkin, Chief Editor, Writers' Unit, April 11, 1940, Entry 32, Box 3 "Records of the Library of Congress Writers' Unit, 1939–1941," File "Personnel File: Sterling Brown," RG 69.

31. Ibid.

32. Gary Mormino asserts that the Slave Narrative Collection consists of 2,358 interviews, compiled from seventeen states, between 1936 and 1938. Mormino, "Florida Slave Narratives," 405.

33. This means the collection reproduced by Rawick as *The American Slave* (and available online through the Library of Congress website) is uneven, as Sterling Brown also noted in an interview. Brown asserts, for example, that Roscoe Lewis, who directed the NWU of Virginia, did not submit the ex-slave narratives to Washington. Rowell, " 'Let Me Be with Ole Jazzbo,' " 301.

34. Hirsch, "Folklore in the Making," 13.

35. Benjamin A. Botkin, "The Folk and the Individual: Their Creative Reciprocity," *English Journal* 27 (1938): 132.

36. Benjamin A. Botkin, May 22, 1941, Entry 21, Box 1, File "Ex-Slaves Correspondence," 5, RG 69.

37. Ibid.

38. Benjamin A. Botkin, "Criteria for Slave Narratives," December 16, 1940, Entry 21, Box 1, File "Ex-Slave Correspondence," RG 69.

39. Ibid., 1–2.

40. Memorandum from Botkin's assistant, Mrs. Wharton, to Miss Prager, "Appraisal of Manuscript 230023," November 15, 1940, Entry 21, Box 1, File "Misc.," RG 69.

41. Botkin to Florida State Director Carita Doggett Corse, February 17, 1939, referred to by Jules Frost on Form A "Circumstances of Interview," sent with his second submission, Rawick, *American Slave*, Florida, II:17:114.

42. Ibid.; see also Rawick, *American Slave*, Florida, II:17:116–19, informant Mama Duck, field worker Jules A. Frost, interviewed March 19, 1937, rewritten March 15, 1939.

43. Memorandum from Wharton to Botkin, "Comments on the Slave Narratives," February 25, 1941, Entry 21, Box 1, File "Ex-Slaves Correspondence," RG 69.

44. Ibid.

45. See appraisals of Florida narratives by J. C. Rogers: October 19, 1940; December 11, 1940; December 12, 1940; December 13, 1940; anonymous October 11, 1940, A897, "Florida—Appraisal Sheets, B–W," FWP-LC.

46. Ibid.

47. See, for example, Appraiser G. Roberts, February 7, 1941, A897, File "Georgia—Appraisal Sheets, B–W," FWP-LC.

48. Most of the appraisal sheet responses to interviews written up in the third person without the incorporation of dialect were recommended for deposit into the archives as reference material only and not recommended for publishing purposes.

49. See, for example, G. B. Roberts, Appraisal, January 27, 1941, A897, File "Georgia—Appraisal Sheets, B–W," FWP-LC.

50. G. Roberts, Appraisal, February 12, 1941, A897, File "Georgia—Appraisal Sheets, B–W," FWP-LC.

51. H. B., Appraisal, February 18, 1941, A891, "Slave Narrative Project—Alabama," File "Alabama—Appraisal Sheets, J–Y," FWP-LC.

52. C. H. Wetmore, Appraisal, January 24, 1941, A891, "Slave Narratives Project—Alabama," File "Alabama—Appraisal Sheets, J–Y," FWP-LC.

53. C. H. Wetmore, Appraisal, January 13, 1941, A891, "Slave Narratives Project—Alabama," File "Alabama—Appraisal Sheets, J–Y," FWP-LC.

54. See, for example, Musher, "Contesting 'the Way the Almighty Wants It,' " 12.

55. H. B., Appraisal, February 12, 1941, A891, "Slave Narratives Project—Alabama," File "Alabama—Appraisal Sheets, J–Y," FWP-LC.

56. C. H. Wetmore, Appraisal, January 21, 1941, A891, "Slave Narrative Project—Alabama," File "Alabama—Appraisal Sheets, J–Y," FWP-LC.

57. H. B., Appraisal, February 8, 1941, A891, "Slave Narrative Project—Alabama," File "Alabama—Appraisal Sheets, J–Y," FWP-LC.

58. H. B., Appraisal, February 10, 1941, A891, "Slave Narrative Project—Alabama," File "Alabama—Appraisal Sheets, J–Y," FWP-LC.

59. C. H. Wetmore, Appraisal, January 22, 1941, A891, "Slave Narrative Project—Alabama," File "Alabama—Appraisal Sheets, J–Y," FWP-LC.

60. Memorandum from Henry Bennett to Mrs. Wharton, "Ex-Slave Narratives," February 21, 1941, Entry 21, Box 1, File "Ex-Slaves Correspondence," RG 69.

61. G. Roberts, Appraisal Sheet, Georgia, January 28, 1941, A897, File "GA—Appraisal Sheets," FWP-LC. For a critique of representations of African Americans found in Shirley Temple films like *The Little Colonel*, see Snead, *White Screens/Black Images*.

62. C. H. Wetmore, Appraisal February 12, 1941, A891, "Slave Narrative Project—Alabama," File "Alabama—Appraisal Sheets, J–Y," FWP-LC.

63. Botkin, *Lay My Burden Down.*

64. Joseph Liss, Radio Research Project, Part II: "Details of Execution of Programs," 1941–42, Radio Research Project manuscript collection, Recorded Sound Reference Center, Music Division, LC.

65. "Hidden History Series: Library of Congress Radio Research Project," Book No. 4, Recorded Sound Reference Center, LC.

66. "Underground Railroad," Program VIII, July 6, 1941, 4, NBC-Blue Network, Radio Research Project, Recorded Sound Reference Center, Music Division, LC.

67. "The Ballad Hunter: John A. Lomax," government leaflet, Federal Radio Education Committee, May 1941, Radio Research Project, Recorded Sound Reference Center, Music Division, LC.

68. Ibid.

69. "Americans Talk Back: Library of Congress Radio Research Project," publicity flyer, Radio Research Project, Recorded Sound Reference Center, Music Division, LC.

70. Memorandum from Harold Spivacke, Chief, Division of Music, Library of Congress, to Dr. Evans, February 25, 1942, Radio Research Project, Recorded Sound Reference Center, Music Division, Library of Congress.

71. Memorandum from Spivacke to Acting Librarian of Congress, May 8, 1942, Radio Research Project, Recorded Sound Reference Center, Music Division, Library of Congress.

72. See letters to the Music Division, Radio Research Project File, Recorded Sound Reference Center, LC.

73. Paramount paid her $100 a week, making it the highest weekly salary Hurston had ever received. Boyd, *Wrapped in Rainbows,* 348–50. For earlier references to Hurston's work in Hollywood, see Marion Kilson, "Transformation of Eatonville's Ethnographer," 112n. Kilson mentions that Hurston "was technical director for a film on Haiti at Paramount Studios" in the spring of 1942. Hemenway also mentions in passing Hurston's time in Hollywood, claiming she worked as a story consultant for Paramount, in *Zora Neale Hurston,* 276.

74. There are many striking similarities between Hurston's descriptions and the film's depictions. For example, much of the terminology, such as "Hounfort" and "Houngan," is virtually the same. More significantly, the zombie guard that appears at the crossroads in the film's celebrated night-walk scene is named Carrefour, the same name as the "Lord of the Crossroads," Maitre Carrefour, that appears in Hurston's description of a Haitian cannibalistic voodoo sect in *Tell My Horse.* For a description of Maitre Carrefour and his role in the Haitian secret society the Sect Rouge, see Hurston, *Tell My Horse,* 211–13. Bansak speculates that the movie's producer and director, Val Lewton and Jacques Tourneur, may have chosen the name Carrefour as a tribute to Renoir's film, *La Nuit de Carrefour* (1932); see Bansak, *Fearing the Dark,* 159.

75. As Hurston recalled on the show: "I'd been out in Hollywood and Ardel hired me after she read my book, *Tell My Horse*"; Mary Margaret McBride, interview with Hurston on WFAF, January 25, 1943, Part IV, MPBRS-LC. Although Hurston severed her connection with Hollywood several months before the film went into production, the studio hired as technical advisor another ethnographer, LeRoy Antoine, a prominent scholar in the field of Haiti and Haitian folk music, and publicized his involvement in the *Hollywood Reporter*. Hurston has yet to receive credit for her contribution to this Hollywood horror classic; instead, the studio, along with the leading contributors to the film, claimed that the movie was based on a "nonfiction" article of the same name written by a Hearst journalist, Inez Wallace. Bansak, *Fearing the Dark*, 146–47.

76. Hurston died on January 28, 1960, and was buried in an unmarked grave in the segregated Garden of Heavenly Rest, in Fort Pierce, Florida, with no headstone, until, in Conjure Queen fashion, her work and literary reputation were resurrected by Alice Walker, who also provided a formal and fitting epitaph in the cemetery where Hurston was buried; her headstone reads simply, "A Genius of the South."

77. My thoughts on the multivalent constructions of black identity have been greatly helped by Favor's insightful study, *Authentic Blackness*, 2.

78. Singh, *Black Is a Country*; Sullivan, *Days of Hope*; and Jacquelyn Dowd Hall, "The Long Civil Rights Movement and the Political Uses of the Past."

79. Ferguson, *Black Politics in New Deal Atlanta*, 268.

80. See Gerstle, *American Crucible*, 162–63. See also Lipsitz, *Possessive Investment in Whiteness*. Roosevelt's decision to not publicly support the anti-lynching bill was for politically expedient reasons; he was justly afraid that white southerners in key positions on the Senate and House committees would retaliate by blocking every other bill he put forth. Jensen, "The Rise of an African American Left," 433–34.

81. Gerstle, *American Crucible*; see chap. 4, "The Rooseveltian Nation Ascendant, 1930–40," 128–86.

82. Roediger, "A New Deal, an Industrial Union, and a White House: What the New Immigrant Got Into," in *Working toward Whiteness*, 199–234.

83. Singh, *Black Is a Country*, 87.

84. The 1930 census listing the number of African Americans in Florida by occupation clearly shows "servants" as the second largest category of employment (31,325), only slightly behind farm laborers (33,752). "Negro Occupations Florida (1930), U.S. Bureau of Census (1935)," Appendix 3b in Antoinette T. Jackson and Allan F. Burns, "Ethnohistorical Study of the Kingsley Plantation," 80.

85. "I Managed to Carry On," Eugenia Martin, WPA Worker–Housekeeping Aide, November 1939, Box A713, "Folklore Project, Life Histories, 1936–40," File "Georgia-Geneva Tonsill," FWP-LC.

86. Nina Silber, reader report, November 12, 2014, University of North Carolina Press.

87. W. E. B. Du Bois, "Segregation in the North," 115.

88. The use of the past as a tool mobilized for anti-pluralistic and reactionary political agendas by competing interests also resonates in current debates over how U.S. history should be taught and the attempts of school boards in states like Texas, Arizona,

and Colorado to erase ideologically inconvenient historical facts from school text-books and curricula. For a discussion of the so-called history wars that surfaced in the 1990s over the History Standard Acts, see, for example, Gary B. Nash, Charlotte Crabtree, and Ross E. Dunn, *History on Trial: Culture Wars and the Teaching of the Past* (New York: Vintage Books, 2000); "Texas Approves Disputed History Texts for Schools," *New York Times*, November 23, 2014, A22. For histories of the Enola Gay controversy, see Richard H. Kohn, "History and the Culture Wars: The Case of the Smithsonian Institution's Enola Gay Exhibition," *Journal of American History* 82, no. 3 (December 1995): 1036–63; and Wallace, *Mickey Mouse History*.

89. "How did you get to be housemaid for such a distinguished Founding Father?" a visitor asks. "Did you read the advertisement in the newspaper?" "Why, yes," Lizzie Mae responds sweetly. "It said: 'Wanted. One housemaid. No pay. Preferably mulatto, saucy, with breedin' hips. Must work 18 hours a day, seven days a week, no holidays.'" *Ask a Slave*, season 1, episode 1, "Meet Lizzie Mae," September 2, 2013, http://www.askaslave.com/season-one.html (July 29, 2014).

Bibliography

Manuscript Collections

College Park, Maryland
  National Archives Regional Office
    RG 69, Records of the Work Projects Administration
Gainesville, Florida
  P. K. Yonge Library of Florida History, Department of Special and Area Studies
    Collections, George A. Smathers Libraries, University of Florida
    Marjorie Kinnan Rawlings Papers
    Stetson Kennedy Papers (consulted at Beluthahatchee)
    Zora Neale Hurston Papers
Iowa City, Iowa
  Special Collections Department, University of Iowa Libraries
    Redpath Chautauqua Bureau Collection
Jacksonville, Florida
  Special Collections, Carl S. Swisher Library, Jacksonville University
    Florida Writers' Project, Papers of Dr. Carita Doggett Corse
New Haven, Connecticut
  Beinecke Rare Book and Manuscript Library, Yale Collection of American
    Literature
    Langston Hughes Correspondence, James Weldon Johnson Collection
New York, New York
  Schomburg Center for Research in Black Culture
Richmond, Virginia
  Eleanor S. Brockenbrough Library, Museum of the Confederacy
    United Daughters of the Confederacy Collection
Tampa, Florida
  Special Collections, University of South Florida Libraries
    Florida Negro Papers and WPA Collection
Washington, D.C.
  Library of Congress
    Archives of the American Folklife Center
      Herbert Halpert 1939 Southern States Recording Expedition
      John A. Lomax and Alan Lomax Papers, 1932–42
      John and Ruby Lomax 1939 Southern States Recording Trip
      Mary Elizabeth Barnicle and Tillman Cadle Interview
      Vertical Files: Benjamin Botkin, John A. Lomax, Zora Neale Hurston

Manuscript Division
   Carter G. Woodson Papers
   Countee Cullen Papers
   Franz Boas Papers
   Lawrence Spivak Papers
   Margaret Mead Papers
   National Association for the Advancement of Colored People Records
   U.S. Work Projects Administration Federal Writers' Project
Motion Picture, Broadcasting and Recorded Sound Division
   Margaret Mead Collection
   Mary Margaret Mcbride Show
   Radio Research Project, 1940–46

Oral History Interview

Stetson Kennedy. Interview by Catherine A. Stewart at his home, Beluthahatchee, in St. Johns, Florida, October 2005.

Online Resources

Both print materials and audio recordings pertaining to the Work Projects Administration collections are available online at the Library of Congress American Memory website, http://memory.loc.gov/ammem/. For the slave narratives from the Federal Writers' Project, photos, and recorded interviews with ex-slaves, see "Born in Slavery: Slave Narratives from the Federal Writers' Project, 1936–1938," http://memory.loc.gov /ammem/snhtml/; for folk song and folklife recordings made by John and Alan Lomax, Herbert Halpert, and Zora Neale Hurston, see "Florida Folklife from the WPA Collections, 1937–1942," http://memory.loc.gov/ammem/collections/florida/index .html (that includes a short clip of Florida state director Carita Doggett Corse: http: //hdl.loc.gov/loc.afc/afcflwpa.3140a2), and "Southern Mosaic: The John and Ruby Lomax 1939 Southern States Recording Trip," http://memory.loc.gov/ammem/lohtml /lohome.html.

Works Cited

Andrews, William. *To Tell a Free Story*. Urbana: University of Illinois Press, 1986.
Babcock, Bernie. *Mammy: A Drama*. New York: Neale, 1915.
Baker, Ella, and Marvel Cooke. "The Bronx Slave Market." *Crisis* 42 (November 1935): 330–31, 340.
Baker, Houston A., Jr. *Critical Memory: Public Spheres, African American Writing, and Black Fathers and Sons in America*. Athens: University of Georgia Press, 2001.
———. *Modernism and the Harlem Renaissance*. Chicago: University of Chicago Press, 1987.

———. "To Move without Moving: An Analysis of Creativity and Commerce in Ralph Ellison's Trueblood Episode." *PMLA* 98 (October 1983): 828–45. Reprinted in Gates, *Black Literature and Literary Theory*, 221–48.

Baker, T. Lindsay, and Julie P. Baker, eds. *The WPA Oklahoma Slave Narratives.* Norman: University of Oklahoma Press, 1996.

Baldwin, Davarian L. *Chicago's New Negroes: Modernity, the Great Migration, and Black Urban Life.* Chapel Hill: University of North Carolina Press, 2007.

Bansak, Edmund G. *Fearing the Dark: The Val Lewton Career.* Jefferson, N.C.: McFarland, 1995.

Beckwith, Martha. "National Folk Festival, Washington." *Journal of American Folklore* 51 (1938): 442–43.

Bederman, Gail. *Manliness and Civilization: A Cultural History of Gender and Race in the United States, 1880–1917.* Chicago: University of Chicago Press, 1995.

Bell, Muriel Barrow, and Malcolm Bell Jr. "Photographers' Note." In *Drums and Shadows*, xxix–xxxi. Page references are to the revised edition.

Bendix, Regina. *In Search of Authenticity: The Formation of Folklore Studies.* Madison: University of Wisconsin Press, 1997.

Benston, Kimberly W. "I Yam What I Am: The Topos of Un(naming) in Afro-American Literature." In Gates, *Black Literature and Literary Theory*, 151–72.

Black Public Sphere Collective, ed. *The Black Public Sphere: A Public Culture Book.* Chicago: University of Chicago Press, 1995.

Blassingame, John W. *The Slave Community: Plantation Life in the Antebellum South.* New York: Oxford University Press, 1972.

———. "Using the Testimony of Ex-Slaves: Approaches and Problems." *Journal of Southern History* 41 (November 1975): 474–92.

Blight, David W. *Beyond the Battlefield: Race, Memory, and the American Civil War.* Amherst: University of Massachusetts Press, 2002.

———. *Race and Reunion: The Civil War in American Memory.* Cambridge, Mass.: Harvard University Press, 2001.

———. "W. E. B. DuBois and the Struggle for American Historical Memory." In Fabre and O'Meally, *History and Memory in African American Culture*, 45–71.

Bold, Christine. *The WPA Guides: Mapping America.* Jackson: University Press of Mississippi, 1999.

Bontemps, Arna. "Famous WPA Authors." *Negro Digest* 8 (June 1950): 43–47.

Bordelon, Pamela, ed. *Go Gator and Muddy the Water: Writings by Zora Neale Hurston from the Federal Writers' Project.* New York: W. W. Norton, 1999.

Botkin, B. A., ed. *Lay My Burden Down: A Folk History of Slavery.* Chicago: University of Chicago Press, 1945.

Boyd, Valerie. *Wrapped in Rainbows: The Life of Zora Neale Hurston.* New York: Scribner, 2003.

Brown, Elsa Barkley. "Negotiating and Transforming the Public Sphere: African American Political Life in the Transition from Slavery to Freedom." In Black Public Sphere Collective, *The Black Public Sphere*, 111–50.

Brown, Sterling A. "The Negro Character as Seen by White Authors." *Journal of Negro Education* 2 (April 1933): 179–203.

———. "Negro Folk Expression: Spirituals, Seculars, Ballads and Work Songs." *Phylon* 14 (Winter 1953): 45–61.

———. *The Negro in American Fiction, Negro Poetry and Drama.* New York: Arno Press, 1969. First published 1937.

———. "Notes by an Editor on Dialect Usage in Accounts by Interviews with Ex-Slaves." In *The American Slave: A Composite Autobiography*, Vol. 1, *From Sundown to Sunup*, edited by George P. Rawick, 176–78. Westport, Conn.: Greenwood Press, 1972.

Brown, Sterling A., Arthur Davis, and Ulysses Lee, eds. *The Negro Caravan: Writings by American Negroes.* New York: Dryden Press, 1941.

Brundage, W. Fitzhugh, ed. *Where These Memories Grow: History, Memory, and Southern Identity.* Chapel Hill: University of North Carolina Press, 2000.

Butler, Judith. "Performativity's Social Magic." In *Bourdieu: A Critical Reader*, edited by Richard Shusterman, 123–24. Malden, Mass.: Blackwell, 1999.

Cade, John B. "Out of the Mouths of Ex-Slaves." *Journal of Negro History* 20 (July 1935): 294–337.

Cantwell, Robert. "Feasts of Unnaming: Folk Festivals and the Representation of Folklife." In *Public Folklore*, edited by Robert Baron and Nick Spitzer, 263–305. Washington, D.C.: Smithsonian Institution Press, 1992.

Carby, Hazel V. *Race Men.* Cambridge, Mass.: Harvard University Press, 1998.

Chadwick, Bruce. *The Reel Civil War: Mythmaking in American Film.* New York: Alfred A. Knopf, 2001.

Clifford, James. *The Predicament of Culture: Twentieth-Century Ethnography, Literature, and Art.* Cambridge, Mass.: Harvard University Press, 1988.

Cohen, Lizabeth. "Encountering Mass Culture at the Grassroots: The Experience of Chicago Workers in the 1920s." *American Quarterly* 41, no. 1 (March 1989): 6–33.

———. *Making a New Deal: Industrial Workers in Chicago, 1919–1939.* Cambridge: Cambridge University Press, 1990.

Cook, Robert J. *Troubled Commemoration: The American Civil War Centennial, 1961–1965.* Baton Rouge: Louisiana State University Press, 2007.

Cook, Walter Henry. "Secret Political Societies in the South during the Period of Reconstruction." *Southern Magazine* 3, no. 1 (July 1936): 3–5, 42–43; no. 2 (August–September 1936): 14–17.

Cox, Karen. *Dixie's Daughters: The United Daughters of the Confederacy and the Preservation of Confederate Culture.* Gainesville: University Press of Florida, 2003.

Cripps, Thomas. *Slow Fade to Black: The Negro in American Film, 1900–1942.* New York: Oxford University Press, 1977.

Cullen, Countee. Review of *Uncle Tom's Children*. *African* (April 1938): 2.

Cullen, Jim. *The Civil War in Popular Culture: A Reuseable Past.* Washington, D.C.: Smithsonian Institution Press, 1995.

Davidson, James West, and Mark Hamilton Lytle. "The View from the Bottom Rail."
In *After the Fact: The Art of Historical Detection*, 187–88. New York: Knopf, 1982.

Davis, Allison, Burleigh B. Gardner, and Mary R. Gardner. *Deep South: A Social Anthropological Study of Caste and Class*. Chicago: University of Chicago Press, 1941.

Davis, Angela Y. *Blues Legacies and Black Feminism: Gertrude "Ma" Rainey, Bessie Smith, and Billie Holiday*. New York: Pantheon Books, 1998.

Davis, Charles T., and Henry Louis Gates Jr., eds. *The Slave's Narrative*. New York: Oxford University Press, 1985.

Davis, John P. "A Black Inventory of the New Deal." *Crisis* 42 (May 1935): 141–42, 154.

Day, Donald. "John Lomax and His Ten Thousand Songs: Symphonies and Operas Come from the Life of the People." *Saturday Review of Literature*, September 22, 1945, 5.

Denning, Michael. *The Cultural Front: The Laboring of American Culture in the Twentieth Century*. New York: Verso, 1996.

Dolinar, Brian. *The Black Cultural Front: Black Writers and Artists of the Depression Generation*. Jackson: University Press of Mississippi, 2012.

———, ed. *The Negro in Illinois: The WPA Papers*. Urbana: University of Illinois Press, 2013.

Douglass, Frederick. *Narrative of the Life of Frederick Douglass, an American Slave*. 1845. Reprinted in *The Classic Slave Narratives*, edited by Henry Louis Gates Jr., 323–436. New York: Signet Classic/New American Library, 1987.

Drake, St. Clair, and Horace R. Cayton. *Black Metropolis: A Study of Negro Life in a Northern City*. New York: Harcourt, Brace, 1945.

Drums and Shadows: Survival Stories among the Georgia Coastal Negroes. Savannah Unit, Georgia Writers' Project, Work Projects Administration. Athens: University of Georgia Press, 1940; revised 1986.

Du Bois, W. E. B. "Criteria of Negro Art." *Crisis* 32 (October 1926): 290–97.

———. "Segregation in the North." *Crisis* 41 (April 1934): 115–17.

Elkins, Stanley M. *Slavery: A Problem in American Institutional and Intellectual Life*. 2nd ed. Chicago: University of Chicago Press, 1968.

Ellison, Ralph. *Shadow and Act*. New York: Random House, 1964.

Ely, Melvin Patrick. *The Adventures of Amos 'n' Andy: A Social History of an American Phenomenon*. New York: Free Press, 1991.

Escott, Paul D. "The Art and Science of Reading WPA Slave Narratives." In Charles T. Davis and Gates, *The Slave's Narrative*, 40–48.

———. *Slavery Remembered: A Record of Twentieth-Century Slave Narratives*. Chapel Hill: University of North Carolina Press, 1979.

Fabre, Geneviève, and Robert G. O'Meally, eds. *History and Memory in African-American Culture*. New York: Oxford University Press, 1994.

Fahs, Alice, and Joan Waugh, eds. *The Memory of the Civil War in American Culture*. Chapel Hill: University of North Carolina Press, 2004.

Fauset, Arthur Huff. "American Negro Folk Literature." In Locke, *The New Negro*, 240–41.

Favor, J. Martin. *Authentic Blackness: The Folk in the New Negro Renaissance.* Durham, N.C.: Duke University Press, 1999.

Ferguson, Karen. *Black Politics in New Deal Atlanta.* Chapel Hill: University of North Carolina Press, 2002.

"Fiftieth Annual Meeting of the American Folklore Society." *Journal of American Folklore* 52 (1939): 209–12.

Filene, Benjamin. *Romancing the Folk: Public Memory and American Roots Music.* Chapel Hill: University of North Carolina Press, 2000.

Fishkin, Shelley Fisher. *Was Huck Black? Mark Twain and African-American Voices.* New York: Oxford University Press, 1993.

Foner, Eric, and John A. Garraty, eds. *The Reader's Companion to American History.* Boston: Houghton-Mifflin, 1991.

"Forty-Ninth Annual Meeting of the American Folk-Lore Society." *Journal of American Folklore* 51 (1938): 102–5.

Foster, Frances Smith. "Historical Introduction." In Keckley, *Behind the Scenes,* ix–xxxiii.

———. *Witnessing Slavery: The Development of Ante-Bellum Slave Narratives.* 2nd ed. Madison: University of Wisconsin Press, 1994.

Fraden, Rena. *Blueprints for a Black Federal Theatre, 1935–1939.* Cambridge: Cambridge University Press, 1994.

Frazier, E. Franklin. *The Negro Family in the United States.* Chicago: University of Chicago Press, 1939.

Fry, Gladys-Marie. *Night Riders in Black Folk History.* Knoxville: University of Tennessee Press, 1975.

Gabbin, Joanne V. *Sterling A. Brown: Building the Black Aesthetic Tradition.* Westport, Conn.: Greenwood Press, 1985.

Gaines, Kevin Kelly. *Uplifting the Race: Black Leadership, Politics, and Culture in the Twentieth Century.* Chapel Hill: University of North Carolina Press, 1996.

Gates, Henry Louis, Jr., ed. *Black Literature and Literary Theory.* New York: Routledge, 1990.

———. "Dis and Dat: Dialect and the Descent." In *Figures in Black: Words, Signs, and the "Racial" Self,* 167–95. New York: Oxford University Press, 1987.

———. "The Signifying Monkey and the Language of Signifyin(g)," in *The Henry Louis Gates, Jr. Reader,* edited by Abby Wolf, 234–286. New York: Basic Civitas, 2012.

———. *The Signifying Monkey: A Theory of Afro-American Literary Criticism.* New York: Oxford University Press, 1988.

———. "The Trope of a New Negro and the Reconstruction of the Image of the Black." *Representations* 24 (Fall 1988): 129–55.

Genovese, Eugene D. *Roll, Jordan, Roll: The World the Slaves Made.* New York: Pantheon Books, 1974.

Gerstle, Gary. *American Crucible: Race and Nation in the Twentieth Century.* Princeton, N.J.: Princeton University Press, 2001.

Giddings, Paula J. *When and Where I Enter: The Impact of Black Women on Race and Sex in America.* New York: HarperCollins, 2007.

Gilkeson, John S. *Anthropologists and the Rediscovery of America, 1896–1965.* New York: Cambridge University Press, 2010.

Gilroy, Paul. *The Black Atlantic: Modernity and Double-Consciousness.* Cambridge, Mass.: Harvard University Press, 1993.

Glymph, Thavolia. *Out of the House of Bondage: The Transformation of the Plantation Household.* Cambridge: Cambridge University Press, 2008.

Gomez, Michael A. *Exchanging Our Country Marks: The Transformation of African Identities in the Colonial and Antebellum South.* Chapel Hill: University of North Carolina Press, 1998.

Gordon, Avery. *Ghostly Matters: Haunting and the Sociological Imagination.* Minneapolis: University of Minnesota Press, 1997.

Green, Elizabeth Lay. *The Negro in Contemporary American Literature: An Outline for Individual and Group Study.* College Park, Md.: McGrath, 1968. First published 1928 by University of North Carolina Press.

Griffin, John Howard. *Black like Me.* New York: New American Library, 1962.

Grossman, James R. *Land of Hope: Chicago, Black Southerners and the Great Migration.* Chicago: University of Chicago Press, 1991.

Guerrero, Ed. *Framing Blackness: The African American Image in Film.* Philadelphia: Temple University Press, 1993.

Hale, Grace Elizabeth. *Making Whiteness: The Culture of Segregation in the South, 1890–1940.* New York: Pantheon Books, 1998.

———. " 'Some Women Have Never Been Reconstructed': Mildred Lewis Rutherford, Lucy M. Stanton, and the Racial Politics of White Southern Womanhood, 1900–1930." In *Georgia in Black and White: Explorations in the Race Relations of a Southern State, 1865–1950,* edited by John C. Inscoe, 173–201. Athens: University of Georgia Press, 1994.

Hall, Jacquelyn Dowd. "The Long Civil Rights Movement and the Political Uses of the Past." *Journal of American History* 91 (March 2005): 1233–63.

Hall, Robert L. "E. Franklin Frazier and the Chicago School of Sociology." In *E. Franklin Frazier and Black Bourgeoisie,* edited by James E. Teele, 47–67. Columbia: University of Missouri Press, 2002.

Hall, Stephanie A. "Preserving Sound Recordings." American Folklife Center, Library of Congress, June 23, 2011. http://www.loc.gov/folklife/sos/preserve1 .html. July 11, 2014.

Harris, Paisley Jane. "Gatekeeping and Remaking: The Politics of Respectability in African American Women's History and Black Feminism." *Journal of Women's History* 15, no. 1 (Spring 2003): 212–20.

Hay, John. *Lincoln and the Civil War in the Diaries and Letters of John Hay.* Compiled by Tyler Dennett. New York: Dodd Mead, 1939.

Hemenway, Robert E. *Zora Neale Hurston: A Literary Biography.* Urbana: University of Illinois Press, 1977.

Herndon, William H. *The Hidden Lincoln, from the Letters and Papers of William H. Herndon.* Edited by Emanuel Hertz. New York: Viking Press, 1938.

Herskovits, Melville J. "The Negro's Americanism." In Locke, *The New Negro,* 353–60.

———. "Some Next Steps in the Study of Negro Folklore." *Journal of American Folklore* 56 (1943): 1–7.

Higginbotham, Evelyn Brooks. *Righteous Discontent: The Women's Movement in the Black Baptist Church, 1880–1920.* Cambridge, Mass.: Harvard University Press, 1993.

Hine, Darlene Clark. *Hine Sight: Black Women and the Re-Construction of American History.* Bloomington: Indiana University Press, 1997.

Hirsch, Jerrold. "Folklore in the Making: B. A. Botkin." *Journal of American Folklore* 100 (1987): 3–38.

———. *Portrait of America: A Cultural History of the Federal Writers' Project.* Chapel Hill: University of North Carolina Press, 2003.

———. "Portrait of America: The Federal Writers' Project in a Cultural and Intellectual Context." Ph.D. diss., University of North Carolina, 1984.

Holloway, Jonathan Scott. *Confronting the Veil: Abram Harris, Jr., E. Franklin Frazier, and Ralph Bunche, 1919–1941.* Chapel Hill: University of North Carolina Press, 2002.

Holloway, Karla F. C. *The Character of the Word: The Texts of Zora Neale Hurston.* New York: Greenwood Press, 1987.

hooks, bell. *Killing Rage: Ending Racism.* New York: Henry Holt, 1995.

Horton, James Oliver, and Lois E. Horton, eds. *Slavery and Public History: The Tough Stuff of American Memory.* New York: New Press, 2006.

Huggins, Nathan Irvin. *Harlem Renaissance.* New York: Oxford University Press, 1971.

Hughes, Langston. *The Big Sea.* New York: Knopf, 1940. Reprint, New York: Hill and Wang, 1993.

———. "The Negro Artist and the Racial Mountain." *Nation,* June 23, 1926, 692–94.

Hurston, Zora Neale. "Characteristics of Negro Expression." In *Negro: An Anthology,* edited by Nancy Cunard, 39–46. London: Wishart, 1934. Reprinted in *Folklore, Memoirs, and Other Writings,* edited by Cheryl A. Wall, 830–46. New York: Library of America, 1995.

———. *Dust Tracks on a Road.* 1942. Reprint, New York: Harper Perennial, 1996.

———. *Folklore, Memoirs, and Other Writings.* Edited by Cheryl A. Wall. New York: Library of America, 1995.

———. *Go Gator and Muddy the Water: Writings.* Edited by Pamela Bordelon. New York: W. W. Norton, 1999.

———. "How It Feels to Be Colored Me." In Hurston, *Folklore, Memoirs, and Other Writings,* 826–29. Originally published in *The World Tomorrow* (May 1928).

———. *Mules and Men.* 1935. Reprint, New York: Harper Perennial, 1990.

———. *Tell My Horse.* 1938. Reprint, New York: Harper Perennial, 1990.

Hutchinson, George. *The Harlem Renaissance in Black and White.* Cambridge, Mass.: Belknap Press of Harvard University Press, 1995.

Irr, Caren. *The Suburb of Dissent: Cultural Politics in the United States and Canada during the 1930s.* Durham, N.C.: Duke University Press, 1998.

Jackson, Antoinette T., and Allan F. Burns. "Ethnohistorical Study of the Kingsley Plantation." National Park Service, U.S. Department of the Interior, Timucuan Ecological and Historic Preserve, Jacksonville, Fla., January 2006. http://www .nps.gov/history/history/online_books/timu/timu_ethno.pdf.

Jackson, Lawrence. *The Indignant Generation: A Narrative History of African American Writers and Critics, 1934–1960.* Princeton, N.J.: Princeton University Press, 2011.

Jackson, Walter. "Melville Herskovits and the Search for Afro-American Culture." In Stocking, *Malinowski, Rivers, Benedict, and Others,* 95–126.

Jacobs, Harriet A. *Incidents in the Life of a Slave Girl: Written by Herself.* 1861. Edited by Jean Fagan Yellin. Cambridge, Mass.: Harvard University Press, 1987.

Jacobson, Matthew Frye. *Whiteness of a Different Color: European Immigrants and the Alchemy of Race.* Cambridge, Mass.: Harvard University Press, 1998.

Jensen, Hilmar Ludvig. "The Rise of an African American Left: John P. Davis and the National Negro Congress." Ph.D. diss., Cornell University, 1997.

Johnson, Charles Spurgeon. "A Proposal for a Regional (or National) Project under the Federal Writers Project (Utilizing Negro Personnel)." New York: Schomburg Center for Research in Black Culture, New York Public Library, n.d. [1930s].

Johnson, Guy B. "Foreword." In *Drums and Shadows,* xxxiii–xxxv. Page references are to the revised edition.

———. Review of *The Myth of the Negro Past,* by Melville J. Herskovits. *American Sociological Review* 7 (1942): 289–90.

Johnson, Walter. *Soul by Soul: Life inside the Antebellum Slave Market.* Cambridge, Mass.: Harvard University Press, 1999.

Jones, Gavin. "'Whose Line Is It Anyway?': W. E. B. Du Bois and the Language of the Color Line." In *Race Consciousness: African American Studies for the New Century,* edited by Judith Jackson Fossett and Jeffrey A. Tucker, 19–34. New York: New York University Press, 1997.

Jones, Jacqueline. *Labor of Love, Labor of Sorrow: Black Women, Work and the Family from Slavery to the Present.* New York: Vintage Books, 1986.

Jones, LeRoi [Amiri Baraka]. *Black Music.* New York: William Morrow, 1963.

———. *Blues People: Negro Music in White America.* New York: William Morrow, 1999.

Joyner, Charles. *Down by the Riverside: A South Carolina Slave Community.* Urbana: University of Illinois Press, 1984.

———. "Introduction." In *Drums and Shadows,* ix–xxvii. Page references are to the revised edition.

Juarez. Directed by William Dieterle. Warner Brothers, 1939; DVD: Culver City, Calif.: MGM/UA Home Video, 1991.

Kammen, Michael. *Mystic Chords of Memory: The Transformation of Tradition in American Culture.* New York: Knopf, 1991.

Kaplan, Carla, ed. *Zora Neale Hurston: A Life in Letters.* New York: Doubleday, 2002.

Keckley, Elizabeth. *Behind the Scenes: Or, Thirty Years a Slave, and Four Years in the White House.* New York: G. W. Carleton, 1868. Reprint edited by Frances Smith Foster. Chicago: Lakeside Press, 1998.

Kelley, Robin D. G. *Freedom Dreams: The Black Radical Imagination.* Boston, Mass.: Beacon Press, 2002.

———. *Hammer and Hoe: Alabama Communists during the Great Depression.* Chapel Hill: University of North Carolina Press, 1990.

———. "Notes on Deconstructing 'the Folk.'" *American Historical Review* 97 (December 1992): 1400–1408.

———. *Race Rebels: Culture, Politics, and the Black Working Class.* New York: Free Press, 1994.

Kellock, Katharine. "The WPA Writers: Portraitists of the United States." *American Scholar* 9 (1940): 473–82.

Kelly, Lawrence C. "Why Applied Anthropology Developed When It Did: A Commentary on People, Money, and Changing Times, 1930–1945." In *Social Contexts of American Ethnology, 1840–1984,* edited by June Helm, 126–28. Washington, D.C.: American Ethnological Society, 1985.

Kennedy, Stetson. "Florida Folklife and the WPA, an Introduction." In *A Reference Guide to Florida Folklore from the Federal WPA Deposited in the Florida Folklife Archives,* compiled by Jill I. Linzee. Tallahassee: Florida Division of Historical Resources, 1990. http://www.floridamemory.com/onlineclassroom/zora _hurston/documents/ stetsonkennedy/. October 15, 2013.

———. "Way Down Upon . . . Gathering Tales of Folklife in Suwannee Country." *Forum: The Magazine of the Florida Humanities Council* 17, no. 1 (Spring/Summer 1993): 22–27.

Kilson, Marion. "The Transformation of Eatonville's Ethnographer." *Phylon* 33 (1972): 112–19.

Kilson, Martin. "E. Franklin Frazier's *Black Bourgeoisie* Reconsidered." In *E. Franklin Frazier and the Black Bourgeoisie,* edited by James E. Teele, 118–36. Columbia: University of Missouri Press, 2002.

Kirby, Jack Temple. *Media-Made Dixie: The South in the American Imagination.* Athens: University of Georgia Press, 1986.

Koenig, Barbara A. "Which Differences Make a Difference: Race, DNA, and Health." In *Doing Race: 21 Essays for the 21st Century,* edited by Hazel Rose Markus and Paula M. L. Moya, 160–84. New York: W. W. Norton, 2010.

Krasner, David. *A Beautiful Pageant: African American Theatre, Drama, and Performance in the Harlem Renaissance, 1910–1927.* New York: Palgrave Macmillan, 2002.

Leadbelly. Directed by Gordon Parks. Paramount Pictures, 1976.

Leong, Wai-Teng. "Culture and the State: Manufacturing Traditions for Tourism." *Critical Studies in Mass Communication* 6 (1989): 355–75.

Leuchtenburg, William E. *Franklin D. Roosevelt and the New Deal, 1932–1940.* New York: Harper & Row, 1963.

Levine, Lawrence W. *Black Culture and Black Consciousness: Afro-American Folk Thought from Slavery to Freedom.* New York: Oxford University Press, 1978.

Lewis, David Levering. *When Harlem Was in Vogue.* Revised edition. New York: Penguin Press, 1997.

Lindbergh, Anne Morrow. *North to the Orient.* New York: Harcourt, Brace, 1935.

Lipsitz, George. *The Possessive Investment in Whiteness: How White People Profit from Identity Politics.* Philadelphia: Temple University Press, 1998.

Litwack, Leon. *Trouble in Mind: Black Southerners in the Age of Jim Crow.* New York: Alfred A. Knopf, 1998.

Locke, Alain, ed. *The New Negro.* New York: Macmillan, 1992. First published 1925 by Albert and Charles Boni.

———. "Who and What Is 'Negro'?" *Opportunity* 20 (1942): 36–41, 83–87.

Lomax, John A. *Adventures of a Ballad Hunter.* New York: Macmillan, 1947.

———. "Adventures of a Ballad Hunter: Iron Head and Clear Rock." *Southwest Review* 30 (1944): 48–55.

———. "'Sinful Songs' of the Southern Negro." *Musical Quarterly* 20 (April 1934): 177–87.

"Lomax the Songhunter." *POV,* American Documentary, August 22, 2006. http://www.pbs.org/pov/lomax/background.php. July 11, 2014.

Mangione, Jerre. *The Dream and the Deal: The Federal Writers' Project, 1935–1943.* Boston: Little, Brown, 1972.

Manring, Maurice M. *Slave in a Box: The Strange Career of Aunt Jemima.* Charlottesville: University Press of Virginia, 1998.

McDonogh, Gary W. *The Florida Negro: A Federal Writers' Project Legacy.* Jackson: University Press of Mississippi, 1993.

McElya, Micki. *Clinging to Mammy: The Faithful Slave in Twentieth-Century America.* Cambridge, Mass.: Harvard University Press, 2007.

Melosh, Barbara. *Engendering Culture: Manhood and Womanhood in New Deal Public Art and Theater.* Washington, D.C.: Smithsonian Institution Press, 1991.

Miller, Herbert A. *Races, Nations, and Classes: The Psychology of Domination and Freedom.* Philadelphia: J. B. Lippincott, 1924.

Miller, Karl Hagstrom. *Segregating Sound: Inventing Folk and Pop Music in the Age of Jim Crow.* Durham, N.C.: Duke University Press, 2010.

Mitchell-Kernan, Claudia. *Language Behavior in a Black Urban Community.* Monographs of the Language-Behavior Research Laboratory, 2. Berkeley: University of California, 1971.

Mormino, Gary R. "Florida Slave Narratives." *Florida Historical Quarterly* 66 (April 1988): 399–414.

Morrison, Toni. *Playing in the Dark: Whiteness and the Literary Imagination.* Cambridge: Harvard University Press, 1992.

———. "The Site of Memory." In *Inventing the Truth: The Art and Craft of Memoir,* edited by William Zinsser, 101–24. Boston: Houghton Mifflin, 1987.

Mullen, Patrick B. *The Man Who Adores the Negro: Race and American Folklore.* Urbana: University of Illinois Press, 2008.

Musher, Sharon Ann. "Contesting 'the Way the Almighty Wants It': Crafting Memories of Ex-Slaves in the Slave Narrative Collection." *American Quarterly* 53 (March 2001): 1–31.

Myrdal, Gunnar. *An American Dilemma: The Negro Problem and Modern Democracy.* New York: Harper and Brothers, 1944.

Natanson, Nicholas. *The Black Image in the New Deal: The Politics of FSA Photography.* Knoxville: University of Tennessee Press, 1992.

Newman, Louise. "Coming of Age, but Not in Samoa: Reflections on Margaret Mead's Legacy for Western Liberal Feminism." *American Quarterly* 48 (June 1996): 233–72.

North, Michael. *The Dialect of Modernism: Race, Language, and Twentieth-Century Literature.* New York: Oxford University Press, 1994.

Odum, Howard. *Southern Regions of the United States.* Chapel Hill: University of North Carolina Press for the Southern Regional Committee of the Social Science Research Council, 1936.

Osofsky, Gilbert. *Harlem: The Making of a Ghetto: Negro New York, 1890–1930.* New York: Harper & Row, 1966.

Ottley, Roi. *"New World A-Coming": Inside Black America.* Boston: Houghton Mifflin, 1943.

Parrish, Lydia. *Slave Songs of the Georgia Sea Islands.* New York: Creative Age Press, 1942.

Penkower, Monty Noam. *The Federal Writers' Project: A Study in Government Patronage of the Arts.* Urbana: University of Illinois Press, 1977.

Perdue, Charles L., Jr., Thomas E. Barden, and Robert K. Phillips, eds. *Weevils in the Wheat: Interviews with Virginia Ex-Slaves.* Charlottesville: University Press of Virginia, 1976.

Phillips, Ulrich B. *American Negro Slavery.* Baton Rouge: Louisiana State University Press, 1966. First published 1918.

Pinky. Directed by Elia Kazan. 1949; DVD: Beverly Hills, Calif.: Twentieth Century Fox Home Entertainment, 2006.

Porterfield, Nolan. *Last Cavalier: The Life and Times of John A. Lomax, 1867–1948.* Urbana: University of Illinois Press, 1996.

Pratt, Mary Louise. "Fieldwork in Common Places." In *Writing Culture: The Poetics and Politics of Ethnography,* edited by James Clifford and George E. Marcus, 27–50. Berkeley: University of California Press, 1986.

———. *Imperial Eyes: Travel Writing and Transculturation.* New York: Routledge, 1992.

Preece, Harold. "The Negro Folk Cult." *Crisis* 43 (November 1936): 364, 374.

Prince, K. Stephen. *Stories of the South: Race and the Reconstruction of Southern Identity, 1865–1915.* Chapel Hill: University of North Carolina Press, 2014.

Prince, Mary. *The History of Mary Prince: A West Indian Slave.* Edited by Sarah Salih. London: Penguin Books, 2004. First published 1831.

Puckett, Newbell Niles. *Folk Beliefs of the Southern Negro*. Chapel Hill: University of North Carolina Press, 1926.

Rabinowitz, Paula. *They Must Be Represented: The Politics of Documentary*. London: Verso, 1994.

Randolph, A. Philip. "The New Philosophy of the Negro." *Messenger*, December 1919, 5.

Rawick, George P., ed. *The American Slave: A Composite Autobiography*. 19 vols. plus 12 suppl. vols. Westport, Conn.: Greenwood, 1972–79. Most references to slave narratives are from this collection. Notes include state, series (I or II), volume, part 1 or 2 (where applicable), and page number(s). For example: Georgia, II:12:1:52. Additional information may include a title, editors of narratives for the state office, and date.

———. *From Sundown to Sunup: The Making of the Black Community*. Westport, Conn.: Greenwood, 1972.

Reinhart, Mark S. *Abraham Lincoln on Screen: Fictional and Documentary Portrayals on Film and Television*. Jefferson, N.C.: McFarland, 2012.

Retman, Sonnet H. *Real Folks: Race and Genre in the Great Depression*. Durham, N.C.: Duke University Press, 2011.

Richardson, Eudora Ramsay. *Little Aleck: A Life of Alexander H. Stephens, the Fighting Vice-President of the Confederacy*. Indianapolis: Bobbs-Merrill, 1932.

Ring, Natalie J. *The Problem South: Region, Empire, and the New Liberal State, 1880–1930*. Athens: University of Georgia Press, 2012.

Robb, Bernard. *Welcum Hinges*. New York: E. P. Dutton, 1942.

Roediger, David, ed. *Black on White: Black Writers on What It Means to Be White*. New York: Schocken Books, 1998.

———. *Working toward Whiteness: How America's Immigrants Became White*. Cambridge, Mass.: Basic Books, 2005.

Rowell, Charles H. " 'Let Me Be with Ole Jazzbo': An Interview with Sterling A. Brown." In Tidwell and Tracy, *After Winter*, 287–309.

Rubio, Phillip F. " 'Who Divided the Church?': African American Postal Workers Fight Segregation in the Postal Unions, 1939–1962." *Journal of African American History* 94, no. 2 (Spring 2009): 172–99.

Sale, Maggie. "Call and Response as Critical Method: African-American Oral Traditions and Beloved." *African American Review* 26, no. 1 (Spring 1992): 41–50.

Sandburg, Carl. *Abraham Lincoln: The War Years*. 4 vols. New York: Harcourt, Brace, 1939.

Savage, Barbara Dianne. *Broadcasting Freedom: Radio, War, and the Politics of Race, 1938–1948*. Chapel Hill: University of North Carolina Press, 1999.

Scarborough, Dorothy. *On the Trail of Negro Folk-Songs*. Cambridge, Mass.: Harvard University Press, 1925.

———. *A Song Catcher in Southern Mountains: American Folk Songs of British Ancestry*. New York: Columbia University Press, 1937.

Schuyler, George S. "The Negro-Art Hokum." *Nation*, June 16, 1926, 662–63.

Scott, James C. *Domination and the Arts of Resistance: Hidden Transcripts*. New Haven, Conn.: Yale University Press, 1990.

Seward, Adrienne Lanier. "The Legacy of Early Afro-American Folklore Scholarship." In *Handbook of American Folklore*, edited by Richard M. Dorson, 48–56. Bloomington: Indiana University Press, 1983.

Shaw, Stephanie. "Using the WPA Ex-Slave Narratives to Study the Impact of the Great Depression." *Journal of Southern History* 69 (August 2003): 623–58.

Sherwood, Robert E. *Abe Lincoln in Illinois, a Play in Twelve Scenes*. New York: Scribner, 1939.

Silk, Catherine, and John Silk. *Racism and Anti-Racism in American Popular Culture: Portrayals of African-Americans in Fiction and Film*. Manchester: Manchester University Press, 1990.

Singh, Nikhil Pal. *Black Is a Country: Race and the Unfinished Struggle for Democracy*. Cambridge, Mass.: Harvard University Press, 2004.

Sklaroff, Lauren Rebecca. *Black Culture and the New Deal: The Quest for Civil Rights in the Roosevelt Era*. Chapel Hill: University of North Carolina Press, 2009.

Slave Narratives: A Folk History of Slavery in the United States from Interviews with Former Slaves. 17 vols. Washington, D.C.: Library of Congress, Work Projects Administration, 1941.

Smith, Felipe. *American Body Politics: Race, Gender, and Black Literary Renaissance*. Athens: University of Georgia Press, 1998.

Snead, James. *White Screens/Black Images: Hollywood from the Dark Side*. New York: Routledge, 1994.

Sprigle, Ray. *In the Land of Jim Crow*. New York: Simon and Schuster, 1949.

Stampp, Kenneth M. *The Peculiar Institution: Slavery in the Ante-Bellum South*. New York: Alfred A. Knopf, 1956.

Starling, Marion Wilson. *The Slave Narrative: Its Place in American History*. 2nd ed. Washington, D.C.: Howard University Press, 1988.

Staub, Michael. *Voices of Persuasion: Politics of Representation in 1930s America*. Cambridge: Cambridge University Press, 1994.

Stepto, Robert B. "Storytelling in Early Afro-American Fiction: Frederick Douglass's 'The Heroic Slave.'" In Gates, *Black Literature and Literary Theory*, 175–86.

Stocking, George, Jr., "The Aims of Boasian Ethnography: Creating the Materials for Traditional Humanistic Scholarship." *Historical Anthropology Newsreel* 4, no. 2 (1977): 4–5.

———, ed. *Malinowski, Rivers, Benedict, and Others: Essays on Culture and Personality*. Madison: University of Wisconsin Press, 1986.

Stott, William. *Documentary Expression and Thirties America*. New York: Oxford University Press, 1973.

Sullivan, Patricia. *Days of Hope: Race and Democracy in the New Deal*. Chapel Hill: University of North Carolina Press, 1996.

Takaki, Ronald. *Iron Cages: Race and Culture in 19th-Century America*. New York: Oxford University Press, 1990.

Taylor, David A. *Soul of a People: The WPA Writers' Project Uncovers Depression America*. Hoboken, N.J.: John Wiley & Sons, 2009.

Taylor, William R. *Cavalier and Yankee: The Old South and American National Character*. New York: George Braziller, 1961.

Thomas, Nicholas. *Colonialism's Culture: Anthropology, Travel and Government*. Princeton, N.J.: Princeton University Press, 1994.

Thompson, Stith. "American Folklore after Fifty Years." Address of the President of the American Folklore Society at the fiftieth anniversary of the Society, December 27, 1937. *Journal of American Folklore* 51 (1938): 1–9.

Tidwell, John Edgar, and Steven C. Tracy, eds. *After Winter: The Art and Life of Sterling A. Brown*. Oxford: Oxford University Press, 2009.

Vanderwood, Paul J. "Introduction." In *Juarez*, by John Huston, 9–41. Madison: University of Wisconsin Press, 1983.

Von Eschen, Penny M. *Race against Empire: Black Americans and Anticolonialism, 1937–1957*. Ithaca, N.Y.: Cornell University Press, 1997.

Walker, Alice. "The Dummy in the Window: Joel Chandler Harris and the Invention of Uncle Remus." In Roediger, *Black on White*, 233–39.

———. *You Can't Keep a Good Woman Down*. New York: Harcourt Brace Jovanovich, 1981.

Wall, Cheryl A. *Women of the Harlem Renaissance*. Bloomington: Indiana University Press, 1995.

Wallace, Mike. *Mickey Mouse History and Other Essays on American Memory*. Philadelphia: Temple University Press, 1996.

Warren-Findley, Jannelle. "Passports to Change: The Resettlement Administration's Folk Song Sheet Program, 1936–1937." *Prospects* 10 (October 1985): 197–241.

Washington, Booker T., Fannie Barrier Williams, and N. B. Wood. *A New Negro for a New Century: An Accurate and Up-to-Date Record of the Upward Struggles of the Negro Race*. Chicago: American Publishing, 1900.

Welke, Barbara Young. *Recasting American Liberty: Gender, Race, Law, and the Railroad Revolution*. Cambridge: Cambridge University Press, 2001.

Wells, Ida B. *Southern Horrors and Other Writings: The Anti-Lynching Campaign of Ida B. Wells, 1892–1900*. Edited by Jacqueline Jones Royster. Boston: Bedford/ St. Martin's, 1997.

Wells, Ida B., Frederick Douglass, Irvine Garland Penn, and Ferdinand L. Barnett. *The Reason Why the Colored American Is Not in the World's Columbian Exposition*. Edited by Robert Rydell. 1893. Reprint, Urbana: University of Illinois Press, 1999.

White, Deborah Gray. *Ar'n't I a Woman?: Female Slaves in the Plantation South*. Revised edition. New York: Norton, 1999.

White, E. Frances. *Dark Continent of Our Bodies: Black Feminism and the Politics of Respectability*. Philadelphia: Temple University Press, 2001.

White, Newman Ivey. *American Negro Folk-Songs*. Cambridge, Mass.: Harvard University Press, 1928.

Wiegman, Robyn. *American Anatomies: Theorizing Race and Gender.* Durham, N.C.: Duke University Press, 1995.

Willis, Susan. *Specifying: Black Women Writing the American Experience.* Madison: University of Wisconsin Press, 1987.

Witt, Doris. *Black Hunger: Food and the Politics of U.S. Identity.* New York: Oxford University Press, 1999.

Wolcott, Victoria W. *Remaking Respectability: African American Women in Interwar Detroit.* Chapel Hill: University of North Carolina Press, 2001.

Wolfe, Charles, and Kip Lornell. *The Life and Legend of Leadbelly.* New York: HarperCollins, 1992.

Woodson, Carter G. "History Made to Order." In Sterling A. Brown, Davis, and Lee, *The Negro Caravan*, 839–46.

Woodward, C. Vann, "History from Slave Sources." In Charles T. Davis and Gates, *The Slave's Narrative*, 48–58.

Wright, Richard. "Blueprint for Negro Writing." In *Richard Wright Reader*, edited by Ellen Wright and Michael Fabre, 36–50. New York: Harper and Row, 1978. Originally published in *New Challenge* 2 (Fall 1937): 53–65.

———. *Uncle Tom's Children.* New York: Harper & Row, 1938. Reprint, New York: Harper Perennial, 1993.

Writers' Program of the Work Projects Administration in the State of Virginia, comp. *The Negro in Virginia.* New York: Hastings House, 1940.

Yans-McLaughlin, Virginia. "Science, Democracy, and Ethics: Mobilizing for Culture and Personality for World War II. In Stocking, *Malinowski, Rivers, Benedict, and Others*, 184–217.

Yellin, Jean Fagan. "Text and Contexts of Harriet Jacobs' *Incidents in the Life of a Slave Girl: Written by Herself.*" In Charles T. Davis and Gates, *The Slave's Narrative*, 262–82.

Yetman, Norman R. "The Background of the Slave Narrative Collection." *American Quarterly* 19 (1967): 534–53.

———. "Ex-Slave Interviews and the Historiography of Slavery." *American Quarterly* 36 (Summer 1984): 181–210.

———. "An Introduction to the WPA Slave Narratives." "Born in Slavery: Slave Narratives from the Federal Writers' Project, 1936–1938." Library of Congress. http://memory.loc.gov/ammem/snhtml/snintrooo.html. March 21, 2013.

———, ed. *Voices from Slavery.* New York: Holt, Rinehart and Winston, 1970.

Zumwalt, Rosemary Lévy. *American Folklore Scholarship: A Dialogue of Dissent.* Bloomington: Indiana University Press, 1988.

Index

Taylor, Cora Mae, 34, 189
Taylor, David A., 250 (n. 5)
Taylor, William, 273 (n. 101)
Tell My Horse (Hurston), 171, 287 (n. 18)
Tennessee Project of the FWP: 1929 oral
history project, 62–63, 268 (n. 4);
dialect use in, 85–86, 87; Lomax's
editorial review of, 77; praise of, 238;
state guidebook for, 46
Terrell, Mary Church, 23
Texas Project of the FWP, 81, 134.
See also Davis, J. Frank
Their Eyes Were Watching God (Hurston),
170, 173
Thompson, Stith, 116, 117, 281 (n. 137)
Thorington, Portia, 180, 296 (n. 32)
Time (magazine), 35, 91, 115
Tonsill, Geneva, 203, 305 (n. 57)
Tourist industry guides. *See* American
Guide Series
Towns, Luke, 184
Transcription in dialect, 8, 78–79, 249
(n. 1)
Travel narrative form, 40–41, 60, 93, 149.
See also American Guide Series
Trickster tales, 165, 201, 214, 302 (n. 17).
See also Folk traditions; Uncle Remus
Truthfulness/untruthfulness, 98,
135–40
Tubman, Harriet, 59
Tunchi (Liddle), 262 (n. 33)
Tupper, Samuel, Jr., 55, 58, 67, 235.
See also Georgia Project of the FWP
Turin, F. E., 35
Turner, Luke, 160
Tuskegee Institute, 54
Twain, Mark, 77

Uncle Ben brand, 13
Uncle Remus, 62, 80, 83, 88, 207, 274 (n.
103). *See also* Harris, Joel Chandler
Uncle Tom's Children (Wright), 11, 24

Unions, 256 (n. 54), 260 (n. 100).
See also Brotherhood of Sleeping
Car Porters
United Daughters of the Confederacy
(UDC): on Civil War, 47; as FWP
employees, 53, 265 (nn. 82–83);
Georgia Project and, 202, 303 (n. 24);
Mammy statue by, 23, 253 (n. 6);
members of, 175, 294 (n. 6), 304
(nn. 31, 44); on play *Mammy*, 73;
representation of slavery by, 5, 52–53,
206–7, 211. *See also* Lost Cause
mythology
University of Georgia Press, 235
*Unwritten History of Slavery: Autobio-
graphical Account of Negro Ex-Slaves*
(Settle Egypt), 62–63, 268 (n. 4)
Urban migration, 11–12, 15

Vernacular vs. dialect, 79–80. *See also*
Dialect
Vesey, Denmark, 59
Vidor, King, 19
Violence: abuse and mistreatment of
slaves, 134, 137–38, 182, 214, 218–20,
285 (n. 72); race riots, 256 (n. 55).
See also Ku Klux Klan; Lynching; Rape
Virginia Guide, 46
Virginia Project of the FWP: Brown's
editorial review of, 76; hiring discrimi-
nation in, 5, 127, 132–33; oral history
project and, 269 (n. 9), 293 (n. 1); state
guidebook for, 55, 60. *See also* Lewis,
Roscoe; *Negro in Virginia, The*;
Richardson, Eudora Ramsay
Voodoo. *See* Hoodoo

Walker, Alice, 62, 279 (n. 106)
Wall, Cheryl, 154
"War Between the States," 47. *See also*
Civil War; United Daughters of the
Confederacy

CPSIA information can be obtained
at www.ICGtesting.com
Printed in the USA
LVOW08s2200101116

512471LV00005B/289/P